Freedom and Religion in Kant and His Immediate Successors

The Vocation of Humankind, 1774–1800

The theologians of the late German Enlightenment saw in Kant's *Critique of Pure Reason* a new rational defense of their Christian faith. In fact, Kant's critical theory of meaning and moral law totally subverted the spirit of that faith.

This challenging new study examines the contribution made by the *Critique of Pure Reason* to this change of meaning. George di Giovanni stresses the revolutionary character of Kant's critical thought but also reveals how this thought was being held hostage to unwarranted metaphysical assumptions that caused much confusion and rendered the first Critique vulnerable to being reabsorbed into modes of thought typical of Enlightenment popular philosophy.

Among the striking features of this book are nuanced interpretations of Jacobi and Reinhold, a lucid exposition of Fichte's early thought, and a rare, detailed account of Enlightenment popular philosophy.

George di Giovanni is Professor of Philosophy at McGill University.

Freedom and Religion in Kant and His Immediate Successors

The Vocation of Humankind, *1774–1800*

GEORGE DI GIOVANNI

McGill University

CAMBRIDGE
UNIVERSITY PRESS

PUBLISHED BY THE PRESS SYNDICATE OF THE UNIVERSITY OF CAMBRIDGE
The Pitt Building, Trumpington Street, Cambridge, United Kingdom

CAMBRIDGE UNIVERSITY PRESS
The Edinburgh Building, Cambridge CB2 2RU, UK
40 West 20th Street, New York, NY 10011-4211, USA
477 Williamstown Road, Port Melbourne, VIC 3207, Australia
Ruiz de Alarcón 13, 28014 Madrid, Spain
Dock House, The Waterfront, Cape Town 8001, South Africa

http://www.cambridge.org

First published 2005

Printed in the United States of America

Typeface ITC New Baskerville 10/13 pt.   *System* LaTeX 2$_\varepsilon$ [TB]

A catalog record for this book is available from the British Library.

Library of Congress Cataloging in Publication Data
Di Giovanni, George, 1935–
Freedom and religion in Kant and his immediate successors : the vocation of humankind,
1774–1800 / George di Giovanni.
p.   cm.
Includes bibliographical references and index.
ISBN 0-521-84451-7
1. Kant, Immanuel, 1724–1804. Kritik der reinen Vernunft.   2. Philosophy and religion –
History – 18th century.   3. Kant, Immanuel, 1724–1804 – Religion.   I. Title.
B2779.D5   2005
193 – dc22

2004051889

ISBN 0 521 84451 7 hardback

for Sheila

Contents

Preface   *page* ix

Abbreviations   xv

1   Introduction: The Vocation of Humankind, 1774   1
     1.1 *The Theme*   1
     1.2 *The System*   6
     1.3 *The Presence of Jacobi*   10
     1.4 *Polemical Notes*   16
     1.5 *The Issue of Religion*   24
     1.6 *Mapping out the Story*   28

2   The Taming of Kant: Popular Philosophy   32
     2.1 *The Brilliant Immodesty of Kant*   32
     2.2 *Popular Philosophy*   37
     2.3 *Popular Philosophy and the Critique*
          of Reason   49
     2.4 *The Culture of Feeling*   55
     2.5 *The Return to Leibniz*   58
     2.6 *Leibniz versus Kant?*   62

3   The Intractable Kant: Schultz, Jacobi, Reinhold   66
     3.1 *The Canonical Interpretation*   66
     3.2 *Jacobi's Realism*   77
     3.3 *Reinhold's Pastiche*   91
     3.4 *The Specter of Naturalism*   104

4   Of Human Freedom and Necessity   108
     4.1 *The Classical Heritage*   108
     4.2 *Reinhold versus Schmid*   118
     4.3 *Rehberg and Kant*   125

	4.4 *Jacobi on Spinozism and Human Freedom*	137
	4.5 *Jacobi, Rehberg, and Reinhold versus Kant*	150
5	Kant's Moral System	152
	5.1 *The Dogmatism of the Critique of Reason*	153
	5.2 *The Gospel According to Kant*	186
	5.3 *Kant's Way*	202
6	The Difference That Fichte Made	205
	6.1 *The Debate on Freedom, Continued*	205
	6.2 *The Gospel According to Fichte*	210
	6.3 *Reinhold on Fichte and Kant*	225
	6.4 *The Scandal That Fichte Was*	237
7	The Parting of the Ways	242
	7.1 *Anno Domini 1799*	242
	7.2 *Reinhold Converts Again*	244
	7.3 *Jacobi's Cri de Cœur*	264
	7.4 *Kant's Anathema*	269
8	The Vocation of Humankind Revisited, 1800: Conclusion	271
	8.1 *New Book, Old Themes*	272
	8.2 *The Critics, Old and New*	285
	8.3 *Back to the Beginning*	293
Notes		301
Bibliography		347
Index		361

Preface

Many of my generation cut their Kantian teeth on Strawson's *The Bounds of Sense* (1966). Strawson's argument was that there is in Kant a powerful critical thesis about the conceptual a priori of experience combined, however, with what Strawson called a 'transcendental story' about an alleged unknown 'thing in itself', and about certain equally alleged a priori sensible intuitions of 'space' and 'time'. According to Strawson, this transcendental story detracts from the analytical force of the first thesis. One should abstract from it if one wishes to appreciate Kant's lasting philosophical contribution. The argument was well presented and convinced many. But then Henry Allison came along (1983). Strawson was no historian of philosophy. He treated Kant as a contemporary in the same spirit (so Jonathan Bennett said somewhere about his own practice) as any of us would read and criticize the work of the colleague down the hall. Allison had, however, historical as well as philosophical credentials, and he argued, referring to Strawson explicitly, that there is no such thing in Kant as a transcendental story. The mirage of such a story appears only if one understands psychologically distinctions that were intended by Kant rather as conceptual markers that delineate the limits of possible human knowledge without, however, restricting human identity to just these limits. Allison based his argument on a close reading of Kant's text, and he convinced many. In North America at least, his position has since become the presupposition of much of Kantian scholarship. One now speaks of Kant's 'modest proposal' (Ameriks, 2000) as denoting precisely the kind of self-limiting, but not necessarily humanly constricting, discipline for which, according to Allison, Kant provided the critical program.

For my part, I was impressed by both Strawson and Allison. The analytical side in me leaned toward Strawson; the historical, toward Allison. But then, my main interest lay in Hegel's *Phenomenology of Spirit* and Hegel's *Logic*. For a long while at least, I was able to indulge both sides. However, precisely as I searched the late German Enlightenment background of these works of Hegel, I had to recognize that, at least so far as Kant's contemporaries were concerned, there was indeed in Kant's critical system something like a transcendental story in Strawson's sense. It is the presence of this story that caused so much confusion in the reception of the system and precipitated what we now refer to as 'post-Kantian Idealism'. It would be presumptuous indeed to believe (without at least first carefully examining the facts) that Kant's contemporaries were all so obtuse as to be universally fooled by a mere mirage. Why would anyone want to claim, as Kant incontestably does, that we do not know the 'thing in itself' at all? To say that the claim is to be understood 'transcendentally' (or 'epistemically', as some might prefer), that is, that the denial of knowledge is only meant to provide a rational space for a moral conception of human nature, begs the question of why one would need the denial in order to allow for such a space. Might the need not depend on a faulty conception of the relation of moral to physical nature? This is what many of Kant's contemporaries thought. Kant spoke of the 'dissatisfaction of metaphysics' – a theme still being played upon today (Stroud, 2003). The metaphysics that Kant had in mind, however, was still that of the schools, and the dissatisfaction that he alleged was due to the impossibility of answering positively questions that metaphysics had been posing from time immemorial. But why would anyone still want to pose them, as Kant did? Critical idealism implied not just the scaling down of the claims of classical metaphysics – a new 'modesty' in things metaphysical, as it were – but its total revolution. It implied that the kind of knowledge its questions invited, but that Kant interdicted transcendentally, is not just impossible *for us* but impossible per se because they are directed at chimerical objects. Could it be that, inasmuch as Kant still experienced metaphysical dissatisfaction, it was because he was still serving the specific interests of the reason typical of the metaphysics he was undermining? To put it another way, could it be that, while recognizing the impossibility of being a 'dogmatic metaphysician', he still hankered to be one and would have been one if it were possible?

These are the questions and the considerations that motivate the present study. However, except for the occasional passage in Chapter 1, I deliberately avoid engaging in polemical discussion with contemporary

interpreters of Kant. This does not mean that I do not have a philosophical agenda. On the contrary, in defense of Kant's idealism, I argue that its
truly revolutionary implications were hidden to Kant himself and to most
of his contemporaries, because, in expounding it, Kant was still being
held hostage to the modes of thought of classical metaphysics. One must
recognize, and effectively suspend, Kant's transcendental story in order
to recognize in full the novelty that the Critique of Reason was bringing to
the philosophical and cultural scene of the day. I have tried to make this
point in the plain language that eighteenth-century 'popular philosophers' would have understood. It is with them, rather than with contemporary commentators, that I am most visibly engaged in discussion.
I make the point, moreover, historically, concentrating on details that,
in Anglophone philosophical literature at least, are normally adverted to
only globally. It was my intention to offer a more nuanced reading of both
Jacobi and Reinhold than is usually provided. If I have succeeded in this, I
will have supplemented, and perhaps even corrected, whatever literature
already exists on the subject. I have also harbored the ulterior motive of
providing the basis for linking Hegel's Phenomenology, and his Logic, to
the tradition of late Enlightenment philosophy, conceptually as well as
historically. If this link were ever to be made, it would provide indeed a
corrective to much traditional Hegel interpretation. In the present work,
however, this last motive remains only adumbrated and the desired link
only a wish.

Many are the intellectual debts that I owe. To acknowledge them all
would require summing up a whole intellectual career. There are two
recent books that I should, however, mention. Both came to my attention
when the present study was already practically finished in script form,
and I was therefore able to retrieve them for the most part only in the
notes. Both nonetheless helped me in crucial ways. The first is Manfred
Kuehn's Kant biography (2001). The book helped, of course, because of
the vivid portrait of Kant, the real individual, that it conveys and the handy
review of all his works that it makes available. For my purposes, however,
it helped especially because it confirmed me in my long-standing belief
that Kant, the real individual, not only claimed not to know anything
about God, he also personally did not care to know anything about him.
For all practical purposes, Kant was an agnostic. Religion and religious
practices were for him just a matter of subjective need, and he apparently
had no such personal need. In that case, however, the question becomes
all the more pressing: why would he have expended so much energy,
and taken so much care, in establishing in his system what he thought

to be a critical basis for both a moral faith and a morally motivated form
of religion? Short of accepting Heinrich Heine's cynical view (as if Kant
were just throwing a morsel of security to poor Lampe), there must have
been serious systematic reasons motivating him. It is these reasons that I
explore in the present study.

The other book is Ian Hunter's admirable *Rival Enlightenments* (2001).
This study confirmed me in my long-standing belief that the critical Kant,
far from reconciling conflicting tendencies of the *Aufklärung*, in fact
brought new conflicts to it. Contrary to the author's opinion, I believe that
these conflicts were creative. I also believe that the Critique of Reason was
not necessarily bound by its conceptual commitments to a reactionary sociopolitical agenda. My estimate of the nature and the intellectual value
of idealism is quite different. Yet it is true, as Hunter's study demonstrates
at length, that the *Aufklärung* was made up of competing mental cultures,
and that the one most responsible for the 'desacralizing' tendencies in
seventeenth- and eighteenth-centrury German society had its origin in
the thought and the political practices of the jurists. Personally, I am
inclined to believe that Kant had ties with this jurist culture that Hunter
ignores. The Critique of Reason even made a contribution to its later development (Negri, 1962). It is nonetheless true that Kant at least played
into the hands of the 'resacralizing' agenda of the academics – though
not necessarily for the reasons, or with the effects, that Hunter adduces.
Whether one agrees or disagrees with its main thesis, *Rival Enlightenments*
should be reading de rigueur for all Kantian scholars.

There are other debts, of a different nature, that I owe and that it is
my pleasure now to acknowledge. The Social Science and Humanities
Research Council of Canada greatly facilitated the research that went
into this study with a three-year grant (No. 410-1998-0802). I had the
opportunity to present the first outline of the study in a series of seminars
at the Istituto italiano per gli studi filosofici di Napoli (October 1998),
and I was given access to much needed but not readily available texts
during a six-month tenure as *Stipendiat* at the *Herzog August Bibliothek zu
Wolfenbüttel* (January to June 1999). I thank all three institutions for their
financial support and the last two for their gracious hospitality as well.
A special note of thanks goes to Dr. Jillian Bepler of the *Herzog August
Bibliothek*.

I am also grateful to my doctoral student, Pierre Chételat, who edited
the final version of my script and saw it through the publication stage. I
consider myself fortunate to have had such a diligent and clear-headed
collaborator.

I have presented some of the themes explored in this study in already published papers, but in considerably different forms and with different contexts in mind. I shall refer to these papers at the appropriate places.

Of a yet different nature is the debt that I owe to my wife, Sheila. I am grateful to her for her companionship in my many travels and her unfailing moral support. This book is dedicated to her.

George di Giovanni
McGill University, Montréal
The Feast of the Epiphany, 2004

Abbreviations

AK = *Immanuel Kant. Gesammelte Schriften*, ed. Royal Prussian Academy of the Sciences: Academy Edition (Berlin: Reimer, 1902 –).

ALZ = *Allgemeine Literatur-Zeitung.*

Between Kant and Hegel = *Between Kant and Hegel, Texts in the Development of Post-Kantian Idealism*, translated with introductory studies, G. di Giovanni and H.S. Harris; revised edition, G. di Giovanni (Indianapolis and Cambridge: Hackett, 2000). Original pagination is indicated in the translated texts.

GA = *J.G. Fichte-Gesamtausgabe der bayerischen Akademie der Wissenschaften*, eds. R. Lauth and H. Gliwitzky (Stuttgart-Bad Cannstatt: Fromann-Holzboog, 1962–2005, projected), cited with series number in Roman numerals, volume number, pagination, and, when appropriate, line number.

GW = *Georg Wilhelm Friedrich Hegel, Gesammelte Werke*, ed. Rheinisch-Westphalischen Akademie der Wissenschaften (Hamburg: Meiner, 1968–), cited with volume number, pagination, and, when appropriate, line number.

Jacobi = *Friedrich Heinrich Jacobi: The Main Philosophical Writings and the Novel "Allwill,"* tr. and ed. G. di Giovanni (Kingston and Montreal: McGill-Queen's Press, 1994), 683 pp.; includes, G. di Giovanni, *The Unfinished Philosophy of Friedrich Heinrich Jacobi*, pp.1–167. The translated texts include original pagination.

KrV = *Critique of Pure Reason*, followed by the pagination of the first edition (A) and the second (B).

KprV = *Critique of Practical Reason.*

Religion = Kant, *Religion within the Boundaries of Mere Reason.*

Spinoza letters = *Über die lehre des Spinoza an den Herrn Moses Mendelssohn* (Löwe, 1785).

Unless otherwise indicated, all translations are mine. Whenever a single reference is cited continuously, the page, paragraph, or column number is included in parentheses within the text.

An English translation of the German titles is included in the Bibliography.

1

Introduction

The Vocation of Humankind, 1774

Everything in nature persuades me that righteousness and happiness belong together, and that they also always come together if external circumstances do not disrupt this otherwise so essential a bond. Such a pervasive
tendency for order must, however, be fulfilled; and only its realization would
remove the confusion and contradiction that would otherwise obtain.

Spalding

1.1 THE THEME

Kant is the most important figure in this book, as one would expect in
a work that deals with late-eighteenth-century German philosophy. He
is not, however, the only or even its main object of interest. As a matter
of fact, Fichte will end up occupying just as much space as Kant. The
main object of interest lies, however, in neither of these two philosophers
but at the intersection of two themes too broad to consider on their
own. One has to do with the reception of Kant between the publication
of the *Critique of Pure Reason* in 1781 and Fichte's publication of *The
Vocation of Humankind* in 1800 – in the period, that is, when transcendental
idealism was being transformed either into what eventually came to be
known as 'post-Kantian idealism' or into that kind of typically German
form of scientific as well as religious positivism that took hold of the
German philosophy faculties in the nineteenth century. The philosophy
of Jakob Friedrich Fries can be cited as a splendid example of this kind
of positivism.[1] The other theme has to do with the revolution in the
traditional conception of 'humanity' that had been underway throughout

1

Europe long before the publication of Kant's Critique. Such a revolution was radical in nature and inevitably posed some formidable challenges to the still deeply religious culture of the late German Enlightenment. The object of this book is to show, on the one hand, how Kant's Critique of Reason[2] was itself part of this revolution, and, on the other hand, how older modes of thought interfered with a proper understanding of its conceptual as well as cultural implications. The fact that Kant himself was not completely clear about such implications, but remained in many respects still hostage to the philosophical language of the older tradition, made things all the worse.

The nature of this revolution in the concept of humanity can be summed up in a simple statement. It consisted in the recognition that it is a mistake for the human being to look for meaning in the world, since his primary mission there is precisely to create this meaning.[3] Of course, nobody could have been expected at the time to formulate as radical a shift in perspectives as this recognition entailed with the same clarity as is possible for us in retrospect. Goethe had, however, come as close to it as anyone could in his famous poem *Prometheus*, the one that was to cause much scandal for Jacobi.[4] And Kant himself was soon to provide the formula for the shift that we still accept today as normative. On the whole, however, the change found expression indirectly in a variety of ways, most obviously in the general tendency to consider human beings precisely as *individuals*. In reaction against what it considered the empty speculations of past metaphysics, the Enlightenment sought to portray humanity mainly in the practical sphere, according to the psychological makeup of individuals, their personal interests and social relations.[5] The late Enlightenment movement of 'popular philosophy' (*Popularphilosophie*) was a widespread and self-conscious expression of precisely this tendency. At the same time, the Enlightenment also endorsed a view of physical nature that in fact negated the most individuating factor of any human being – namely, his capacity to determine his existence independently of physical compulsion. This was a view consistent with the old scholastic metaphysics, for which the possibility of human freedom vis-à-vis God had always been a source of difficulties, but one that now found revamped justification in the new physics that the Enlightenment also accepted enthusiastically. The problem was that, on the view of humans as individuals, the human being emerges as the responsible master of his own destiny; on the deterministic view, as a piece of the greater organization of matter[6] by which he is determined from beginning to end. Or again, on the one view, God – if a human individual still cares for him – has to be sought within the individual's own heart, as if an extension of his private conscience; on the other, the same individual finds himself externally caught up in this God's cosmic designs without having any effective say about them at all. The two views were incompatible. Goethe might have indeed found a poetically acceptable way of reconciling them in the vision of a humanity that attains freedom in the resolve to create a progeny of happy individuals – such that can laugh and play, and behave before the gods as if free, albeit in full awareness that they are in fact bound to them by chains.[7] This was the vision that he had forcefully expressed in the poem *Prometheus*. It might have been poetically viable, but it did nothing either to resolve the conceptual problem at hand or to relieve the moral predicament that it posed.

Kant, as we have just suggested, had hit upon the perfect conceptual formula for expressing the new humanism now taking shape. The radical rearrangement of ideas that this humanism required was implicit in his relentless polemic against traditional eudemonism, or the belief that the pursuit of a naturally preappointed happiness is what motivates moral life and therefore also defines the principles of moral science. It was made explicit in the claim, which Kant advanced in opposition to the other traditional and widely accepted position, that the idea of the law is itself the beginning of all morality, and of moral science accordingly. This appeared to his contemporaries as a strange claim indeed, counterintuitive and too empty of content to provide any significant guide to conduct. In fact, its formalism had wide-ranging material implications, for it made the 'law' itself – or 'lawfulness' as such; or again, in more concrete language, reason's capacity to legislate – into the one overriding value according to which all other values are to be measured. The pursuit of the realization of this value becomes, therefore, the highest end to which every rational being is to be committed; and the maintenance of the conditions that promote this pursuit, the highest duty to which such a being is bound. The inversion of priority of terms in the previously assumed relationship between reason and nature was clear. Nature does not determine what constitutes moral value. Rather, it first acquires moral significance only inasmuch as it becomes implicated in the task of establishing the universal rule of law. As Kant put it most graphically, it is not because the law abides by an alleged naturally determined distinction between 'good' and 'bad' that it acquires validity as law. On the contrary, that distinction arises in the first place when an action and its product either conform to the rule of law and are then deemed good or do not conform to it and are deemed bad. The pursuit of any naturally defined happiness loses, therefore, every semblance of constituting by itself a moral principle, since what counts as a happiness worth pursuing is itself an issue to be resolved on independent moral grounds.

This shift in perspectives was as radical as it was unmistakable. It came across most strikingly in the context of Kant's moral theory. But Kant's contemporaries had already been given notice of it at the very beginning of the _Critique of Pure Reason_, where "in place of the old presupposition, namely _that the understanding conforms to things_, Kant [had] laid down the new presupposition _that things must rather conform to the understanding_."[8] I am quoting from Reinhold (about whom much more in due time), who made this comment at the close of the century while lamenting the sad misappropriation to which Kant had been subjected at the hands of the 'popular philosophers'. The point is that after Kant reason was no longer to be conceived as the discoverer of meaning, whether in a theoretical or a practical context, but as the creator of it.

The question, however, is whether Kant had also succeeded in reconciling the two otherwise contradictory tendencies of the Enlightenment. In his own mind, and those of his first followers, it seemed that he had. His famous distinction between 'thing in itself' and 'appearances' allowed him an added intelligible space on the side of the thing in itself within which he could conceptually situate the human subject when considered as an agent responsible for self-determined activities, while still conceding that, when an object of external observation, that is, as appearance, the same subject is just as much ruled by the mechanism of nature as any other physical entity. That extra space could also be furnished with all sorts of what Kant called 'noumena' – _entia rationis_, as they were known in traditional scholastic philosophy, or 'constructs of reason'.[9] The ideas of 'God', the 'soul', and the 'world' all fell into this category. But there were many other instances as well – such entities, for instance, as 'courts of law', 'contracts', 'juries', and 'wills and testaments'.[10] These are all ideal objects that do not admit of strict empirical definition but that (according to Kant's scheme of things) the moral agent can nonetheless postulate as having a place in the ideal world of morality that is conceptually made possible by reference to the thing in itself. He must treat them as quasi-physical things for the sake of conducting his rationally determined human affairs. The scientist as well, according to Kant, produces his own set of ideal constructs – in his case, however, in order to regulate and thereby advance his own scientific activities of systematizing experience.[11] In either case, whether the issue is the broader goal of promoting humanity as such or the narrower one of promoting scientific discovery, the motivation for constructing these noumena and treating them as if they were real things lies, according to Kant, in reason's interest in its own program of formal rationality. In brief, it appeared indeed that Kant had hit upon the right formula for restricting knowledge to the limits of the science of the day, without, however, thereby embarking on any reductionist program on the broader pragmatic side of human existence. There was still ample logical room for legitimately treating the human individual as an autonomous subject of action.

But was the formula truly successful? It did not necessarily imply a two-worlds view of reality – one sensible and the other supersensible. This is an interpretation no longer in favour. It has now rather become commonplace to say that, according to Kant, "there are not 'two worlds', [i.e., one phenomenal and the other noumenal,] but rather one world which must be conceived in two different ways. [. . .]. When we view ourselves as phenomena, we regard everything about ourselves [. . .] as part of the natural world, and therefore as governed by its laws. But in so far as we are rational, we also regard ourselves as *active* beings, who are the authors of our thoughts and choices."[12] This is a fair claim. But its fairness should not blind us to its limitations. The metaphor on which it plays of conceiving one and the same world from two different points of view remains inherently opaque until two questions are answered: *Who* is the 'we' (call it the 'I') who assumes the two allegedly different points of view and considers himself, on the one hand, as *homo phaenomenon* and, on the other, as *homo noumenon*;[13] and *from where* are these points of view to be assumed? The obvious reply is that this I is the individual human self, and that the two points of view are assumed by him as he engages historically in different forms of activities. Though obvious, however, the reply begs the important questions of what constitutes the unity of this individual who can nonetheless regard himself in such totally disparate and apparently irreconcilable manners; and of how this same individual manages to stand outside of himself, so to speak, in order to regard himself in these ways. As I shall try to show in the rest of this book, this is the question that controlled the first stage of Kant reception in Germany. It explains in large part why the Critique of Reason met such vehement opposition in many quarters, and why so many attempts were made by those who at least thought they were its friends to interpret it along more familiar modes of thought or to reshape it radically along more idealistic lines. It even explains why many might even have thought that Kant was committing himself indeed to a two-worlds view of reality. In all cases, the problems that the question posed found expression in a debate concerning the adequacy of Kant's system for safeguarding the reality of human freedom. And this debate unavoidably brought in its train the further issue of the nature and importance of religion in human affairs.

1.2 THE SYSTEM

Why the system should have been implicated in the first place is a question worth considering.[14] One place where the philosopher comes to grips with the individual as such is precisely in the construction of his system, that is, at the juncture where all the more particularized conceptions that he has otherwise developed independently are deployed together in a single view of reality. System building is the philosopher's reflective way of regaining conceptually the experiential unity that the historical individual achieves pragmatically in the moment of decision taking. It is the philosopher's way of reaching back to actual history while still operating at the abstract level of reflection. In the medieval past, a theologian such as Thomas Aquinas could make this move by combining logical genealogy and historical narrative in a single conceptual structure. The *Summa Theologiae* is at once the deduction of things from their first principle of being and the story about an original event (creation) that was followed by another (man's fall through disobedience), which then necessitated another whole series of events (the incarnation and redemption) that marked the slow return of a fallen nature back to the creator. In the case of the critical Kant, since the principle of being is now thought itself, and since the original creative event is the positing of a world of meaning, the move back to historical experience is made rather in the second part of the *Critique of Pure Reason* in the Dialectic of Reason and the Transcendental Method. There Kant tries to reconcile apparently contradictory conceptions of nature by limiting each, and thereby rejoining, as Kant believed, the vision of common wisdom (A831/B859). Reality is now to be represented by individualizing, albeit ideal, constructs such as the Soul, the World, and God, with respect to which the historical subject of experience can define his own place within that reality precisely as individual. It is in the system, as Kant well knew, that one finds the philosophical resolution to such an existentially pressing question as "What may I hope for?", and thus it is in the system that the existential relevance of a philosophical position is being tested.

Such an existential view of 'system' might appear odd to us today. It is certainly at odds with the relentless polemic waged by existentialists and poststructuralists alike in the recent past against anything systematic. But it was not one that was foreign to Kant. On the contrary, there is good reason to believe that this existential view was uppermost in his mind, and that it was precisely to such a view – common in his day – that he wished to provide scientific reflective limits. Take, for instance, the title, *The Vocation of Humankind*,[15] that Fichte affixed to his already mentioned philosophico-devotional tract of 1800. In choosing that title, Fichte was harking back to a central theme of Enlightenment literature by unabashedly appropriating it from the book that in 1748 had given expression to the theme in the first place. The author, the pietist theologian Johann Joachim Spalding,[16] had then kept a record, so to speak, of the pulse of the Enlightenment by restating the theme in many subsequent revised editions of the book, each time in terms that reflected the most recent philosophical developments. The book won immediate and widespread popularity from the beginning and was to maintain it to the end of the century. It had been written in the language of the eudemonism of the day, and, as the author openly acknowledged in the preface of a later edition,[17] it reflected the modes of thought of the first half of the eighteenth century.[18] We shall have many occasions to return to it. Of interest to us right now is that, as stated in the edition of 1774, the purpose of the book had been to determine the nature and the purpose of human existence – to establish a "system of life," as Spalding says – in an effort to defend religion against what the author perceived to be the growing encroachments of materialism into people's lives.[19]

Here is a taste of what Spalding, writing under the thin cover of a fictional character, had to say.

Having suffered long enough the plague of an unstable mind, one troubled by opposing impressions, he [i.e., the writer] had resolved in earnest and with equanimity to examine what he should be, starting from the beginning. He had resolved not to accept anything as true, or reject anything as prejudice, which would not appear as such by this rigid new test; to collect and join together all that he found in this way undeniable, and to draw from it the necessary consequences . . . ; thus to establish for himself a secure system of life by which he could abide for all times. . . . (3)

Surely it was a worthwhile effort, the writer goes on to say, "to know why I am here, and what I should rationally be" (4). In this enterprise, moreover, he had been guided by the belief that "in a decision regarding such an important issue, truth would yield even to the plain but healthy human understanding the evidence sufficient to impart certainty and peace to a honest enquirer" (3–4). The writer was already in possession of the fruits of much experience; he had, moreover, the power to reflect and to choose. His task was only a matter of putting things in order. To this end, he would have had to avoid both the poetic pictures of an overheated imagination and "the aridity of unduly subtle thought" (*trockene Spitzfindigkeit*). As he concludes, "Let plain uncomplicated nature speak by me; surely its decisions are the most reliable" (4–6).

And what does this honest inquirer find as a result of his self-examination? First, he discovers that the satisfaction of the senses cannot be his only aim in life, since by itself such a satisfaction can easily lead to destruction. There are such things as the pleasures of the spirit (1–13). Second, he recognizes that he is a social being – that the satisfaction of his own needs cannot be divorced from that of the needs of others (25). Third, he observes that he reacts differently to the behavior of an animal, a child, or an idiot than to that of a man who acts with premeditated and possibly evil intentions, even though in both cases the behavior in question might be a threat to him. On the basis of this observation, he concludes that there must be, as he says, "a type of inclination, a source of actions, essentially different from self-love yet just as essentially part of my nature. Something is right and good and praiseworthy in itself, also without reference to my particular satisfactions and advantages; and something else is not" (31–2). Fourth, once this discovery has been made, he further recognizes that he finds in himself a deep satisfaction in the presence of order of any type, whether physical, aesthetic, or moral. This satisfaction is just as certain a fact for him as his need to sleep. At this point, therefore, he also discovers that his desire for happiness – his own and that of all others – follows from his awareness of being part of an overall order. "I am myself a part of the whole," he exclaims (33). It follows that, whenever his desire for happiness is thwarted by evil or other circumstances, his integrity as a human being is still left undisturbed, provided that in his actions he has remained attuned to the order of the universe. "Whatever evil might afflict me, cannot make me essentially [*in der Hauptsache*] unhappy, so long as I can say to myself: I do what I should do; I am what I should be. This alone is the inexhaustible source of the equanimity and the peace which, in their silent ways, are worth more than all the din of sense amusements" (38). Fifth and last, he discovers that his belief in God – a belief that follows naturally from his recognition of universal order (41) – also affords him the certainty of a future life. For the order itself of the universe requires that happiness be distributed

according to righteousness of conduct, and if the right proportion between the two is not achieved in the present life – and we know that it is
not – then it must be achieved in a future one.

The writer concludes:

Everything in nature persuades me that righteousness and happiness belong
together, and that they also always come together if external circumstances do
not disrupt this otherwise so essential a bond. Such a pervasive tendency for order
must, however, be fulfilled; and only its realization would remove the confusion
and contradiction that would otherwise obtain. If I were to consider this life as
the final human state, I would not be able to make my thinking on the matter
fall in one piece. The moment I however expand my vision [. . .], everything falls
conceptually into place [. . .]. The moment I am assured that the great originator
of all things – the one who at all times acts according to the strictest of rules and
the noblest intentions – cannot possibly be willing to annihilate me, I need not,
so I believe, fear any other destruction. (54–6, passim)

Now, at least as of 1774, in the medium of the popular philosophical language of the day heavily influenced by British empiricism and
Scottish 'commonsense' philosophy,[20] Spalding had in effect already formulated both the questions and the substance of the answers around
which Kant was to construct his system. He had done it, moreover, by
undertaking an inventory of the mind, exactly how Kant proposed to do
it (Axiv). What can I know? Answer: what my finite yet rational nature
allows me to know. How must I act? Answer: according to a distinction between right and wrong that is more fundamental than any distinction between the pleasurable and the repugnant. In what must I believe? Answer:
in my freedom and in a universal order. What can I hope for? Answer:
in a future life. These are Spalding's questions and answers no less than
Kant's. I am not suggesting that Kant drew his inspiration from Spalding
or, for that matter, that he even knew of him – though it is very unlikely that he did not.[21] The point, rather, is that, though the 'system'
might appear to us to be the aspect of Kant's critical work most removed
from actual experience because it is the aspect most dependent on ideal
constructs, it was in fact the place where he was addressing the most
pressing existential questions posed by his age. It is the system, moreover, where his critical revolution had the most devastating effects. To
all appearances he was simply restating Spalding's questions in their culturally accepted form, and also giving to them the culturally accepted
answers. He was rejoining 'common wisdom', as he himself might have
thought, though by way of his new critical instruments. But in fact, precisely by deploying these instruments, he was explicitly bringing into play

the assumptions of the new humanism that had already been interfering with the accepted beliefs of his day. While speaking the language of Spalding, Kant had in fact already undermined the easy transition from a presumed universal order of nature to the moral perfection of the human individual that Spalding took for granted. To be sure, in his system Kant had sought to reestablish on a critical basis the possibility of that transition. But the resulting universal harmony of things could no longer have the same meaning that it had for the audience to which Spalding was addressing himself. Nor could the ideal of rationality that Kant now promoted, or the faith and hope he counseled, have the same meaning.

Here is where the potential for confusion lay. For Kant was couching his system in traditional language. It was easy to assume that, after Kant, things in the cultural universe stood exactly where they had always been, except that the method for justifying their place had become more complex. As a matter of fact, things had not been the same for some time, and Kant's Critique of Reason, far from reestablishing them in the old order, only served to destabilize them all the more. Whatever order it brought about had to be radically new. One man who was clearly to understand these deep cultural implications was Fichte. But he paid the price for his insight in 1800. At the very end of the first stage of the reception of the Critique of Reason, he found himself leaving the university and the city of Jena under suspicion of atheism. Kant himself had just disavowed him as a would-be disciple.[22] Apparently Kant also was not in the clear about the radicalness of his own conceptual revolution.

1.3 THE PRESENCE OF JACOBI

We shall eventually return to these events. Here we must retrace our steps and add one more circumstance that affected the first stage of Kant reception. In the course of the events that eventually led to Fichte's departure from Jena in 1800, there was one man whom Fichte thought was an ally but who, though trying to come to his aid at the personal level, came out against him in public. This man was Friedrich Heinrich Jacobi, the same man we have already mentioned in connection with Goethe's *Prometheus*. He is important because, although he became a factor in the reception of Kant only after 1785 – after the publication, that is, of his correspondence with Moses Mendelssohn on the subject of Spinoza and Spinozism[23] – from that time on he set the tone of the reception of Kant on both the pro and the contra side. Jacobi might not have been an exceptionally creative philosopher. He was, however, a perceptive one. He had long recognized the incompatibility of the Enlightenment's interest in the 'individual' and its scientific agenda. He was also aware that the latter entailed a rejection of the God-centered Christian humanism, and was greatly disturbed by some of its already visible cultural manifestations. The heroic pantheism of Goethe's *Prometheus* was a case in point. But Jacobi placed the blame for this unfortunate turn of events squarely on the shoulders of the philosophers because of what he took to be their perverse conception of 'reason' and 'rationality'. Astute cultural propagandist that he was, he sought to bring the issue to public debate by orchestrating a dispute with Moses Mendelssohn that, though private at first, would eventually break – as Jacobi must have planned – into the public arena. And this is indeed what happened in 1785.[24] From that time on, the fate of Kant reception was inexorably intertwined with Jacobi's diagnosis of the malady that in his opinion affected the Enlightenment and with the etiology that he offered for it.

Mendelssohn was at the time the leading German Enlightenment philosopher and, until Lessing's premature death in 1781, the close friend of that other great artificer of the *Aufklärung*. The original point of the contention that Jacobi had raised with Mendelssohn was whether Lessing had been a Spinozist; and whether all philosophy entailed Spinozism and hence (as Jacobi claimed) was by nature atheistic. This final link in the chain of argumentation was made by way of definition, since at the time most took it for granted that Spinozism equaled atheism. In defense of his recently deceased friend, Mendelssohn had argued that Lessing could not have declared to Jacobi in an alleged private conversation that he was a follower of Spinoza, at least not in any seriously philosophical sense; and that, even if he had, Spinozism could be interpreted in ways perfectly consistent with such deeply held religious beliefs as that God is transcendent and that he created the world *ex nihilo*. There was nothing in what Jacobi had been recounting about Lessing, according to Mendelssohn, that could detract from the reputation that Lessing enjoyed among his contemporaries of being an enlightened, but still basically Christian, personality. Jacobi, for his part, had been arguing the very opposite. And his argument, as he and Mendelssohn, as well as the public at large, well knew, had implications that far exceeded the immediate issue of Lessing's alleged Spinozism. It was in effect an attack on the Enlightenment ideal of humanity, of which the two great friends – Lessing and Mendelssohn – had been the leading promoters. Jacobi was now saying that in the end this humanism, based as it was on an abstract idea of rationality, artificially construed for the sake of satisfying the speculative needs of philosophers, denied in fact the reality and the moral significance of human individuality. And since freedom, according to Jacobi, was nothing apart from the individual, this humanism thereby also undermined the possibility of freedom itself. The upshot of the much vaunted Enlightenment humanism, according to Jacobi, was an atheistic antihumanism.

The bitterness of the dispute and the wide, at times violent, reactions that it provoked attest to the relevance to the culture of the day of the issue it had raised. Reflecting on it over fifty years later, Goethe was to describe the event as a "veritable conflagration" that affected everyone and pitted even the closest of spirits against one another.[25] At first it was waged in the language of classical Enlightenment scholasticism, that is, the Wolffian version of Leibniz's philosophy further modified through the influence of British empiricism. That had been Spalding's language also. But it was Mendelssohn himself who gave notice at one point that the situation had come to such a confused state that the "all-crushing" Kant (Mendelssohn's word)[26] was alone in a position to resolve it. Soon after, in 1786, for reasons and under circumstances that we need not detail here, Reinhold began publishing in the *Teutscher Merkur* the first version of the eight letters on the subject of Kant's critical philosophy that have since come to be known as the *Kantian Letters*.[27] In these letters Reinhold portrayed Kant in the way the latter was himself to do in 1787, in the Preface to the second edition of the *Critique of Pure Reason*, namely, as the one who, by limiting the claims of reason, had thereby made room for faith (Bxxx). In the context of the then raging Jacobi–Mendelssohn dispute, Reinhold was deliberately casting Kant in the role of mediator between the otherwise contradictory claims of the two parties. As we shall see, the possibilities that critical philosophy offered for reformulating traditional theological doctrines on a new conceptual foundation, one immune to skeptical attacks, had already not been lost on at least some theologians. Reinhold was not being, therefore, particularly original. But the Jacobi–Mendelssohn dispute had raised the issue of whether the Enlightenment humanism was a viable one – or, more precisely, whether the Enlightenment was capable, on the strength of its given intellectual resources, of defending the very ideals of humanity that it professed to champion. Kant himself had always been a promoter of these values. By casting him in the role of mediator, Reinhold was now positioning him front and center in the debate over the Enlightenment – in effect testing the strength of his critical assumptions against Enlightenment ideals. By the same stroke, however, he was placing Jacobi and his criticism of philosophical reason in the same position.

What was this criticism? If one is to believe Jacobi's report of his 1779 conversation with Lessing, the point he had been arguing with him was that the philosophers, driven by their enthusiasm for explanation, are given to mistaking conditions of explanation for conditions of existence, and hence to assuming that reality conforms to the abstractions that philosophers have created. Since such abstractions leave behind the individuality of actual human beings, and since, however, it is only as individuals that these beings can be the subjects of action, it follows that the philosophers' view of reality does not allow for genuine action. As Jacobi famously put it, in a world such as the philosophers conceive it, one should not say that Raphael painted the *School of Athens*, but rather that an anonymous efficacy has made its way across the world and had resulted in something that we call the *School of Athens* and associate with the name of Raphael.[28] That, according to Jacobi, was the ultimate implication of the Spinozist formula of the *hen kai pan* ('one and all'). Lessing, for his part, had declared his general agreement with this formula, at least to the extent that he saw no alternative to it. And Jacobi had responded by suggesting that Lessing redress his position through a *salto mortale*. This was a jump, head over heels, to be performed on the strength of faith alone.[29] In the manner of philosophers, Lessing now stood and walked on his head, confusing abstractions with the solid ground of reality. In virtue of the jump that Jacobi was now proposing to him, he would find himself redressed, standing again upright on real ground.

There were personal factors – notably his peculiar relation to Goethe – that had motivated Jacobi's whole course of action from the beginning. It might well be that Goethe, and the cult of nature that the latter had been championing, were Jacobi's primary target of attack, and that Lessing and the philosophers were only secondary targets.[30] Inasmuch as Jacobi's criticism was to degenerate, moreover, into a personal attack on Mendelssohn, Jacobi was being especially unfair. As a matter of fact, Mendelssohn had always been a staunch defender of the primacy of the individual. On one occasion in which he had disagreed with his friend Lessing, the disagreement was due to the latter's conception of history.[31] Mendelssohn could not accept the image of history as a slow progression toward a final revelation of reason that Lessing was proposing because, in his view, such an image made the individual subjects of history of secondary importance to the unfolding of reason itself. Nonetheless, whatever the historical complexities of the case, the claim that Jacobi had made regarding philosophical reason using Lessing as a foil was emotionally powerful and not without conceptual merit. It brings us back to the point with which we began. The Enlightenment could not have it both ways. It could not idolize human individuality yet endorse a scientific view of the universe in which everything is determined externally, and hence where no room is left for true human autonomy. Jacobi was now arguing that this picture of the universe was part of the legacy of traditional metaphysics. And this is the claim that set the tone for the subsequent reception of Kant. From 1785, after the publication of Jacobi's correspondence with Mendelssohn, the central issue became precisely whether, as Reinhold claimed, Kant had truly succeeded in reconciling the rational aspirations of traditional metaphysics with the personalistic demands of Jacobi's faith – in effect, whether one could indeed perform the jump that Jacobi had urged on Lessing, but on grounds provided by reason itself – or whether, on the contrary, Kant had rendered an old problem even more intractable than ever before. Lessing, incidentally, had declined the suggested jump with his usual irony citing the infirmities of old age as his excuse.

Jacobi himself came out against Kant. It is true that his attitude toward the great philosopher was never totally unambiguous. In the course of the Spinoza dispute, as we shall see, he made a point of declaring the close affinity to his own thought that, when still a young man and an innocent seeker of philosophical wisdom, he had discerned in Kant's way of treating metaphysical questions.[32] By contrast, he had always found Mendelssohn's rationalism suspect.[33] Late in life, Jacobi suggested that he himself had been the first to propose the kind of argument that Kant later used in his refutation of idealism.[34] Yet, despite the ambiguities, Jacobi had come out strongly against the critical Kant from the beginning, treating his transcendental philosophy as one more example of the philosophers's method of replacing real things with abstractions. In his view, Kant had pushed that method to its limit. He had extended it to the realm of subjectivity, thus substituting, even more insidiously than ever before because now done in the language of a pseudo I, the 'self' of real individuals with an empty abstraction. The result was that, while talking about freedom, Kant was in fact denying it.

The irony is that, in one important respect at least, Jacobi and Kant were both pursuing the same agenda. Both were making an issue of the possibility of human agency. Kant's reason for rejecting eudemonism, or any other form of ethical naturalism, was precisely that, to the extent that the human individual relies for his motivation on factors established for him by nature – be these internal or external – he behaves as a spectator with respect to his own actions. He observes the natural factors that ply their influence on him and even decides, perhaps, which among them are most likely to determine his conduct, but ultimately lacks the control over them that would establish a direct connection between himself and the resulting actions.[35] Any such connection is rather mediated by a nature that transcends him as an individual. More like observer than agent, he remains detached from his own supposed actions. This was exactly the point that Jacobi also had been making against the philosophers. In the universe as they conceive it, action must remain anonymous. The personal link between individual and action is broken by being reduced to a moment in a system of abstract cosmic relations; moral responsibility, therefore, is abolished. Translated into Kant's language, this amounted to saying that, on any form of naturalism, moral doctrine fails to capture the practical attitude, that is, the ground of an individual's responsible engagement in his activities that morality demands. Though parading itself as 'practical', it remains mere 'theory'. On this issue at least, Jacobi and Kant shared common ground. Any commonality between the two, however, ceased there. For they each drew from their identical insight radically opposite conclusions. Kant, as we have seen, felt obliged to invert the long-accepted relation of reason to nature, and assumed that reason, according to its formal requirements, sets the norm for what nature 'ought to be'. Jacobi, by contrast, took the autonomy that reason displays at the hands of the philosophers, and on which Kant was now relying for establishing a direct link between the human agent and his actions, as the philosophical fiction that preempts precisely this link from the start. Since it abstracts from the agent's individuality, it makes impossible the intimate relation between the agent and his God. But it is only in the presence of this God, according to Jacobi, that the human individual is forced to acknowledge who he is, and can therefore take responsibility for what he does. Kant might have thought of safeguarding on rational grounds the religiosity of a Spalding. In Jacobi's view, he was striking the final blow against it. Rather than remedying a cultural malady, Kant was compounding it.

The situation must have been complex indeed when, on the basis of an identical insight, two serious cultural commentators such as Kant and Jacobi could reach directly opposite diagnoses for a commonly perceived malady and offer contradictory remedies for it. One cannot fault Kant's contemporaries if, whether they opposed Kant or sided with him, many equally thought themselves as at the same time promoting Jacobi's

cause. The facts of the case were inherently ambiguous. One thing is,
however, clear. In the many debates that ensued, whatever the different
shades of opinion held by the participants, the question we raised at
the beginning – who might possibly be this individual who assumes the
different transcendental points of views required by Kant – remained at
center stage throughout. Jacobi kept it there. In one way or another, as
we shall see, the debates were to be fought on the issue of the possibility
of human freedom. In one way or another, moreover, they all brought
religion into play. This is one more factor to consider in the early reception of Kant's critique of reason. Religion was everywhere in everybody's
mind, and for understandable reasons. The German Enlightenment was
obsessed with the subject. Jacobi had recently made the charge that all
philosophy necessarily leads to atheism. Reinhold had made religion the
leading theme of his *Kantian Letters*. And Kant himself had played on
the theme from the beginning, giving one to understand that his critical
claims of ignorance opened up new conceptual possibilities for defining the place of faith in human experience. But again, it was Jacobi who
sounded the alarm regarding the implications for religion of the new
idealism.

1.4 POLEMICAL NOTES

With his penchant for the bon mot, Jacobi had first publicly summed up
his reaction toward Kant in 1787 (on the occasion of the publication of
the second edition of the *Critique of Pure Reason*) by saying that without
Kant's 'thing in itself' he could find no entrance into the transcendental
system, but, once there through that opening, he found himself already
out of the system.[36] His argument was that Kant's peculiar brand of idealism was based on the assumption of a thing that exists in itself but of
which we have absolutely no knowledge. One cannot, however, assume
such a thing, and assign to it a relevant role within the system, without
thereby giving a content to it, that is, without attributing determinations
to it that belie the original claim of ignorance. It is taken, for instance,
as the cause of immediate sensations. The argument, incidentally, was
not original to Jacobi. It had already been raised in the earliest reviews
of the Critique,[37] and was to be repeated after Jacobi in different contexts and for different purposes. Schulze/Ænesidemus, for one, made a
great deal out of it in defense of skepticism.[38] It was not, moreover, a
fair argument. It took for granted that Kant conceived the thing in itself in the same spirit as Locke had assumed the existence of particular

physical entities outside the mind – the mind itself being conceived also as a particular entity, albeit of a special kind. But in fact Kant was only concerned with the structure of the universe of meaning. The object of his system was reason and rationality; the system itself was a transcendental logic rather than metaphysics or psychology in any traditional sense. The thing in itself was accordingly an idea – a norm of objectivity in general, the counterpart of the thinking subject, that allowed him to clarify otherwise opaque distinctions. It made possible the notion of a 'phenomenal object' on which Kant's whole system depended. It explained the sense in which the whole field of sense experience appears to us as irreducibly contingent. For, as contrasted with what the objects that appear to the senses *might be* from the ideal standpoint of the thing in itself – or with what they *ought to be* from a practical standpoint for which the thing in itself makes room ideally – how such objects are de facto constituted for the mind in experience depends on factors over which the latter has no complete control. Sense objects are therefore in principle always reformable; whether taken singly or collectively, they are always contingent. By the same token, however, just because they are nothing definite on their own, they can always be ideally referred, in toto, to the thing in itself; singly, to other equally single phenomenal objects, in a series extending *in infinitum.* Within the confines of actual experience, in other words, they can be subjected to the laws of external, strictly mechanical, causation.

In brief, the thing in itself allowed Kant to exploit the notion of 'facticity' in its double sense of 'contingency' and 'external necessitation'. In professing ignorance regarding it, Kant was denying 'knowledge' only in the sense in which a dogmatist might claim or disclaim to possess it. His thing in itself simply escaped the parameters of 'knowing' or 'notknowing' in that sense. Jacobi's criticism was misplaced precisely because it was still being advanced on dogmatic grounds. Yet there was a point to his bon mot, though not necessarily one intended by him. Kant was filling the logical space provided by the thing in itself with conceptual constructs that defined the limits of the universe within which the human being must establish his self-identity and thereby realize his vocation. This was a perfectly legitimate move on his part. However, for the reasons just stated, to claim either knowledge or ignorance with reference to these constructs, or to the universe they defined, made no sense at all. Since the meaning of things – I mean, the kind of meaningfulness humans expect in life – is not to be presupposed ready-made in a preestablished physical cosmos, but is rather to be produced ideally by reason, any difficulty that such a production presents is itself to be resolved at an ideal level of reflection.[39] As it happened, there was a difficulty in the ideal universe as defined by Kant's system – the difficulty, namely, of reconciling the two at least apparently contradictory ideas of 'physical' and 'moral nature'. And Kant was appealing to 'critical ignorance' as a means of resolving the difficulty. He thereby made himself vulnerable to the charge that either he was still presupposing the thing in itself as understood by the dogmatists, while at the same time denying knowledge of it, or, alternatively, dissembling in his use of 'ignorance'. He was not being forthright about what the ignorance in question was the ignorance of. In either case, Jacobi's bon mot applied. Kant had stepped outside his own system.

The difficulty in question went deeper than was evident from Kant's already mentioned attempt to remedy it by restricting physical nature to the realm of appearances and thereby opening up an ideal space for moral nature. A telling symptom was the radically different meanings that the modal categories – notably that of 'possibility' – acquire when applied in the context of each of the two presumed natures. In a theoretical frame of reference, with respect to physical phenomena, such categories do not signify anything about the content of an intended object but define, rather, an observer's relationship to it (A219/B266). This observer must, on the one hand, presuppose his intended object in order to be able to recognize it once it appears in experience (in other words, in order to judge that *it is* indeed as *it is said* to be); on the other hand, he cannot know that it truly is as intended until it is de facto given in experience and immediately apprehended as such. Confronted by these contrasting conditions, the observer has no choice but to assume the object first as a theoretical possibility and then to seek to see it realized in actual experience piecemeal in the medium of the senses (thereby also testing the validity of his original assumption). In this theoretical framework, possibility thus denotes an observer's original material ignorance with respect to his intended object. It denotes the limitation imposed upon him by the fact that he must approach the object from the outside, so to speak; or, as Kant puts it, the fact that he must determine the content of his object discursively, starting from a universal concept for which he must then find particular instantiations in actual experience. If one were capable of approaching an object from the inside out, from the standpoint of the thing in itself – or, as Kant normally puts it, if one had an intellectual intuition of it – any such distinction between abstract intention and particular realization would disappear. Possibility would fall, and, along with it, the other modal categories as well. Kant was quite explicit on this point. As he says:

It is absolutely necessary for the human understanding to distinguish between the possibility and the actuality of things. The reason for this lies in the subject and in the nature of its cognitive faculties. For if two entirely heterogeneous elements were not required for the exercise of these faculties, understanding for concepts and sensible intuition for objects corresponding to them, there would be no such distinction (between the possible and the actual). That is, if our understanding were intuitive, it would have no objects except what is actual. Concepts (which pertain merely to the possibility of an object) and sensible intuitions (which merely give us something, without thereby allowing us to cognize it as an object) would both disappear. Now, however, all of our distinction between the merely possible and the actual rests on the fact that the former signifies only the position of the representation of a thing with respect of our concept and, in general, our faculty of thinking, while the latter signifies the positing of the thing in itself (apart from this concept). Thus the distinction of possible from actual things is one that is of merely subjective validity for the human understanding.[40]

The situation is radically different in a moral context. The object there cannot even be conceived without thereby implicating the category of possibility. For unless things may *possibly* be otherwise than they de facto are, there will not arise the idea of measuring them against a norm that transcends them in order to determine what they *ought* to be as contrasted to what they are. The whole of moral language – such concepts as 'responsibility', 'obligation', 'guilt', or 'merit', all of which are essential to such language – depends precisely on the assumption that, in any given situation, moral possibility as defined by an 'ought' trumps whatever motivation for action the de facto natural content of the situation might otherwise warrant. It was primarily for this reason that Kant, on his own testimony (Bxxx), had declared the objects of experience as 'appearances' – in order, that is, to allow at least the purely logical possibility of interpreting them as being in themselves the product of freedom, which would in turn allow investing them by extension with moral meaning.[41] Here is, however, where the difficulty lay. Kant was working with two ideas. One was that of a community of intelligible beings acting autonomously in an attempt to establish nature as it 'ought to be' – a *corpus mysticum*, as Kant occasionally calls it,[42] based on possibilities opened up by the idea of a pure reason. The other was the idea of the thing in itself as something that just is to which Kant's category of possibility led him in a theoretical context. And the two ideas did not fit together by any conceptual stretch. Kant's universe of meaning thus ineluctably tended to fall apart. Kant could convey the impression of having reconciled, in principle at least, its two principal components, the theoretical and the practical, only by equivocating in the use of the concept of 'causality', that is, by treating it in a moral context as the work of reason and in a theoretical context as 'efficient force'. In this last sense, whether understood phenomenally or extrapolated ideally into a noumenal world, the concept still depended on the image of physical exertion. How the two senses held together by the use of a single term – indeed, whether causality applied to 'freedom' understood as a work of reason at all – was a question that remained begged.[43]

Nor was Kant addressing the question when he insisted that we have no knowledge whatsoever of the thing in itself, and that the logical possibility of reconciling with reference to it the theoretical demands of science with the moral demands of freedom is therefore purely negative, a denial of contradiction rather than the assertion of anything positive (A558/B586). Even while disclaiming knowledge, Kant was in fact making at least two claims that had significant material consequences. For one thing, Kant granted that one must start by postulating a reality that somehow transcends anyone's experience of it. And inasmuch as one hypothetically assumes the standpoint of this reality and considers all things from it, Kant was saying that from that standpoint all the distinctions that define rationality no longer hold – notable among them the modal distinctions, and the distinction between the theoretical and the practical. They would all be absorbed into a simple 'is'. But this is to imply that, in itself or before it is subjected to the conditions of consciousness, reality transcends not just the limits of human reason (a claim that no religious metaphysician would have been likely to deny); and not just the knowledge that dogmatic metaphysics pretends to display; it transcends rather *reason as such*. It is to imply, in other words, that the fiction of assuming the standpoint of the thing in itself is just a rhetorical device, since the very concept of 'knowledge' no longer applies from that standpoint. It follows that, in contrast to the thing in itself, the universe of meaning that reason creates and we as humans live in is just an epiphenomenon; in itself, reality is neither rational nor irrational, but simply *there*. This was, however, as far-reaching a metaphysical commitment as any Enlightenment philosopher would have dared to advance.[44] Kant was making it while claiming critical modesty at the same time. He was not just denying the validity of the knowledge professed by the dogmatists but also opposing their claims with a positive claim of his own – namely, that what they claimed to know was, on his critical terms, *intrinsically* unknowable.[45]

Kant was himself making a metaphysical claim. Jacobi's bon mot applied again.

From Kant's claim, there followed a significant practical consequence. If the distinction between actuality and possibility is strictly a function of human cognition, yet this distinction is essential to moral language, it follows that, when tested against the ideal thing in itself, moral language loses all meaning. One should, of course, expect such a result, since under the same test the whole universe of meaning comes into question. Kant acknowledged this point quite openly, but by framing it in a way that hid (perhaps even to himself) its devastating consequences for moral theory. As he says:

Just as in the theoretical consideration of nature reason must assume the idea of an unconditioned necessity of its primordial ground, so, in the case of the practical, it also presupposes its own unconditioned (in regard to nature) causality, i.e., freedom, because it is aware of its moral command. Now since here, however, the objective necessity of the action, as duty, is opposed to that which it, as an occurrence, would have if its ground lay in nature and not in freedom (i.e., in the causality of reason), and the action which is morally absolutely necessary can be regarded physically as entirely contingent (i.e., what necessarily **should** happen often does not,) it is clear that it depends only on the subjective constitution of our practical faculty that the moral laws must be represented as commands (and the actions which are in accord to them as duties), and that reason expresses this necessity not through a **be** (happening) but through a should-be: which would not be the case if reason without sensibility (as the subjective condition of its application to objects of nature) were considered, as far as its causality is concerned, as a cause in an intelligible world, corresponding completely with the moral law, where there would be no distinction between what should be done and what is done, between a practical law concerning that which is possible through us and the theoretical law concerning that which is actual through us. Now, however, although an intelligible world, in which everything would be actual merely because it is (as something good) possible, and even freedom, as its formal condition, is a transcendent concept for us, which is not serviceable for any constitutive principle for determining an object and its objective reality, still, in accordance with the constitution of our (partly sensible) nature, it can serve as a universal **regulative principle**. . . . [46]

This is a line of argument that Kant exploited in other contexts as well. He prided himself, for instance, on having been able, unlike Spinoza,[47] to save the teleology of nature precisely by relying on the distinction between nature as it de facto appears in experience and as it ought to be and *might* be indeed in a purely intelligible world. The distinction allowed him to treat the ought (but, of course, only ideally, in the manner of a regulative principle) as an end toward which nature is internally

directed to realize. 'Internally' is the key word here, since interiority of
direction is the necessary condition for any genuine idea of teleology.
Spinoza, according to Kant, lacked the conceptual basis for attributing
such an interiority to nature in any way, even if only ideally. In one of
his earlier critical essays, Kant had also employed a similar strategy when
suggesting the principle of a possible critical philosophy of history. In his
view, nature is to be conceived as promoting the realization in this world
of such conditions as would obtain ideally in a purely intelligible world.
It does so mechanically, according to laws governing phenomena, but
under the steering of a secret internal plan. It is as if, under the guide
of a benevolent Creator, it worked for the realization in time, but at an
infinitely remote future, of ends that are consistent with the realization
of freedom in the human race.[48]

Kant's was indeed an imaginatively compelling line of argument – one
that could indeed convey the impression, which many accepted, that the
critical system saved, even protected, the otherwise threatened spiritual
world of Spalding. There was, however, an intractable problem lurking
in it. It lay in Kant's use in the cited text of 'intellectual' and 'intelligible' in such expressions as 'intellectual intuition' and 'intelligible world',
and also (to return to a point already broached) in Kant's supposition in
other places of a presumed 'efficient causality of freedom'.[49] According
to Kant's own account, inasmuch as we can think of an 'intellectual intuition' at all, we must construe it ideally as an act of cognition that, in
being performed, creates its own object. So construed, the act is reminiscent of the theological notion of God's creative act; or, closer to home, of
Descartes's and Spinoza's *causa sui*.[50] On such a construal, however, intellectual loses all recognizable meaning, since all the distinctions on which
intelligibility depends – notably the distinction between 'subject' and
'object' that allows for conceptualization and recognition (*Erkennen*) –
no longer apply. It is only metaphorically, therefore, that the intuition
is called intellectual. No less than the sense-intuition to which Kant denies any cognitive power per se, intellectual intuition would be more
appropriately characterized as 'blind'. It could just as well be imagined
as an infinite force that unknowingly issues forth in an endless stream
of effects. In this sense, it might then be identified, perhaps, with the
presumed 'efficient causality' that Kant attributes to freedom as a thing
in itself. But here again, when imagined in this way, freedom no longer
has any recognizable connection with the freedom required for moral
purposes. The latter is inextricably bound to reason's conceptual ability
to establish values and, along with values, possibilities of choice. In either

case, whether intuition or efficiency is at issue, the use of intellectual and of freedom has at best only rhetorical meaning.

To be sure, Kant did not claim much more, if any more, than such a meaning. As he insists, we cannot conceive even the conceptual possibility of a would-be intellectual intuition, or of an infinitely efficient causality, let alone assert any knowledge of either.[51] It makes a difference, however, to the quality of the moral life one espouses – I mean, to the kinds of commitments to which one is thereby bound, or the kind of doubts and temptations to which one is exposed – if, in order to define the nature of that life, one has to bring into play ideal constructs that in fact escape the bounds of meaning as required by its practice. It makes a difference, in other words, if a moral agent must subject himself to the rule of an ought that, were it ever to be realized, would transpose him to a world where that ought would no longer have any meaning. What is there, apart from purely subjective motivation, to prevent the agent from wondering whether, from the standpoint of the reality that the ought itself defines in principle, that same ought and the whole moral life dependent on it is just an epiphenomenon, an illusion that is given credibility only by his own commitment to live by it? But then, what difference would there be – rhetoric and subjective preferences apart – between Kant's moral vision and that which, to Jacobi's great scandal, Goethe had vividly championed in his *Prometheus*? In both cases, the human being acts *as if* he were free, in full awareness that, while engaged in his human designs, another force that transcends even the meaning of 'design' is fatefully working itself out.

Ironically, Kant himself unwittingly gave voice to this aporia. In a passage in which he distinguishes between nature as a system of externally necessitated events and 'nature' as the product of moral activities, he says:

if the proficiency of choice in accordance with laws of freedom, in contrast to laws of nature, is also to be called *art* here, by this would have to be understood a kind of art that makes possible a system of freedom like a system of nature, truly a divine art were we in a position also to carry out fully, by means of it, what reason prescribes and to put the idea of it into effect.[52]

Suppose now, as Kant does in another passage at the end of Part I of the *Critique of Practical Reason* – that we could *per impossibile* realize this idea, in virtue of an insight into things that, as Kant says, would make "God and eternity in their awful majesty [...] stand unceasingly before our eyes (for that which we can completely prove," Kant adds, "is as certain as that which we can ascertain by sight)."[53] In that case, we would be indeed in a position to avoid the many conflicts to which moral life is necessarily prone, since it is guided by ideal intentions rather than anything immediately present. We would be in a position to allow the natural dispositions to have their way according to their external play of forces, but in full view of their otherwise merely intended goal, thereby achieving mechanically and infallibly what we would otherwise have to strive for internally under the guidance of moral imperatives. There we would have indeed the consummation of the 'divine art' of which Kant speaks in the earlier passage. But then, Kant admits,

the moral worth of actions, on which alone the worth of the person and even of the world depends in the eyes of supreme wisdom, would not exist at all. The conduct of man, so long as his nature remained as it now is, would be changed into mere mechanism, where, as in a puppet show, everything would gesticulate well but no life would be found in the figures.[54]

One should not therefore complain – Kant concludes – if "a stepmotherly nature"[55] has not given us the insight into things we might otherwise wish to have (and many wrongheadedly claim to possess), but should rather revere the inscrutable wisdom that has on the contrary denied us that knowledge in order to allow us the worth of moral persons.[56]

One might balk at the image of a wisdom that is hidden from humans because, if it were ever revealed to them in full, they would see what they thought was the substance of their existence vanish before them. The more important question, however, is whether the term 'wisdom' has any place here at all; whether a more appropriate figure would not be that of a demonic force that escapes the bounds of rationality. The image of a wisdom that hides itself is nonetheless instructive, because it is the counterpart of the image of a human being who hides from what might be the truth of his situation in fear that, if the truth were ever revealed, the situation would become for him intolerable. But again, how would a humanity figured in such a being differ from the one celebrated in Goethe's *Prometheus*, except for the element of self-deception present in the one but happily absent in the other?

1.5 THE ISSUE OF RELIGION

Jacobi had good reasons indeed to be worried about the new critical philosophy. He had entered the philosophical fray in the first place because of religious concerns, even before the specifically critical notion of 'rationality' had been in play. So far as he could see, the God of the philosophers only served the purpose of safeguarding the supremacy of the universal. The God to whom he addressed his prayers was rather the infinitely transcendent 'Thou', the great 'Other' who forces the human individual to recognize his own finitude and thereby realize his individuality. Jacobi liked to portray himself as the champion of the exception – one who would not hesitate to break every ethical prescription if the integrity of the individual was at stake.[57] He would have nothing to do with a philosophical cosmic principle that was in fact reason itself, thinly disguised under the figurative image of a person. In the critical version of the same figure, God now stood for 'practical' rather than purely speculative reason. It was now being said that religion is "the representation of the laws of reason as divine commands, and of virtue as the conformity of a will with the will of a holy and generous creator of the world – which creator has the will and the power to bring about the most accurate balance of happiness and morality." "Through religion," it was further claimed, "consciousness of merit turns therefore into hope of enjoyment of happiness." This definition was provided by Carl Christian Ernst Schmid – the same Schmid who was the author of the first and at the time very popular Kant-Lexicon.[58] It was widely accepted by the Kantians of the day, and apparently satisfied the religious interests of those among them – the Jena theologians at first and then Reinhold – who had turned to Kant precisely because they thought that his critique of reason offered a rational safeguard for their faith. But it could hardly satisfy Jacobi, since God was still being portrayed as the enforcer of universal principles.

Jacobi eventually accused the new idealism that Kant had originated of atheism. He directed the charge against Fichte in the course of the dispute that was to surround the latter at the end of the century. It was clear, however, that for Jacobi, Fichte's idealism was only a logical extension of Kant's. Indeed it was, and the threat that it posed to Jacobi's piety was in fact even subtler, and therefore more threatening, than Jacobi himself might perhaps have realized. It was not the same threat as the one posed by the Enlightenment rationalism that had been Jacobi's original foe. Kant's strategy of critical ignorance had changed things radically. A quite different interest now hid behind the figure of God that idealism (whether critical or otherwise) was advancing, and quite different the faith that it evoked.

According to its traditional meaning, 'faith' is the assent to a presumed truth that escapes the comprehension of the believer, but that the latter nonetheless accepts on some subjective ground.[59] (In Christian theology, this ground is the love of God.) The object of faith is thus something presumably intelligible per se, though not necessarily intelligible *for us*. Faith, accordingly, is not essentially opposed to knowledge. On the contrary, it is already knowledge, though based on insufficient evidence, hence dependent on nonnoetic factors for its assent. This is how faith was understood in orthodox Christian theology and how the Enlightenment also understood it – except that, in the case of the latter, the object of faith was no longer the saving God to whom Jacobi still prayed, but a vision of things that could be, and would eventually be, totally consummated through conceptual means. The faith that the pious but unenlightened folk took to be the product of divine revelation constituted rather, despite all pious protestations to the contrary, already an immediate, unreflective, nonconceptual form of rationality – already knowledge, albeit a knowledge that did not know itself as knowledge.

Lessing, of course, had exploited this notion of faith in order to explain why there can be many historical faiths and how they can be reconciled.[60] But the notion no longer fitted the sense in which Kant was now using the term 'faith' for reasons already given. In the context of Kant's critical system, if a believer could *per impossibile* assume the standpoint of the thing in itself, he would not be bringing his knowledge to completion; he would not be transforming whatever faith still encompasses that knowledge into vision. Rather, since the conditions that make for knowledge in *any* sense would no longer apply, he would instead annul the possibility of meaning. It followed that, whatever the more pious among the Kantians might have wished to the contrary, the idea of an 'intelligible kingdom of ends', of 'God', of a 'future life', or, for that matter, any other construct of reason that Kant had introduced in order to help the individual human being find his way across the critically redefined universe of meaning had absolutely nothing in common as objects of a critically purified faith with the apparently corresponding imagery of traditional theology. They no longer stood as surrogates for a knowledge yet to be achieved but as devices that, while conveying the illusion of completeness of meaning, only served to stave off the irrationality that always threatened at the boundaries of meaning. The theologian Flatt called it 'blind faith' and reproached Kant for wanting to put it in place of the less pretentious but more reliable certainty born of centuries of speculation.

You must concede [he argued against a fictional Kantian] that [...] your moral faith amounts to blind faith. Should you opt for this kind of faith, you might indeed be able to hold on to it, provided you are comfortable with it, and stand by Kant's reassurance that it is legitimate for the righteous to say: **I will that God exist**. But then you must not ask me to approve of a system that, short of falling into contradiction, can leave nothing for the most important of truths but blind faith, or to believe that **such a system is of greater use** than all what has been done in speculative philosophy over half and two thousand years.[61]

Faith was no longer "vision through a glass darkly,"[62] but a commitment to abide by Kant's moral vision whatever the existentially impossible consequences for the individual that it entailed. Again we are led (now for the last time) to Goethe's *Prometheus.* The poem's emotional tone was definitely non–Kantian, and the lifestyle it counseled would hardly have met with Kant's moral approval. But the quality of faith that the poem voiced, namely, commitment in the face of the impossible, was nonetheless identical with the quality of the faith Kant was now advocating.

It is significant that Mendelssohn objected to Kant's theory of history just as he had objected to Lessing's, and on the same ground.[63] The theory did not respect human individuality. So it appears that Jacobi had picked the wrong adversary in his fight against the philosophers. In this he showed bad judgment. But Mendelssohn also showed bad judgment when he suggested that Kant alone was in a position to resolve the confusion caused by the Spinoza controversy. Before the dispute broke out, the Jena theologians had already made the same error,[64] thinking that Kant's Critique of Reason offered a new rational defense for their faith (granted, of course, that theirs was faith in any traditional Christian sense). Or perhaps Mendelssohn was right. The "all destroying Kant" could indeed resolve the confusion that Mendelssohn was decrying, but not necessarily with the results that the latter expected.[65] The fact is that Mendelssohn, Jacobi, the Jena theologians, and (as we shall see) Reinhold as well all still belonged in their different ways to the conceptual and emotional universe of Spalding. Their reason was still the reason of the Enlightenment. The difficulty that this reason faced in saving a place for the individual in its universe of meaning had been inherited from Christian theology. Although formulated in a more abstract form, it was still the difficulty of reconciling human freedom with God's almighty power. But Kant was now advancing a completely revolutionary notion of reason and rationality. The problem that the Critique of Reason now posed for the individual was of a completely different kind. It was a problem of defining the limits of the universe of meaning of which that individual's reason was itself explicitly the creator; in which, therefore, all the problems mooted in past metaphysics lost their conceptual basis. Kant was indeed all destroying. Any appearance that he could or, for that matter, could not resolve old problems was due to an equivocation in his use of language. Kant was simply no longer operating with traditional categories. This was the deeper meaning of his Copernican revolution.[66] As of 1800, at the conclusion of the final episode in the first stage of Kant reception, the only thinker to be fully aware of this turn of events was Fichte.

It is fitting that this final episode should have involved the issue of religion. Religious practices respond at the social and personal levels to the same existential needs that the philosophers try to satisfy conceptually through their systems. In both cases, the individual is explicitly at issue. That was precisely the issue that stood at the center of the reception of Kant beginning with the eruption on the scene of Jacobi. It is interesting to note how the many personalities implicated in the episode reacted to the unfolding of events. Kant repudiated all his would-be disciples. Jacobi accused Fichte's idealism (if not Fichte personally) of atheism, thus condemning the new philosophy of which he took Fichte to be the most logical exponent. Reinhold, in one more attempt at playing the role of mediator (this time between Jacobi and Fichte), began to talk about the necessarily paradoxical nature of all philosophy. Fichte himself, of course, had no choice but to leave Jena. He was later to enjoy a new philosophical life in Berlin.

1.6 MAPPING OUT THE STORY

We shall consider the episode of Fichte's departure from Jena, and the issue of religion that goes with it, at the end. Before that, we must, however, examine the debate regarding the nature of human freedom that led up to it and, ahead of anything else, the attempt on the part of the Enlightenment's popular philosophers, whether they stood for or against Kant, to reduce his categories of thought to their own conceptual universe. It was this bid to inject new wine into old skins that was to be throughout the cause of the greatest disarray.

Since the story that follows is a complex one, it might help if it is mapped out in advance.

Chapter 2 provides a general picture of *Popularphilosophie* while giving an account of how some typical representatives of this tradition failed to recognize the originality of the Critique of Reason. Whether they sided with Kant or opposed him, these popular philosophers all ended up refashioning his new system according to their own well-worn patterns of thought. I must stress that, in saying that the popular philosophers misunderstood Kant, I do not in any way mean to detract from the conceptual integrity of their tradition. On the contrary, the point is that the position on which they held their ground was so well laid out, and so firm, that it was difficult indeed to see how Kant's critical distinctions could bring anything new to it except unnecessary new conceptual problems.

Chapter 3 expands on the same theme, but with a different strategy and a different stress in view. Here I bring on the scene three well-known personalities of the day: Pastor Schultz, the already mentioned Jacobi, and Reinhold. As it will emerge even more clearly in the rest of the book, these three men had strong cultural and intellectual ties that bound them to *Popularphilosophie* – in the case of Reinhold and Jacobi, even in spite of their contrary judgment on the matter. Each approached Kant with a different project in mind. Pastor Schultz's intention was to give a faithful but plain exegesis of the *Critique of Pure Reason* in order to make it more accessible to the general public. Jacobi, for his part, wanted to show that it is possible to safeguard the normative element of experience without accepting the a priorism of Kant's Critique. Reinhold, by contrast, wanted to validate precisely this a priorism by reforming Kant's Critique of Reason on the basis of a new systematic principle. As it happened, Jacobi and Reinhold each hit in the course of their particular efforts upon models of experience that, as will emerge later in the story, were to contribute to the development of post-Kantian idealism. In all three cases, however, whether one intended simply to expound Kant, or to criticize him, or to reform him, the Critique of Reason was still being brought back to older patterns of thought. This is essentially still the result of Chapter 2, but the stress now is on the fact that there was something about the Critique of Reason itself that fated it, so to speak, to this result. This something is Kant's 'transcendental story' – a point that is only adumbrated in Chapter 3 but is further developed in the two following chapters. An added aim of Chapter 3 is to offer a more nuanced picture of both Jacobi and Reinhold than is normally found in the literature. In their different ways, the two men were very sophisticated thinkers.

Chapter 4 revisits the Critique of Reason in the medium of a controversy on the nature of freedom that broke out at the time. All the characters introduced so far will make an appearance again, together with one added figure whom I shall mention in a moment. The controversy was in principle unresolvable because it was based on an ambiguous, even internally contradictory, concept of freedom. Freedom stood at once for a sort of presumed hyperphysical source of causality and for an ideally determined form of conduct. The two meanings were not reconcilable and, when not clearly distinguished, necessarily made for confusion. Kant's 'transcendental story' promoted precisely this kind of confusion. The

new personality introduced in Chapter 4, W. R. Rehberg, is important
because, so far as I know, he was the first to criticize Kant for not having sufficiently relinquised the ways of metaphysics. Kant had failed to
sufficiently insulate ethics and religion from the confusions caused by
metaphysical speculation and, as a consequence, his Critique of Reason
was still being held hostage to this kind of speculation. This was the element that made it so susceptible at the hands of the critics to being led
back to the traditional patterns of thought of *Popularphilosophie.*

Chapters 1 to 4 presuppose a general acquaintance with Kant's Critique of Reason. Chapter 5 focuses on his moral theory, and in particular
on the idea of freedom that governs it. This idea harbors metaphysical
assumptions that, though allegedly critically neutralized, in fact affect
Kant's whole moral theory. It makes for an element of irrationality that
has far-reaching consequences for Kant's vision of moral nature. In effect, Chapter 5 develops the point already made by Rehberg *in nuce.*
There is indeed a transcendental story in Kant, and his moral theory is
the place where its deleterious effects are most noticeable. The upshot
is that, although Kant seems to be restating on stronger critical premises
Spalding's idea of the vocation of humankind, he is in fact subverting
it by altering completely the meaning of the Christian faith that still inspired Spalding. In Spalding's religious universe, reason's function was
to clarify truths already held instinctively on faith. In Kant's new moral
universe, faith is brought in instead to remedy otherwise impossible existential difficulties that confront every individual operating within it. In
spite of Kant's personally held optimistic views regarding the future of
humankind that were also typical of the Enlightenment, his moral theory
led to a somber view of human nature that, as it happens, was much more
in tune with the culture of Pietism of which he was himself a product.

The merit of Fichte is that he clearly saw this aspect of Kant. He also
understood that Kant's critical project was still affected by metaphysical presuppositions. His first effort was precisely to expunge from Kant's
Critique of Reason the dogmatic residues that he thought still affected
it. It does not follow that Fichte, however, rejected Kant's moral vision
of humankind. On the contrary, his effort was to defend it on what he
thought were more self-consistent idealistic grounds. The net result was
the vision of the vocation of humankind that Fichte expounded in his
1800 tract entitled precisely *The Vocation of Humankind.* In this little book,
Fichte seemed indeed to be committing himself to the same idea of a
physically harmonious universe that Spalding had advanced in his own
tract over a half century before. But any affinity between the visions of the

two men was only superficial, for the harmony of the universe in which Fichte now put his trust was based on a completely different and even antithetical conceptual basis, and was animated by just as different and antithetical a spirit, as it ever had been in the past. Chapter 6 presents Fichte's effort to purge Kant's Critique of Reason of all metaphysical residues. Chapter 8 brings the whole study to a conclusion by contrasting Spalding's optimistic vision with Fichte's heroic one. The advent of Kant's Critique of Reason was the crisis that had precipitated, conceptually at least, the transition from the one to the other. Harking back to moves already made by the early critics of Kant, Chapter 8 also hints at another way of exploiting the conceptual and moral resources of idealism than Fichte's. Hegel comes on the scene in this context, but only peripherally. Before this concluding chapter, however, Chapter 7 parades again all the main characters introduced earlier, this time in order to gauge their various reactions to Kant's idealism now that Fichte had exploded any illusion that it could be reconciled with traditional metaphysics. Spinoza will have a conspicuous presence in this chapter, but so he does throughout the book. One theme that this study develops is that of the influence of Spinoza's thought on the reception of the Critique of Reason. There was at least some justification to Jacobi's claim that the figure of Spinoza still lurked behind that of Kant.

2

The Taming of Kant

Popular Philosophy

2.1 THE BRILLIANT IMMODESTY OF KANT

Before turning to the popular philosophers and explaining why they have
as visible a part in this study as they do, it is important to elaborate on
a theme we only began to develop in the previous chapter. If one failed
to understand where the novelty of Kant's Critique of Reason truly lay,
it was easy to denigrate its originality or to reabsorb it into more traditional molds of thought. The popular philosophers, as we shall now see,
did both. There was, however, inherent in the nature of that Critique,
a conceptually even more significant reason for its vulnerability to reab-
sorption. The fact is that the Critique needed both the Leibnizian model
of experience, the kind that the popular philosophers instinctively presupposed, and the kind of phenomenology of experience that the same
popular philosophers were pioneering – provided, of course, that both
(the model and the phenomenology) were played in a critical key. How
to hit this new key was precisely the problem. This last point is the more
important and will emerge only at the end of the present chapter. But
first, to the Critique of Reason itself.

The opposition between 'critique' and 'metaphysics' can easily be over-
played. Even Kant saw himself as opposed not to metaphysics as such, but
to what he called 'dogmatic metaphysics.'[1] His goal was not to abolish the
science but to reestablish it on a critical, therefore more secure, foundation. To this end he exposed the sophisms that underlay the syllogisms
with which school metaphysics pretended to establish scientifically such
tenets of mere belief as the incorruptibility of the soul or the existence
of a personal creator of the universe. The force of his criticism had the

salutary effect of forever marginalizing, where not eliminating altogether, long-standing topics of metaphysical argument.[2]

But, however notable this achievement, the true significance of Kant's reformation of metaphysics lay at a deeper level. It rested not in the exposure of the limits of reason (as Kant himself might have thought while engaged in polemic with metaphysicians, and so many of his commentators still think) but, on the contrary, in the revelation of the full extent of reason's involvement in human experience. After all, Kant's portrayal of school metaphysicians was not altogether fair. These metaphysicians, despite their many sophistic arguments, were well aware that their representations of suprasensible objects were at best analogical constructs intended to give *some* rational expression to realities that escape conceptualization per se but must nonetheless be posited on other existential grounds. They did not naively hold, as Kant sometimes leads one to believe, that their representations actually determined their intended objects. They treated them, rather, not unlike Kantian noumena, as conceptual constructs that carry no objective evidence on their own but must be put in rational circulation nonetheless in order to satisfy other pressing nonconceptual yet existential ("subjective," as Kant says) needs. One must not forget that metaphysics developed in the Christian West in the matrix of theology; that it was implicated from the beginning in the larger Christian cultural project (still apparent in Spalding's essay) of finding some rational expression for truths already held on faith yet admittedly escaping strict conceptual determination. *Fides quærens intellectum* (faith seeking understanding) stood at the origin of metaphysics. Nor should one forget that for believers living in a world still perceived by them in the shape of classical cosmology, the objects of faith were a lot more intuitive (hence, a lot less in need of conceptual definition) than we can possibly imagine nowadays. One only had to look up at the sky to see "the Heavens above." To be sure, by the eighteenth century much had occurred to the cosmological sciences, as well as to metaphysics and to the Christian faith motivating both the sciences and metaphysics. It was time for a conceptual revolution of the type Kant was proposing. The point, however, is that classical metaphysicians would not have disagreed with Kant that the determination of the objects of reason is purely logical. How much such a determination had value *realiter* was at least a matter of dispute among them. For the more nominalist, conceptual determination was merely a matter of assigning names.[3]

The more innovative, and ultimately more revolutionary, aspect of Kant's reformation was rather to show that the faith that had traditionally

governed metaphysics was not as original as the believers professing it assumed. The picture of a supreme mistress summoning to its service the
lower power of reason that the motto *fides quærens intellectum* evokes is
misleading, at least to the extent that it hides how much reason in fact
determines faith from the beginning – how much it has 'infected' it all
along, as Hegel will say.[4] For it would not occur to anyone to invent
myths of creation, or to fabricate stories about man's journeys in the beyond before and after this earthly life, and to put trust in them contrary
to every available evidence, were it not for the fact that such myths and
stories satisfy a deeply embedded need of human nature. This is a need
for meaningfulness, for completeness of explanation, for finality of existence, as Kant himself argued in setting up the architectonics of his
system. Its source is none other than reason itself. It follows that in seeking intellection through ratiocination, faith is actually retrieving its own
rational origin. It is unearthing the interest that originally set the imagination into motion in constructing its explanatory devices. The subtext
of the history of *fides quærens intellectum* is that of an intellect inspiring
faith in an effort to understand itself. The medieval theologians would
not have had much difficulty accepting this conclusion, since they took
the 'intellect' to be itself a reflection of God in man – the spark of the
Divine in the human soul that the task of ratiocination was to bring to
consciousness. To the later rationalistic metaphysicians whom Kant had
especially in mind, the case would have been even clearer, since the traditionally held faith no longer provided the obvious intuitive matrix for
their accepted scientific pictures of the universe. As a result, reason had
already acquired an autonomy of exercise that it did not have in earlier
theological contexts, and the tendency had already long set in of treating
faith as a stand-in, so to speak, for truths that reason already held in principle but that needed further conceptualization. Yet, in both instances – I
mean, in earlier Christian theology as well as in later rationalistic metaphysics – the fundamental assumption still held that the origin of the
meaningfulness that faith groped for darkly, and reason presented lu-
cidly but abstractly, lay in reality itself, in God and his creation, both of
which it was reason's vocation to mirror in its representations. And it was
precisely this assumption that the critical Kant was now challenging by
arguing that, on the contrary, reason – that is, formal reason – is at the
origin of the meaning we seek in experience and ideally project onto
the things we otherwise come in contact with only physically. This is what
I meant when I just said that the most innovative aspect of Kant's Critique of Reason lay in revealing the full extent of reason's involvement

in human experience. Kant was bestowing on reason an autonomy it had never been granted before, and, by the same token, raising again, but now in an essentially different frame of reference, the issue of the nature of faith and its relation to reason. The already strained edifice of *fides quærens intellectum* was finally collapsing.

There was nothing 'modest', as is sometimes said,[5] about Kant's reformation in metaphysics. His new assumptions were thoroughly immodest – and all the more brilliant because of their immodesty. To portray them as modest is to understand Kant falsely, in the way many of his contemporaries did, as still operating within the parameters of the old metaphysics but with scaled-down expectations. In effect, Kant was putting an end to any naive representational theory of knowledge. On his new critical assumptions, to know a thing does not mean, as it does in a typical representational theory, to generate a picture of it in the mind, a sort of analog resembling it. This is an assumption based on a metaphor that ultimately fails to stand up to critical examination and that, as a matter of fact, has invariably given rise to all forms of skepticism. To know means rather to make a thing, with which we have otherwise hitherto interacted only unconsciously at some physical level, reexist in the medium of conceptualization and language in such a way that its presence can thereby be 'recognized' or 'acknowledged' – rendered meaningful, in other words. It is made into an 'object'. The medium within which such a transformation occurs is subject to laws and conditions that are typically its own, and that can therefore be established by us a priori, since it is *we*, the knowers, who provide the medium in the first place. This is the fundamental thesis of all idealism, whether Kantian or post–Kantian. Its net effect, contrary to initial appearance, is that all thought, far from being freed to roam at large because of its newly recognized autonomy, is in fact restricted in its operations to the limits of experience. To be sure, the thesis implies that there is no such a thing as a supposed 'bare fact', the type that common sense might expect to find. Every fact carries a theoretical interpretation from the beginning, since it is admitted as fact only to the extent that it answers to questions that we, the knowers, pose to nature. Nature, in turn, becomes an idea, the fundamental theoretical construct on the basis of which more pointed questions can be raised about particular facts. Yet, the truth of any theoretical construct, or the validity of any question we pose to the things of nature, is measured by the success that each has in transforming what would otherwise be a mere physical affection into an intelligible presence – where the presence in question, though intelligible indeed, must satisfy nonetheless all the existential conditions that the

word 'presence' connotes. It must be immediate. This means that conceptualization necessarily involves a moment of intuition; in effect, that
all cognition is ultimately perceptual. Though there is no such a thing as
a 'seeing' (*Anschauung*) that is not already conceptually interpreted, any
conceptual construct that would not in principle resolve itself into an
'intelligent seeing' is empty fiction.

It is in this sense that Kant trimmed the wings of classical metaphysics.
It was not just a matter of scaling down earlier claims to knowledge, but of
altering the meaning of 'knowledge' itself. Sense representations are now
made to play a totally new role in the process of experience. They differ
from 'concepts', not as obscure in contrast with clear representations, but
as providing the place where conceptual representations realize in immediate intuition (i.e., by way of recognition) the objective presence that
such representations otherwise can only intend. Concepts, for their part,
can measure their truth precisely by the degree to which they succeed
in thus achieving intuitive realization. This difference in roles is irreducible and would have to hold, according to Kant, for all knowledge –
including that of an intelligence equipped with a different sense apparatus than the human. A purely intellectual intuition, the kind that Kant
occasionally envisages, whatever it might be, would constitute knowledge
only equivocally.

It is again in this sense that the ideas of classical metaphysics differ
from Kantian ideas essentially. The difference is not a matter of whether
one either grants or denies to purely conceptual constructs the capacity to determine their intended objects, but of the significance that one
attributes to such constructs in the process of cognition. In classical metaphysics, the significance lay in the capacity ideas allegedly have to give
discursive expression to truths originally held only on faith but eventually
also buttressed by argumentation. In the Kantian scheme of things, on
the contrary, the significance lay in the power ideas have to bring the
process of realizing conceptual intentions by instantiating them in immediate sense intuition – a process that would otherwise remain always
open-ended – to at least putative completion. Such a process, however
rational in origin, requires nonetheless the generation of a faith. This is
a condition that applies, according to Kant, to the theoretical as well as
to the moral realm of experience, though, as we shall see in due time,
to the moral realm in a special way. The function of Kantian ideas is to
give expression to just this rationally generated faith. What we have with
Kant, in other words, is no longer *fides quærens intellectum*, but, if anything,
intellectus quærens fidem, that is, an intellect that generates its own faith, as

expressed in rationally constructed ideas, for the sake of realizing itself as intellect. The ancient trope had indeed been overthrown. This is the point that is now to be developed.

2.2 POPULAR PHILOSOPHY

The so-called popular philosophy (*Popularphilosophie*) of the German late *Aufklärung* was just as complex a phenomenon as the *Aufklärung* itself. Witness to its resilience is the fact that the man who took over Kant's chair of philosophy at Königsberg when Kant died – the same Traugott Krug who challenged the idealists to deduce his writing pen from the idea[6] – was a notorious representative of precisely this school. The popular philosophers were the self-professed boosters of the Enlightenment, the vigilant defenders of the latter's program of rationalization of all things social and religious in the face of what they took to be the ever-present but hidden forces of 'obscurantism' (i.e., in their minds, the Jesuits and their supposed emissaries). In the name of freedom of the press, they won in 1787 a famous court case against these alleged forces in the person of a certain Johann August Starck – an intriguer at large who operated in the admittedly less reputable circles of the Free Masonry. Starck had sued the editors of the *Berlinische Monatsschrift* for defamation of character.[7] Together with the *Allgemeine deutsche Bibliothek* and the *Allgemine Literatur-Zeitung*, this journal was at the time the vehicle of much of the popular philosophers' propaganda. Of course, to their opponents these same self-professed promoters of reason and rationality appeared in quite a different light. Jacobi regularly referred to them contemptuously as "Messrs the Enlighteners." Hegel was to dub them "the gossipers of the Enlightenment." To such opponents, their name was synonymous with shallowness of mind and deviousness of intent.

It would, however, be just as historically misguided to accept at face value this characterization of the popular philosophers as to accept in the same vein the characterization that they advertised of themselves and their foes. The popular philosophers liked to think of themselves as the friends of the Enlightenment; of their foes, as the Enlightenment's own foes. Their opponents, for their part, accused them of diluting with their abstract talk about reason in general values that had long provided the moral basis of society. Yet, despite their mutual recriminations, to an impartial observer both parties would have to appear to be equally members of the same Enlightenment household, each contributing in its own way to the same ideal of social rationalization. On the one side, the popular philosophers were extending rational discourse to all aspects of social existence, thus bringing to reflection distinctions that once were taken for granted. Their rational 'gossiping' created the conditions of conceptual fluidity necessary for any social change. Their opponents, on the other side, defended the rationality that they saw implicit in long-standing customary practices, fearing what might take their place if undermined by abstract criticism. Jacobi, who sided with the plaintiff in the Starck affair, objected to the Enlighteners on the ground that they had given rise to a new kind of popery, one that was just as intolerant of dissenting views as the Roman popery but lacked the validation of traditional wisdom on which the latter could rely.[8] The Enlighteners, however, did not really contest the legitimacy of this assumption of an implicit historical rationality, at least not in principle. Unlike their French counterparts, their aim was to bring about social reform without disturbing the Christian ethos that still permeated German society at the time. The obscurantism that they fought was, in their minds, just as detrimental to true (i.e., enlightened) Christianity as their opponents thought the Enlighteners' social tactics were. The conflict between the two sides spawned a whole new genre of literature that took the form of a fictional dialogue between the representatives of the new rationalism and the defenders of the old faith.[9] Whether slanted in favor of one side or the other, the point in each case was that there was ultimately no conflict between reason and religious belief.

Reinhold perhaps summed up the situation best in 1798 – in a late work that still reflected his recent association with the by then proscribed Illuminati.[10] In his opinion, the two parties approached the same goal of constituting an enlightened society from two different perspectives. The Enlighteners did it *in abstracto*, fixing their gaze on ideals of rationality in general; their opponents, *in concreto*, concentrated rather on the weaknesses of human nature and the kinds of dangers to which any program of social reform is inevitably exposed. The many conflicts between the two parties were the results of differences in strategy rather than of basic beliefs. We shall return to this essay of Reinhold later in connection with Fichte.[11] That was not, however, the only place where Reinhold dealt with *Popularphilosophie*. He had reflected on the phenomenon in earlier essays, and his comments there are more to the point for us now, since they were explicitly addressed to the connection between popular philosophy and Kant's Critique of Reason.[12] We must keep in mind that in the expression *'Popularphilosophie,'* 'philosophy' is being used in a very broad sense. It encompasses areas of discourse that we would nowadays more comfortably associate with literature, religion, and social criticism.[13] Reinhold's earlier reflections were restricted to the more philosophical side of the phenomenon – the one that was more directly, though by no means exclusively, implicated in the reception of Kant.

In brief, this is Reinhold's account of the genesis and nature of German popular philosophy.[14] The phenomenon owed its origin to the one-sidedness of both Leibniz's and Locke's systems. These were both based on two apparently inconsistent assumptions regarding ideas (*Vorstellungen* or 'representations', as Reinhold most commonly refers to them in keeping with the German scholastic tradition). The first was that knowledge originates in the conformity of ideas to reality in itself; the second, that the object of a representation is the representation itself. Granted these assumptions, each system adopted a radically different strategy for determining how a representation, in having itself as object, could nonetheless conform to external reality. Leibniz relied on the further assumption of a universal harmony of everything in the universe with everything else. Such a harmony would in principle ensure that the mind is from the start already in tune with reality at large. Quite consistently, therefore, he could also assume the presence in the mind of certain innate representations that define its basic relation to reality and that can thus also serve as criteria for judging which other representations (especially those drawn immediately from experience) truly conform to their intended objects. The whole problem of cognition thus devolved into one of recognizing which representations are truly innate because original and, consequently, also universal and necessary. And this was a question to be resolved, according to Leibniz, by testing the credentials of a representation precisely as representation – that is to say, on the basis of its internal coherence. The principle of contradiction sufficed for the purpose. It was thereby raised by Leibniz to the status of the highest among all principles.

Locke took a directly opposite tack. According to him, all cognition depends on representations originating in actual experience. What Leibniz considered universal and necessary ideas were for him, rather, derivatives of original sense impressions. Such ideas lacked, therefore, the convincing power of these impressions, and were also likely to have had their representative character falsified in the process of derivation. Locke accordingly concluded that only the simplicity of a representation – in effect, its being an original 'sense impression' – guaranteed its truth, and this made it the only possible criterion for justifying the validity of other representations constructed on its basis. Any such process of justification was thus reduced to accounting for the origin of a representation from original sense impressions. Theory of knowledge in general became a historical account of the genesis of the mind.

It did not take long for someone like Hume (thus Reinhold's account proceeds) to come along, and to raise the obvious objections to which both Leibniz's and Locke's systems were vulnerable. Against Leibniz, Hume argued that the principle of contradiction is sufficient to demonstrate only the formal coherence of a representation or the formal correctness of an inference. It can say nothing about the material truth of either – that is, whether either a representation or an inference has any real bearing to the real world. This is an objection, Reinhold points out, that the German Crusius had already raised, and much more insightfully than Hume; one, moreover, that Kant was to raise again by distinguishing formal from transcendental logic.[15] Against Locke, Hume argued that it is impossible to assert the objective truth of a sense impression (i.e., its conformity to external reality), no matter how simple the impression is, without actually comparing it with what it is supposed to represent. But such a comparison would require bringing yet another representation into play, and this would be in turn subject to the same condition. Locke's demonstration of the truth of any cognition thus becomes necessarily entangled in a circular argument with no hope of resolution. Reinhold points out, moreover, that Leibniz had already struck a serious blow against Locke's theory by arguing that there cannot be such a thing as a simple sense impression. Upon careful analysis, the examples on which Locke had relied all turn out to be in fact made up of a complex of representations, each amenable to further analysis.[16] (This is a point that must be kept in mind because, as we shall see, it will come up again in connection with Reinhold.[17])

Skepticism was, of course, the upshot of Hume's criticism. It was a skepticism totally immune to rational argument once the assumptions regarding the grounds of cognition behind it had been accepted. Philosophy had reached a dead end. It had exhausted the conceptual possibilities inherent in both Leibniz's and Locke's assumptions and, by the same token, had destroyed itself by undermining the grounds of truth. Such being the situation, Reinhold proceeds,

nothing was more natural than the course that Reid, Oswald, Beattie [the three names commonly associated at the time with the so-called commonsense philosophy], and others embarked upon to refute Hume. They summoned the common sense of mankind against him, for it was the only course open to them given the stage of reason's philosophical advance at the time. They evoked in their writings all the *feelings* at whose tribunal Hume would necessarily stand convicted – even if he had championed the strict requirements of reason more opportunely than was actually the case. They were the feelings that for the largest segment of even cultivated people take the place of *thought* [*-determined*] principles. Some of them, the *moral feelings* (as expressions of *practical reason*), are the one single means of possible orientation for *theoretical* reason in its unavoidable internal dissensions on its way *to* (hence *before*) the discovery of *ultimate* grounds.[18]

Since the judgments of common sense are determined more by will than by thought, more by inclinations than by insight, more by felt than by thought [*-determined*] grounds, they are to this extent, not seldom indeed, an unfailing remedy against the aberrations of *thought*. [...But] man's common understanding was all too readily misjudged and misused by philosophers. [...They] mistook it for the power of judgement itself [...], and used its one-sided judgements to snub reason's philosophizing. The proposition: '*Thus says man's common understanding,*' became the *first principle* of an alleged new philosophy which its followers dubbed *eclectic*, since it allowed them the most complete freedom. [...] The common sense[19] of academic teachers demonstrated the existence of God, the immortality of the soul, and, in words at least, the freedom of the will (indeed, it would have proved not to be a human common sense if it had demonstrated the contrary, thereby forfeiting for its man his professorial chair and the meagre living attached to it), while the common sense of the tougher–minded French spirits corroborated the nonexistence of God, the mortality of the soul, and the fated necessity of all human actions.[20]

This is thus the genealogy of popular philosophy according to Reinhold. At its root there lay a misunderstanding about the nature of representation that both the rationalists and the empiricists had in common despite their otherwise totally opposite analyses of experience, namely, the erroneous assumption that the object of a representation (whatever the source of the latter) is the representation itself, yet that truth consists in its conformity to a reality external to it. This assumption, coupled with Locke's critique of rationalism, necessarily led to skepticism. This skepticism led in turn to common sense as the only possible nondiscursive defence against it. And since common sense has no single internal self-limiting principle, it led to eclecticism. It is this latter trait – its being by nature eclectic – that defines popular philosophy most typically according to Reinhold.[21] The phenomenon originated in England, spread among France's *Schöne Geister* (elegant wits), and had of late been adopted wholesale by the German philosophical luminaries. Among these, Reinhold singled out Plattner as one whose arguments based on common sense did not even begin to meet Hume's skepticism.[22] But he equally included under the heading of popular philosophy just about everyone with any philosophical reputation at the time – Eberhard, Tiedeman, Reimarus, Feder, Meiners, Selle.[23] What he decried most about them all was that, aping "the rhetoric and the satire of the English and the French against systems," they had brought into disrepute among the Germans the spirit of systematicity, which is indispensable to true science and was the proud German heritage of both Leibniz and Wolff. "Hardly a more brilliant crown could adorn the century," Reinhold concludes, than the regaining of precisely this spirit. "With such a radically foundational step, Germany could undertake the work of its sublime vocation as *future school of Europe.*"[24]

We can ignore this final jingoistic outburst.[25] It was part of the ethos of the day. The emphasis on system and systematization is, however, important. Reinhold was obviously promoting his own agenda, and it is this circumstance that distorted what would have been otherwise not an altogether inaccurate account of the historical and conceptual situation. Reinhold was portraying the chaotic intellectual situation of which popular philosophy was symptomatic as historically necessary in order for Kant to emerge and restore order by means of a new set of distinctions. Reinhold himself could then follow up and bring systematicity to these distinctions by establishing representation as the one fact of consciousness upon which they all depend. The age of true science would then finally be at hand. For philosophy learns about itself, and is thus made ready for a new leap forward, only when its own earlier one-sided assumptions collapse under the pressure of their mutual discord. Popular philosophy was a necessary stage in the progression of philosophical thought.[26]

This was an attractive historical vision that itself reflected the Enlightenment's passion for discovering sense in history. More to the point right now, however, is that, in his grand historical sweep, Reinhold was either failing to recognize or outright misrepresenting several crucial factors. For one thing, he was being unfair to both the English and the French by laying the blame for the alleged eclecticism of popular philosophy exclusively at their door. There was, of course, an element of eclecticism in the German philosophy of the time, and nobody would deny the dependence of this eclecticism on foreign influences.[27] But there were also much more significant home-grown precedents for it deeply rooted in the distrust of reason that was part and parcel of the Evangelical religious tradition. Christian Thomasius, the great opponent of Wolff at Halle, was an eclectic in matters philosophical, deliberately and on principle. A jurist and a moralist, he sought truth first of all in divine revelation and in the positive evidence of the senses – two sources that defy systematization. Granted that these were his only principles of cognition, he had no choice but to accept truth *wherever* and *however* he found it.[28] Christian Crusius, on whom Reinhold lavishes praise because of his critique of the principle of contradiction, was part of the same tradition of thought.[29] Mendelssohn, writing in 1759, expressed fear that with Crusius serious philosophy was at an end in Germany. As he complained, "Philosophy, 'the poor matron' who, according to Shaftesbury, had been 'banished from high society to the schools and colleges' had to leave even this dusty corner. Descartes expelled the scholastics, Wolff expelled Descartes, and the contempt for all philosophy finally expelled Wolff; and it appears that Crusius will soon be the philosopher in fashion."[30]

Eclecticism, moreover, was not necessarily synonymous with frivolity, as Reinhold apparently thought. In its German form at least, because of its religious origins, it possessed a legitimate principle for selecting the elements it drew from its various sources, namely, the effectiveness that a supposed truth has in the promotion of right living. It was a pragmatic rather than a speculative principle – yet a principle nonetheless. Reinhold was no stranger to it. His pro-Enlightenment activities when still a priest in his early Vienna days, before fleeing to Protestant Germany, were shaped by the expressed conviction that the heart is the best witness to truth. Truth demonstrates itself best in the positive effects that it has on the lives of individuals.[31] Later, when he set out to systematize Kant's critical idealism, he adduced as evidence of Kant's failure to cast his thought in adequately scientific form the fact that, though indisputably valid internally (*gültig* per se), the Critique of Reason had failed to command indisputable universal assent, that is, it had not become common coin (*allgemein geltend*).[32] Reinhold was at the time engaged in a speculative project a whole world removed (in appearance at least) from his earlier sociopolitical propaganda in Vienna. Yet, his still pragmatic bend of mind was unmistakable. As we shall see,[33] it was to be equally unmistakable in his activities leading up to the project of social reform of which the late essay we previously mentioned was the product.

It is also open to question whether, at least as practiced by the German popular philosophers, eclecticism truly lacked even a theoretical (as contrasted with a purely pragmatic) principle of internal coherence; whether, in other words, it was truly antithetical to systematization – unless, of course, one understands the latter in Reinhold's strong sense of the deduction of a whole science from an original simple fact (about which more in due time). Without denying, in other words, that there was a shallow side to German *Popularphilosophie* to which the title 'eclecticism' applied, one can wonder whether the title unequivocally covered its more serious manifestations. An important witness in this respect is a

certain Adam Weishaupt – not because he was one of the luminaries of the
day but because, despite his many faults, he was a perceptive observer of
the contemporary philosophical scene. He was himself, moreover, a self-
professed popular philosopher and an eloquent promoter of a position
that was paradigmatic of much of what passed for popular philosophy.[34]
Reinhold does not include him in his list of popular philosophers, though
the lives of the two men crisscrossed at significant points. Weishaupt was
the founder of the secret society of the Illuminati, of which Reinhold had
become a member and an agent of propaganda when inducted into the
Masonic Lodge at Vienna.[35] His philosophical views, in Weishaupt's own
opinion, constituted the perfect conceptual blueprint for, as well as justification of, his social activities. As we shall see, however much Reinhold
was to criticize these views, he in fact remained intellectually bound to
their assumptions from beginning to end.

These historical adumbrations aside, of interest now is a booklet that
Weishaupt published in 1786 under the title *Über Materialismus und Idealismus (Concerning Materialism and Idealism).*[36] It consists essentially of an
exercise in worldmodeling. Weishaupt begins by defining an object of
experience as the product of a compact struck (so to speak)[37] between
the energy of a mind and the energy impinging on the latter from things
outside. Then, taking as his starting point the various worlds of objects
that the five human senses construct, each in virtue of its specific energy
(for instance, the visual world and the aural world), Weishaupt proceeds
to envisage a whole series of other possible worlds, each as would appear
to a mind endowed with two or more of the senses that we know. And
the series can be expanded with reference to other possible senses that
we do not know but that might exist just as well, all of them in a variety
of combinations. Add to these possible sense-worlds such other worlds
as would appear to minds whose senses are modified by reason, or to
minds endowed with reason alone, and the series can be made to extend
in infinitum.[38]

This is by itself an already interesting conceptual construction.
Weishaupt's next step was, however, even more interesting. On that construction, by running across all the envisaged possible worlds, starting
from the ones for which immediate empirical evidence is available,[39] one
should *ex hypothesi* be able to identify elements that are common and necessary to all, since without them each would not be a world (175ff.). These
elements would thus constitute a necessity that is at once empirical (since
derived from observation of experience), yet a priori (because, once recognized, it is recognized as necessary). This result had the far-reaching

implication that it was possible to meet Hume's skepticism by capitalizing on the notion of factual necessity that was the heritage of the Leibnizian–Wolffian type of scholasticism without having to fall back dogmatically on either Descartes' rationalism or Locke's empiricism. Weishaupt repeatedly expanded on this consequence in his many subsequent works.[40] Against Descartes, it can be argued that there is continuity between sensation and conceptualization, since in both cases there is at work the same basic complex of factors (i.e., according to Weishaupt's particular account, a compact between the mind and its immediate surrounding). These factors are, however, brought to greater explicit expression in the medium of the concept. The distinction between truths of fact and truths of reason is thus relative. The same argument holds against Locke as well. In his case, however, the stress is on the autonomy that the concept enjoys even though continuous with the senses. The concept is governed by requirements that are specific to it and that affect how the original play of factors present in experience is represented conceptually. In either case, whether arguing against Descartes or Locke, the important consideration is that the mind is part of a greater world to which it is connected organically. On the one hand, one should expect that common patterns will develop across the effects that objects of experience produce upon one another as things in themselves, since they are all parts of one world. On the other hand, one should equally expect that these common patterns will be reflected in the human soul when it is acted upon by those same things, since the soul is also part of the one world to which they belong. It is therefore possible to justify *theoretically* the belief in the truth of empirical representations that all men share *in fact*. As Weishaupt says, "The ground of my representations [. . .] lies *in the position that the soul holds at different times among the other parts of the world; in the differing self-manifesting influence that the objects with which the soul coexists exercise according to that position.*"[41]

Each side, that is, the soul and the objects, must express the other. Any other assumption leads to theoretical as well as practical absurdities.

One more consequence that Weishaupt liked to stress, and that was perfectly in tune with the general aspirations of popular philosophy, is that his constructions did not abstract from the individuality of things. On the contrary, his argument depended on the assumption that the objects of experience are radically individual in form, both as things in themselves and as objects of cognition.[42] Weishaupt went to great lengths elaborating on this point. Each object (the soul included) is both an individual world by itself and an individual part of a greater common world. According to Weishaupt, the root cause of all skepticism is the false step, commonly made in the course of representation, of abstracting from the individual traits of the original data of experience. In so doing, one produces new ideas that do not represent anything in particular, and one assumes, as a consequence, that there are in reality universal entities corresponding to them. But any such assumption destroys itself because of the absurd results it generates. Skepticism is the unavoidable result. The proper route to follow in the ascent from the immediate experience of objects to the more embracing representations of them is rather to discover patterns[43] that are common to them all but that respect their individuality. It is, in other words, a matter of advancing from simpler to more complex representations of what are still individual objects – all of them part of one individual world. But again, this process would not be possible unless one assumes that all that there is to know about the world is in principle already present in the soul's constitution (*Lage*) in virtue of the soul's position with respect to the things with which it coexists. True knowledge, therefore, consists in the process of clarifying through ever more sophisticated representations a content of experience already present in the soul obscurely, even unconsciously.[44]

As all popular philosophers did, Weishaupt was drawing from commonly accepted scientific views of the day. One can easily recognize in his metaphysical disquisitions echoes of Charles Bonnet's extrapolations to possible future worlds made on the basis of biological observations. Scientific evidence was not, however, what counted most for Weishaupt. So far as he was concerned, the most unimpeachable evidence in favor of his system was that the picture of the world it conveyed was the most conducive to human happiness. Relevance in this respect was, according to him, the ultimate criterion of all truth. More than any other, his system encouraged individual human beings to accept their particular worldly situation. It therefore promoted the peace of mind in the face of even the worst calamities that is the essential ingredient of all happiness.[45] As it happened, Weishaupt was to use his system to justify theoretically a program of extreme social action that most of his contemporaries found unacceptable. Today we might even judge his program as bordering on the paranoid.[46] This circumstance, coupled with the fact that Weishaupt was greatly influenced by d'Holbach's materialism and that the latter was just as unacceptable to many of Weishaupt's contemporaries as Weishaupt's own social ideas, makes him a popular philosopher in a sense that is admittedly very distinctive. Yet, all things considered, in making human welfare the ultimate criterion of theoretical truth, Weishaupt was again showing how much he was in fact in tune with the fundamental attitudes of all popular philosophy.

It is with his system in mind that one can detect the distortions in Reinhold's view of popular philosophy caused by Reinhold's own distinctive conceptual agenda. Reinhold was indeed right in thinking that Locke and Leibniz had figured prominently in the genesis as well as the content of *Popularphilosophie*. Each presented his own contrary strategy for explaining the rise of human knowledge – the one, a priori and analytical; the other, a posteriori and historical. But he was wrong in thinking that, though contrary, the two strategies were opposed, or that the German philosophers had no choice but to opt for either the one or the other. Nor was he correct in suggesting that, since each position led to impossible consequences, they had to settle at the end for some eclectic combination of elements drawn from both. On the contrary, the two strategies converged naturally. On the one hand, there was a historical dimension to Leibniz's theory. His innate principles of reason presided over a temporal process of elucidating obscure perceptions drawn from experience. On the other hand, Locke had allowed that there were innate fundamental dispositions (*Grundbestimmungen*) in the soul that made it capable of apprehending (*empfinden*) necessary truths immediately. In this sense, he too allowed for a type of a priori.[47] Weishaupt (as we have just seen) had accordingly used Locke's psychology to integrate the internal organization (*Organization*) of the human mind with the organization of the world at large. He had re-created in a more empirical form that harmony of part with part that Leibniz had instead postulated a priori on the basis of purely logical necessities. What Locke's historical method had offered to the German philosophers, in other words, was precisely a means of forging a more systematic unity between the a priori and a posteriori elements of their theory of knowledge that in its traditional scholastic form was left inchoate; it had provided them with a means of developing it psychologically.

Reinhold, who apparently had Locke's *Essay on Human Understanding* in front of him when penning his own work, *The Foundation of Philosophical Knowledge*,[48] never quite understood this systematizing role that Locke had played in traditional scholasticism. Nor did he ever appreciate how and why British theories of common sense could so easily be assimilated into the German discourse of popular philosophy. This is a topic to which we shall return in the following chapter in connection with Jacobi and also with reference to Reinhold's own effort at reforming Kant.

The point right now is that it was false to think that the German popular
philosophers had resorted to common sense as an ad hoc defense against
Hume's skepticism – a sort of medicament of last resort, not necessarily
a bad medicament but deadly if administered in place of food.[49] As a
matter of fact, the Germans never really took skepticism to be a serious
threat precisely because they took it for granted that, when transposed
into the more sophisticated framework of Leibnizian theory, Locke's psychology was immune to it. In that framework, common sense (or 'healthy
human understanding') denoted the rationality that even feelings might
have just because they reflect in their own way the organization of the
whole. Common sense can therefore serve at least as a negative criterion
of truth, though, as a would-be positive criterion, it would lack the determination that only the reflective concept can provide. This was the sense
in which Mendelssohn used the notion in his dispute with Jacobi. There
are questions, as he argued, that the philosophers might indeed pose but
need not answer, since any answer would require jumping from one's
own shoulder. Such questions offend common sense. The latter is like
a rational instinct that helps the philosopher orient himself in thought
by precluding lines of investigation not likely from the beginning to lead
anywhere.[50] Kant seemed to agree with Mendelssohn in his late contribution to the dispute – making use, however, of his own critical terminology.
Common sense is in effect identical with the felt interests of reason – interests that, though in the form of subjective dispositions of the mind,
already delineate in principle the sphere of the possible objective use of
the concept.[51]

In sum, a less self-serving view of *Popularphilosophie* than Reinhold's
might give reasons to wonder whether Kant's Critique of Reason had
failed to win universal acceptance or, inasmuch as it had been accepted,
had had so many different results, because, as Reinhold thought, it lacked
adequate systematic form, or rather because, as a system, it did not prima
facie offer much more than the mainstream of *Popularphilosophie* already
did. Both – that is, the critical system and popular philosophy – traded
on a notion of 'factual necessity'; both met Hume's skepticism at its
basis; both assumed that rational activities constitute an organic whole
(an *Organization*); both treated and accepted common sense as a sort of
instinct of reason; both gave speculation a definitive moral intonation,
taking as the ultimate test of a metaphysical system whether it satisfied
certain inalienable needs of the human spirit. As we must now see, it is no
surprise that those unsympathetic to Kant would have seen the Critique
of Reason as offering nothing new except distinctions that caused new

difficulties without resolving any of the old. Nor is it surprising that those sympathetic to him could easily have conflated these new distinctions with the older.

2.3 POPULAR PHILOSOPHY AND THE CRITIQUE OF REASON

The objections raised against Kant's Critique of Reason in the earliest reviews came from the side of the academics of the time, all of them in some way connected with *Popularphilosophie*. Most notable among the reviewers were Feder, Pistorius, Garve, and Ulrich.[52] Their objections were mostly directed at Kant's distinctions between the thing in itself and appearances, sense and understanding, understanding and reason. These distinctions were hardly new to them, and they had no problem accepting them in principle. They could not understand, however, why Kant should now reintroduce them in what seemed to them an unduly exclusive sense. Most of all, they could not understand how Kant could at once assume a thing in itself yet deny any knowledge of it, as if the assumption did not already entail at least some cognition; or again, how Kant could claim that we have experience of this thing as it appears, yet deny that, in apprehending its appearances, we do not thereby also gain at least *some* knowledge of it in itself, however limited and indirect. So far as these reviewers were concerned, Kant's distinctions, and his total denial of knowledge of the thing in itself, made for a formalism of cognition – an unacceptable split in experience between form and content that detracted from the organic unity of accepted doctrine without contributing any new advantage. As for the limitations of human cognition that Kant had made his special vocation to stress, their claim was that such limitations had always been well recognized, and duly allowed for, within the parameters of traditional metaphysics.

Objections of this kind were repeated, and enlarged upon in the years to come. J. A. Eberhard was to press them in a new and strident tone on the pages of a magazine that he founded in 1788 at Halle, in association with others, for the explicit purpose of counteracting Kant's influence.[53] In *Letters Concerning the Moral Ground of Knowledge of Religion* of 1789, these objections were summarized with rare brilliance by the already mentioned theologian Flatt, who gave special reference to Kant's moral philosophy.[54] And we find them again in G. E. Schulze's *Aenesidemus* of 1792[55] – this time, however, marshaled in defense of skepticism. As we know, Kant replied to Eberhard in public, thus bestowing special notoriety on the latter's claim that the Critique of Reason added nothing to Leibniz's philosophy.

Much as these objections caught Kant's attention, and caused him aggravation, they are not our concern here. They reasserted in opposition to Kant the already adumbrated theses of popular philosophy. Of more interest is how self-professed disciples of Kant could believe that they were defending their master's alleged position while in fact, just as much as his critics, also reasserting the same theses. The point of contact between the two sides, that is, Kant and the popular philosophers, and where the blending of the two could easily take place, was in the way each side developed the concept of a 'subject of experience' – in the area, in other words, where Locke held his own in popular philosophy. In their respective analyses of experience, both sides gave priority to the subject, since in their different ways they both conceded that whatever representation we have of reality is mediated by the de facto position that this subject occupies within this reality. They each based their particular notion of 'factual necessity' on precisely this consideration. If one had failed to grasp where Kant's revolutionary move truly lay, it was easy to confuse what for Kant was a theoretical model of the mind – one required for the logical construction of the concept of an object of experience in general – with a physiological explanation of the genesis of such a mind, despite Kant's explicit warnings against it.[56]

Reinhold is the one usually regarded as responsible for this psychologizing of Kant. In fact, as we shall see in the following chapter, Reinhold's Kantian reform was both more complex and, in some respects, more confused than any such popularization of the master. For an earlier and much more telling example of the process of domesticating Kant for popular purposes, one should rather look to Carl Christian Ernst Schmid, notorious for his Kant-Lexicon fame.[57] In an essay appended to the second edition of the Lexicon (1788),[58] Schmid defined the difference between, on the one hand, what he refers to simply as *Empirismus* – to all appearances the classical empiricism of Locke – and, on the other, a so-called new Kantian *Purismus*. According to Schmid, the key to the difference is how 'sensibility' (*Sinnlichkeit*) is understood by each. According to Empiricism, it is the mind's (*Gemüth*) capacity to receive impressions from external things by means of certain specialized organs that we call the 'senses'. An immediate impression is called 'sensation' (*Empfindung*), and the consciousness of it after occurrence, 'representation' (*Vorstellung*). According to Kantian Purism, by contrast, sensibility is the mind's capacity to be passively affected by its objects – where by 'objects' (*Gegenstände*) one must, however, not understand anything outside the mind but certain products for which the mind is itself responsible. The whole process is from the start all a matter of the mind's self-affection. Sensibility constitutes the passive aspect of the mind's relation to these products – hence, indirectly, its relation to itself. What the Empiricists call 'sense organs' are counted by the Kantian Purists, rather, as also among such products; what the Empiricists call sensations are counted by the Kantian Purists, rather, as passive and transient conscious states totally immanent to the mind (5–15).

This, according to Schmid, is a difference with important immediate consequences. Empiricism recognizes that the mind contributes to the content of an external affection through its own capacity of being affected. However, because of its original assumption, Empiricism is both bound to and unable to draw any clear line of demarcation between what in the affection supposedly derives from the external things and what is instead contributed to it by the mind's organs. Any such differentiation is for Empiricism an impossible task, since its success would presuppose knowledge of the very difference that is to be established. It also follows that any connections that Empiricism draws inside the mind between its various sense representations remain irreducibly accidental. For to the extent that the distinction between the mind and the things external to it remains unclarified, equally unclarified must remain the attribution of these representations to either side of the divide. In the case of Kantian Purism, by contrast, the situation is totally different. Since the assumption now is that the object is exclusively constituted by the activities that the mind exercises over its own passive states (its *Empfindungen*), it is always possible on the strength of self-reflection both to draw a clear line of demarcation between the mind's passive states and its active contributions to the constitution of an object and, by means of further reflection on these contributions, to establish a priori the essential determinations of an object in general.

This fundamental difference has further consequences for how *Empirismus* and *Purismus* each conceives the faculties of 'understanding' and 'reason'. According to a pure Kantian position, the objects of these two faculties are not abstractions artificially drawn from the content of sensations – as they must be for Empiricism. They are the products of connections actively drawn by the two faculties between otherwise merely passive states of the mind. According to Schmid, the great advantage that Kant's *Purismus* thus offered over classical Empiricism is that it rid the latter of any reference to extramental things (15–23, 33–4). Kant could not therefore be accused, as he had been from the beginning, of asserting the existence of things in themselves while at the same time removing every ground on which to make the assertion. This is an inconsistency that is rather the flaw of Empiricism. For Kant, according to Schmid, the thing in itself is an idea totally internal to the mind, and one construed for purely mental purposes. Moreover, Kant could retain a clear distinction between objective and 'nonobjective' (i.e., between 'objective' and 'subjective' in the sense of 'private') in virtue of standards of objectivity set a priori by the mind through its activities. And since these activities are 'constructive' rather than 'abstractive' – that is, they control passive content rather than depend on it – they can in principle reach out to every detail of the experienced world. There need be no appeal in Kant's reconstruction of experience, therefore, to the abstractness and the vagueness of empirical conceptual representations.[59]

Capitalizing on Kant's transcendentalism, Schmid was thus carrying the subjective implications of the Lockean side of popular philosophy to extreme, but at the same time more consistent, conclusions. The restriction to which all mental representations are subject, namely, that they reflect reality only from the standpoint peculiar to the human being, is now taken as the basis for a systematic form of subjectivism. In this system, Leibniz's metaphysical concepts find a place again, but as categories structuring a purely mental, rather than physical, universe. So transformed, however, Kant's Critique of Reason was made all the more vulnerable to the attacks of those who, on the contrary, wanted to hold on to the spirit of realism that animated Leibniz's metaphysics and was also part (however inconsistently, perhaps) of Locke's empiricism. The Critique was criticized for being an extreme form of subjectivism – dishonest because of its pretensions to objectivity, and ultimately just as self-destructive as dishonest.

Weishaupt is again a clear case in point. He repeatedly attacked Kant on precisely this ground – most forcefully in a book published in the same year as Schmid's essay (1788).[60] He advanced arguments there that ran in direct opposition to Schmid's. According to his reading of Kant, transcendental idealism had indeed to be 'pure' in order to be self-consistent. Its purity, however, brought its true nature to light all the more clearly. It was in fact nothing short of a conceptual trick – in effect, a way of redefining objective in terms that, according to accepted usage, are already subjective. Every detail of any picture of reality that a realist would offer as 'true in itself' is thus saved, but only under the new modality of 'true for a subject only'. The skeptics had tried a similar strategy in the past, according to Weishaupt – in their case, by accepting everything people normally accept as unqualifiedly true under the variant modality of 'possibly true.'[61] These were for Weishaupt, however, nothing but ruses that did nothing to further the cause of truth. For one thing, he saw no sense in introducing abstruse new assumptions, or in engaging in singularly subtle reasonings, only for the sake of having all things fall in place at the end exactly as common sense takes them at the beginning – except that now they bear the empty, and in practice useless, coefficient of being for a subject or of being possibly true. Even more important, Weishaupt thought that the ruses were ultimately self-destructive. They all came to grief on the requirement that, in order to be known, an object must be identified. For that, it must be placed in a definite context. It must be related to other objects, with respect to which it stands as a distinct individual that nonetheless bears elements in common with them. To the extent, however, that one qualifies the object as being for a subject only, or as only possibly true, one detracts from its individuality, thereby making it impossible to relate it significantly to anything external to it. By the same token, one also makes it impossible to identify it as object. Just like the skeptics, the Kantians were thus caught in a vicious circle. By failing to retain enough of a distinction in experience between subject and object, they precluded the possibility of inserting the latter into the greater universe on which it depends for its identification. But in thus failing to identify it, they also precluded the possibility of any serious distinction being drawn between it and a subject. It was the identity of this subject, hence its reality, that the Kantians, exactly like the skeptics, were ultimately undermining. They were caught up in a solipsistic position, and solipsism is by nature self-destructive. In sum, Kant's categories were empty subjective instruments that stood in the way of the mind's discovery of itself in the world where it actually belonged.[62] They were like an opium (an *opiat*, as Weishaupt says with respect to the antinomies)[63] distracting it from the richness of experience.

Weishaupt was raising a powerful objection. Important to note, however, is that, despite their radical differences, he and Schmid both considered as the final test of the validity of their respective position whether it saved the reality of the individual. And in this they were both bearing witness to their shared roots in popular philosophy. Schmid had thought that, in reforming Lockean empiricism by injecting into it elements from Kant's a priori constructivism, he would overcome the formalism for which empiricist abstractions were rightly denounced. His arguments were intended to deflect from Kant the charges of formalism that Kant's critics (Weishaupt included) were leveling against the Critique of Reason. Weishaupt, for his part, thought that with his move, that is, by systematically translating the language of objectivity in subjective terms, Schmid, or anyone else pursuing the same tack, was in fact erecting a phantom kind of reality.[64] The move only sharpened the nagging doubt that, as Weishaupt believed, haunts individual consciousness constitutionally – namely, the doubt that experience might just be a dream; that the individual is totally alone, caught up in a purely private world. A doubt of this sort disturbs the peace of mind; if taken seriously, it even leads to despair.[65] The fact alone that the Kantians were adding credence to it constituted for Weishaupt – again, true popular philosopher that he was – sufficient ground for dismissing the lot once and for all. Of course, Schmid could have retorted that Weishaupt's realism hardly afforded greater comfort to the individual. For in the real universe that Weishaupt assumed, everything that an individual did or that happened to him was strictly determined by universal necessary laws. Whatever happens must happen. Weishaupt was quite explicit about this consequence of his system and even welcomed it. In his opinion, fatalism made for peace of mind.[66] But one could then have reasonably asked him, as Jacobi had already done to Lessing with reference to Spinoza, how an individual who is thus totally absorbed in the mechanics of a greater universe is 'individual' in any recognizable sense of the word; how, in Weishaupt's realism, consciousness of one's individuality is any less illusory than on Schmid's subjectivism.

Schmid never raised the question for obvious reasons that we shall consider in due time.[67] The point now is that it was easy indeed to view Kant with a mind to the set of problems that drove popular philosophy – notably the problem of how to reconcile individual identity with the overriding mechanism of nature; or the contrary problem of how to safeguard the presumed necessity of the laws governing this mechanism, granted that whatever representation we have of them has been gained from the limited standpoint of an observer immersed in experience. It was easy because Kant himself had addressed himself in his Critiques to precisely these problems. But he had thereby given rise to new ones of a specifically critical nature. And to the extent that one interpreted both his attempted solutions to the old problems and the new problems he had created as a variation of the accepted problematic, whether one capitalized on the new problems in order to attack Kant (as Weishaupt and the academic critics on the whole were doing); or whether one capitalized on his attempted solutions to the old ones to optimize the extant resources of *Popularphilosophie*; or again, whether one relied on these resources in order to mitigate the specifically Kantian problems (Schmid was in fact doing these last two at once); in all cases, the net result was that, far from bringing closure to the current debates, the presence of Kant only served to exacerbate them. In the process, the flaws that afflicted all sides became all the more evident.

2.4 THE CULTURE OF FEELING

There is one more factor in this reception of Kant that needs attention before we bring the whole discussion back to the theme with which we began. We must remember that the late Enlightenment culture put great emphasis on the moral and even epistemological significance of 'feelings'. And in this respect also the Critique of Reason came under revisionist pressures as it became part of the general debate. Kant had made the feeling of respect for the law a centerpiece of his moral theory, even though the notion of a state of mind that is inextricably bound to the mechanism of nature – as any feeling would have to be – but is nonetheless determined a priori by the idea of the law, was indisputably problematic. It was precisely this notion that opened the way for the appropriation, along traditional lines, of even the moral side of his system, exactly where the revolutionary character of 'critique' should have been most evident.

A splendid example of this aspect of the process is to be found in the prolific production of J. H. Abicht.[68] A theologian and professor of philosophy at the University of Erlangen, Abicht's doctoral thesis had been nothing but a faithful reproduction of the earliest religiously motivated interpretation of Kant.[69] But Abicht soon began to assume a critical distance with respect to Kant – or more precisely, of what he thought was Kant. In company with most of the early critics, he especially objected to the alleged extreme formalism of the Critique of Reason that made it ultimately useless so far as any insight into the psychological and moral constitution of the human mind was concerned. Abicht's project was to reform the same Critique in the shape of a psychology – one, moreover, that was to satisfy the requirements of an 'elementary philosophy' (*Elementarphilosophie*). This meant, in effect, that it was to be based on what Abicht describes as "a complete internal fact, i.e. something that gives itself over to me in cognition immediately."[70] Such a fact (*Tatsache*) would have to be 'internal' as well as 'complete' because only then would it constitute an immediate object of cognition, one not in need of further deduction, and would therefore provide the ultimate answer to the ultimate 'why?'

The term 'elementary philosophy', as well as the description of the program and the principle of the new science that was to bear it, were borrowed. Reinhold had already embarked on a similar project and had already defined the parameters within which it had to be realized. As we shall see, Reinhold had, however, chosen representation (*Vorstellung*) as his absolutely immediate fact on which to base his reformation of the Critique of Reason. Abicht thought, on the contrary, that representation was too complex a mental fixture to satisfy the required criterion of simplicity. It presupposed more fundamental operations and simpler elements on which to exercise them. This had been, incidentally, one of Schulze/Ænesidemus's more compelling objections to Kant and Reinhold in his skeptical attack of 1792.[71] And Abicht was now trying to preempt it by positing as his first fact 'consciousness' itself – that is, such immediate presence of a self to itself that, because of its immediacy, defies definition yet is the tacit starting point of any self's awareness of anything else in itself. Abicht described it in one place – obscurely, to be sure – as *"die unabänderliche Gewißheit von der Beseelung in mir,"* that is, "the irrevocable certainty of my being animated [or 'ensouled']."[72] Granted this presence as fact, Abicht proceeded to establish the first group of more particularized forms in which it is realized. These forms also constitute a set of fundamental (though not original) facts. They are the capacity of the soul 'to represent', 'to feel', and 'to will'. Abicht's theory of mind unfolds along these lines.

We need not dwell on the details – uniformly unoriginal as they are[73] – but can proceed instead directly to Abicht's treatment of 'feelings'. These phenomena, according to Abicht, are distinguished from sensations inasmuch as they constitute a soul's consciousness of generating something within itself actively rather than, as in sensation, of receiving something passively. Feelings are, however, always directed to a presupposed object; they are pleasant or unpleasant in accordance with the way this object is perceived. The consciousness of their being entirely generated from within the soul can be due, therefore, only to the fact that, though dependent on an external object, they are nonetheless elicited by the object only indirectly, by means of a *representation* of it. This representation is itself an internally generated product of the soul. In brief, a feeling is the soul's pleasant or unpleasant reaction to an object, in accordance with whether this object is represented by it as contributing either positively or negatively to its representation of itself. As an object of feelings, that is, inasmuch as it becomes material of either desire or aversion, the object of a representation thus acquires a new meaning by being incorporated into the economy of a soul's image of itself.[74]

But how is this transformation possible? How can objective representations that, at least on the face of it, are directed to things external to the soul become part of the soul's self-image? How can the soul's original awareness of itself in the form of a strictly self-directed feeling of well- or ill-being be transformed into a complex of aversions and desires putatively directed to external objects? Now, according to Abicht, Kant had already provided the answer to this question. It has to be sought in his theory of transcendental apperception. Though the content of an object refers to something external to the soul, the object itself cannot be represented *as object* except in virtue of the categories. But these categories are in the first instance determinations of the representation of an I in general. Therefore, even when representing a presumed external object, the soul is in fact still representing itself. In other words, the process by which the soul, through its conceptual activities, shapes otherwise undifferentiated sense materials into a world of objects is only the other side of the process by which the same soul establishes limits to its image of itself. What originally was an immediately self-directed feeling of well- or ill-being becomes, through the conceptual shaping of a world, the well-articulated system of desires and aversions that defines an individual person. The two processes – defining oneself and defining a world – thus proceed *pari passu.* On the one side, the soul's capacity for feeling embraces its capacity for representation, since the soul's original self-relation is the source of the efficacy of all its desires and aversions. It is also the source, therefore, of the sense of effective reality that the objects of such emotive states assume before it. On the other side, it is the faculty of cognition that elicits and directs the soul's particularized feelings insofar as through that faculty the soul excogitates different possible objects and depicts them as either contributing to or detracting from its well-being. The concepts of good and evil depend on the 'pre-sentiments' (as Abicht calls them) of how envisaged objects fit within a subject's conception of itself.[75]

Moral life represents only a more developed stage of this process. The will is a soul's capacity (*Fähigkeit*) to allow itself to be determined by different kinds of objects. Once developed into a stable and effective power (*Kraft*) of self-determination, this capacity becomes what, according to Abicht, we call 'moral nature'. The whole issue of the possibility and the realization of moral life thus devolves on the question of whether, and to what extent, one is capable of playing an active role in the shaping of effective desires once the soul's original undifferentiated feeling of self-love has been transformed into desires for other things as well. And this is a role that requires a very complex concept of one's self-identity. According to Abicht, Kant's idea of duty, and of self-imposed maxims of conduct, are all components of precisely this complex concept of self-identity. In the end, therefore, morality consists in an art (*Kunst*) of living – in the art, that is, of constructing as complete and as rationally well-balanced an idea of oneself as possible.[76]

There are, of course, important social and political consequences that follow from this conclusion. For instance, it follows that 'right' (*ius*) cannot be based on a government's supposed absolute prerogative to coerce the members of a society but on its capacity, rather, of detecting what is good for them. This good is determined by their nature, and this nature is in turn constituted by an individual's felt responses to given situations. Legislation is only part of the art of good living. Basically this art is a process of educating feelings, and, just as in all cases of education, coercion should enter into it only to the extent that reason has yet to establish its rule on the one being educated. According to Abicht, coercion defines only 'imperfect duties' or externally imposed demands.[77]

2.5 THE RETURN TO LEIBNIZ

Such, in bare outline, was Abicht's theory of the mind as he developed it in his Erlangen lectures and, starting from 1789, as he published it in a series of books.[78] To be noted is how the theory stood with respect to the Kantianism of a Schmid and the anti-Kantianism of a Weishaupt. On the one hand, Abicht was treading the well-defined path of Schmid's subjective Purism. A subject's perception of the world ultimately depends on his image of himself. Since Abicht had, however, made feeling the centerpiece of his theory, and since feelings are phenomena of consciousness in which the well-being of a subject – the subject's existential standing, so to speak – is at issue, he could defend himself against any accusation of solipsism. Any representation of reality – a mere theoretical possibility otherwise – acquires existential relevance the moment it becomes engaged in the economy of a subject's feelings. These feelings are responsible for the heavy weight of reality that some representations convey in contrast to others. They are the last judge of how realistic a subject's perception of the world, as well as the subject's image of himself on which such a perception is based, truly are. This is a strategy that, as we shall see, is also pursued, albeit in different ways, by both Jacobi and Fichte.[79] On the other hand, to Weishaupt, Abicht could have pointed out that he too (i.e., Weishaupt) grounded his realism on the witnesses of feelings. As a matter of fact, Weishaupt had based his whole theory of knowledge, as well as of moral perfection, on the premises that 'heart and head cannot stand in conflict'; that the human being spontaneously seeks perfection;[80] that his feelings are so disposed by nature as to respond positively to anything that promotes happiness; that, since the human being finds satisfaction in clarity of representations, this clarity must itself be implicated in his search for perfection and consequent happiness. Weishaupt's final conclusion was that we must trust our first principles of knowledge because without them we could not even begin to define the nature of our happiness, let alone strive for it.[81] And this was a conclusion that Schmid could easily have recognized as his own. Abicht, Schmid, and Weishaupt were in fact all operating within the same conceptual framework of popular philosophy. Any disagreement between them could only have been a family squabble.

With respect to Kant, toward whom Schmid and Weishaupt had assumed diametrically opposed attitudes, one should also note the reform to which Abicht was subjecting the Critique of Reason. Abicht might have believed that he was supplementing it with psychological elements drawn from Locke. In fact, he was using Kant to complete Locke's physiology of the mind. Starting from the assumption that philosophical reflection must be based on some primitive facts of consciousness, and from assumptions regarding the nature of these facts drawn from classical empiricism, Abicht was using Kant's transcendental method of construing objects a priori in order to show how a subject's original feeling about itself can be transformed into a world of physical and moral objects. Gone are any inferences from impressions found within the mind to the existence of supposed things external to it – inferences that Schmid as well as Weishaupt had also found dubious. Gone also are the claims that, by this process of inference, one can determine at least the primary qualities of these things. Such inferences were dogmatic remnants in Locke's empiricism that interfered with its consistency. In Abicht they are replaced by an alleged descriptive account of how, through conceptual activities and the mediation of feelings, modifications internal to the mind can *immediately be taken as* external objects or, for that matter, how self-love can be *seriously taken as* the love of others. However clumsily (and there is indeed much spurious thinking here), Abicht was transforming Locke's empiricism into a genetic phenomenology of the mind. And he was using conceptual tools borrowed from Kant in order to perform the task.

There should be no doubt that Abicht thought of himself as a Kantian. In 1794, in response to Schulze/Ænesidemus's notorious skeptical attack

on Kant and Reinhold, he published a book entitled *Hermias* in which he
took up the cause of Hermias, the Kantian character in Schulze's dialogue
left speechless at the end by the onslaught of the skeptic Ænesidemus.[82]
In Abicht's version of the dialogue, Ænesidemus is the one left speechless. Moreover, in 1790–1, together with F. G. Born, he edited two vol-
umes (eight issues altogether) of *Neues philosophisches Magazin*, a journal
specifically dedicated to the explication and application of the Kantian
system.[83] Yet Abicht did not hesitate also to criticize Kant, and his criticisms grew in number and tone as his position developed over the years.
He was aware, of course, of the changes that the Critique of Reason was
undergoing at his own hand. He could not, however, understand – this
was the main point of his criticism – why Kant might have objected to
them. To the suggestion, which he himself mooted, that Kant would not
have accepted his theory of the faculty of the will because it was based
on an empirical concept, he replied that he (Abicht) knew of no other
will except an empirical one.[84] To base the theory on an a priori concept
would have resolved none of the difficulties encountered at the empirical
level of conceptualization but would have rather reintroduced them all
in a transcendental form. And Abicht was especially hard on Kant for
claiming that happiness had to be added to morality as an external in-
ducement to right behavior offered by God. So long as the connection
between moral action and reward was based on what had to appear as the
arbitrary and hence accidental intervention of a third party, there could
be no effective motivation for the action. True moral life had to be – so
Abicht argued – its own reward.

This was the strength of the appeal of the originally Leibnizian ideal of
a universal harmony that reflects itself in individual minds and finds subjective fruition in their individual contentment. Kant's theologian friends
had not really abandoned it, though they had tried to think about it
anew by placing it on moral/pragmatic grounds. Abicht – himself one
among them – had now provided a whole psychology for this new interpretation. Feeling was the immediate yet already complex component of
consciousness in which a harmonious totality of human existence and
of a greater world beyond was in principle already reflected. The important point is that Abicht was applying this model of rationality as a
harmony of relations to his own descriptive reconstruction of the mind
as a matter of course, such that he could not even understand why or
how Kant could object to it. That Kant might have been operating on the
assumption of quite a different idea of rationality simply was not an issue
for him.

It is to Schmid again, however, that we must finally turn for the classical example of what still was, fundamentally, a Leibnizian model of the mind, but was now being both restated in psychological language and argued for – only superficially, of course – transcendentally. We find it in his *Philosophische Dogmatik* of 1796[85] – a book in which, as Schmid says in the first page of the Preface, he meant to fulfill the promise of an earlier book "to make clear the relation of this noblest part of philosophy [i.e., the philosophical doctrine of religion] to all its other parts; to clarify the connection of its principles with one another and with the fundamental principle of all philosophy, and also, finally, to make clear its relation to humanity in general, its fundamental laws, its drives, and purposes."[86] Now, as Schmid goes on to say, "'unity' is the highest law of the spirit; more specifically, 'the unity of the I'." In his own words (§44, pp. 34ff.):

Thus the highest law (drive) of our spirit – the one to which all other laws (drives) are subordinated – is this: To produce the unity of the 'I' with itself. This law – that we be at one with ourselves – acquires because of our finitude and our being bound to the conditions of time the sense of a command, namely: **there should come to be in us the highest unity**, all manifold in us should agree with itself. This highest law of law is, precisely because of that, the *highest objective law* of all the products of the spirit, including science or philosophy.

The first principle of every science follows directly from this "highest law of law" (§45, pp. 35–7). Thus, our thinking should agree with itself (principle of logic); our willing should agree with itself (principle of morality); our thoughts and their objects should agree with one another (principle of the metaphysics of nature); our will and its objects should agree with one another (principle of the metaphysics of morals); finally – this is the first principle of theology – our willing should agree with our cognition. Belief in God and the immortality of the soul is based on this requirement. Moral belief forges the final link that brings the harmony of the self with itself to completion. And the moral veneration of a God thus morally adhered to in belief marks the fruition of a life animated from the beginning by feelings. Again, to cite Schmid's own words:

The first principle of a theoretical doctrine of religion is this: There shall (*soll*) be the highest conceivable condition for the highest possible realization of the highest purpose of being in agreement with oneself, and, through this condition, all manifold shall be raised to the highest theoretical unity. – The first principle of a practical doctrine of religion is this: Our striving shall (*soll*) be directed to the [the realization of] the highest condition of the will's purpose (*Zweck*), and this condition shall be the highest objective (*Ziel*) of all our striving, i.e. we shall venerate God morally. (36–7)

At Schmid's hand, the 'I think' that in Kant was the principle of the transcendental unity of apperception is transformed into a principle of organic unity of individual existence. The principles of the sciences that together should have constituted for Kant an ideal universe of reason become commands that derive their force from an individual's striving after harmony of existence. As for religion, it is the celebration of the contentment thus finally achieved in this harmony. The absorption of the Critique of Reason back into the tradition was complete.

2.6 LEIBNIZ VERSUS KANT?

But was this Leibnizian recasting of Kant necessarily disastrous for the Critique? The answer is not as straightforward a "yes" as one might think at first. Kant himself would have resisted it, and with good reason. The popular philosophers were conflating the reflective reconstruction of the conditions of a universe of meaning with the theoretical explanation of a physical universe. They were conflating grounds of meaning with causes of existence; logic with cosmology; subject of predication with subject of psychology. In this, they were 'dogmatic' in the new specific sense that Kant had given to the term, and were still entangled in the same sophisms for which Kant had criticized past metaphysics. From the new standpoint defined by the Critique of Reason, they were hopelessly old-fashioned. For the same reason, they all failed to appreciate the new intuitive role that Kant had assigned to the senses in experience. The products of the latter, that is, sensations, cannot be, as they all still assumed, just a case of obscure representation. They are the place rather where the otherwise merely reflective intentions of the mind are brought to existential consummation. They constitute the immediate presence of hitherto only logically intended objects.

This last point is one that the *Popularphilosophen* never quite grasped. Yet the story does not end there. For it is at least simplistic, if not outright wrong, to interpret the kind of psychology that in their different ways they all practiced as mere 'physiology' – that is, as some sort of empirical discipline for which Kant's Critique of Reason must provide the transcendental principles, just as it provides them for every empirical science. This is how Kant himself characterized Locke's theory of the mind, and how one would have to characterize all of the psychologizing of the popular philosophers on a narrow positivistic reading of the Transcendental Logic. On that reading, one either reflects on concepts or theorizes about the 'real', whether mental or physical. But this would be to miss the true nature of what the popular philosophers were actually doing, and what Locke, from whom they all drew inspiration, had done as well.

The fact is that it is not possible to reflect upon the intentional activities of the mind without thereby envisaging a concrete subject who is responsible for them. Such a subject is not an object of strict empirical description, for it operates in the midst of noumenal entities (say, as we already have, courts of law, treaties, wills and testaments, markets, experimental laboratories) that are in fact the product of its own intentional activities and for which no strict empirical reality test can ever be set. We nonetheless presume in common experience that this subject is to be found, along with the things that populate its intelligible realm, within the same spatiotemporal world where we find any physical entity. Nor can it be taken to be an explanatory principle, at least not in any causal sense – though, again, we normally treat it as if it had explanatory causal power. This 'subject' is rather the product of an idealizing imaginary construct – one that is indeed imaginary and, as such, admits of a high degree of latitude yet need not therefore be arbitrary. Different cultures may well come up with different variations of this construct, as in fact they have done. In the modern world we have long been operating with a variety of them, all nonetheless mutually related. *Homo œconomicus* is not quite the same as *homo juriducus* or *homo politicus* or *homo theoreticus;* yet we are constantly forced to adopt now one such construct of 'being a human subject', now another, and to negotiate the shift from the one to the other as we move from arena to arena of activity. The truth of any of them (the limit to their arbitrariness) depends precisely on the pragmatic value that each demonstrates in bringing to subjective awareness the lived engagement we have in these arenas of action. They make possible at a practical level the transaction between conditions of meaning and conditions of natural existence that action indeed requires, as well as transactions from one arena of action to another. They stand, in other words, as the subjective points of reference that make it possible for an individual being to negotiate his way across a cultural world of meanings with the same ease that the natural body allows him to make his way across the physical world. Of course, they can just as well hinder us from grasping the theoretical and moral conceptual commitments that each tacitly presupposes. They can thereby also mask the shortcomings that such commitments might well harbor.

I am saying, in brief, that the figurations of mental life along Leibnizian lines into which the popular philosophers were absorbing Kant's Critique of Reason were not the empirical theories of psychology or physiology that Kant or, for that matter, the popular philosophers themselves were inclined to take them to be. They were rather ideal imaginary constructs – figures of the mind that derived their persuasive force exclusively from their success in portraying in quasi-objective shapes a human being's lived experience of acting, though physically, nonetheless in a world of meaning. The limitation that made them a source of confusion lay precisely in the fact that, since they were all devised after cosmological models, they blurred the distinction between physical and meaningful existence, as if the latter were simply a more complex variation of the former. This was just as true for someone like Weishaupt, for whom the mind was just a segment of the physical cosmos, or for someone like Schmid, whose so-called *Purismus*, while reducing the physical cosmos to the mind, still conceived the latter as ruled by the laws of causality just like any physical thing.

Now, Kant was ill advised in dismissing offhand this Leibnizian psychologizing. His Transcendental Logic required a psychological model. It required the idea of a subject to whom the operations typical of that Logic would be attributed. As a matter of fact, Kant was operating with some such model. It was the model of faculty psychology that he was borrowing without compunction from the scholastic tradition. And it stood to the credit of his critical genius that he was able to recognize it for exactly what it was. It was a schema of the mind that derived all its meaning in virtue of the logical operations that it helped to define, and was not to be confused with any physical or metaphysical theory of mental life. What was not clear, however, is whether, in adopting it, Kant had sufficiently modified the traditional model he was borrowing from to allow *both*, the irreducible distinction between the physical and the intentional that he had introduced but the popular philosophers had failed to take seriously, *and* a conceptually easy transition from the one to the other that would reflect the ease with which the transition is performed in actual experience. The distinction between *homo phænomenon* and *homo noumenon* that he introduced did not do that job in any obvious way. And to the extent that, in order to explain the transition from logical intentions to objects of actual experience, Kant famously appealed to some 'secret art of the imagination', he could easily convey the impression that he was still operating on the same assumptions regarding being and knowledge typical of dogmatic metaphysics. In that case, he would have been scaling down the pretensions of the latter without revolutionizing it from within.

It might well be that the Leibnizian model of the mind, if duly reformed, would have been an apt medium for embodying Kant's new critical standpoint, perhaps even better than the one he actually adopted. As we shall see in the following chapter in connection with Reinhold, the irreducible distinction between intuition and reflection, sensation and concept, which is crucial to that standpoint, could have been saved in the Leibnizian model. More about this in due time. The mention of Reinhold, however, leads to a further consideration that is again only an adumbration of things to come. History was an object of great interest during the *Aufklärung*. Kant himself shared in this interest. It was Reinhold, however, who first drew an at least de facto connection between the truth of any philosophical system and the history that had led up to it. It might well be that Kant's Transcendental Logic, and to an even greater extent his revolutionary moral theory, were precisely in need of a historical, genetic model of the mind. Historical events are inextricably the products of both nature and human intention. Hegel will be the one to bring this line of thought to fruition. It is noteworthy that his early teachers were popular philosophers and that, as a young man, he thought of himself as a pedagogue of humanity, as the popular philosophers did. But Hegel does not fall within the purview of the present study. Fichte does, and, as we shall see, he explicitly drew the connection between nature, conceptual reflection, and the genesis of the human mind – though not necessarily in a form we are likely to accept. We shall return to this subject. The immediately pressing question that has now emerged is how to forge a satisfactory conceptual connection between Kant's logical subject (his transcendental I) and a concrete individual self, that is, between Transcendental Logic and a new, critically inspired anthropology. Popular philosophy, as we have just seen, had brought the Critique of Reason back to well-worn Leibnizian paths. The question is whether it could instead be made to travel the new critical way.

3

The Intractable Kant

Schultz, Jacobi, Reinhold

3.1 THE CANONICAL INTERPRETATION

Abicht, Schmid, or Weishaupt might not have been philosophical luminaries, but in their varying reactions to Kant they all gave clear expression to a naturalism typical of the late *Aufklärung*. By contrast to other
contemporary more crude reactions, their efforts appear even elegant.[1]
Weishaupt was notorious in his day mostly because of his connections with
the Illuminati and because of some shady aspects of his life. Reinhold
wondered why Weishaupt wrote so much against Kant when, as Reinhold
thought, he misunderstood him altogether.[2] The judgment was not altogether fair. There were difficulties in Kant's system on which Weishaupt
capitalized. But the judgment was also the expression of a general tendency to shun Weishaupt because of his materialistic views[3] – the kind
that would have been widely regarded in Germany as morally reprehensible. Schmid is remembered today mostly because of his quarrels with
Reinhold and Fichte, while Abicht is not remembered at all. In their own
time, the two men (Schmid and Abicht) made an impression nonetheless
because of their teaching activities and the sheer massiveness of their publications, all of them intended as textbooks. At any rate, whatever their
actual philosophical merit, and perhaps even because of their lack of it,
they provide for us today a perfect illustration of how *Popularphilosophie*
was able to remold the Critique of Reason according to its own presuppositions. The flaw that made the Critique vulnerable to this remolding
was its need for a model of the mind that reflected the transition from
the transcendental I to the individual self in a way that was recognizable
in actual experience. And the source of the power that *Popularphilosophie*

was able to exercise lay in a misunderstanding of the Critique of Reason that made it possible for it to interpret the transcendental I simply as one more psychological dimension of the individual self. The fact, however, that the popular philosophers gave a false solution to a Kantian problem did not make the latter any less of a problem. The degree to which the problem interfered with the new critical position was visible even in the very first, and arguably still the clearest, commentary on the *Critique of Pure Reason*. The commentary was all the more important because it was commissioned and approved by Kant, and therefore carried, so to speak, canonical status.

The commentator I am referring to is the Court Chaplain Johann Schultz.[4] Kant was not happy with the first reviews of the *Critique of Pure Reason*. He thought that he had been seriously misunderstood, and assumed that he was misunderstood because he had failed to communicate properly with the public. The complaint everywhere raised that the technical language of the book created undue difficulties – to the point that, for practical purposes, the book stood sealed[5] – reinforced this opinion of his. His *Prolegomena to Any Future Metaphysics*, which was his attempt at remedying the situation, did not fare any better. The same complaints of obscurity were raised against it, and the same misunderstandings persisted. Kant's eventual reaction was to enlist the help of Chaplain Schultz, also professor of mathematics and a colleague at the University of Königsberg. Kant had the highest respect for the intellectual abilities of "honest pastor Schultz." When the latter wrote to him shortly after the publication of the *Critique* announcing his intention to review it, he responded by offering some suggestions on how the book should be read, and also by encouraging Schultz to write an "independent piece," something more substantial than just a review. The result was a short commentary entitled *Elucidations of Professor Kant's Critique of Pure Reason*, which Schultz first published in 1784.[6] Upon reading the text still in manuscript form, Kant wrote to Schultz congratulating him for its comprehensiveness and accuracy, and testifying in conclusion that, in his words, "as far as the correct presentation of my meaning is concerned, I find almost nothing in it to change."[7]

Schultz's little book was indeed a paragon of clarity and accuracy. Its intention, as stated in the Preface, was to avoid Kant's technical language altogether (12). In fact, it stayed very close to it.[8] But it presented Kant's position in such a simplified and straightforward form that it brought out its meaning with a forcefulness that Kant's own text never attained. It had the merit, moreover, of confronting the reader straightaway with two crucial theses of the *Critique* and the problem that they generated together.

The first thesis is that sensations and concepts are two radically different products of the mind. Their difference defines the very nature of human knowledge, inasmuch as the latter is dependent on experience. The starting point of the *Critique* is the simple acknowledgment of the fact that the objects of human cognition derive from experience. They are *given* in experience. Something cannot, however, be 'given' in any relevant sense of the word without at the same time being actively received, that is, 'recognized' or 'acknowledged' as being given. (The German word for 'knowing', *erkennen*, conveys precisely this extra meaning of recognition or acknowledgment.) Now, judgment is the mental operation through which the required recognition or acknowledgment is attained. A judgment asserts (or denies) that something, as immediately given in experience, is exactly what the judgment says that it is. In a judgment, a subject of experience reflectively takes hold of (i.e., 'comprehends' or 'perceives') what would otherwise be a merely subjective state of mind. He comprehends it as the determination of an object that, in turn, he recognizes as *given* through it. Thus the subject stands related to his object at once *directly*, in virtue of an immediate representation that we call a sense intuition or sensation, and *indirectly*, in virtue of another type of representation that is the mind's exclusive product and that we call a concept. In judgment the subject of experience brings the content of his sensations *under* certain presupposed concepts, thereby understanding what this content truly is, namely, a particular determination of the object intended by the concepts. At the same time, the subject recognizes this object as actually present in experience (cf. pp. 188, 203–6).

Thus from the start Schultz stressed a point that Kant's contemporaries – whether rationalist or empiricist, or, as most often the case, a mixture of the two – found difficult to understand, namely, that the difference between sensation and concept cannot be just a question of degree of clarity and distinctness of representation.[9] Sensation is not just an obscure concept, nor is the concept just a duly explicated sensation. The two play roles in judgment that are supplementary and, precisely for that reason, irreducible. Because a subject must presuppose his objects as existing prior to him and as given to him from outside, his representation of them must entail the double function of 'immediate presentation' and 'reflective apprehension'. It must be discursive or based on judgments. The irreducible difference between sensation and concept is needed precisely in order to satisfy this requirement.

The second of Kant's theses that Schultz underscores follows from this same requirement of human knowledge. The thesis is in two parts: (1) there must be some fundamental concepts that a subject applies to the content of experience a priori; (2) such concepts, though logically prior to experience, are nonetheless restricted to it (cf. pp. 205ff., p. 213). The argument in defense of both parts is plain enough. To the extent that judgment entails the recognition (or apprehension) of an object as given in experience, the object thus recognized must have been intended in the first place – that is to say, it must have been conceived at least in some respect prior to its actual apprehension in experience. Otherwise, it could not be *recognized* as given. As a matter of fact, most concepts are themselves representations derived from experience, the result of repeated associations of sense impressions. Many others are artificial combinations of such impressions put together for who knows what pragmatic or other purposes. If these were, however, the only types of concepts at work in judgment, as the empiricists claim, all our supposed apprehensions of objects in experience would be in fact purely subjective or fictitious. There would never be anything necessary about them. The belief accompanying all our experiences – namely, that, albeit in a limited sense, such experiences are objectively true – would therefore not be saved. The alternative is to grant, as Kant does, that underlying all sense experiences there are certain rules, reflectively conceived independently of these experiences, in virtue of which it is, however, possible to judge what elements in these experiences can be appropriately attributed to objects as their determinations and how these attributions can appropriately be made.

These rules are Kant's well-known categories of the understanding. Together they constitute the concept of an object of experience in general – the most fundamental norm for what counts, in experience, as either the true or merely illusory apprehension of an object. This norm is necessarily reflective or a priori, which follows from the requirements of judgment in general. The first part of the thesis is thus established. By the same token, the second part also follows, namely, that the categories only define the possibility of objects that can be given in sense experience. For how the object is actually apprehended in experience, and what it actually looks like when thus apprehended, necessarily depend on sense conditions over which the subject himself has little, if any, reflective control. There might be senses different from those that the human being happens to possess. And, as regards the actual human senses, the only necessary thing about them is that they determine a subject's immediate relation to his objects in the forms of space and time. At what determinate point in either space or time, however, and under what circumstances such a relation is realized, and whether it is realized at all – actual experience alone can determine that. In brief, the categories define only the marks of the genuine *appearance* of an object – not the object as it would be *in itself* apart from its having come in contact with a subject in sense experience.

It is a mark of Schultz's perspicacity that he does not advance Kant's famous distinction between appearance and thing in itself as an independent thesis, but rather as the consequence of other, more fundamental and more immediately demonstrable ones. Everything depends on the nature of judgment as the apprehension of an intended object in experience. The implications of this definition also give rise, however, to the great problem that the *Critique*, according to Schultz, must resolve. Why is a subject of experience justified in applying his logical order of intentions to the sense-content of experience? Might this application not be an arbitrary imposition?[10] The question arises, according to Schultz, because of the great disparity – perhaps even incompatibility – between reflective order and immediate appearance that naturally gives rise to the doubt about whether it is legitimate to extend the one to the other. Here is where Schultz reproduces, in a brilliant six-page précis, Kant's transcendental deduction of the categories as follows.[11]

(1) A subject could not become aware of his sensations – he literally could not 'take them in' or 'apprehend them' – without simultaneously going through them and holding them together. This step consists in a 'synthesis of apprehension'.

(2) Such a synthesis requires an extra faculty over and above that of sensation, for the senses are bound to the transitoriness of impressions; hence, though capable of receiving such impressions momentarily, the senses cannot retain them. Sensations must therefore be reproduced in a stable medium in which they can be held together. The faculty responsible for this operation is what we call the 'imagination' – *Einbildungskraft*, literally, the power of picture-making. Its product consists in a 'synthesis of reproduction'.

(3) But how does one know that, in thus reproducing the content of sensation, one is being faithful to what was originally given? Here is where the factor of 'recognition' comes in. In the process of reproduction, the subject must have in mind some object – an object that he assumes is already given, or at least capable of being given, and that he takes as his norm of truth. The original impressions are thus no longer simply taken in or apprehended. They are also perceived as apprehended, that is, they

are comprehended in what we call a 'synthesis of apperception'. The subject's faculty responsible for this already reflective operation is what we call the understanding, and the representations that the subject uses as a norm of objectivity in the discharge of this operation are concepts.

Although Schultz does not mention here either Locke or Hume, it is important to note that any sophisticated empiricist could have accepted his (and Kant's) analysis of the process of experience that Schultz has presented so far. Schmid, as we remember, had accepted it precisely in order to make empiricism more consistent with itself. The only difference is that an empiricist of the Lockean type would consider the representations used as the medium for the synthesis of recognition in apprehension to be merely mental fictions dependent for their effectiveness on custom or some other pragmatic factor, whereas a Kantian would take them rather as possessing logical validity a priori. In either case, it is still open to doubt whether the order that they express is actually given in sense experience. The main issue of the deduction, namely, the justification of the a priori use of the categories, is therefore being confronted in Schultz's formulation of the Deduction only at this point. And it is here that the unity of the subject of experience, already assumed from the beginning, comes in for official consideration (cf. pp. 36–7).

(4) Recognition requires a subject's reference not just to his object, but to himself as well. For 'to recognize something' is to declare that what a subject knew under one set of circumstances is now present to him again (and is recognized by him) under a different set of circumstances. The process presupposes, therefore, that a subject is aware of his own identity across a variety of experiences. It is the same subject who once saw or heard something and now sees it or hears it again. Such a sense of identity cannot, however, be derived from experience a posteriori, because, inasmuch as a subject is an object of experience, he is subjected to the same flux of temporality as any other object. Hence his own representation of himself, just like any other representation, would have to be the product of a synthesis of reproduction and apperception. But it is the a priori legitimacy of such a process of synthesizing that is now in question.

(5) One must therefore presuppose another synthesis of apperception. Or more precisely, one must presuppose that at work in any synthesis of apperception is a purely reflective awareness of self-identity – one based on the activity of the concept alone, on the 'I think'. Since this awareness transcends temporal self-consciousness, we call the unity of experience that it produces 'transcendental unity of apperception'. The I think itself constitutes its a priori principle.

(6) The crucial move in the whole deduction comes at this point. If, as we have just seen, the subjective unity of representations must rest on a necessary a priori principle, that is, if it has to be transcendental, the same applies to the unity of the manifold that is the object of such representations. Their objective unity too must rest on transcendental principles, namely, on a priori conceptual intentions. These are the categories. Hence their objective validity is justified.

This is the clinching move in the argument. But why this last inference? Why the move from 'necessity of a transcendental principle of subjective unity' to 'necessity of principles of objective unity'? Schultz's only laconic comment is that if it were otherwise – if the manifold of our representations were the product of mere apprehension, association, and reproduction – there could not be the kind of subjective unity that was required in the first place.[12] Now, on the face of it, this is not much of an explanation. It leaves at least two questions unanswered. We shall turn to the second in a moment. The first has to do with the necessity of the alleged connection between subjective and objective unity of apprehension. On Schultz's argument, if the categories deployed in the exercise of the I think were not effective as principles of objective unity, the I think of which they are the functions would not be effective either as a principle of subjective unity. Why should this be so?

Now, short of assuming that Schultz has fallen into the subjectivism of Schmid's *Purismus*, we might find the basis for an answer if we turn to a later section of the commentary, where Kant's Analogies of Experience are being considered (cf. pp. 57–60). There, Schultz defends the objectivity of the category of causality by arguing that, unless there were objective causal links connecting certain events, a subject of experience would have no reliable criterion for distinguishing between chains of internal and chains of external events – these latter being determined by a necessity that transcends the subject. Contrary to actual experience, he would not therefore be capable of safeguarding his immediate and irreducible sense of being a real subject making his way across an external, and just as real, world. This is a strong argument, all the stronger in Schultz's shortened form, as compared with Kant's. It presupposes, however, that the subject deploying the categories in the process of experience is, from the start, a spatiotemporally determined self. Of course, for this kind of *real* subject of experience, a merely formal principle of unity, though indeed necessary, would not by itself be sufficient. A material content is equally required for it, and such a content is not available except with reference to an equally *real* and equally *ordered* world. A stable self of experience, in other words, can be realized only with reference to an equally stable world as its object of experience. It follows that one cannot *really* engage in the activity of judgment, and thus implicate one's transcendental sense of identity, without at the same time necessarily intending, and also expecting to recognize as given, a well-ordered world of experience. But the categories define this order. Inasmuch as a self attains true subjective unity through its exercise of the I think, the effectiveness of the categories as principles of objective unity is thereby necessarily implied. Schultz, and presumably Kant as well, simply take the connection for granted.

If we were to take this reading of the Analogies of Experience as normative for an interpretation of Kant's Transcendental Logic, then it would follow that the kind of subject that both Schultz and Kant have in mind from the beginning is precisely the concrete self of actual experience. It would indeed be peculiar if this were not the case. Just like the popular philosophers, or, for that matter, every philosopher, Schultz and Kant are interested in real subjects. It would also follow that already at work in the *Critique of Pure Reason* is a model of this self. Such a self, just like the one of the popular philosophers, refers indeed to immediate experience, but, unlike it, neither is nor claims to be the product of psychological observation. It is rather an idealized model of its operations that a self deploys in the course of experience. In virtue of it, the self retains the sense of identity that it requires as it makes its way across its spatiotemporal world while discharging there its intentional activities. Kant, in other words, had already begun to give a phenomenological account of how this model is construed in the course of experience, while at the same time demonstrating the de facto effectiveness of the categories in bringing the objective order of that experience to reflective awareness.

The problem, however, in taking this reading of the Transcendental Logic as normative is that, with its adoption, the great disparity that allegedly separates sensibility and reflective conceptualization vanishes. The doubt also vanishes regarding the applicability of the categories to immediate experience that the Transcendental Deduction was supposed to dispel. It would follow that, so far as experience is concerned, the categories have meaning from the start *only* as schematized (to use Kant's language), that is, as already entailing reference to a sense content. This is not to say that one should therefore abandon the critical distinction between 'immediate' and 'reflective representation' of an object, but to claim rather that the reflective representation is from the start implicated in the process of presenting an object as *given* in experience to a *real* subject. Any other meaning that the categories might have independent of this function would be the artificial product of a philosophical abstraction that itself creates the alleged gap between the form and content of experience, and in turn creates the consequent possible doubt as to whether the one applies to the other. Indeed, the image itself of experience as a process of applying categories to an external sense material is the product of a falsifying abstraction. In other words, any demonstration of the objective validity of the categories, inasmuch as any such demonstration is required at all, could only consist in an exposition of the structure of experience that simply brings to reflective awareness the degree to which the categories are indeed implicated in the experience of things from the beginning. In fact, this is all that Kant ever accomplishes in much of the Transcendental Deduction and, even more clearly so, in the Analogies of Experience. And, to the extent that this is what he accomplishes, he does it brilliantly. In the Leibnizian tradition of the popular philosophers, concepts add to a supposed sense-content a clarity that this content otherwise lacks, and thus attain a knowledge that transcends the senses. Kant now interprets these same conceptual products rather as instruments in virtue of which the sense-presence of objects in experience is attained in the first place. This presence alone constitutes knowledge proper. 'Phenomena' never are, therefore, *mere phenomena* (unless, of course, they are the localized product of illusion) but reality as made manifest to a subject, that is, as *present* to the subject. 'Noumena', for their part, have no meaning except as implicated in precisely this process of objectification in sense experience. The very idea, therefore, of a thing in itself inherently unknowable in possible experience also becomes meaningless. The thing, rather, is known in experience precisely in itself, albeit within the limits to which its presence is realizable. There might be indeed limits to *our* senses, but not to sensibility as such.

In brief, on this reading of the Transcendental Logic, Kant would turn out to be an even more radical empiricist than any of the classical empiricists ever were, for he would be rejecting the assumption that classical empiricism shared with rationalism and that made it prone to skepticism. This is the assumption that sense experience is inherently lacking because of its presumed subjectivity and contingency. For Kant, on the contrary, nothing would be more self-justifying, clearer, and more distinct than a well-executed sense-experience of an object. But again, the problem with this reading of Kant is that he, as Schultz faithfully reports, *does* think of phenomena as *mere* phenomena; *does* operate with the image of the categories being applied to an independently obtained sense content, as if externally; *does* believe that there is gap between products of the understanding and sense-content requiring a transition from one to the other (indeed, Kant wrestled with this problem of an *Übergang* until the end of his life);[13] most of all, *does* assume a thing in itself inherently unknowable through experience, and, though denying that the intellectual intuition posited by the rationalists is possible for human beings, Kant still maintains its possibility at least in principle. All these assumptions hardly square with the picture of Kant as the phenomenologist of experience that one might otherwise gather. His critical distinction between the senses and the understanding gives rise to the problem that the Transcendental Deduction is supposed to resolve only if still understood in a Leibnizian context, as if the categories still made some sort of ontological commitment. And the alleged irreducible unknowability of the thing in itself makes sense only if this thing is still being understood, again in a Leibnizian sense, as the possible intelligible object of would-be purely intellectual intentions. This is how intractable Kant is. The more crystal clearly his position was stated, as in Schultz's commentary, the more he confronted the reader with problems that were either no problems at all or, if truly problems, the consequence of assumptions still drawn from the empirico-rationalist tradition of the popular philosophers.

Sigismund Beck was one philosopher, and an early self-professed disciple of Kant, who explicitly tried to reshape the Critique of Reason by taking the already schematized categories (which he accepted as original) as his starting point, and by thus describing the structure and genesis of experience from the standpoint of an observing subject without having to take recourse to any transcendental argument. Unfortunately, Beck's theory always remained peripheral in the general discussion of the day and must therefore remain equally peripheral here.[14] Of greater concern now is the second question, still left in abeyance, that arises in connection with the last step of Schultz's exposition of the Transcendental Deduction. What should lead Schultz to believe that the I think, the effectiveness of which as a principle of subjective unity necessarily brings in train the effectiveness of the categories as principles of objective unity – that this principle is the effective subjective principle that it is assumed to be? Why should the threat of formalism that otherwise affects the exercise of the categories not affect it also? Why should the unity that the I think provides be more than a fiction with no real counterpart in actual experience? Of course, all these questions vanish if, just like the categories that regulate its thinking, the I think is conceived from the start as part of a real subject's awareness of its real identity in a real world of experience. This might be precisely how Kant and Schultz do conceive it. But, just as in the case of the categories, unless the I of the I think is properly schematized, the way in which this I contributes to a self's robust sense of its own real identity in just as real a world remains problematic. What is needed, again, is a proper phenomenological model of the genesis of the self, exactly the kind that the popular philosophers thought they were providing but were held back from developing by their traditional modes of thought.

The need of such a model, this time enriched with a moral component, comes through again later in Schultz's commentary, where he proceeds to ask why the subject of experience, though naturally bound to the limits of the senses, seems just as naturally driven to seek knowledge of objects that necessarily transcend these limits (cf. pp. 233–8, 189). This question constitutes, according to him, another great problem that the *Critique* must resolve. At this point Schultz brings into play Kant's notion of a 'subjective interest of reason' and proceeds to explore the extent to which such a purely subjective factor is sufficient justification for committing oneself to certain admittedly undemonstrable, yet apparently invincible, beliefs. In all of this, Schultz remains very close to Kant's text both in terminology and in line of argument. Interest of reason, however, is at best only a metaphor. Not 'pure reason', but a rational individual human being, is the subject of interests in actual experience. As part, however, of the mental makeup of such an individual, an interest, under whatever title one appeals to it and however rarefied one conceives it, still denotes the kind of subjective attitude of mind that has feeling as its prototype. And feeling cannot be divorced from the senses. Of course, whether in his precritical or his critical period, feelings, especially moral feelings, were for Kant always an object of reflection. From very early on, however, his tendency had been to distinguish sense-induced feelings sharply from interests of reason, thus introducing a split in his moral model of the human being that his contemporaries found even more difficult to accept than the split between sense and understanding. Is there a way of connecting feelings and interests of reason internally? The question is all the more important because feelings carry with them a more immediate and robust sense of a self's reality, and therefore of its involvement in a real world, than even the senses do. Feeling, as we remember, was Abicht's deliberately chosen starting point for his reconstruction of the Critique of Reason in a phenomenological mode. Fichte will follow a similar strategy, as we shall see, but with a clear understanding of the implications of Kant's Critique. Hegel will be greatly indebted to him. But, before Fichte, and even before Abicht, Jacobi had already tried a similar move. He had done it by offering an alternative position to Kant's and by expressly bringing into play themes derived from the British philosophical tradition. We have reached the point where we must retrieve the already mentioned commonsense component of *Popularphilosophie* that, as we remember, was one of the many aspects of this cultural phenomenon that Reinhold had badly misunderstood.

3.2 JACOBI'S REALISM[15]

3.2.1 Polemical Notes

In 1787 Jacobi published a little book entitled *David Hume on Faith, or Idealism and Realism, a Dialogue.*[16] The book was published at the height of the controversy caused by his Spinoza-Letters of 1785 and was itself, in many ways, a contribution to it. It made its appearance, moreover, at a time when the *Berliner* (whom Jacobi identified with the worse type of Enlighteners) were indulging in what he considered an unseemly paroxysm of grief at the sudden death of Mendelssohn.[17] Some were hinting that Jacobi had been responsible for it because of the stress his attack had caused on the aging invalid.[18] The main part of the book, as the title indicated, took the then popular form of a dialogue. As an appendix to it, Jacobi also published his already mentioned influential criticism of Kant.[19] It was added as an afterthought, occasioned by the recently published revised edition of the *Critique of Pure Reason*. The attention that it, however, attracted obscured the fact that Jacobi had already been addressing Kant in the body of the dialogue. There he had tried to offer an alternative to his idealism that would have saved its transcendental standpoint while at the same time avoiding its alleged subjectivism and excessive a priori formalism.

The complexity of the dialogue's title reflected its complex production. According to Jacobi's prefatory account, the final text had been put together from what were originally intended as three distinct dialogues, to be entitled respectively "David Hume on Faith," "Idealism and Realism," and "Leibniz, or Concerning Reason." Jacobi was obviously dissatisfied with how the final product hung together and seemed hesitant about its main line of argument. Much later, in 1815, in the Preface to its second edition, he distanced himself from it explicitly. He then declared the dialogue inconclusive and blamed this flaw on the fact that at the time of its composition he had not yet clearly distinguished between understanding and reason – the one allegedly being a reflective faculty, the other an intuitive one – and hence was not in a position to bring his argument against subjectivism to a satisfactory ending. By that time Jacobi had changed philosophically (not necessarily for the better). He had fallen in line with the new religious positivism of Schleiermacher and Fries. This was a positivism that he had himself indirectly inspired but that nonetheless bore direct connections with the more scholastic and, ironically, more rationalistic currents of *Popularphilosophie.* In that frame of mind, Jacobi was, of course, no longer capable of recognizing that there had been in fact an impeccable logic driving the original text. The discomfort with the dialogue that he had felt from the start had much more likely been due not to any particular lack of insight regarding the nature of reason but to his instinctual realization that that logic led ineluctably to conclusions unacceptable to him. The fact that in the second edition Jacobi disingenuously altered the original text to suit his new views (disingenuously, because he claimed to have left it untouched) made the dialogue all the more confusing for all future readers.[20]

We shall see, at the end, the nature of these consequences that Jacobi found disturbing. Let us turn now to the text itself. The dialogue falls into three clearly recognizable parts suggestive of the three distinct dialogues originally planned. The first is the most polemical and the one also most directly connected with the ongoing debate. Jacobi had been accused by many of being an irrationalist because, in his Spinoza-Letters, he had claimed that all knowledge depends on a more fundamental faith. '*Schwärmer*', that is, 'fanatic' or 'enthusiast', was the term at the time reserved for those who subordinated human science to divine revelation. In this part, Jacobi's goal is to counter this accusation of being a *Schwärmer* by clarifying the sense in which he had used the term 'faith' (*Glaube* in German) when addressing himself to Mendelssohn. The use, as he claimed, had been imposed on him by his adversaries. These claimed that all cognition is achieved through reflective conceptualization. Jacobi held, on the contrary, that reflection presupposes the prior intuitive apprehension of an object, for it is impossible to re-present anything in a concept unless that thing is somehow already present to a subject intuitively. But since his adversaries had preempted the use of 'cognition' for what was in fact from Jacobi's point of view only the product of reflective or derivative representation, Jacobi himself had no choice but to call faith what for him was, on the contrary, genuine and original cognition.[21] The object of this kind of primordial apprehension would indeed appear to a subject of experience as the product of a revelation, since its presence to him is immediate. Used in this sense, however, the term did not have to carry any irrationalistic connotations. 'Faith' amounted to immediate or direct cognition of an object. To this line of defense Jacobi then added – tongue in cheek, and obviously poking fun at his academic adversaries – what he calls the most persuasive of all arguments, namely, one from authority (29ff.). Citing extensively from Hume, Jacobi points out that he too had used the term belief in exactly this sense of 'faith'. This was a notable coincidence, even if obscured by the circumstance that the English language has two words, namely 'belief' and 'faith', for the one German word *'Glaube'*. If Jacobi had been writing in English, he would have used the work 'belief' in exactly the same sense as Hume had used it. Nobody, however, had ever accused Hume of being a *Schwärmer*. On the contrary, in the eyes of Jacobi's adversaries, Hume stood as the model of rational good sense. Why then accuse him, Jacobi, of irrationalism when he had in fact simply followed a practice sanctioned by none other than Hume?

Jacobi's case, so stated, had some merit. It could, of course, have been pointed out to him that there was more to the accusation than he alleged. In the Spinoza-Letters, he had made profuse use of clearly recognizable enthusiastic rhetoric. He had also repeatedly invoked the name of Lavater – of all the *Schwärmer* of the day, certainly one of the most notable. Even the present dialogue, despite all its rational argumentation, was to end by hinting at the possibility of private revelations of a world beyond. Whatever his true philosophical intentions, in other words, Jacobi had certainly done his best to invite the charge of irrationalism. And if one took as evidence the dialogue's conclusion, he still did not seem inclined to deviate from this path even as he was making his case.[22] This opening polemical sparring was nonetheless leading up to a definite and interesting philosophical theory that begins to take shape only in the second part, where Jacobi begins to develop his notion of 'immediate knowledge' still left vague in his opening polemic.[23] For polemical purposes, he had just allied himself with Hume. His problem now was to show that, even though he was using Hume's language, he was, unlike Hume, not a skeptic but a realist. The challenge, in other words, was to explain what he meant when he alleged the possibility of an apprehension that is immediate and, like belief (*Glaube*) even revelatory, but that constitutes genuine knowledge rather than the blind and irrational commitment to a presumed object that faith (*Glaube*) normally denotes. It is here, as Jacobi tries to meet this challenge in the second part of the text, that it becomes apparent how much not Hume, the eponymous hero of the dialogue, but Kant was the primary object of Jacobi's interest.

3.2.2 Jacobi's Theory of Experience

The rhetoric of dialogue tends to disperse the steps in Jacobi's argument against skepticism. Yet an argument is there, complete and compelling. The starting point of the argument is the denial of the fundamental assumption of classical empiricism that Jacobi takes to be contrary to fact. This is the assumption that experience begins with purely subjective representations, and that the belief in external objects is arrived at only by way of an inference based on the passivity of some of these representations. This is the assumption that inevitably led to Hume's skepticism. Jacobi rejects it offhand on the ground that, as a matter of fact, a subject could not be aware of himself and, consequently, aware of the alleged subjectivity of some of his representations without defining his self in opposition to some admittedly external object, that is, without immediately referring his representations to something other than himself. The very possibility of subjectivity entails the possibility of objectivity. Jacobi's classical formula for this position is that there is no 'I' without a 'Thou' (65). The most important Thou for Jacobi is that of another subject, first of all God. But it is clear that the formula here defines first and foremost the structure of all consciousness, whatever the object. Subject and object, activity and passivity, are for Jacobi inextricably and immediately given in consciousness together. As he says, "the internal consciousness and the external object, must be present both at once in the soul even in the most primordial and simple of perceptions – the two in one flash, in the same indivisible instant, without before or after, without any operation of the understanding – indeed, without the remotest beginning of the generation of the concept of cause and effect in the understanding" (65).

Jacobi is aware that Hume had doubted whether we have any definite representation of the presumed self in us. Even if we had one, it would have no stronger claim to objectivity than any other representation. Thus Jacobi's argument could be deflated by the simple move of denying the presence in any subject of the kind of self-awareness that would necessitate, according to the argument, the immediate awareness of an external object. Here is where Jacobi makes his second move. Hume's doubt about the objective reality of the self makes sense only to the extent that we assume a purely speculative, that is, distanced, attitude with respect to our subjectivity and that we thus entertain a purely theoretical representation of our self. Such a representation would entail an equally theoretical representation of a possible world external to the self, and both – that is, representation of self and 'external world – would equally be susceptible to Hume's doubt. But in fact, as he proclaims with a rhetorical flourish, we do not just think. We also act (102). And in action there is implicated a much more fundamental kind of self-awareness – one that is not open to doubt, since our own existence is at issue in it. Feeling is the form that this kind of self–awareness assumes; more precisely, the feeling of 'power'. Hume himself had acknowledged this much, Jacobi points out, but had failed to work out the implications of this insight (107). Jacobi proceeds, therefore, to make up for what Hume had left undone by repeating his opening argument, but at a much more existential level of analysis. A feeling of power would amount to nothing unless, in the exercise of the felt power, an obstacle were met that renders the exercise problematic and, by that token, also significant. A serious obstacle can only proceed, however, from an external source – external, that is, to the subject exerting the power. The source must therefore be immediately experienced by the subject as something existing outside him *in itself*. Of course, in order to be the target of a force, the obstacle must be somehow susceptible to the subject's influence; it must be 'penetrable' by him, as Jacobi puts it. But it cannot be totally penetrable, for otherwise it would cease to be a significant obstacle. The awareness of its existence in itself, in other words, is inextricably bound with a subject's feeling of power. It follows that the existence of a world external to the subject is both immediately experienced and conceptually justifiable (107ff.).

Jacobi's third move is to retrieve and integrate in the more existential context just defined his first comments about representation in general. It is granted that a subject's reflective representations of himself are all bound up with, and dependent upon, the subject's feeling of power associated with action. Such representations must all proceed pari passu with the representations of an opposing external world of objects. Since the representations in the two series – namely, of self and of external world – are both reflective, both are equally susceptible in particular contexts to challenges and doubts. But they cannot be prey to Hume's generalized doubt, or to the radical subjectivism that follows from empiricistic assumptions, for they all are in some way implicated in a subject's attempts to assert his own existence in action. In fact, based on the requirements of action, a number of indisputable claims can be made regarding the structure of the objective world confronting the subject. Jacobi proceeds

to state these claims, in each case sketching an argument in their defense, and boldly summing them up at the end with what amounts to
the definition of an object in general. This definition, though abstract,
depends nonetheless for its meaning on the interaction in actual experience between a sentient body and its immediate environment. Here are
his words:

So it would seem that we have shown the concepts of reality, substance or *individuality*, corporeal extension, succession, and cause and effect, to be concepts that
must be common to all finite, self-revelatory, beings; and we have shown also that
these concepts have their concept – independent object in *the things in themselves*.
In other words, they have a true, *objective*, meaning. (118–19)

To the further question of whether these concepts can be said to be
necessary, Jacobi replies by drawing a distinction. If the required necessity
is conceptual, and is demanded on the assumption that actuality derives
from possibility, and hence that the existence of anything is justified on
the basis of its concept, then, of course, the concepts he has just derived do not meet the criteria of either necessity or universality. Such
criteria, however, are mere fictitious products of reflective reason, nothing of real consequence insofar as actual experience is concerned. If,
on the contrary, by necessary and universal one means that, granted an
actual fact of experience, one has identified and defined in suitable representations the essential elements constituting it, then, Jacobi argues,
his concepts defining the fundamental structure of experience enjoy as
much necessity and universality as anyone could possibly wish. To be sure,
the necessity now in question is a factual one, dependent for its validation on actual experience and limited in its universality to the boundaries
of the latter. But again, anything more than that would be mere fiction
(110–20).

It is here, in making this last move, that Jacobi explicitly refers to transcendental idealism (123), thus finally betraying that Kant, rather than
Hume, had been his main object of interest all along. Jacobi boasts that
he has been able to save the possibility of judgments of experience that
are necessary without, however, having to presuppose the existence in
the mind of a priori categories. Such categories, to the extent that there
are any, are nothing according to Jacobi but prejudices of the mind
(119–20). Applying them reflectively to actual experience only detracts
from the evidence already immediately inherent in the latter. It is important to note that Jacobi is not here contesting Kant's or even Hume's
method of defining the objects of experience always from the standpoint

of a subject that is himself immersed in experience. He is not denying that it is impossible ever to transcend the limits of experience. Kant's and Hume's phenomenological method was also Jacobi's, at least insofar as the present dialogue is concerned. Jacobi's contention is rather that he, and he alone, has succeeded in discovering the right formula for representing how an experiencing subject, in becoming aware of himself, equally becomes conscious of the presence of an external world. This objective consciousness is the necessary condition of any subjective self–apprehension. The true transcendentalist, it is implied, was Jacobi himself. He – not Kant – had truly overcome Hume's skepticism while still honoring Hume's subjective method.

Distilled from the many twists and turns of the dialogue, the formula that Jacobi had discovered thus includes three claims.

(1) Self-awareness originates in a subject's feeling of power.
(2) This feeling immediately implicates the presence for the subject of an external something that exists in itself and interferes with the felt power, but at the same time provides the feeling with a reality check.
(3) Representation is called into play as the reflective attempt on the part of the subject to sort out the difference between his own self and the external thing resisting his power.

This formula brought together in an original unity the three components of consciousness, namely, feeling, sense representation, and reflective conceptualization, that Kant had instead sought to synthesize externally by imposing the admittedly formal constructs of reason upon the content of already conceptualized experience. It is the same formula that we found in Abicht. We would equally find it at work in the many attempts by other popular philosophers to overcome what they perceived to be Kantian formalism. Specific to Jacobi is that, by defining feeling as originally a feeling of power, he was saving the robust sense of realism that is part and parcel of all lived experience. He was circumventing the danger to which both Abicht and Schmid were vulnerable and that Weishaupt had had occasion to decry – namely, that in defining the external world as the counterpart of an internal world, one was thereby fabricating a counterfeit objectivity, something real *for us* but not *in itself*. For the external check on the internal feeling of power that Jacobi now assumed as the basis of his conception of objectivity was in principle irreducible to anything purely subjective. In effect, Jacobi was discounting as fictitious and irrelevant the distance between the I of transcendental apperception and the self of a concrete subject of experience that on Schultz's version of the transcendental deduction had to be overcome in order for the deduction to succeed. But he was not in any way diluting the specifically existential significance of the senses that Schultz had been at pain to stress. The opposite was the case. From the beginning Jacobi's strategy vis-à-vis Kant had been to recognize that there is indeed an element of necessity in experience. But, instead of seeking its source in concepts external to the senses, he had taken it rather as a structural component of sensation *as sensation.* He was thus reinforcing, rather than detracting from, the existential contribution of the senses to experience. In the course of experience, conceptualization must naturally intervene in order to develop this structural component of sensibility, but it cannot ever leave it behind.

Of course, the price for all this was to abandon the formalism of reason that Kant had adopted to combat the dogmatism of scholastic metaphysics. Jacobi was no less opposed to this dogmatism than Kant. His next challenge in the dialogue is precisely to develop a theory of reason that avoids Kant's formalism yet preempts the claims of dogmatism. We have seen that Jacobi acknowledged Hume as his source of inspiration when he attributed the origin of self-awareness to feeling (105–8). But he also gave credit to Spinoza, at least for providing what he thought was a more adequate definition of the relation between representation and action than any found in Hume. As he says:

According to Spinoza, although representations only *accompany actions*, the two still *implicate* one another; they are inseparably joined together in one and the same indivisible being and consciousness. [. . .] The individual wills and acts in accordance with the constitution of his particular nature, and in conformity with the requirements and relations of this nature. And he displays all of this for his viewing in his consciousness [i.e., in representation], with more or less obscurity, or clarity. (108–9)[24]

There, in Spinoza, Jacobi thought that he had already found defined the synthesis of being, will (of which feeling is a mode), and representation in which, according to him, experience consists. This reference to Spinoza is important (and should not be forgotten) because, as we shall see when we come to Fichte, it will have wider consequences than Jacobi expected. However, as he now moves to the final part of his argument with reason and rationality in mind, the source of his inspiration will clearly be neither Hume nor Spinoza, but Leibniz and Thomas Reid.

3.2.3 Jacobi on Reason: The Nature of 'Common Sense'

Even before turning the reader's attention to transcendental idealism, Jacobi had already brought Kant onto the stage – accidentally, as it were, in an autobiographical digression that marks the transition from the first to the second part of the dialogue (67ff.). The purpose of the digression is manifold. It provides a kind of relief from the polemic tension of the first part. It gives an account of Jacobi's early training in philosophy, thus establishing his credentials as a serious philosopher, and it sets the theme for the discussion to come.

Even as a young man, still new to things philosophical, Jacobi had instinctively assumed that existence, or actuality, precedes possibility; that existence is the source of possibility. This assumption, according to his account, had from the beginning blocked his advance in the study of philosophy, since all the recognized authors of the time (Mendelssohn included) derived actuality from possibility instead. They sought to demonstrate the existence of a thing from its concept, whereas Jacobi thought that the concept is a derivative product totally dependent for its content on the actual thing it is supposed to represent. The net result was that in the standard textbooks the *principium compositionis* was inevitably being confused with the *principium generationis* (93). That is, it was assumed that the demonstration of the components of the concept of a thing by way of analysis is equivalent to the explanation of the process by which that thing comes to be, as if its generation were equivalent to the derivation of the properties of a triangle from its definition. The further result was that temporal succession, which depends on the actual becoming of things, was reduced to a mere subjective apprehension, nothing real in itself.

This method of demonstration explained why the Cartesian proof of God's existence from the idea of God was universally accepted by the authors of the day (again, Mendelssohn included) (74ff.). So far as Jacobi could see, the step from the idea to existence is separated by an infinite divide, since the one is a reflective product of reason, while the other is something in itself. The proof could not therefore succeed unless, of course, one assumed with Spinoza that God is the substance of all things, and took the idea of God as the first and most general idea of reality as such. This is not an assumption that the same authors were willing to accept, yet they all unquestionably granted the validity of the Cartesian demonstration. Hence Jacobi's delight and excitement when he discovered that Kant, in an essay that had been shabbily reviewed in the literary journal edited by Lessing and Mendelssohn, had criticized the demonstration, and had also argued that the only rationally demonstrable necessity is that of some actuality in general, since whatever possibility we conceive would have to entail some prior actuality. One can call this necessarily presupposed actuality 'God', if one so wishes. However, as Kant pointed out, *what* the attributes of this God might possibly be are nothing that can be deduced from the original assumption. Therefore this actuality could not be the basis of theology as expounded in the metaphysics textbooks of the day. This was a thesis that neatly coincided with Jacobi's own instinctual belief that existence precedes conceptual essences, or that actuality precedes possibility. His enthusiasm upon discovering Kant's essay was therefore understandable. The young Jacobi, still intimidated by authors whom he could not, however, bring himself to accept, had finally found an authority vindicating him.

Kant was thus being introduced in Jacobi's dialogue on a polemical note, with the ongoing controversy still in sight (84ff.). Jacobi was hinting that he, not Mendelssohn, had true affinities with Kant. In view of what immediately followed in the dialogue, however, the polemical note was being struck in the direction of Kant as well. The further implication of Jacobi's autobiographical story was that in the *Critique of Pure Reason* Kant was not being true to his own earlier insight, since transcendental methodology reversed his previously asserted order of thought and existence. It made the objectivity of experience depend on the a priori requirements of formal thought. But this is precisely what the authors whom the young Jacobi had been unable to accept had also been doing. In effect, Jacobi was lumping Hume and Kant together, and was criticizing them both for still viewing experience with the same distanced attitude of theoretical reflection on which metaphysics is based. They both construed the objects of experience ex post facto, on the basis of already presupposed representations – in the case of Hume, according to the alleged psychological mechanism governing these representations; in that of Kant, according to the logical requirements of judgment; in either case, abstracting equally from the actual process in which an object appears to consciousness. The process itself was consequently made to appear inherently mysterious. In either case, the reflective reconstruction of experience remained strangely disconnected from the robust sense of realism that accompanies the latter, and equally disconnected from a subject's immediate awareness of being existentially involved in his objects. This is not to say that the two philosophers did not both acknowledge this irreducible natural realism or that their analyses did not in fact rely on it. In their different ways, they both sought the source of this realism on the emotive side of human nature. Hume especially made a lot of alleged naturally induced beliefs about the reality of things. At the end, however, neither philosopher had been successful in capturing this belief conceptually.

This flaw signaled that something was amiss with both philosophers' conceptions of reason. Leibniz's name is rhetorically invoked by Jacobi – 'invoked' literally, as if by way of incantation (144–5) – precisely at this point, when the issue of reason is put on the table. We shall turn to this figure from the past in just a moment. First, we must take note of yet another theme being played by Jacobi in the dialogue. We must remember that in 1786, one year before the publication of *David Hume*, Kant had published an essay entitled "What Does It Mean to Orient Oneself in Thinking?" It was to be his only contribution to the ongoing Spinoza controversy. The title played on an expression used by Mendelssohn in one of his replies to Jacobi. Mendelssohn, typical Wolffian metaphysician that he was, had accepted Locke's assumption that sensations are purely subjective mental states, but had at the same time tried to stave off the Humean skepticism that logically follows from it by claiming that it is possible to argue from these mental states to their presumed causes outside the mind. Jacobi had challenged the reliability of inferences such as these; they belie the immediacy of our certainty about the reality of things. To this, Mendelssohn had replied that there are questions that should not be asked simply because they cannot be answered. When such fundamental matters as the existence of things outside the mind are at issue, for instance, one must ultimately turn to what he called 'common sense' and rely on it as a guide for orientation on how to deal with such matters in thought.

Now, in his essay Kant had set out to define this notion of common sense critically, openly siding with Mendelssohn against Jacobi, whom he considered a religious enthusiast, but finally coming down with a notion typically his own.[25] Common sense is an extension of reason. It consists of inclinations that are indeed subjective, but that are nonetheless reliable guides for orientation in the pursuit of truth since they respond to reason's interests. They are themselves the product of these interests; hence, though subjective, they possess objective relevance. They direct us to objects for which we have no evidence, and might not even be possible so far as our comprehension goes, but that we are led to accept ideally nonetheless, because they are required for our rational reconstruction of the totality of experience.

This was Kant's definition. Jacobi, who must have been pigued by Kant's siding with Mendelssohn, was tacitly advancing in the dialogue a competing definition. And for this he was relying on Thomas Reid, whose name was generally associated in Germany with common sense.[26] To be sure, Reid's presence in the dialogue is not very visible. His name occurs only once, and incidentally at that (26–7).[27] Yet we know from other sources that Jacobi had the highest respect for this Scottish philosopher and that he was well acquainted with his rejection of Hume's skepticism.[28] His own defense of realism in the dialogue was clearly inspired by the same conception of sense and sensation on which Reid had made his stand against Hume. Reid's argument, in brief, had been that, inasmuch as sensations enter into mental life – whatever their nature as purely physical events – they function in the manner of natural signs, immediately making manifest to a subject the presence of something external to him.[29] Sensations, in other words, are 'perceptions' in both the Latin and German sense of 'apprehensions' (*Wahrnehmungen*). They are complex events because, even as subjective states of the mind, they entail a judgment and hence have objective significance. However indeliberately, they take up (*nehmen*) a certain position with respect to something and hold it for what it is (*Wahr*).[30] Sensations are thus inchoate perceptions – even though, because of the vagaries of English philosophical usage at the time, Reid was forced to deny that perception is what he called 'simple apprehension', precisely in order to restore to the term the meaning of the Latin *apprehendere* or of the German *wahrnehmen*.[31] This was exactly the meaning also assumed by Jacobi in defense of realism. It was clearly entailed by his opening remark in the second part of the dialogue that experience begins with an original distinguishing between a self and an external presence apart from which there is no consciousness in the first place. In other words, experience originates in some sort of judgmental activity.

    With this claim, echoing Reid, Jacobi had already forged in principle the link between theory of sensation and theory of reason. For it followed from his (and Reid's) understanding of sensations that reason's conceptions do not have to be the faintest among the copies of sense representations that Hume had taken them to be. Nor, as on Kant's model of experience, do conceptual representations have to be either categorial forms applied to sense materials a priori, as if externally, or ideal constructs further applied to these categorized materials equally a priori. They are rather representations that reflectively articulate, and hence enhance, distinctions already found in sense perceptions.[32] All forms of conceptual representations, but notably those produced by reason, cannot indeed function apart from the senses – or more precisely, they might, but only at the risk of generating illusions. This was a fundamental thesis of empiricism on which Hume, Reid, Jacobi, and Kant could all equally agree. For Reid and Jacobi, however, this only meant that reason must continue, and never abstract from, the work of reflective apprehension already in principle performed by the senses. Within this restriction, reason can claim its own objective significance, for its rationality is in essence only a heightened, that is, a more self-aware and hence deliberate form of sensibility.[33]

Jacobi drew this conclusion in the dialogue explicitly when arguing that, even according to the witness of common language, to be rational really means to have some form or other of good sense. As the leading character (the 'I') says,

You must have noticed that whenever I want to express what is most eminent about a man, I speak of his *sense*. *One never has more understanding than one has sense.* I: The common use of language which, whenever philosophy tries to make a laughing-stock of it, usually turns out to be the wiser one, teaches us the same lesson. [. . .] We derive from *Sinn* ('sense') the most characteristic forms of understanding as well as of the lack of it. *Unsinn* (or 'nonsense'), which is the extreme lack of understanding, is its opposite. Then come *Schwachsinn* ('feeblemindedness' or 'dullness of sense'), *Stumpfsinn* ('insensitivity'), *Leichtsinn* ('frivolity'), and their opposites, *Scharfsinn* ('sharpness of sense') and *Tiefsinn* ('profundity of sense'). (133)

In drawing this conclusion, Jacobi did not refer to Reid explicitly, but he did the next best thing. He practically paraphrased key passages from his major work. "The Latin words *sentire, sententia, sensa, sensus,* from the last of which the English word *sense* is borrowed," thus Reid had said, "express judgement or opinion, and are applied indifferently to objects of external sense, of taste, of morals, of the understanding." And again, "I have endeavoured to show that sense, in its most common, and, therefore, its most proper meaning, signifies judgement. [. . .] From this it is natural to think that common sense should mean common judgement."[34]

I leave aside the question of which sources Mendelssohn draws upon in his particular use of common sense. The notion had wide currency in Germany at the time and owed its many different shades of meaning to a variety of sources.[35] The point is that, as used by Reid, and now in the dialogue by Jacobi as well, common sense was not at all that vague remedy of last resort against skepticism that Reinhold had taken it to be. On the contrary, it had a definite and effective meaning. Common sense is one form of the sense that, on both Reid's and Jacobi's accounts of experience, runs across all forms of consciousness, originates in the complex relation in principle already established in sensation between feeling and representation, and emerges again in the ever more complex derivative relations further established in consciousness. This sense pervades all aspects of mental life. Common sense has the form that it takes inasmuch as it depends on inclinations for its validation. In this form, its certainty is therefore immediate. But it is not any the less reliable because of that, since the inclinations on which it is based are themselves the products of an essentially rational form of life, in virtue of which even the most primordial feelings are already affected by reason.

This is the link between sensibility and reason that Jacobi had slowly been forging in the second part of the dialogue. Once forged, the slide into Leibniz in the third and final part – "our Leibniz," as Jacobi refers to him in contrasting him to Spinoza (145) – was only too natural. Jacobi's incantation worked for the simple reason that Leibniz had been present in the dialogue in spirit all along. For long before Kant and the present controversy, Leibniz had already provided, according to Jacobi, the conceptual model for the link just forged. The two, sensibility and reason, represent two forms of life (154ff.), differing in degree yet both expressing the same fundamental 'energeia' that, according to Leibniz, constitutes the substance of every monad. The Greek root of the term 'energeia' means precisely 'force'. Common sense negotiates the exchanges between these two components of the monad inasmuch as, though the expression of an essentially rational life, it retains nonetheless the immediacy of feelings bound to the senses.

Much of the last part of Jacobi's dialogue is dedicated to a long discussion of Leibniz's Monadology, obviously intended as a display of Jacobi's scholarship, but also serving the more substantial purpose of demonstrating that Leibniz's theses could be read without accepting their dogmatic conclusions. In effect, Jacobi was interpreting Leibniz phenomenologically, just as the popular philosophers had also long done. He accepted his distinctive theory of the monad in the sense that for him existence is radically individualized, yet every existent reflects the whole universe according to its particular form of life. On the strength of that same doctrine, however, Jacobi was also restricting Leibniz's vision of the universe to one that is reflected in human existence – qualified as the latter is by human sensibility. One cannot therefore perform the dogmatic conceptual leaps of standard scholastic metaphysics – certainly not on the strength of such formal constructs of reason as this metaphysics could deliver.[36] On the face of it, Jacobi's was an exciting rereading of the great German philosopher, totally dedicated to a rehabilitation of his metaphysics. But note how, while discussing Leibniz, Jacobi was just below the surface still relentlessly carrying on his polemic against both Mendelssohn and Kant. These revered philosophers had both played on a notion of common sense that still carried the typically Leibnizian meaning of a generalized sound sense rooted in a human being's essentially rational form of life. But, while playing on this meaning, both had in fact undermined its possibility. Contrary to anything Leibnizian, they had both accepted a false (basically Humean) view of the senses that made impossible the vital connection between sensibility and reason essential to it.

Kant had divorced reason from existence. This was the message underlying much of the main body of *David Hume.* Jacobi was to shout it again, as if from the rooftops, in the Appendix added to the dialogue just before publication. Yet, from the beginning, Jacobi had felt uncomfortable about the theory he had just advanced and was ultimately to repudiate it explicitly – more precisely, to attribute a meaning to it that it originally did not have. There were good reasons for this. But before we consider them, we must turn to Reinhold's attempt at reforming Kant.

3.3 REINHOLD'S PASTICHE

Essay of a New Theory of the Human Faculty of Representation[37] was the result of Reinhold's notorious plan to reshape Kant's Critique of Reason in a rigorous systematic form, taking the fact of 'representation' as first principle. In an age in which verbosity was the rule, Reinhold would have easily counted as more verbose than most. The present essay was no exception to this norm. Nonetheless, despite the usual prolixity, and after a long Preface detailing the fate to which Kantian philosophy had been subjected to date,[38] the *Essay* was presented in three books and 88 numbered propositions in what purported to be strict scientific form.[39] At the very end,[40] there were a few pages added containing the "outlines of the theory of the faculty of desire." This first sketch of a moral theory was to become important for Reinhold, and we shall return to it in due time. The *Essay* was immediately attacked on many grounds. Reinhold's strategy of assuming an allegedly simple fact of consciousness as a starting point seemed to mark a radical departure from Kant's critical method, which was based rather, as Schultz had clearly recognized, on an analysis of the conditions for judgment in general.[41] Reinhold's choice of representation (*Vorstellung*) as his original fact, moreover, seemed arbitrary. And, as defined by Reinhold, representation did not seem to be either the simple fact that he took it to be or sufficiently complex to account for all the manifold aspects of consciousness.[42]

These criticisms were not altogether fair; but then, neither were they altogether unfair. Here we are faced with a problem that confronts the reader of Reinhold at every turn. There is no singleminded reading of his texts. On the one hand, they give evidence of deep insight. On the other, they are marred by moves that, on the face of it, are breathtakingly naive. The constant problem is to winnow the chaff from the wheat, so to speak. But again, the mixture of the two, though obviously a sign of confusion on Reinhold's part, is nonetheless symptomatic of a greater problem that was not exclusively of his making. This was still the problem of integrating Kant's Critique of Reason into the tradition in order to remedy its apparent formalism. A sympathetic reading of his *Essay* requires, therefore, that we first distinguish the various faces that it presents and then ask how in Reinhold's mind they might possibly have appeared to present a single view. We shall first consider it at its best, so to speak, in an effort to uncover the true insights that inspired it. Next, we shall look at Reinhold's bad arguments that distort these insights. Finally, we shall try to identify the extra factor that caused Reinhold to remain blind to this unfortunate mixture of insight and bad argument. At that point, we shall find ourselves also broaching the reasons for Jacobi's hesitancy about the results of his own redoing of Kant's Critique of Reason.

3.3.1 Reinhold's Insights[43]

Reinhold never defined representation.[44] Since it was being posited by him as the most basic fact of consciousness, he claimed that its concept could not be subsumed under simpler ones but had to be included, rather, in the definition of any other fact as an essential component. Reinhold, however, gave several descriptive accounts of the function that representation plays in consciousness, first in §VII of the *Essay* and then again in later, more precise formulations – these last in response to critical reactions. According to a formulation of 1790, representation is "distinguished in consciousness by the subject from both subject and object, and is referred to both."[45] Representation is the one product (*Wirkung*) of the mind that all levels of consciousness have in common – whether as 'sensing', 'thinking', 'intuiting', or 'conceptualizing' (§IX). It is present in all of them as the medium of a process of distinguishing and referring in which consciousness consists.[46]

Reinhold's critics objected, on the one hand, that representation was itself the product of more primitive mental operations, and hence that it could not be taken as the first principle of a science of consciousness. On the other hand, they argued that representation was not broad enough to cover all aspects of consciousness and that, because of this particularity, it could not serve as the required universal principle. To these critics, Reinhold's answer was twofold. (1) The mental product that we call representation performs its function of representing indeed only in connection with the complex transaction of 'distinguishing' and 'referring' between subject and object in which consciousness consists. But, inasmuch as consciousness proper begins only when this representing is achieved in virtue of that process, phenomenologically speaking, or rather – since Reinhold himself does not use this term – so far as a descriptive account of the facts of consciousness is concerned, representation must count as the first fact from which all the rest derive their meaning. (2) For this same reason, representation must be at work at all levels of consciousness. On the basis of what we mean by 'consciousness', the burden of proof for the opposing thesis, namely, that there can be consciousness without the distinguishing of subject and object that representation makes possible, rests on the one proposing it. It should be noted that with this account of representation Reinhold was making the same point as Jacobi in his *David Hume*, namely, that consciousness proper begins only inasmuch as a certain distance is achieved between a subject and an object and the one is referred to the other. This distance, and the concomitant distinguishing and referring, are achieved in the medium of representation.

With this account at hand, Reinhold is easily able to introduce Kant's signal concepts of thing in itself and appearance. In the assumed process of distinguishing and referring, the thing in itself stands as an empty term x that transcends the whole process but that the subject responsible for it intends throughout. This intended x allows the subject to recognize his representations both as being his own products and as instrumental in making a transcendent 'somewhat' present to him. In one respect (i.e., as his own products), he refers the representations back to himself; in the other (i.e., as the medium of an external presence), he refers them to the assumed transcendent x.[47] In this way the idea of appearance (*Erscheinung*) is generated. An appearance is the manifestation of this transcendent x in the otherwise purely subjective medium of representations. It requires the double activity on the part of a subject both of referring this medium back to himself and of taking it also as the place where something external is made present to him.[48] Neither side of this activity is, of course, possible without the original transcending reference to the presumed x. Still in virtue of the same activity, the subject can then further distinguish among a variety of subjective determinations, each according to the extent and degree to which it can be taken to be also an objective reflection of the x. The subject can then further organize these determinations together in an ever-expanding phenomenal representation of the same x. The net result is that, while 'truth' is still defined in general as the conformity of the mind to a given state of affairs, in actual experience the problem of attaining this required conformity is translated into one of developing two internally coherent and mutually compatible *particular* models of reality, namely, that of a world as it actually appears to a subject and that of the subject's mind to which such a world thus appears.

This is a neat reconstruction of Reinhold's position ('neat' in the sense that it 'tidies' it) as stated in §XVII of his *Essay*.[49] We shall soon see that Reinhold runs into difficulties of his own making. For the moment, I am suggesting that Reinhold's much maligned opening moves, if restricted to their strict logical import, could have provided a solid basis for a nonmetaphysical, purely phenomenological account of the genesis of experience. Essential to Reinhold's program is the distinction that he introduces right at the beginning between what he calls 'internal' and 'external' conditions of representation and his contention that, so far as his theory of representation is concerned, he is restricting himself solely to the former.[50] In other words, Reinhold is not denying – on the contrary, he is openly admitting – that the whole process of representation is conditioned by external factors possibly subject to the laws of physical or hyperphysical causality. His theory, however, deliberately abstracts from this aspect of the process in order to focus attention on representation as an already conscious occurrence – on conditions, that is, specific to it precisely as representation. To the extent that the external factors figure in the theory at all, they must enter it under the formality of 'objects of representation' – as deriving their meaning strictly with reference to the process of representing. Reinhold can therefore avoid the type of naive causal inferences from representations to a supposed external reality that Locke and Mendelssohn had posited, and that many popular philosophers still commonly posited, without, however, falling prey to any form of psychological subjectivism. For it is itself an essential condition internal to representation that an x external to it is nonetheless made present through it to a conscious subject. This is a condition immediately apprehensible in consciousness itself.

Two crucial consequences logically follow from these moves. The first has to do with the critical distinctions that, according to Reinhold, Kant had introduced only ad hoc but that Reinhold now wished to derive systematically from his first principle. If one is to take seriously Reinhold's claim – a claim that he defended against repeated critical attacks – that representation is, in his words, a 'generic concept' that applies to all levels of consciousness,[51] then it must follow that these critical distinctions, since they define components essential to representation, are to be found at all levels of representational activity, though realized under different particular modalities in each. Such distinctions as between 'form' and 'content', a priori and a posteriori, 'intuitive' and 'reflective' would have to be taken as various aspects of the one activity of representing rather than as defining radically different mental products or outlining different regions of the mind, so to speak. The inevitable further consequence is that the difference among such representational products as sensations, concepts, or ideas is relativized, since each would have to exhibit all the generic distinctions inherent in representation as such precisely in order to count as a particular type of it. Functionally speaking, so far as the development of a mind is concerned, some types of representations might indeed presuppose others for their existential basis; and, within the overall economy of the mind, each will indeed supplement all the rest, and some perhaps will also play a more significant role than others. Yet none should be taken as being subsumed under another externally, as if one needed the other in order to be a representation.

In other words, given Reinhold's model of the mind, the need for a transcendental deduction of the categories in Kant's sense is being undermined from the very opening moves of the *Essay*. Just as it had happened to Jacobi's model in *David Hume*, Reinhold's is being driven from the start in the direction of Leibniz. This is a consequence confirmed by the particular Theory of Cognition developed in Book 3 of the *Essay*. There, Reinhold *does* relativize Kant's distinctions. The theory's starting point is the definition of 'clear' and 'distinct', two attributes of the consciousness that accompanies every representation. The definition has already been prepared at the conclusion of Book 2 as the culmination of the general theory of representation. Consciousness is said to be clear to the extent that, given a representation, a second is added to it that *explicitly* qualifies it as the representation of the object of which it is the representation *in fact* (step 1).[52] When a third is further added (step 2) that reflectively qualifies the representation as the product, qua *representation*, of a representing subject (i.e., when it raises it to self-consciousness), consciousness then is said to be distinct as well.[53] The move to cognition proper is made by adding yet another reflective representation (step 3) – one, namely, in virtue of which the object itself of the original representation is now apprehended by itself precisely as such an object.[54] In other words, by becoming explicitly aware of what it intends subjectively in representation (step 1), and of how it does it (step 2), the mind can then determine in judgment what it has in fact achieved in representation objectively (step 3). Cognition thus develops by virtue of a process of ever more reflective representations of distinctions that are at work in the process of representing from the beginning. This process culminates in the kind of abstract reflection on the whole process that Reinhold performs with his theory of the faculty of representation.[55]

This model of how cognition unfolds is explicit in Reinhold's *Essay*. On his own account, what counts as 'form' at one level of representation (and thus functions there as an a priori internal to the subject) becomes the 'material' at another level that makes explicit the objective implications of the preceding one (and functions there a posteriori, in the manner of an external object in need of representation). All the complexities stipulated in the original generic definition of representation apply equally at all the more specific levels of representations, albeit at each in a form appropriate to its particular status. One cannot therefore single out certain representations as falling exclusively on one side of any of the thus generically defined distinctions and other representations as falling exclusively on the other. Rather, they should all be expected to fall, in different mental settings, now on the one side, now on the other – exactly as they do in Reinhold's Theory of Cognition.

This is a consequence, moreover, that should also extend to Kant's most crucial critical distinction, the one between concept and sensation.[56] Inasmuch as sensations enter into the process of representation in any significant way and perform their intuitive role in experience,[57] they too must be assumed to be intentional in character, that is, to exhibit as sensations an internal distinction between content and form, between immediate reference to an object and reflective apprehension of it. To the extent that they fail to do so, they would be at best only physical modifications of sense organs – premental ('blind') states rather than already a part of the cognitive process itself.[58] The net result is that the line of demarcation in experience between conceptual and intuitive, between reflective and immediately given, cannot be drawn univocally but must be negotiated within a broad range of still unclarified representations where common sense is often the only norm available. What counts as 'theoretical construct' in one context may well count as 'given fact' in another. The true problem of experience is precisely to determine what counts in any given context as sufficient evidence for the presence of an object – in effect, what counts in that context as a reliable sense 'datum'. And this is a problem that cannot be resolved univocally across the whole field of experience but depends in each case on the particular frame of reference subjectively relevant to it. In all cases, the resolution of the problem must ultimately rely on the idealizing functions of reason.

The great merit of Reinhold's *Essay*, if one were to follow the logic of its starting point, is thus that it brings to light what should be, after Kant's Critique of Reason, the fundamental problem of experience. This is the second crucial consequence that follows from Reinhold's opening moves. The problem of experience is how to bring to explicit consciousness what is already present to the mind, but still unconsciously, in the form of its naturally given body. In other words, the thing in itself is no longer outside the mind – as it was, though in different ways, for both Descartes and Locke – but in the mind itself as its unconscious past. The problem is one that can therefore both be posed and resolved within the mind without, however, having to resort to either Cartesian or Lockean subjectivism. Or, in other words, the problem of experience is indeed how to bring sense representations and feelings to reflective conceptualization – not, however, by imposing foreign forms on them, but by developing according to the logic of the concept forms that are already implicitly present in them. Restated in this way as a problem of ever clarifying a subject's consciousness of himself and his world, Kant's critical agenda was one that the popular philosophers could well have understood. It brought that agenda back to Leibniz's organic view of the relation between mind and nature or, within the mind, between its conscious and unconscious components. Jacobi had been driven back to this view in *David Hume* in an effort to defend commonsense realism. Reinhold – at least as we have presented him so far – might well be taken as working out in detail Jacobi's theory of mind that was only adumbrated in his dialogue in the name of Leibniz. But Reinhold explicitly resisted this course of action. Jacobi's scruples, perhaps, were also troubling him.

3.3.2 Reinhold's Bad Arguments

Solomon Maimon had been the first to note that sensations, the supposed material that according to Kant's critical model of experience must be brought under conceptual determinations, are not anything immediately detectable in consciousness. Like the infinitesimals of calculus, they are rather an artificial construct introduced for theoretical purposes – in the case of Kant's model, to express the complex intuitive-reflective character of human consciousness. Sensations are hypothetical points at which intuition and reflection presumably coincide. In any actual experience, however, the distinction between the sensible and the conceptual, the immediate and the reflective, cannot be drawn absolutely. Maimon rejected Kant's project of synthesizing these two supposed components of consciousness, as if it were a matter of uniting two otherwise heterogeneous factors. Cognition is rather a process of dissecting analytically the content of given experiences until the infinitesimal units that lie at their basis are brought to conceptual expression and the conformity of reflective thought with actual experience is thus finally exhibited. Of course, this is a process that only God could bring to completion. So far as human experience is concerned, Maimon allowed for science only in principle. Mathematics apart, which is a special case since its objects are purely imaginary, he restricted de facto human knowledge to objects dependent on such psychological factors as Locke had already discovered. The content and the truth value of these objects can therefore be determined only empirically. This last restriction was the source of Maimon's peculiar kind of skepticism – a skepticism 'of fact' that he coupled with a rationalism 'of principle'.[59]

Maimon knew that in taking this step he was bringing Kant's project back at once to Leibnizian Monadology and Lockean psychology – not an unusual step in popular philosophy, as we have seen. But this deliberately taken step put him directly at odds with Reinhold, who, on the contrary, deliberately resisted it. The exchange of letters between the two that followed the publication of Reinhold's *Essay*, and that Maimon eventually published without Reinhold's permission, would make the subject of an interesting study all by itself.[60] Maimon became Reinhold's most strident critic. Reinhold resented him and often took umbrage at what he considered his opponent's rude lines of questioning. In all fairness to Reinhold, it must be said that Maimon was an eccentric character, one not easy to deal with. Yet his astuteness was just as great as, if not greater than, his petulance, and Reinhold would have been better advised to listen to him carefully instead of treating him patronizingly, as he normally did. Maimon's objections regularly hit their target. In Reinhold's theory of representation, Kant's transcendental idealism tended to slide in the direction of Leibniz no less than it did at the hand of Maimon, and Reinhold was most vulnerable to attack precisely where he tried to resist the slide. Quite apart from Maimon's objections, which must be mentioned but cannot be treated in detail here, Reinhold was showing bad judgment in many ways.

One example of bad judgment was to be found in the signal importance that Reinhold gave to his argument purporting to prove that the thing in itself exists, yet is unknowable. Kant's failure to demonstrate this key tenet of critical doctrine was the cause, according to Reinhold, of much of the doctrine's failure to win acceptance. Now, if one takes as normative Reinhold's own definition of the concept of the thing in itself in §XVII of the *Essay*, the thesis that he was proposing to demonstrate was nonsensical on its own terms. According to that definition, the thing in itself derives its meaning exclusively from the function it plays in determining an external condition of representation in general. It makes explicit one aspect of the process of representing, namely, that there are external factors conditioning it. It is a reflective or (in Reinhold's terminology) a 'logical' concept,[61] the object of which is representation itself qua representation. It follows that the thing in itself lacks all content, hence conveys no knowledge of anything in particular, for the simple reason that it is not meant to represent anything in particular but is rather a component of the concept of representation in general. What it says about representation is all that it is supposed to say, and what it says (namely, that there are external factors conditioning representation) is perfectly comprehensible. To say that we have no knowledge of it is therefore nonsensical, unless the claim is made in an empirico-psychological sense – in which case this claim would be just as subject to the stricture of dogmatism as the contrary claim that we have an intuition of it. In either case, whether one grants or denies knowledge of this thing in itself, it would be a matter of confusing logical with real entities, 'concepts of concepts' with 'concepts of particular things' – in either case, of falling victim to what Kant called a transcendental illusion.

If the thesis was confused, the argument intended to demonstrate it could not fare any better. It played on the two elements included in the claim that the thing in itself is a (1) necessary yet (2) external condition of representation. In brief, since it is necessary, the thing's existence must be presupposed; since it is external, it must escape the reach of representation, hence remain unknowable. This is an argument that might have been justifiable in a physiological frame of reference, where representation is treated as a physical process for which some external thing is assumed to be the cause. But Reinhold's intention was to proceed phenomenologically, as we would say nowadays or, in his words, to restrict himself to the internal conditions of representation as such. In that case, however, to say that the thing in itself is a necessary external condition of representation is to mean that, to the extent that a representation is successful, to that extent the presence in consciousness of a thing external to it must have been achieved through the means of the representation – albeit internally, that is, subject to the internal conditions of representation in general. But this is to say that knowledge of the thing in itself is indeed attained in actual experience, precisely as knowledge of the object matter of experience (*die Sache selbst*, as the Germans would say) – although, of course, within the contextual limits of a given representation and on the ascertained merit of such a representation as representation. This last stipulation in no way detracts from the possibility of real though limited knowledge, since such terms as thing in itself and appearance, internal, and external, are contraries rather than contradictories. The difference between the two admits of degree, and it is the task of actual experience to negotiate precisely the difference between such degrees. If anything, Reinhold's argument thus demonstrated the contrary of what it purported to do. There is knowledge of things, and representations make it possible.

Reinhold was also showing bad judgment in the way he tried to avoid the consequence of his original claim (the one we have taken particular care to stress) that representation is a generic fact – namely, that all the distinctions assumed in it would have to apply to all of its more particularized forms. He did it by distinguishing between a wide generic meaning of the concept and such narrower meanings as 'sensibility', 'understanding', and 'reason', and by then reserving for these particular faculties the specialized functions that Kant had already attributed to them.[62] This was itself a naive move. One may not avoid a logical consequence simply on the strength of nominal definitions. But then Reinhold compounded his difficulty by distinguishing between different types of alleged 'materials' of representation – a priori and empirical, subjective and objective, internal and external[63] – and by treating these materials as if they were fixed components of consciousness of which one can make an inventory once and for all. He also curiously denied that we have knowledge of the 'form' and the 'material' (*Stoff*) that belong to representation in itself.[64] This was a strange claim indeed, only explainable on the assumption that Reinhold was again confusing logical with real intentions. There is no such thing as a generic representation in itself; there is only the generic concept of a representation that is presumably defined by these alleged materials that Reinhold discusses. Reinhold's claim that we do not know representation in itself, that we do not know its form and content in themselves, was just as plainly meaningless as his earlier claim that we do not know the thing in itself.

However, nowhere was Reinhold's position as dubious as on the subject of consciousness and how this differs from representation.[65] Here also Reinhold appears inexorably driven to the very Leibnizian model of the mind from which, on the contrary, he thought he was distancing himself. His starting point is the claim that there cannot be representation without consciousness, just as there cannot be consciousness without representation.[66] This is perhaps an indisputable but certainly uninformative claim. More revealing is the following passage:

Mere representation is indeed not consciousness itself but *only* makes something present *in* consciousness – [something that] is represented in consciousness *only* through it. For *something is made present through representation* only when the representation is attached [*verbunden*] to this *something*, i.e. the object, and to the representing *subject*. Apart from this combination [*Verknüpfung*] (this actual connection [*Zusammenhang*] with object and subject), representation is called mere representation only to the extent that it is something distinct from subject and object – something however in which the possibility of the double being-in-relation [*Bezogenwerden*] through which something is actually represented is determinedly at hand.[67]

Now, the prima facie meaning of this passage is that representation first brings an object *to consciousness*, as well as the subject representing the object, by combining these two – presumably through the distinguishing and referring function of representing. Consciousness is the product of this 'making present' of an object to a subject, prior to which it can be nothing more determinate than a nebulous state of mind. Representation, for its part, deserves the name of representation insofar as it actually discharges this function of making present, or at least inasmuch as it provides the 'possibility of the double being-in-relation' that such a presence entails. Apart from this making present, it too is nothing determinate – a premental, physical somewhat, to be investigated empirically.

Here is where the slide into Leibniz's model begins. For it follows, on Reinhold's statement of the case, that the more sophisticated a representation is, the more developed the object would be that this representation brings to presence in the mind; and the clearer and more distinct, therefore, the consciousness would be that accompanies it. In this sense, there is indeed a symmetrical relation between representation and consciousness. But one can then think of representations so primitive that whatever consciousness they afford is at best only inchoate; and, following the same

line of reflection, of others still more primitive – so primitive that any connection they might have to actual mental life is only potential, and are best
described, therefore, as physical states rather than intentional events. The
net result is that the concept of consciousness, just like that of representation, runs across a line of degrees of ever-increasing complexities and
thus bridges the difference that otherwise separates the physical and the
mental.[68] This was, of course, a result totally in keeping with Leibniz's
Monadology. It is interesting that Reinhold explicitly saw its possibility
but dismissed it deliberately; even more interesting, that he did it while
addressing himself to Plattner – a notorious representative of popular
philosophy and an influential critic of Kant.[69] Driven by the same desire
to overcome the apparent formalism of Kant's critical distinctions that at
the time also motivated much of the popular philosophers's reaction to
the Critique of Reason, Reinhold had instinctively reached back to these
philosophers' conceptual heritage. But his explicit intention was not to
overcome these distinctions, but to remain faithful to them by grounding
them on more basic principles. The result was an unfortunate mixture of
older concepts dependent on Leibniz's and Wolff's more organic vision
of the human mind and the new critical distinctions intended precisely
to deny that vision. Reinhold never saw himself clear of this confusion.[70]
Ultimately he abandoned his Kantianism altogether, as we shall see, making his way again – after an ambiguous brief interlude in company with
Fichte – to his own roots in popular philosophy.

Reinhold should have taken to heart the criticism that Leibniz had
raised against Locke, namely, that it is impossible to find in experience
such a thing as a simple sense impression. As we remember,[71] Reinhold
had seconded the objection when discussing Locke's contribution to the
situation of philosophy just prior to Kant, but he was now failing to recognize how relevant it was to his own theory of representation. There,
on the issue of sensation, lay precisely the divide between two possible
interpretations of Kant.

According to the first interpretation, one took sensations in a Lockean
sense, as simple impressions caused in the mind by who knows what external cause, and devoid of any internal differentiations that would make
them, however primitively, conscious events in their own right. This is
the sense in which Kant seemed to take them. Sensations per se are
blind, a material of cognition rather than cognitions. In that case, however, the conceptual determinations that, according to Kant, must be
brought to them a priori in order to turn them into proper representations remain external to them, even though, again according to Kant,

such determinations depend for existential validation on the alleged empirical material the sensations provide. But on their own, sensations do not represent anything in particular. The doubt therefore necessarily arises as to whether the objects thus created by conceptually informing sense materials are more than just fictions instantiatable only at the level of the imagination and never in actual sense experience. The basis of post-Kantian skepticism lay precisely in this doubt. Maimon's kind of skepticism was perhaps the most imaginative case in point. But one must not forget the Schulze/Ænesidemus defense of Hume's skepticism against Kant and Reinhold that appeared shortly after the publication of the latter's *Essay.* Arguing specifically against Reinhold, Schulze contended that sensations are not representations, since they are simple impressions. It followed that Reinhold's alleged first fact of consciousness, namely, representation, did not cover all the other facts of consciousness and was not, therefore, the first fact that it was supposed to be. Reinhold's much vaunted science was no science at all. As for Kant's Critique of Reason, it constituted, according to Schulze, a formalism of reason that in no way improved on Hume's skeptically tempered acceptance of natural beliefs.

According to the second interpretation of Kant, one did not take literally Kant's opposition between the immediacy of sensation and the reflectivity of conceptual representation, and one considered sensations, rather, as obscure representations that only need clarifying in order to reveal their implicitly rational content.[72] This is a move that Kant explicitly rejected and one that, as we have seen, popular philosophers normally followed in their appropriation of the Critique of Reason. Jacobi had also traveled this road by deriving all sense from sensation. On that strategy, since intelligibility would have to be developed out of sense experiences rather than being applied to them a priori, metaphysical knowledge, whether of things in themselves (as in the dogmatic tradition) or of phenomenal nature (as per Kant), was no longer possible – unless, of course, one was willing to revert to the dogmatism of a Leibniz. This is not to say that true science was therefore not possible or that one would have to give way to skepticism. Jacobi had tried to prove exactly the opposite. It is to say, rather, that science would always have to be limited to, and subjected to the vagaries of, human experiences. In general, the popular philosophers did not object to this limitation.

Jacobi was, however, hesitant about his Leibnizian-inspired program of defining levels of experience as ever more complex forms of life. Reinhold, for his part, while being pushed in this direction both by the logic of the opening moves of his theory and by the architectonic of its development, resisted the pressure and instead restated all of Kant's critical distinctions, albeit in his own terms. The result, as we have seen, was an unfortunate conceptual pastiche. When we find philosophers in such uncomfortable positions, and we assume that lack of logic was not their weakness, it is only fair to wonder whether there were perhaps extra factors operating below the surface and influencing their stand. Perhaps there were reasons, other than purely scientific ones, that troubled the judgment of the one man and obscured that of the other.

3.4 THE SPECTER OF NATURALISM

It is instructive at this point to recall Weishaupt. What is remarkable about him is that, while still working within the general conceptual framework of Leibniz's Monadology, he had transposed the framework into more empirical terms. He had restricted the view of the universe that the sciences can achieve to one that is conditioned by the limitations of the human senses, and hence can be developed only on the basis of information drawn from the latter. Weishaupt had insisted on the radical individuality of real things. We have seen that, according to him, the proto-error of all types of idealistic metaphysics was to confuse real things with fictional entities that are in fact only the object of conceptual abstractions. We should add that, just like Thomas Reid and Jacobi, Weishaupt also rejected the assumption that the object of a sense representation is the sensation itself. In the manner of natural signs, rather, sensations render immediately present to the mind the real things that they signify. Weishaupt's realism was based on precisely this thesis.

Now, what is also remarkable about Weishaupt in all this is that, while thus translating Leibniz's metaphysics into more physically manageable terms, he had also remained faithful to Leibniz's still basically Christian view of the human vocation as one of self-purification by way of self-knowledge. While cutting Leibniz's Monadology down to more physical size, so to speak, he still conceived of moral ascesis as a matter of overcoming the dispersion of sense-induced passions by means of rational reflection. This reflection reveals to the human individual his true place in the universe. To this extent, it releases in him the image of divinity that Weishaupt, in common with Leibniz, still took for granted. Weishaupt, however, now made this image depend on the convergence of the many physical factors that together constitute the specifically human situation. And he was clear about the naturalism that this position entailed. This is the feature of his thought that ultimately made him so remarkable.

There is nothing in Weishaupt of the dissembling regarding the question of human freedom of which Leibniz was guilty; nothing of the impossible attempt to claim at once that the human will is free, that there is moral evil, yet that everything is exactly as it must be, and that, as it is, it is for the best.[73] According to Weishaupt, there is no freedom of the will. Everything is fated to happen as it does. On this, Weishaupt is explicit. Peace of mind, which is the essential component of happiness, consists in recognizing and accepting, through rational reflection, the fatalism of human existence.

It was the specter of this naturalism, and of the fatalism that it entailed, that must have been uppermost in Jacobi's as well as Reinhold's mind and must have troubled both. This is not to say that they had Weishaupt necessarily in mind, since there was no need of his lesson on this score. That of Leibniz sufficed. The situation was especially embarrassing for Jacobi. In the third part of *David Hume*, he had found himself expounding a basically Leibnizian doctrine, and even citing Spinoza with approval, while defending his own realism against Hume's skepticism – thus sliding into the very naturalism that had been the cause of his criticism of metaphysics, of Spinoza's in particular, in his original conversation with Lessing. His brief against speculative thought had been that philosophical abstractions negate the possibility of human individuality, since they make all individuals cogs in the greater organization of nature; in effect, therefore, they negate the possibility of human freedom. Philosophy leads to a nihilistic form of antihumanism. Now in the dialogue, however much he qualified his acceptance of Leibniz's Monadology, Jacobi was in fact siding with a philosopher whom he had only recently accused of being no less of a pantheist than Spinoza. He was explaining human consciousness as the product of a play of opposing forces, each representing in turn a form of life. The slide into naturalism was obvious. To be sure, the abrupt note on which the dialogue ended, evoking as it did the possibility of immediate, natural revelation of the supernatural, disrupted the slide. But it did so at the risk of making Jacobi again vulnerable to the charge of irrationalism that it had been his goal to allay at the beginning of the dialogue. This is how paradoxical his position was. He had begun by appealing to Hume's authority to clear himself of the charge of irrationalism. He had then moved in the direction of Leibniz to distance himself from Hume's subjectivism and also to provide an alternative to Kant's formalism of reason, but in the end shrouded the naturalism that the move entailed by sounding notes that brought the theme of irrationalism back in play. It is no wonder that Jacobi should have felt uncomfortable with the dialogue.

As for Reinhold, he had broken through to public center stage in his new career in Protestant Germany by portraying Kant as the one who could mediate the difference between Jacobi and Mendelssohn.[74] He had then gone to great lengths to reinterpret the history of Western philosophy as a process in which opposing positions had methodically arisen, each in reaction to its opposite, and all driven by the inner logic of conceptual possibilities. These possibilities had finally been exhausted, and the stage had been set for Kant to appear on the scene to reconcile all prior oppositions in virtue of his critical distinctions. The most crucial of these oppositions, the one that had recently been the focus of the Jacobi–Mendelssohn dispute and had precipitated Reinhold's intervention, was precisely the one between the claim of freedom and the requirement of rational explanation. Reinhold's historically appointed task (according to Reinhold's own perception of himself) was to ground and systematize Kant's critical distinctions, and thus to take the final step that would put to rest past oppositions – that between freedom and nature in particular – and in so doing usher in the final kingdom of enlightened reason. Reinhold could not abandon Kant's critical distinctions, however badly they fit into the scholastic context he was trying to fit them into, without abandoning his own conception of his task.

I am saying, in other words, that the extra factor that motivated Jacobi as well as Reinhold, and influenced the judgment of each, was still the role that each man had been playing, and saw himself as playing, in the defense of Spalding's still basically Christian humanism. The justification of the possibility of human individuality, hence of human freedom, was still the fundamental issue throughout. But the same issue had also been the one that had motivated Kant's critical distinction between the senses and reflective conceptualization. The distinction signaled that the realm of meaningful intentions that we presuppose when we act as morally responsible individuals requires an irrevocable breach with nature. Christian humanism is ultimately unnatural and hence cannot be saved on the assumption of purely natural inclinations, the kind that Kant identified with the senses and sensibility. The formalism of the understanding, such as Kant now assumed, was not the product of a merely abstractive reflection but of a reflection that set up a new norm of what counts as significantly real – as setting up, in other words, a radically new realm of nature. The real problem, on these terms, was not the challenge of synthesizing an abstract I and a supposed already given self, but that of constituting such a self through reflection in such a way that both its originality and the physical limits to which it is nonetheless bound are respected. The models of experience that both Jacobi and Reinhold advanced – Jacobi quite deliberately, Reinhold as if in spite of himself – had the advantage of avoiding the at least apparent abstract formalism of Kant's own model. Both could have been adapted to promote Kant's critical turn, as long as each had made it clear that when reflection determines the boundary between self and external reality in experience or brings to reflective awareness the otherwise natural processes that give rise to experience (both models actually amount to the same thing), a breach with nature occurs that gives rise to a radically new mode of existence, namely, that of human intentions. In other words, Kant's formalism necessarily gave rise to the problem of a synthesis that threatened a slide into either naturalism or skepticism only when interpreted within the traditional conceptual limits of popular philosophy. But Kant himself had stated the terms of the synthesis in this impossible way. This is how intractable he was. He was drawing original, new distinctions, but at the same time distracting from their originality and actually falsifying them, by stating them in all too traditional terms. We must further develop this point. The issue now on the table is that of the possibility of human freedom. The self of experience must be considered in the first instance as an agent, exactly in the way Jacobi had made an issue of it in his conversation with Lessing. For this, we must turn to a debate on human freedom that broke out shortly after the publication of Reinhold's *Essay* and Jacobi's second, much enlarged edition of his Spinoza book.

4

Of Human Freedom and Necessity

4.1 THE CLASSICAL HERITAGE

In 1788, Johann August Heinrich Ulrich, respected professor at Jena, published a little book entitled *Eleutheriologie oder über Freiheit und Nothwendigkeit (Eleutheriology, or Of Human Freedom and Necessity)* as a text for his Michaelmas lectures of that year.[1] As we shall see, the text became normative for the debate on freedom that was soon to break out. In response, Kant wrote a small essay that was then turned by his friend Kraus into a review published in the *ALZ* in an April issue of 1788.[2] One year later, in 1789, Jacobi published a second, much enlarged edition of his Spinoza book,[3] which he prefaced with fifty-two propositions – twenty-three purporting to defend the thesis 'Man does not have Freedom'; the remaining twenty-nine, the opposite thesis 'Man has Freedom' He also added to it eight lengthy supplements in which he restated his views regarding Spinoza and Leibniz, clarified his own position with respect to both, and sharply criticized Herder – in all instances with the issue of human freedom clearly in view We shall return to this contribution of Jacobi in due time and to Ulrich's in just a moment. First, however, we should recall the origin of the terms in which the issue of 'human freedom', paramount to both works, was being discussed at the time. And, for this, we must again turn to Leibniz, for he had been the one responsible for setting them.

In a Christian context, the problem in any theory of freedom was how to safeguard the Christian belief that the human being is a free individual, responsible before God and his fellow human beings for his decisions and actions, in view of the other equally Christian belief that God is an omnipotent creator – that all things, therefore, including human actions, ultimately depend on him. In a Christian sense, sin is understood as a human being's deliberate turning away from God; as a privation, therefore, rather than a mere limitation or negation, of the good willed in him by God. How can sin then be possible, granted that its presence in creation entails a check to God's otherwise invincible will to bring only the good into existence? The juxtaposition of the two beliefs, in man's capacity for sin and God's omnipotence, is easy enough when entertained in the medium of religious language, where immediate experience is the norm and the imagination the instrument of representation. However much God is portrayed in biblical narration as infinitely transcending the work of creation, he is still being treated as someone intimately engaged in human affairs, and hence as displaying all the traits typical of a powerful yet caring father. So long as the relation between him and the human race is imagined on the analogy of the human relation between a father and his children, there is no conflict that necessarily arises between the power of the one and the freedom of the other. Though totally dependent on their father, children still have a will of their own that can lead them to transgress the father's might and thus to incur his consequent wrath. This is exactly how the prophets depicted the turbulent relation between God and the house of Israel. It is a long story of covenants made out of God's munificence and broken by human perversity; of punishments incurred by God's wrath and of grace regained at his mercy.

The situation is quite different when immediate experience gives place to metaphysical reflection, and the representations of the imagination yield to the supposedly pure concepts of reason. There a conflict necessarily arises. Leibniz's classical attempt at staving it off proceeded along two distinct but related lines of reflection.[4] According to one, God is conceived, on the one hand, as *ens realissimum* (to use Kant's expression), that is, as the ontological reservoir of all possible and copossible beings; on the other hand, as *ens perfectissimum*, that is, as the one being whose existence is absolutely necessary because, since it holds all possibilities within itself, there is nothing external to it that might prevent its being actual. Two questions arise. The first is why this God – ontologically infinite and existentially complete – would ever want to create a world distinct yet dependent on him (i.e., one ontologically finite and existentially incomplete); the second, granted that he has created one, one must ask why, of all the worlds he might have created by assembling a specific group of copossible beings, he chose the one he has actually created. There is no answer to either of these questions on the basis of God's

[margin note: paternal God]

attribute of *ens realissimum.* An answer is, however, possible based on his other attribute of *ens perfectissimum* (For, just as God cannot but exist, since there is nothing to hinder it, so he cannot but do all that he can do.) Since he can create, he will create. And, since he will create, he will exercise this power to the utmost limit, that is, of all the possible worlds that he might create, he will create the best. De facto, therefore, though not de jure, the present created world is both existentially necessary and, so far as created worlds go, ontologically perfect as well. There are, of course, evils present in it. But these are the consequence of the limitations that conflicting possibilities, all of them necessary for the composition of the best of all possible worlds, necessarily impose on one another as the condition of their existence. God does not will them as such. He simply allows them as an unavoidable consequence of his perfect creative act [In the language of modern warfare, evils (of all sorts) are the unfortunate collateral damage of an otherwise well-intentioned and well-performed operation.]

According to Leibniz's other line of reflection, a creature's situation in the created world is considered from the point of view of the creature itself. As an actually existing albeit finite entity, every creature strives to maintain itself in existence and to maximize its capacities for being. Insofar as the human individual is concerned, since he is endowed with reason, this striving takes the form of a desire informed by the rational recognition of his place in the universe. Freedom consists in the special degree of spontaneity that attaches to an existence motivated by precisely such a desire [According to Leibniz, here is where the possibility of sin or moral evil arises.] For an individual's reason might well be obscured by a false conception of himself and the world because of the limitations of his sensible nature. He will then strive to achieve ends not in conformity with the general harmony of the whole, thereby setting himself against God and, by implication, also against his own well-being. Hatred of God, in which the damnation of an individual human being consists, arises out of this subjectively induced disharmony between whole and part. Freedom is thus the function of rational knowledge; sin, the consequence of a failure in the exercise of reason.

This is Leibniz's repeatedly stated position on the subject of sin and human freedom. It is a position perfectly in accordance with the conclusions regarding divine perfection that he reached in his first line of reflection. It also makes perfectly apparent, however, Leibniz's incapacity to recapture in metaphysical terms, whether along one line of reflection or the other, the Christian sense of sin and responsibility. For it follows, proceeding according to the first line, that a human being's knowledge depends on the place he occupies in the universe. This is a place, however, over which he has no say, since it is determined rather by the architectonics of the alleged best among all possible worlds within which he happens to find himself. He cannot therefore be held responsible for standing in opposition to God when choosing forms of conduct contrary to God's supposed idea of right human nature. His choice is due to a lack of adequate knowledge – a lack due in turn to the place in the universe that he occupies and over which, as was just said, he has no control. One can even dispute the allegation that there is any real opposition between him and God, since his situation, however 'evil' in the sense of pathologically affected or diseased, actually contributes to the realization of the divine creative plan. It makes for the best of all possible worlds that God willed and would have been impossible without his evil. Even if his 'sin' were to take the form of a depraved refusal to see the light of truth, its evil would still follow from the imperfection that defines a certain group of beings. It cannot be sin in a strict Christian sense.

The medieval theologians who had pioneered Leibniz's lines of reflection could avoid the full brunt of this conclusion because, when claiming that God must tolerate evil in order to create the greatest good, they understood this to mean that, for the sake of human perfection, God had to create man free; this freedom, however, entailed the possibility that he might culpably fail to exercise it.[5] This was a view still bound to anthropopathic representations. It envisaged God as taking man as partner in his work of creation, still on the analogy of the relationship between a father and his children. His dealings with the often wayward children of Abraham were portrayed by the biblical prophets precisely along the lines of this analogy. And he was equally portrayed by this analogy in the Christian myth of the incarnation and redemption. But Leibniz, in keeping with the spirit of the time, had methodically cleansed his metaphysics of any such imaginary residue. He had reduced his conceptions of the Divinity to bare logical abstractions. The net result was that the same logic inherent in the idea of the invincible harmony of the universe that absolved God from evil in Leibniz's first line of reflection equally absolved the human being from moral responsibility in his second line. Despite all of Leibniz's efforts to the contrary, his metaphysics did not save the Christian experience of freedom and sin.

One can get a sense of the conceptual quandary in which Leibniz was entangled, but that he stubbornly refused to acknowledge, from the frustration, even irritation, with which he responded to the pointed questions that Bishop Nicholaus Steno raised to him on precisely the issue of moral evil.[6] The bishop was the Catholic vicar to the court of Hannover, where Leibniz was employed. To the question of how the human individual can be held responsible for his turning against God, since his conduct is determined by ignorance, Leibniz replies that the individual is himself responsible for such an ignorance. To the further question of how this is possible, unless the individual has freedom in the exercise of his reason – in which case the prior assumption that freedom depends on reason, and that its misuse is due to a failure of reason, would be abrogated – Leibniz retorts with, "As if anyone seriously denied this freedom of the use [of reason]!"[7] This was obviously a rhetorical way out of the argument rather than an answer, since Leibniz had in fact denied the possibility of that freedom. The embarrassing truth was that Leibniz had no satisfactory answer.

Now, in 1788, one hundred odd years after Leibniz's retort to Bishop Steno, we find Ulrich in his little book reiterating the same doctrine as Leibniz's, but with Kant's moral theory clearly in view and without the deliberate ambiguities of Leibniz's language. Gone are the intricate conceptual plays that, though they made Leibniz vulnerable to the charge of dissemblance, were also signs of his sensitivity to the full meaning of the Christian conception of sin. Ulrich is quite single-minded about his position. On the one hand, he denies categorically the possibility of freedom of choice, understood in the sense of a capacity on the part of the human being to initiate radically new courses of action. On the other hand, he declares that nothing is lost in the language of necessity that is otherwise expressed in the language of freedom and responsibility.[8] His auditors, as he exhorts them to do in the dedicatory note, are "to show through their example that a properly understood determinism does not do away with morality but rather protects it" (5–6).

How is determinism so to be understood? Ulrich begins by defining it in opposition to indeterminism. The one posits complete determinations of grounds, even regarding human choices; the other imagines the possibility that a rational being, given identical circumstances, can indifferently will to act in one direction or another (§8). Determinism recognizes that there are two kinds of necessity, namely, physical and ethical. The one means that, given certain circumstances, certain results inevitably follow. The other means that, on the assumption of certain rational cognitions, certain results should follow even though they do not always do so. This is the case, however, only because the cognition from which the results are expected to follow is not strong enough to determine the efficacious willing of them. Should such a cognition acquire the required strength, the efficacy of the thought 'I should' that follows from it has, according to Ulrich, all the traits of 'true necessity' (*wahre Notwendigkeit,* §5, p. 17). It is true natural necessity. With reference to Kant, Ulrich says that he will not discuss here the question of whether there is a 'categorical imperative', that is, a knowledge that binds absolutely, or whether its presence is to be ascertained a priori. The only important consideration, so far as he is concerned, is that we know from experience that sooner or later (for some sooner, for others later) the thought of an ethical necessity occurs to all of us, and that it is strong enough to counter the force of natural desires at least some of the time. The efficacy of such a thought is, however, still a matter of natural necessity.

Armed with these definitions, Ulrich has easy play dismissing the arguments usually advanced in defense of indeterminism. There is no immediately available evidence based on inner experience that we have the capacity to act differently under perfectly equal circumstances (§18). The evidence drawn from our alleged ability to move our limbs at will, or to focus our attention at will, is inconclusive. In fact, the phenomena adduced as evidence can in all cases be explained more convincingly on deterministic grounds. There is, on the contrary, much to support determinism, on theoretical as well as experiential grounds (§§26–37). 'Moral freedom' can coherently and exhaustively be understood as a human being's capacity to achieve the kind of rational perfection to which he is disposed by nature and for which he strives also by nature. Though one cannot help being what one is at any given moment, one can always strive to become otherwise (§26). Human freedom lies precisely in this capacity to improve oneself through moral means, that is, by improving one's knowledge and refining one's senses (§31). This is a slow process that requires much education and discipline. Its goal – in effect, the goal of human freedom as well – is to gain 'moral necessity', that is, the capacity to be effectively necessitated to act in accordance with the right thought of what is good for the human being as determined by nature (§37). The much touted concepts of 'duty' and 'law', which the determinists are accused of abolishing, all in fact lead back to the one concept of 'obligation' *(Verbindlichkeit)* – a concept that is, however, the equivalent of the just defined concept of moral necessity. Such a concept consists in the "the insight *(Einsicht)* that I should act in this or that way." It is an effective concept, even though it is admitted that we are not, nor can we become at once, all that we should be. "It suffices that we can be so if we earnestly will it, and that this earnest willing can, and will, be promoted through the influence of the motivating grounds to which the representation of moral necessity, or of the 'should', of 'obligation', also belong" (§58).

Ulrich reiterates his core position in a variety of formulas. As he says, everyone is responsible for his action, since everyone acts according to what he is and wills accordingly (§§64–7). Perfect freedom would consist in the capacity to act infallibly according to reason independently of all sensible inclinations. This is the ultimate theological definition of freedom (§83). There is no luck involved in the matter of virtue (§64). To be sure, since God is the ultimate cause of all things, he is ultimately responsible for the differences among human beings (§§89–90). But it can be shown that he could not have created the world otherwise than he did. Here Ulrich repeats Leibniz's arguments (§§68–71). One cannot therefore blame God for what one is (§71) any more than (as Ulrich might have said, quoting Leibniz) a peasant can blame his father for not having married a princess.[9]

In brief, there is little, according to Ulrich, to recommend indeterminism and much to be said against it (§§84–5). Its main flaw is that it denies the universality of the principle of sufficient reason, thereby limiting the power of God and thereby also undermining his providence. The opposite holds for determinism (§86). It provides the perfect foundation for a justification of God's acts. We can be sure that whatever evil there is had to be there, and that it will work for the good of the whole. This is an assurance that, while upholding the power of God in everything, also makes for the peace of mind that is necessary to happiness.

This last claim is one that we have already heard from Weishaupt. The two, Ulrich and Weishaupt, belonged to the same scholastic tradition of thought, though Weishaupt rests his case in the defense of fatalism, as we have seen, ultimately on the practical need of accepting it as a way of life. Ulrich, on the contrary, defends it on more metaphysical grounds. There is absolutely no middle ground between determinism and indeterminism, between necessity and accident (§9), for to accept a modicum of accidentality even within a restricted sphere of being is to deny the universality of the principle of sufficient ground – in effect, to deny the principle completely. And since indeterminism is thus unacceptable, determinism must therefore win the day. The problem of Kant, according to Ulrich, is that he tried precisely the impossible. He sought a middle way between the two, and in doing so he gave rise to a tangle of confusions that Ulrich frankly admits he cannot sort out.

In Ulrich's book, Kant figures prominently from the beginning (§§10–13), though we have deliberately neglected his presence so far.

Ulrich introduces him by saying that he finds him more difficult to understand than Spinoza, and that he suspects him of a new kind of Neoplatonism (§10, p. 22). He rehearses Kant's well-known distinction between the noumenal and the phenomenal, and then proceeds to define on its basis what he takes Kant to mean by 'freedom'. So far as he can understand, freedom, according to Kant, is an agent's capacity to initiate action absolutely. The human being possesses such a capacity inasmuch as he belongs to the world of noumena, that is, inasmuch as he acts as a thing in itself (pp. 23–4). Freedom is thus a kind of causality – one that an agent exercises through reason according to ideas and that, in exercising it as he actually does, the agent knows he might equally exercise otherwise (§11, pp. 27–8). Freedom is therefore the source of the agent's responsibility for his actions. The same actions initiated through its causality, however, have effects that fall within the realm of the phenomenal. And these, as empirical events occurring in time, are subject to the laws determining the sequence of all such events. To this extent, they are totally dependent on external conditions. Kant's peculiar position, according to Ulrich, consists in this attempt at reconciling a free agent's supposedly complete independence in initiating action with the external determinism to which the temporal effects of the same action are necessarily subject. Ulrich tries repeatedly to find a formula that might capture it in full. One might say, for instance, that, according to Kant, a human free agent acts all by himself, without his actions, however, having their beginning with him (§10, pp. 26–7); or again, that freedom is a cause, "of which the effect begins in time, though the causality does not begin" (§12, p. 31).

Kant is a determinist of such a unique nature, Ulrich says, that a Linneus would make him a species of the genus philosopher all by himself (§10, p. 22). Kant's motivation is clear. Since he has made of time something purely subjective, he needs an intelligible causality to complete the otherwise indefinite sequence of temporal events. But, Ulrich contends, one need not accept Kant's assumption regarding time. On a different assumption, it is God's creative act that brings the temporal series to completion (§12, pp. 35–6; §13, pp. 36–7). Kant also needs the intelligible causality because, in his opinion, without it the 'ought' (*sollen*) of reason would never be an efficacious source of actions. These actions could never therefore be imputed to a subject deemed responsible for them. But here again, one need not follow Kant. This is the claim that Ulrich then proceeds to elaborate in the rest of the book. All that is needed to save the meaning of the ought is to recognize that man is not perfect but strives after perfection; that at each stage of this striving, while he acts and even more so at a later moment of calm reflection, he can recognize the possibility of acting otherwise, however aware he is that de facto he must act, or must have acted, exactly as he does or did (§13, pp. 39–40).

According to Ulrich, Kant's position is also internally inconsistent. Even granted that the human agent has the capacity to initiate action absolutely in accordance with his intelligible or noumenal character, there still is a difference, Ulrich contends, between a capacity and its exercise. The question is why this agent exercises his capacity in certain instances but fails to do so in others. What causes this difference of conduct? If the difference is due to a failure to use reason properly, as Kant himself seems to imply, then, either there is a cause for this failure or there is not. If there is not, then Kant is positing the presence of 'accidentality' *(Zufall)* in the intelligible world, thus denying the universal validity of the principle of sufficient reason. If there is a cause for this failure, is Kant thereby implying that the failure is due to an original weakness inherent in reason itself? This weakness would to be unalterable, since it is intelligible. Is he also implying that a proper use of reason would be due, on the contrary, to another factor also inherent in reason, and equally original and unalterable, but in this case the cause of special strength? On this assumption, the exercise would be subject to a play of opposing intelligible factors, and this play would be subject to as strict a determinism as any play of empirical factors. We would find ourselves back with a system of determinism just as universal, and natural, as Ulrich wants to defend (§12, pp. 33–4). Kant's detour into the realm of the intelligible, in other words, turns out to be redundant. What is 'reason' as Kant conceives it anyway? Is it a dark, undeveloped, disposition *(Vernunftanlage)*? Or is it rather a certain activity, and if so of what kind? These are questions that cannot be answered on Kant's terms (§12, pp. 35–6). As the earliest critics of Kant had already argued, his distinctions add new difficulties without solving any of the old.

Ulrich, no less than the earliest critics, had, of course, totally misunderstood Kant's distinction between the moral and the natural, and the kind of 'efficacy' that his morality required. The distinction had nothing to do with the traditional distinction between 'physical' and 'hyperphysical' entities – a typically cosmological distinction that Kant was, on the contrary, trying very hard to supersede. His own distinction referred rather to the difference between the 'physical' and the 'intentional'. As we shall see, Jacobi was clear on this point. But, as we shall also see, he claimed to have learned the distinction in the first place from Spinoza. One can therefore appreciate the reaction of the anonymous reviewer of Ulrich's book in the *Allgemeine Literatur-Zeitung* – that is, of Kraus, who was in fact writing for Kant.[10] He denied that Ulrich had succeeded in rendering in purely natural terms the full meaning of the Kantian ought, and found very curious Ulrich's attempts at saving human freedom by arguing that, though at each moment we cannot be otherwise than what we are, we ought nonetheless to become better in the future. Given a series of alterations from A to C, this is the same as saying that, when we are at C and see how we got there from A, we cannot allow that we could have become otherwise than C. When still at A, however, we have an obligation of actually becoming other than C.[11] The reviewer finds this line of argumentation unsatisfactory. And indeed, there is something at least paradoxical, if not outright nonsensical, in Ulrich's claim that we are free inasmuch as we recognize that we might be otherwise than what we are, in full awareness, however, that we must be exactly as we are. There is no less question begging here regarding the reality of freedom than there was in Leibniz's reply to Bishop Steno.

Yet, without in any way trying to attenuate Ulrich's failure to understand Kant, there is nonetheless something disingenuous in the reviewer's criticism. He balks at what he sees as Ulrich's paradoxical claim. But is there any real difference between it and Kant's claim, which we remember from Chapter 1,[12] that we are fortunate not to see things from God's point of view, because, if we did, "the conduct of man would be changed into mere mechanism," and "the moral worth of his actions [. . .] would not exist at all"? Do not both claims amount to saying that we act *as if* we were free, though in fact we are not? And was not Kant fated, so to speak, to hold this position because, just like Ulrich, he too had defined freedom as a kind of efficient causality – one that, according to him, escapes the limitations of temporally conditioned causality, since it operates in a purely intelligible realm, but that nonetheless rejoins in the products of human actions the effects of the other, temporally conditioned, line of causality? One cannot bring into play this kind of theoretical construct without at the same time at least inviting, if not altogether sanctioning, a concept of the moral law that is analogous to physical law, thereby incurring the kind of aporias that Ulrich was raising against Kant.

Of course, Ulrich's reading of Kant in purely naturalistic terms was predictable. It was part of his mental universe. He did not need any prompting on Kant's part. But there is again something disingenuous in the *Allgemeine Literatur-Zeitung* reviewer's accusation that Ulrich had made nonsense of Kant's position by raising questions about the mechanics of the free will's operations that, on Kant's assumptions, can neither be asked nor answered, since no knowledge is possible of things that transcend the phenomenal realm. There is no hiding here behind the veil of critical ignorance, since the issue is not one of knowledge but of meaning. If Kant's idea of freedom as an efficient, yet intelligible causality originating in a noumenal realm is totally devoid of meaning, then Kant should simply drop it and seek systematic unity through other means. Even if advanced as a mere hypothesis, the idea must still be subjected to the test of internal coherence and completeness of meaning. Ulrich found it wanting on precisely this last ground, and not without reason.

One cannot therefore blame Kant's self-professed disciples if they still argued about the nature and the possibility of human freedom in the terms dictated by Ulrich, even when they understood what Kant meant by moral law in a way that Ulrich himself did not. Kant himself had opened the way for this confusion. The debate over human freedom concentrated on two issues. One was whether the idea of the law could have, simply as idea, the efficacy to affect feelings and thus initiate action in the empirical realm of existence – that is, whether the idea could in fact act as an efficient cause. The other issue, granted that the idea of freedom had the required efficiency, was whether its exercise and effects were caught up in a universal system of determinism, be it phenomenal, intelligible, or both. This second issue brought in its train the question of the universal validity of the principle of sufficient reason. Both issues were misguided. But, as we shall see, it took the perspicacity of a Jacobi to see through the conceptual confusion that gave rise to them and the dialectical skills of a Fichte to propose an alternative that, though perhaps unsatisfactory in other respects, had at least the virtue of being internally consistent.

4.2 REINHOLD VERSUS SCHMID[13]

One cannot speak of a debate on human freedom in the same historically circumscribed sense as one can speak of the Jacobi-instigated Spinoza debate or the debate on atheism later to flare up around Fichte. There were no exceptional circumstances to set it apart from normal academic discussion; no broader social circumstances to influence it or broader social consequences to flow from it. Human freedom was a commonplace of philosophical discussion at the time, and, since the publication of the *Critique of Pure Reason*, Kant's unique moral position was routinely taken into consideration in the discussion. Ulrich's little book that we have just considered, and a much larger and more scholastic work that he had published only a few years earlier,[14] were cases in point. Yet there was a flurry of essays and books published on the subject in the first years of the final decade of the eighteenth century that, though neither reflecting nor necessarily influencing the wider nonacademic world, nevertheless played an important part in the development of post-Kantian idealism. To this extent at least, and in a broad sense, these publications can be taken as constituting a specialized debate on human freedom.

The starting point was a textbook on moral philosophy that Schmid (our well-known Schmid) published in 1790.[15] The book contains no surprises. It further develops Schmid's program, already defined in his essay on Kantian Purism, of interpreting Kant's transcendental idealism along purely phenomenal lines by extending it now to the realm of moral experience. The self-identity that a subject of experience first achieves by establishing a unified world through theoretical means is now expanded to encompass the subject's feelings and motives for action. The world to be established in this way must be conceived as responding to the subject's desires and ultimately to his quest for happiness. What follows is a moral psychology not unlike in content that of Abicht, which we have already considered.[16] The point of interest is that, just as in the earlier essay Schmid had accepted as a matter of fact the a priori origin and the formality of Kant's categories of the understanding, so he now accepts the formality and the unconditional authority of the moral law, apparently as defined by Kant.

This is how Schmid defines the task of morality:

> To determine, through an extended function of the understanding in general, a higher unity in what has already been bound together through the first action of the understanding, i.e. there arise through **reason in general** higher rules that bind the many in one, i.e. principles in a more general meaning. [...] **Practical principles** come to be out of several practical rules united in one more general proposition. (§25, p. 20)

How is this higher unity to be achieved? It is done through the establishment of a higher rule – one that is the work of reason, and that apparently gives rise to the kind of conduct exclusively motivated by the demands of lawfulness in which, according to Kant, morality consists. Here are again Schmid's words:

> According to formal moral principles, I will something, not because I will something else, but exclusively because I am a rational being. An action [*Handlung*] is combined with my will, not as means to a further goal, but rather because of the

necessary relation in which a manner of acting stands to a rational nature as such. There is a material (whether internal or external) being acted upon [*behandelt*], not immediately because of the connection which this object has in itself to my receptivity (this can be only a remote ground of my choice), but in the first place because something given is thereby rationally **handled upon** [*behandelt*.] Supplementary thought: This acting can itself modify my sensibility. Thus arise **moral feelings**. (§38, p. 26)

It is obvious here that Schmid is making an effort to preserve Kant's idea of a formal law that binds strictly because it is a law. The lawfulness of an action, that is, its ideality, not its particular content, constitutes its moral nature. Just as obvious, however, is the interference that more traditional moral language still exercises on his effort. Schmid has a choice. On the one hand, he can follow up on the implications of Kant's standpoint. In this case, a new world of meaning would open up for him, one in which the apparently mere physical component in the description of human behavior carries from the beginning a completely different meaning than it would have in purely theoretical discourse. The character of an action is defined first and foremost ideally, with reference to the law. This is a world where 'killings' are relevant only inasmuch as they are to be adjudicated as either 'manslaughters' or 'murders', and, in the last case, whether as 'first' or 'second degree'; or again, where otherwise physically induced 'sexual drives' have meaning only as either 'lustful' or 'romantic' or some other variation on the two. None of these characterizations are reducible to purely physical predicates. The concept of natural determinism is relevant here only as a test, itself ideally constituted, of whether a given individual rightfully belongs to this world of meaning, that is, whether the individual is *compos* or *non compos mentis*. On the other hand, Schmid can revert to Ulrich's traditional conflation of physical and moral – that is, he can consider the law, however much now formally defined in Kantian style, as still the conscious by-product of a given particular nature. As a conceptual product, it is part and parcel of a human being's striving for the kind of self-identity that such a being requires because of his given nature. The way is thus open to treating the law as a mental cause that, in ways unknown to us, give rise to a special quality of feelings – the two, the law and the thus newly generated feelings, being part of an enhanced mechanism of nature in general.[17]

There is no doubt that Schmid opted for this second alternative – or, more precisely, since it is doubtful that he ever understood the possibility of the first, that he fell in line with it as if instinctively. Once one is committed to naturalism in things moral, however, one is subject to its well-known limitation, namely, its difficulty in retaining such all-important moral categories as 'freedom of choice', 'obligation', and 'personal responsibility'. Schmid himself was aware of this inevitable consequence. He officially repudiated 'naturalism' precisely for this reason (§223). A repudiation in words, however, has little meaning if one is still subject to the effects of what is being repudiated. Schmid spent a good portion of his treatise – indeed, some of its most interesting paragraphs – trying to stave off the implications of his officially denied naturalism. The attempt took two forms, neither of them particularly original. In the first place, Schmid relied on the notion of 'comparative freedom' that was widely accepted at the time. Since the representations of external stimuli, rather than these stimuli themselves, are the direct causes of human desires, it follows that, in virtue of the rationality of such representations, the human agent achieves a certain freedom *from* the otherwise strictly necessitating force of the stimuli. He need not, therefore, be the slave of sense-induced passions (§§226–7). This limited sense of freedom, however, does not in any way detract from the necessity that pervades the whole of nature (§228). That a man should represent his objects as he does, and that these representations should induce certain desires, and that these produce in turn certain actions – this is still part and parcel of the overall organization of nature.

In the second place, Schmid relied on the Kantian theme of 'critical ignorance'. Nature is but a system of appearances. One can therefore at least think of (though not comprehend) the possibility of a kind of causality that, since it transcends time, does not itself have a beginning in time, yet issues in temporal and hence temporally determined effects. When one speaks of an 'I', one must therefore distinguish between two senses of the pronoun. One refers to a phenomenal subject of actions (one, therefore, that is subject to the necessitating laws of nature); the other, to a transcendent subject that is, on the contrary, a member of a purely intelligible realm. It is to this intelligible I, Schmid then argues, that we refer in moral language and to which – since it is by definition free of the necessitating influence of phenomenal nature – the language of moral responsibility can be applied (§§239–42). When all is said and done, however, it still does not follow, according to Schmid, that this transcendent I acts arbitrarily. We must, on the contrary, think of it as governed by such laws as would belong to an intelligible world, so that nothing, whether in the phenomenal or the intelligible world, can be said to happen without sufficient reason. *"Yet,"* Schmid concludes stressing his words, *"necessity everywhere. If we do not want to make room for anything with no reason, then, there is nothing left but necessity, for between the two* [i.e., being with or without reason] *there is absolutely no middle way"* (§255, pp. 209–10).

If there were any doubt that Schmid was still being caught up in Ulrich's metaphysical categories, this last passage should dispel it. Schmid is citing from Ulrich's *Eleutheriologie*, as he duly acknowledges in a footnote.[18] Although in deference to Kant he duly follows the detour into the intelligible realm that Ulrich thought redundant, he still comes to rest on Ulrich's starting point. His flagrant naturalism, however much Schmid disavowed it, was not acceptable to Reinhold. Starting in 1791, first on the pages of the *Teutscher Merkur*, and then in 1792, in the second volume of his Kantian Letters, Reinhold published a series of articles on the subject of human freedom,[19] obviously written in response to the determinism endorsed by Schmid in his recently published textbook. He returned to the theme again in the *Contributions* of 1794, one of which he addressed to "my dear friend" Schmid.[20] We have here the core of our debate.

In the 1791 essay, Reinhold argued that morality presupposes freedom, and that freedom consists in the capacity of the human being to act (*handeln*) in abstraction from all his otherwise natural desires for sensible objects. These desires are governed by laws over which the human being has no control and with respect to which, therefore, he cannot be said to be ultimately free. Now, reason is at the origin of this capacity to act, for reason is the faculty of law-making (*Gesetzgebung*); as such, it is therefore capable of reflective acts (*Handlungen*) that have no other motive except the maintenance (*Wahrung*) of the conditions necessary to their law-making. "According to our conception," he says,

morality is a totally free and entirely disinterested willing of the lawful (*des Gesetzmäßigen*). This willing has its motive force exclusively in the autonomy of our spirit from which our personality depends, and which we designate with the name of reason – this last in the strictest sense of the word, 'theoretical reason' inasmuch as such reason is engaged in thinking, 'practical' inasmuch as it is engaged in willing.[21]

The acts that flow from this autonomy are 'useless' (*uneigennützig*), in the sense that they have no motive that transcends reason itself. Yet, precisely because of this, they provide the transcendent factor, in virtue of which otherwise purely natural instincts are suspended as 'natural' but are put into play again, so to speak, exclusively within the limits of reason's interest in establishing the rule of law everywhere. "The pure interest of reason is *lawfulness* (*Gesetzmässigkeit*) willed for its sake, *disinterestedly decreed* (*beschlossene*)" (239). This interest of reason is what defines moral life.

This, in a few words, is the substance of the essay. In effect Reinhold was reaffirming, but in a more psychological language, the autonomy of the principle of morality that Kant had already asserted. Without this autonomy, it would have been impossible to avoid naturalism. The problem was that Schmid had also asserted it, and, on its basis, had also denied naturalism, in words at least. Yet, by interpreting this autonomy as an expression of the spontaneity that follows 'being rational', he had ended up with a system of universal determinism that for all practical purposes was identical with Ulrich's naturalism. It was not clear that, in his position as stated in 1791, Reinhold could avoid being caught in the same slide. At that time, he was still operating on the Kantian assumption that the will is the same as practical reason subjectively considered – that freedom, in other words, is identical with the spontaneity that reason enjoys in establishing its own law of action. This assumption, of course, allowed him to bypass the problem of whether, and how, the idea of the law can be by itself an efficacious principle of action. But it also brought Reinhold face to face with the question of how it is possible for anyone to transgress the rule of reason *knowingly*. The problem is that, if moral life presupposes freedom, but freedom is an attribute of reason, to act as a morally responsible agent and to follow the rule of reason amount to one and the same thing. But reason cannot but follow its own law. Hence, either an action falls under the rule of reason or it escapes its compass altogether, becoming morally irrelevant in this latter case. The possibility of moral evil – as the contradictory of the moral good – is thus abolished, and so is moral life as we normally understand it. Though Reinhold was following a different conceptual route, and deliberately opposed Schmid, the consequences of his position were not unlike Schmid's and by implication not unlike Ulrich's as well.

This is the problem that Reinhold was to address in the subsequent Kantian Letters. The obvious first step was to distance himself from Kant by clearly distinguishing the will from reason.[22] Reason is a faculty of formal rules that become effective commands only by virtue of the intervention of the will. This was a long-standing scholastic position. But how was one to understand the 'will'? Here Reinhold had a conceptual choice. He could take it as a capacity (dependent on the intelligible force that reason exercises on it) to act either in conformity or nonconformity with selfish desires. On this assumption, however, he would have been endorsing Schmid's determinism and implicit naturalism – something that Reinhold would not do.[23] He opted, therefore, for a second alternative. He defined the will as a faculty that renders the human being indeed indifferent to sense desires and, in this sense, free from them. But it renders him also indifferent to the formal rules of reason, so that, whether these become his effective principles of action or not, depends on a freely undertaken decision on its part. 'Freedom' now acquires for him the meaning of *Willkühr* – namely, a self-determined commitment (*Entschluß*), in virtue of which one chooses (*whälen*) as the motive of one's action *either* the objects of selfish (*eigennützig*) sensible desires (thus subordinating reason to them) *or* the unselfish (*uneigennützig*) interest of reason (in this case, subordinating the desires to it).[24] This was a meaning of freedom – of not being "in any way exclusively *bound* either to the law of the unselfish or the law of the selfish drive" – that Reinhold had already included in his list of possible meanings in his first sketch of a theory of the will in 1789. But it was a meaning that had no proper place in such a theory at that time, since Reinhold still assumed that will and practical reason were the same faculty.[25]

There was in fact a third possible alternative – one of which Reinhold should have been aware, as we shall see in due time, but that he did not consider. Be that as it may, by thus defining the will, Reinhold had in effect introduced a source of indeterminacy in the intelligible realm of the thing in itself, a move that few at the time would have dared. He was summoning up the image of a transcendent human history, so to speak – one that takes place in an intelligible realm unknown to us, somehow becomes part of the economy of God's creative activity, and, together with it, has consequences at the temporal level. This was an image perfectly in accordance with biblical language, but hardly compatible with the philosophical instincts of his contemporaries. Reinhold tried to respond to his many critics by arguing that he was not denying the universality of the principle of sufficient reason, since there was an explanation for every individual arbitrary choice, namely, the actual choice itself.[26] But, since he was not identifying this choice with God's creative act, he was in fact positing a multiplicity of first and possibly conflicting principles – in effect, therefore, threatening the universality of the order that the principle was supposed to guarantee. And for this he was roundly condemned by many[27] – most notably by Kant himself, as one should have expected.[28] Though Ulrich had been hesitant regarding Kant's position on the question of whether there is a middle way between accidentality and necessity, Kant himself stood in fact squarely on his side, allowing no room between these two modal categories. His objection to the classical metaphysics that Ulrich represented was that it understood 'sufficient reason' in a univocal sense, in some variation or other of 'physical efficacy'. It was therefore necessarily bound to naturalism, as Ulrich and Schmid clearly demonstrated. According to Kant, on the contrary, sufficient reason carried at least the two radically different and mutually irreducible senses of moral and physical, noumenal and phenomenal. Whether understood in one sense or the other, however, the principle still called for determinism everywhere. There was no doubt for Kant on this score.

Of course, Kant's position suffered from the new, and apparently intractable, problem of reconciling the different meanings he now attributed to sufficient reason. His equivocating on the use of the concept freedom, as we have already noted, only made for confusion. One must therefore give credit to Reinhold for at least trying to remedy the situation by introducing bold distinctions that respected, at least on the face of it, the commonsense meaning of 'choice'. The problem, unfortunately, was that his attempt failed miserably, and for more profound reasons than that it contravened the accepted philosophical wisdom of the time. We shall return to these reasons in a moment. First, we must, however, introduce another personality whom Reinhold must also have had in mind while debating with Schmid. This character is August Wilhelm Rehberg.[29]

4.3 REHBERG AND KANT

4.3.1 Introducing Rehberg

Rehberg is best known for his political activities and political polemics.[30] He belonged to the much Anglicized Hannover school of political thought.[31] A self-professed metaphysical skeptic and conservative politician, he was to be a bitter critic of the French Revolution. Though not an academic philosopher, we find him nonetheless appearing regularly on the philosophical scene. Supplement III of the 1789 edition of Jacobi's Spinoza-Letters was in response to Rehberg's review of *David Hume* in the *ALZ*.[32]

In his younger days, moreover, Rehberg had exhibited philosophical ambitions as well as philosophical promise. In 1780, he had anonymously published a dramatic dialogue entitled *Cato* – to which we shall return at the end of the chapter – on Spalding's well-worn subject of the 'vocation of humankind'.[33] Even before then, as he was to claim in 1828 in a retrospective summary of his literary and political career, he had been the first to state the thesis, later popularized by Jacobi, that metaphysics necessarily leads to Spinozism.[34] He had advanced the thesis in an essay submitted in response to the Berlin Academy's call for the 1779

Prize Essay Competition. According to this later statement, he had done it in a skeptical spirit, hoping to cast doubt on the reliability of school metaphysics indirectly. The announced theme of the competition was 'On the Essence and Limitations of Forces'. It had been intended, as Rehberg thought, to promote the authority of Leibniz, the founder of the Academy. As it happened, the young Rehberg found Leibnizian philosophy highly unsatisfactory. And since he could not express this opinion openly, he tried the stratagem of defending Leibniz on the totally negative ground that his metaphysics was the only possible alternative to the Spinozistic conclusions to which a metaphysical analysis of the concept of 'force' necessarily leads. The exercise, according to Rehberg, had been a tour de force – an underhand way of criticizing Leibniz by defending him only as an ad hoc escape from the very consequential, though universally unacceptable, results of Spinoza's philosophy.[35]

In 1787, Rehberg was also the author of a little book, entitled *Concerning the Relation of Metaphysics to Religion*,[36] in which, so far as metaphysics was concerned, he proposed a peculiar Kantian adaptation of Spinozism and, with respect to ethics, a Spinozistic adaptation of Kant's moral theory. All this was done again with polemical intent. Rehberg's main intention was to insulate ethics from theology and metaphysics in order to protect it from the doubts that always trouble these last two while safeguarding at the same time its vital connections with religion (9–10). The book had been written in the wake of the Spinoza dispute, and it clearly showed Rehberg's sympathies, though not with Jacobi himself, at least with Jacobi's claim that metaphysics necessarily leads to Spinozism. Rehberg had himself already advanced the claim (17–18). It is in this book that we find raised against Kant[37] the criticism that, albeit in different ways, was later also voiced by both Jacobi and Fichte, and that is also at the heart of the present study. Kant had not gone far enough in criticizing classical metaphysics; he was still being held hostage to its assumptions.

More about this in a moment. To be noted now is that, shortly after his 1787 book, Rehberg published a long review of the *Critique of Practical Reason* in the *ALZ* (1788).[38] It was arguably the most philosophically perceptive of all the reviews of Kant's recent work to be published at the time. Reinhold, who had already recognized the importance of Rehberg's earlier book and had dedicated a long and careful review to it,[39] also did not fail to notice the importance of this latest piece. Rehberg, for his part, had responded to Reinhold's review of his book with an article in *Der Teutsche Merkur*,[40] at the conclusion of which he suggested that the question, "whether it is possible for a human being to renounce reason *knowingly*" runs parallel to the other question, "whether it is possible for a human being to ignore the natural satisfaction [that we take] in order and rationality" (233). The point being made, at the conclusion of a long criticism of natural theology, was that, insofar as human conduct is concerned, the question of its motivation cannot be reduced to that of a human being's relative knowledge of the truth. This was how the question was ultimately resolved in the Leibnizian conceptual universe. Rehberg contended, on the contrary, that there are other factors, such as desire for order, which, though implicating rationality and therefore knowledge, cannot be reduced to the latter. They belong to the voluntary side of human nature and thus involve needs that transcend mere knowledge. The two stated questions run parallel in the sense that, though involving one another, they must remain separate.

The point was not lost on Reinhold. In 1792, in the Introduction to the second volume of his Kantian Letters, he referred to the review of the *Critique of Practical Reason* in the *ALZ* of 1788,[41] as "marvelous" and admitted that he had derived important hints from it. Reinhold then went on to say: "I cannot think of true freedom as restricted to the efficacy of reason any more than [the author of the review, i.e., Rehberg] can; nor can I, any more than he, call reason *practical* in the sense that it contains the complete, self-determining ground of an action of the will" (ix–x). It appears, in other words, that the distinction between reason and will that Reinhold introduced at that time, and the corollary claim that the will can determine itself to a course of action independently of reason, had been inspired by Rehberg. There was an extra dimension, in other words, to Reinhold's attack on Schmid. While trying to counter the latter's de facto naturalism, Reinhold was also trying to escape the full force of Rehberg's objections against Kant's moral theory raised in the *ALZ* – objections that he apparently felt had hit the mark. We have just suggested that Reinhold's innovation failed to offer a viable alternative to Schmid's naturalism, but we have still not considered why this is the case. Reinhold was not to fare any better in his response to Rehberg. He failed miserably to dodge his objections just as he failed to undercut Schmid. And, as we must now see, he proved vulnerable with respect to the one for the same reasons that he was ineffective with respect to the other.

4.3.2 Rehberg's Antimetaphysics

Where did Rehberg stand? In his already mentioned intellectual retrospect, when reflecting on the fascination that Spinoza was to have for the German mind soon after the publication of his earliest essay in philosophy, Rehberg attributed it to the fact that Spinoza offered even the most disparate casts of mind an easy point of access to his philosophy. To someone like Goethe, he offered the irreducible immediacy of experience; to the philosophers, systematic thought; to the *Schwärmer*, the possibility of mystical intuition. There was something for everyone (9–12). Rehberg does not mention what Spinoza specifically offered to him. However, from the general tenor of his remarks, one can conclude fairly that the attraction he felt for him was due to his belief that Spinoza had de facto put an end to metaphysics. On the one hand, Spinoza had driven to an extreme reason's tendency to ascend from individual objects of experience to ever more abstract and hence universal representations of them. His concept of 'substance' represented the highest peak of abstraction possible. On the other hand, Spinoza had resisted the temptation of trying to explain the existence of individual things on the basis of any such abstraction – a temptation that, if unchecked, leads to dogmatic metaphysics. To be sure, the existence of the visible world requires an explanation, and one can provide it by positing a cause for it in general. When it is a question, however, of explaining individually the existence of the singular things that make up the world, referring them to such a general cause is of no use. Rather, one must explain them by referring each to other equally singular and finite things. And since the explanation thus obtained does not exceed the limits of these things, the explanation itself remains bound to phenomena. It reaches only as far as it reaches – never as far as things might be apart from any particular representation of them. One can, of course, turn for a complete explanation to the highest abstraction of substance. But, in that case, one would no longer be considering things in their singularity – that is, as the finite objects that one was to explain in the first place. As Rehberg says, "the individuality of a singular can indeed be placed under the universality of a concept, but never be derived from it."[42] This, according to Rehberg, was exactly Spinoza's position. One further implication – one that Rehberg does not, however, draw explicitly – is that each science is bound in its explanations to the particular level of abstraction determined by its principles. Although the objects of any science might reflect and parallel the order of the concepts of any other, they are not thereby being explained by those concepts. Insofar as immediate experiences are concerned, this means that their validity ultimately rests on their immediacy alone. In brief, by pushing metaphysics to its highest abstraction, Spinoza had in fact rendered it innocuous insofar as the things closest to us are concerned, thus in effect laying it to rest.

Judging from his 1787 book, it also appears that Rehberg had found in Spinoza his point of access to Kant. The Critique of Reason was, in his opinion, a more consistent form of Spinozism. Its greater consistency lay in the fact that Kant explicitly denied that we can say anything about the thing in itself – this latter being the highest form of abstraction possible and, therefore, the equivalent of Spinoza's substance. It can only stand for existence in general, and existence (as Rehberg says, citing the authority of Kant)[43] cannot be the object of any representation. 'Thought' and 'extension', therefore, must be conceived as attributes that belong exclusively to phenomena, that is, to things as represented rather than as in themselves (60 3).

Kant also had another advantage over Spinoza, this time in moral theory. This advantage was due to Kant's clear recognition that morality is based on autonomous principles,[44] independent of either physical or metaphysical considerations. As Rehberg thought, this independence of moral principles was part of Kant's more general program, with which he agreed wholeheartedly, of insulating ethics and religion from both metaphysics and theology in order to protect the former two from the vagaries of the latter two.[45] As autonomous, moral principles provide a point of reference that transcends any de facto situation (whether such a situation be conceived in physical or even metaphysical terms), and hence can serve as an undisputed measure of moral value. For Kant, therefore, evil need not be defined as a mere negation of the good, as it was done in dogmatic metaphysics and as Spinoza also did. Evil is not just a limitation of the good but the privation of it, the lack of something that should rather be there.[46]

This was undoubtedly a great advantage, since it saved some of the most elementary moral intuitions. It was here, however, precisely in the realm of moral theory, where Kant should have completed Spinoza's task of putting an end to metaphysics, that he also seriously overstepped the limits of his insight, thus falling prey again to metaphysical speculation. According to Rehberg, Kant made the serious mistake of assuming that the idea of the law – the first moral principle – is by itself an efficacious principle of action.[47] In effect, Kant had thereby failed to respect the cardinal rule that Rehberg thought one should learn from Spinoza – namely, that any representation can explain its object only within the limits of its particular level of abstraction. Precisely because the idea of the law transcends the whole realm of individual experiences, it explains the possibility of moral conduct in general without, however, sufficiently explaining any single moral action in particular.[48] Any such explanation has to be derived, rather, from particular principles established at the level of experience at which moral conduct actually occurs. All such principles, Rehberg insists, must take into consideration the satisfaction of sensible desires. Or again, even granted *ex hypothesi* that the idea of the law is by itself an efficacious principle of particular action, one would still not be able to recognize its alleged efficacy except as the object of phenomenal consciousness – that means, in effect, in the medium of appropriately modified sensible desires and their satisfaction. So far as a theory of particular actions is concerned, therefore, the hypothesis would not do any significant conceptual work. Hence, rather than trying to draw a direct line of efficient causality from the idea of law to actual conduct, one should try instead to define how the moral ideal, as expressed abstractly by the law, is reflected at the level of actual experience in a form congruent with the sensibility of the latter.

But how is this to be done? Here is where Rehberg's originality shows best.[49] On the face of it, he seemed to have fallen back on the well-worn idea of comparative freedom that we have already encountered in Ulrich and Schmid (121, 132). In fact, however, Rehberg was going well beyond it. His important new claim was that the human agent cannot pursue his greater good without at the same time also expecting that the satisfaction of any of his desires will harmonize with the satisfaction of all other desires, his own as well as those of all other agents (122–3). This is an expectation that follows naturally from the agent's rationality. In the context of actual experience, the otherwise purely formal principle of lawfulness in general thus acquires the extra meaning of a principle of universal harmony of desires. Moreover (and this is the most important point), since the moral ideal of lawfulness in general, even when reinterpreted as a principle of universal harmony of desires, transcends any particular form in which it might be perceived as realized in experience, any system of harmonious desires that the agent assumes in the course of his actions must be considered as one among many other possible ones. It constitutes one possible moral world among a potentially infinite number of others (111–12). In the eye of a pure intelligence – one, however, not to be confused with any metaphysical God, since it would be conceived with direct reference to phenomena – there would actually be many such worlds, all of them phenomenal because each is dependent on a particular capacity of representation (111, 113).

Rehberg thus tried to save the sense of absoluteness that Kant had rightly ascribed to the law and to the duties that follow upon it while at the same time transposing it into a more immediate, experiential medium. Since in moral action the agent commits himself to a whole world of desires, there is an expectation of completeness in his conduct that cannot be derived from immediate experience. Through the action, therefore, the agent transcends the latter. He is actively engaged in experience. He is not the mere instrument of anonymous natural forces, as he would have to be in any form of eudaimonism. Kant was right on this last score. But he did not need to attribute to his action the kind of absolute value that would require that the action both originate and terminate outside experience. Its particular value is definable in terms of an interplay of actual desires. In another phenomenal world – granted some other form of sensibility and a different set of consequent desires – the same action might have a completely different value (148–9).

The liberalizing[50] political implications of this claim were obvious, and Rehberg did not fail to make them explicit.[51] So far as moral conduct is concerned, the essential point is that the moral ideal of lawfulness can never be abstracted from the interplay of actual desires. Rehberg also refers to this ideal as the moral equivalent of the principle of noncontradiction, drawing an analogy between moral action and discursive argument.[52] This is an interesting analogy worth expanding on. It is assumed that in theoretical discourse one is bound in an argument to abide by the demands of the principle of noncontradiction. Since these demands are absolute, one is equally bound to consider the argument as in principle connected to a whole set of other arguments, all of them coherently developing one single theme. With respect to this stated theme, the discourse claims total truth. But, in the case of another theme, all the arguments in the discourse could well become altogether irrelevant. In this sense, there is nothing absolute about the discourse. Now, the moral law stands to moral conduct in the same way that the principle of noncontradiction stands to theoretical discourse. It defines the standard of coherent moral action without in any way dictating its material content.

Rehberg thus never abandoned – not even in a moral context – his phenomenal standpoint. His moral theory was worlds removed from Spinoza's, since it assumed that the desire for lawfulness in general is an overriding motive for action that makes individuals social in principle – not just by default, only to promote selfish interests. Yet, he was operating on Spinozistic principles, at least in the sense that, according to him, moral explanation has to be confined to the limits of visible human situations. Schmid's problem of determinism does not arise, since there is never any question of either performing or adjudicating action as if one stood on the side of the thing in itself, or of expecting the results of any action to terminate there. Rehberg had suspended all such possibilities from the start. He had insulated ethics from metaphysics by relegating the concepts of the latter to abstractions that, though perhaps conceptually regulative, are incapable of explaining actual events. This result applies also to moral actions. Though performed with the harmony of a whole world in mind, they are to be taken as unfolding, and also terminating, within the limits of phenomenal existence; and hence, like all phenomena, as not allowing of strict determination. Their limits are open-ended. Every agent might always have acted differently than he de facto did, and why he did not act otherwise is a fact open only to historical explanation, the kind that admits personal responsibility as a factor. The fact *is* explainable but, *in principle*, never totally explainable. This is a limit of explanation in general, not just of 'human explanation' – though the latter is, of course, affected by specialized limits when contrasted with the equally limited, though differently limited, explanation proper to (say) a rational nonhuman race.

Rehberg's refusal to accept even the terms of the classical problem of human freedom was the third alternative (alluded to previously) open to Reinhold to counter Schmid's determinism if he had just seen it. Within the limits of a moral context, it is perfectly feasible to speak of individual responsibility, since it is perfectly possible to think of a human being whose actions are rational – that they implicate moral principles in Kant's strong sense – but that, because of historical circumstances that affect their immediate motivation, lead to results that contradict such principles. The issue of responsibility is always to be raised, and resolved as far as is possible, within the limits of precisely these defined circumstances. It does not help to bring physical or metaphysical models of reality into the picture (the kind that raise the issue of a physical or hyperphysical form of free agency), whether such models are introduced dogmatically or just hypothetically. For, apart from their theoretical unreliability, the moral relevance of any of them would depend on the already historically taken moral decision of what constitutes an orderly human society. This was the ultimate burden of the position that Rehberg had first expounded in his 1787 book[53] and that, in reply to Reinhold, he had then summarized again at the end of the *Teutscher Merkur* article by linking the question of whether one can knowingly disregard reason with the more historically oriented question of whether one can disregard the natural desire for universal order.

4.3.3 Rehberg's Criticism of Kant and Reinhold

It might be argued that Rehberg was being unfair to Kant, since his moral theory is not at all unlike Kant's own. Nowadays, at least, we are inclined to interpret Kant's idea of law as a regulative principle that defines the limits of moral action without in any way determining its actual content. For the latter, one must turn to the world of sense experience. Indeed, at its most interesting, Kant's moral theory does deal with a world of moral phenomena, all centered on the feeling of respect for the law, in the midst of which otherwise exclusively physical entities are reinterpreted in moral terms and are subjected to typically moral rules of explanation. Rehberg, however, was reading Kant's texts in a cultural context in which metaphysical thinking was still the rule and in which, therefore, it would have been extremely difficult to perform the textual abstractions necessary for that purified reading of Kant's theory. Moreover, Kant had said that the law typically defines the conduct of a free will. He had also defined freedom as a kind of efficient causality that operates independently of phenomenal causality in an ideally conceived realm of existence. And he had relied on the albeit purely negative idea of this causality, and of the noumenal nature it would create, in order to guarantee the ultimate success in the noumenal realm of moral actions that in the sense realm cannot even begin to be realized. These claims made sense only against the background of traditional metaphysical notions. They were now being reintroduced in the new epistemic guise of theoretical regulative ideas. But, though no longer pretending to convey actual knowledge of anything in particular, they still gave rise, precisely as theoretical constructs, to conceptual aporias, and these in turn made a difference to how moral life was being understood. Even the idea of such a morally fundamental phenomenon as 'respect for the law', a feeling at once sensible yet morally determined, became problematic.

We shall have to return to the quality of a moral life defined in specifically Kantian terms. Fichte, as we shall see, did not stray far from it; he only made its theoretical underpinnings more consistent. The point now is that Rehberg was justified in complaining that Kant had failed to insulate ethics from metaphysics but had still held it hostage to the conceptual prejudices of the latter. On Rehberg's theory, the law either has purely logical regulative meaning or is defined from the beginning in social terms.

It denotes a special class of human desire. Kant's problem of demonstrating its efficacy does not therefore arise. Rehberg, as far as I know, did not draw any explicit connection between Kant's practical aporias and the difficulties that had attended his transcendental deduction of the categories in the *Critique of Pure Reason*. It is nonetheless instructive to note the parallel between the two. If Kant had restricted the categories to their purely logical function of determining the concept of an object in general, that is, as defining the parameters of meaning in general, rather than taking them also, as he in fact did, as the most generic predicates of all objects, then the need of a transcendental deduction would not have arisen at all. There is no need to validate the applicability of the categories to actual physical objects as these appear in experience, since the predicates of such objects are rather to be determined on their own merit in the course of experience itself – within, of course, the framework of meaning stipulated by the categories. The idea that they could ever be determined by adding a schema, that is, an imaginative content, to the logical categories a priori makes sense only if one has already defined these categories materially by assuming that they constitute in principle the outlines of a real world rather than of just a world of meaning. Only on this assumption, which already implies a metaphysical extension of the function of the categories, does the possibility also arise that cognition of another world – that of the thing in itself – would be indeed possible if one could just add to these categories an intelligible intuitive content that we humans do not, however, have. I am saying, in other words, that Kant's dependence on metaphysical modes of thought that Rehberg was decrying in the context of moral theory was already at work on the theoretical side of the Critique of Reason and had already had its deleterious effects there.

Rehberg made his case against Kant most conspicuously by applying two particular strictures to his moral theory. One was directed at Kant's theoretical construct allegedly justifying the belief that human moral intentions, though unrealizable in the sensible world, are nonetheless being invisibly realized in a noumenal one. The other stricture was directed at the form in which the final realization of moral life was presented by Kant. Regarding the first, Rehberg argued that, since on Kant's own terms there is an infinite logical gulf separating the noumenal and the phenomenal, any connection postulated between the two for systematic purposes is *in principle* equivocal. Whatever effect a noumenal cause might have, be this cause God's creative act or some other source of free causality, it would have to be itself noumenal and hence could bear no relation to the phenomenal world. It could hardly constitute a credible basis, therefore, on which to pin the belief that what we do here, though bound to the mechanics of phenomenal events, is having its moral fruition in a noumenal beyond.[54] The net result, Rehberg concluded, was that Kant courted the dangers of *Schwärmerei*, because, by distracting man's moral aspirations from the only world in which he may ever hope to see his actions having results, and by directing them instead to a world that has no relevance to the present one, he made man prone to scrupulosity and self-castigation.[55]

Regarding the second target of his strictures, that is, the end of moral life, Rehberg sharply criticized the idea of the 'perfect good' in which, according to Kant, such an end consists. This good, according to Kant, is allegedly made up of two factors. The first, and more important, is moral perfection itself, that is, purity of heart; the second is the happiness that Kant held is the deserved and necessary by-product of a morally upright life. Kant also thought, however, that this happiness consists in the satisfaction of sensible desires. And it is here that Rehberg found cause to complain. For, on Kant's own premises, moral perfection is attainable only in an allegedly intelligible world. But, since a noumenally conceived agent cannot be the subject of a phenomenally conceived happiness (as happiness would have to be if dependent on sensible satisfactions as understood by Kant), it followed that Kant's idea of a finally consummated moral life was just as internally inconsistent as the moral theology he had devised in its support was irrelevant.[56]

It might sound strange to hear Kant – the hypercritical Kant, as he was sometime called – being accused of *Schwärmerei*. Rehberg was perhaps being carried too far by his Tory instincts. The strictures he had applied to Kant's moral theory, however, were both valid and fair. And they applied to Reinhold's theory as well, with added relevance in his case because of his newly devised assumption that we have arbitrary choice. The problem with Reinhold was that he was battling Schmid's de facto naturalism on Schmid's own naturalistic grounds. If one is seeking the natural causes of moral phenomena, it makes little difference whether such causes are conceived as possible sense objects or are projected into an invisible, hyperphysical realm of existence. In either case, one is still caught up in Schmid's conceptual framework. And, granted the accepted cosmology of the day, there was no conceptual room for this kind of individual and also absolutely originating sources of efficient causality that Reinhold was postulating. Moreover, even if there had been conceptual room for them, they would still not have performed a morally useful explanatory function in real life of determining the distinction between 'selfish' and 'unselfish' desires on which Reinhold was basing his theory. For granted that a moral agent has exercised his assumed noumenally appointed privilege of arbitrarily choosing one line of conduct over some other, how is he to know *phenomenally* which choice he has made noumenally in a given case, that is, how is he to know whether he has opted to act 'for' or 'in abstraction from' the law? The base of the distinction must lie in the visible historical circumstances accompanying his actions. To shift it to an invisible noumenal realm is to place it beyond the reach of human judgment. On Reinhold's theory, a moral agent would at best only be able to guess at his assumed transcendent motives of action, thereby becoming all the more vulnerable to the kind of scrupulosity and self-castigation for which Rehberg had accused Kant of fomenting *Schwärmerei*. In brief, by supplementing any historical account of conduct with a transcendent history of its motivation, Reinhold contributed nothing morally significant to the account. He only catered to misguided metaphysical interests. Reinhold's theory of arbitrary choice added extra difficulties to Schmid's naturalism without resolving any.

Yet Rehberg's theory was itself not immune to difficulties. On the contrary, there were good reasons why it would have appeared puzzling to his contemporaries or why Jacobi should recoil from it in abhorrence.[57] For one thing, though Rehberg was justified in wanting to restrict moral explanation to moral phenomena as such without running incursions into metaphysical theorizing, the fact remains that, according to his Spinozistic principles, there is a realm of physical events that admits only of physical explanation. Can one simply allow the two lines of explanation, the moral and the physical, to run parallel without making any effort to find a point of contact between the two? Rehberg himself was willing to leave the matter at that. He was satisfied with what he thought was a kind of Platonic dualism.[58] The supposed impossibility of resolving this dualism was at the core of his repeatedly professed skepticism. But was this claim of skepticism any different from Kant's claim of critical ignorance? If it was, how did it differ from it? There was also the question of what Rehberg meant by 'religion'. Restricting religious beliefs to the phenomenal realm, as he apparently did, must have sounded unsettling, if not blasphemous, to the typical pious believer of the day. It at least needed explaining.

We shall turn to this issue of religion in the next chapter. As for the other question, we shall revisit it shortly, after we let Jacobi have his say on the issues of Spinozism and human freedom.

4.4 JACOBI ON SPINOZISM AND HUMAN FREEDOM

4.4.1 Of Things Spinozistic

In Chapter 3 we left Jacobi in an embarrassing position. He had tried in *David Hume* to offer an alternative to Kant's critical model of experience – one that would save the factual necessity for which that model provided a basis without, however, incurring its undue formalism. In the attempt, Jacobi had been led to conceive experience as a play of opposing forces and reason as an especially highly developed form of life. These were not bad moves in themselves. On the contrary, they were highly promising. But conceptually they implied a Leibnizian model of experience, and this in turn tended to reduce the human subject, however much one took his individuality as existentially primordial, to a reflection of the greater organization of the cosmos. In effect, therefore, the two moves led to the same kind of abstractive explanation that Jacobi had accused of nihilism in the Spinoza-Letters. Jacobi brought his dialogue abruptly to an end. Much later, as we said, when he assigned an intuitive function to reason, Jacobi declared his early position to be unsatisfactory and even tried to mask it. In 1789, however, in the second edition of the Spinoza-Letters, obviously with Kant's *Critique of Practical Reason* in mind, he had already restated his position in a way that would certainly not have satisfied a rationalist but that a man of faith could have found internally coherent.

David Hume was not Jacobi's most obvious preoccupation in the many additions to this new edition of the Spinoza–Letters. His main concern was to clarify his position as he had stated it in the first edition, and above all to explain how he could have defended Spinoza as the most consequential of all philosophers – to the point that Mendelssohn had taken him to be himself a Spinozist – while rejecting him in toto precisely because he was a philosopher. Clarification of his position in *David Hume* came only indirectly, by implication. Why, then, could Jacobi praise Spinoza so highly? The reason, in brief, is that of all the philosophers, Spinoza alone had had the intellectual courage to abide strictly by the assumption that, according to Jacobi, has governed philosophical explanation from the beginning. This was the classical assumption that nothing can come from nothing and nothing can revert to nothing – *gigni de nihilo nihil, in nihilum nil potest reverti*.[59] It is the assumption that is at the basis of the principle of sufficient reason. On this assumption, 'being' must be conceived as a self-contained whole, 'infinite' in the double sense that it

does not allow room for anything outside it (i.e., it has no external boundaries) or inside it (i.e., it has no internal determinations). For in either
case, in order to draw any distinction between 'it' and any alleged 'other'
(whether this other be internal or external), one would have to bring
in 'nothingness' as a factor, thus transgressing the accepted principle.
This being is what Spinoza calls substance or God. It obviously follows,
for the reason just stated, that there cannot be any coming-to-be of finite
creatures really distinct from it, whether such a becoming is conceived
by way of creation *ex nihilo* or by emanation.

It does not follow, however, that one cannot speak of substance or
God (to now use Spinoza's language) in many ways, or that one cannot
meaningfully speak of finite individuals, as we obviously do. The important point is to understand exactly what we are saying when we speak in
this way and how God is being implicated in what we say. Jacobi makes
his point using the analogy of the relation of space to its parts. Space is
infinitely divisible. Suppose now that we delineate one segment of it by
arbitrarily introducing some limits within it. Inside this arbitrarily chosen
segment, space is still infinitely present in the sense that all of its properties *as space* are still to be found there infinitely, including its possible
divisibility *in infinitum*. While talking about this segment of space, in other
words, we are still talking about space in general. To refer to the segment
precisely as such, we would have to speak of it with reference to some
other segment – strategically chosen with the explicit purpose of defining the boundaries of the first, but ultimately just as arbitrarily chosen as
the first. This other segment would have to be defined in turn with reference to some other strategically chosen segment; and so on *in infinitum*.
It is in this way that Jacobi thinks that we should consider the relation
between finite things and Spinoza's notion of God or substance. When
talking about these things, we are still talking about God, but abstractly –
picking out, so to speak, something positively real but at the same time
leaving out of consideration all that is in fact being implied by what we
are saying. *Omnis determinatio negatio.* The determination of the one thing
we are considering is in fact the function of our ignoring the rest. It is
the product of the abstraction that is the necessary condition of all representation, be it imaginary or conceptual. The illusionary reality of space
and time, of becoming, or of engendered nature in general (*natura naturata*, to use Spinoza's term) emerges precisely in this way as the result
of the abstractive function of representational knowledge.[60] Such is the
paradoxical position in which philosophers land themselves. Once their
first principle has been established by way of abstraction and taken as the

original 'reality', they must consider as products of abstraction the very individual entities from which their reflection made its start. Weishaupt, as we remember from Chapter 2, produced a similar argument against the philosophers from his materialistic point of view.

It so happens, Jacobi proceeds, that 'extension' and 'thought' are the two properties that define essentially all the finite things that are the immediate objects of our representations. Hence we attribute the two to God precisely as his 'attributes'. But it must be clear in what spirit this is done. The attribution does not in any way imply that God has either a body or an intellect. These, even if conceived as infinite, would already be determinate things. They would be the products of abstraction and would belong by right, therefore, to the realm of *natura naturata*. Extension and thought are rather the two forms under which all finite things are to be defined precisely as 'modes', or aspects, of God, and can thus be referred back to him as their only reality. They are principles of explanation with respect to these finite things, hence distinguishable from one another, and from God, only on the ultimately arbitrary assumption of such finite things. In reality the two (thought and extension) are identical with one another, and each is identical with God. Thought is extension as 'represented'; extension is the content of thought; and both are ways of conceiving things as essentially modes of God.

Jacobi enters into long disquisitions regarding Spinoza and his relation to Leibniz.[61] Apart from these scholarly arguments, which do not interest us now, the important point is that, according to Jacobi's reading of Spinoza, just as space is present in toto in any of its segments as much as in any other, so God and his attributes are present in each of the finite things that are the objects of experience as much as in any other. And, just as space indifferently and totally explains the properties of each of its presumed segments – so that, to define any of these precisely as 'that particular segment' one would have to do it with reference to some other segment *in infinitum* – so God and his attributes explain each and every presumed finite thing indifferently and totally, with the result that, in their case also, to determine any of these finite things, one would have to do it only with reference to some other finite thing *in infinitum*. This is not a case of God and his attributes being unable to reach out to finite things in their individuality but, on the contrary, of their reaching them, so to speak, in one fell swoop from the beginning, so that from God's own point of view (i.e., *sub specie aeterni*) any other explanation of these things would be de trop. To consider them exclusively as finite, and to explain them as such, one must abstract precisely from God and his attributes.

This is indeed what we normally do, and hence we are restricted in our explanations to the endless chains of limiting relations that constitute finitude. But even then, when explaining things in this way, we are in fact still speaking about God. Such is the logic of a universe conceived strictly on the basis of identity. For the same reason that we cannot say that God has a body or an intellect, for that reason, in seeing natural bodies and in thinking them, we can truthfully say that we are seeing God and thinking him.

Rehberg, in his own way, had also seen this dimension of Spinoza's doctrine, and had drawn his peculiar conclusion from it that in ethics one must abstract from metaphysical considerations altogether. This part of Jacobi's exposition of Spinoza in the first edition of the Spinoza-Letters was, however, the one that Mendelssohn, bound as he was to the modes of thought of school metaphysics, found especially difficult to understand. He could not understand how it could be both the case that thought was an attribute and that God could not be said to think or, for that matter, to will. And, had he heard it,[62] he would have been especially puzzled by the argument that Jacobi was to put in Lessing's mouth in the second edition of the work in a fictional dialogue between Lessing and Herder. In the dialogue, Lessing is made to take up the defense of Spinoza against some unwarranted objections by Herder. He reproves the latter for wanting to attribute the power of representation to God, contrary to Spinoza's own opinion. Lessing's argument, as imagined by Jacobi, is that representation entails consciousness. But consciousness is nothing unless it is the consciousness of being. It must therefore presuppose this being, and must inevitably determine it or limit it by making it its object. Taken in itself, as the cause of all things or as God, being cannot exhibit a feature of which it is in fact the presupposed ground and by which it would be rendered finite. Jacobi has Lessing ask Herder, "Does thought implant eyes into your God?"[63] – a memorable turn of phrase, because we shall find it again in Fichte. Mendelssohn, we repeat, would have found it totally incomprehensible. His strategy, even before the Jacobi imbroglio, had always been to bring Spinoza's thought in line with Leibniz's or, more precisely, with Leibniz's thought as interpreted by school metaphysics. Jacobi's intent, on the contrary, had been from the beginning to demonstrate that Leibniz's metaphysics, if consistently construed, leads straight to Spinozism. And he had been using Lessing's alleged Spinozism as an authoritative witness to the validity of his claim. He had already made this argument in the first edition of the Spinoza-Letters, and he was now buttressing it more firmly in the second edition. Among the many additions to the original text, he included a long disquisition on the subject of whether Leibniz had in fact derived his doctrine of the universal harmony of being from Spinoza himself.

These scholarly excursions aside (which, again, do not interest us in the present context), the main reason Jacobi could not accept Mendelssohn's strategy regarding Spinoza is that, on the standard scholastic understanding of Leibniz, possibility is prior to, and even exceeds, actuality. A thing is actual only to the extent that it is, in the first place, possible. And one can think of unrealized possibilities – that is, of possibilities that are held in check by the realization of other, inherently more possible, ones. To Spinoza, however, any such line of argument would have been anathema, since it posits a distinction between the actual and the possible that in turn implies – in defiance of the first principle of all thought – that being is affected by 'nothing'. On his position, actuality is, on the contrary, prior to possibility. Indeed, nothing is possible unless, and to the extent that, it is already actual. God is *causa sui*, an infinite source of actuosity in which all things that only *might* be, when considered from the standpoint of representational cognition, or only *will* be already actually are. All talk of yet unrealized, or even unrealizable, possibilities is only the function of human ignorance. Either Leibniz's Monadology, therefore, is brought into line with Spinoza's thought or it runs into absurdity. Either God's idea of all possible worlds that constitute, according to Leibniz's *Theodicy*, the ground of the actuality of our present world is only a conceptual construct – in which case Leibniz is led back to Spinoza – or, if the distinction between possibility and actuality is seriously maintained, Leibniz is guilty of transgressing the principle *gigni de nihilo nihil, in nihilum nil potest reverti*, which he accepts as much as Spinoza.

The issue of human freedom arises in this context. If, according to Spinoza, nothing is possible unless it is already actual, then any idea of a freely undertaken action loses all meaning. It loses meaning even if understood in Ulrich's and Schmid's minimalist sense of a de facto necessary act that is nonetheless accompanied by the idea that it could possibly have been otherwise. And it would be positively absurd in Reinhold's sense of arbitrary self-determination. At best, freedom means every existing thing's tendency to maintain itself in existence. It is the *conatus* of existence, the expression of its actuosity. Any other conception would have to depend on the limitations of representational cognition. It would be in effect the product of ignorance regarding the actual causes of actions. Already in the first edition of the Spinoza–Letters, in an interpolated fictional dialogue between himself and Spinoza, Jacobi represents the latter as rejecting offhand all the accepted philosophical theories of freedom. The one, however, that he has Spinoza reject with special odium is precisely the one that was at the time typical of school metaphysics and that Ulrich was shortly to restate in its crispest form. For the theory commits a double sin. On the one hand, it does not deliver what it promises, since all actions are according to it predetermined *in fact* and any alternative scenario that an agent envisages in the moment of acting, or ex post facto, is a mere hypothetical play of abstract concepts. On the other hand, it locates the source of this necessity of action in the wrong place. It posits it on the side of an agent's intended ends, thus making this source of necessity depend on the special efficacy that some of these ends allegedly have, though still merely possible and *as possible*, to affect an agent's conduct. But this is again to give possibility priority over actuality. The source of the necessity should be sought, rather, in the actuosity of the causes driving an action from behind. All causality is, according to Spinoza, efficient causality. This applies first and foremost to God's all-pervasive efficacy. It applies as well, however, to the kind of causality that we witness in the world of spatiotemporal events when we consider them in abstraction from any reference to God. Everything that happens is mechanically driven *ab ante* from external anterior causes.

"Under 'mechanism'," Jacobi says, "I include every concatenation of purely efficient causes. Such a concatenation is *eo ipso* a *necessary* one, just as a necessary concatenation, *qua* necessary, is by that very fact a *mechanistic* one."[64] Jacobi's argument in defense of the thesis that 'man has no freedom' is based on the assumption that human affairs are organized according to precisely this definition of mechanism. In defending the thesis (only hypothetically, of course), Jacobi follows Spinoza closely. The mechanism at issue applies to the cognitive side of man just as much as it applies to his bodily side. Consciousness, or representational being, is only a mirror of extended being. Whatever happens in the latter is repeated on the side of thought, though it does so according to thought's own modality of existence. Thus, according to Jacobi, syllogistic thinking is mechanistic in nature, being driven by principles *ab ante* no less than any corporeal sequence of events.[65] Between this system of mechanical causes – be they extended or representational – and the system of freedom that Jacobi then proceeds to develop in another twenty-nine paragraphs, there is, as he contends, no middle ground.[66] Here Jacobi seems to be repeating Ulrich's injunction against trying to force a third way between determinism and indeterminism. But he is in fact saying something quite different. For the system of freedom that he will defend has nothing to do with the indeterminism that Ulrich denies. This indeterminism is the denial of *Ulrich's* 'determinism' and is conceptually dependent on it. Whether one accepts this indeterminism or denies it, it makes sense (or nonsense) only if one assumes the idea that a universal mechanism of being is possible in the first place. If Jacobi were to state his position in these terms, he would be playing into the hands of his naturalist adversaries, thus making the same mistake that Reinhold was to make in his debate with Schmid. The middle ground that Jacobi is now denying is rather between freedom as he understands it and the philosophers' conception of both determinism and indeterminism. His goal is to escape the whole philosophical conceptual framework within which the issue of human freedom has traditionally been debated.

But exactly what did Jacobi mean by freedom? How did he defend the thesis 'Man has Freedom'? And why, in order to make his point, should he have taken the trouble, to Mendelssohn's great mystification and to that of many others as well, of defending Spinoza – of all philosophers the one who had denied human freedom most unequivocally and consequentially? We shall take up this second question first. The answer will lead directly back to the first.

4.4.2 Of Human Freedom

The first and most obvious reason that explains Jacobi's predilection for Spinoza is the one already repeatedly stated. Spinoza was a consistent philosopher, unafraid to carry the principles of conceptualization to their logical conclusions. But there were other reasons as well, clearly discernible in the second edition of the Spinoza-Letters. On at least three counts, Spinoza stood in Jacobi's mind on the same side as Leibniz in opposition to Descartes. First, contra Descartes and in accordance with Leibniz, Spinoza had refused to identify extension with space (357ff.). He had not defined bodies as mere spatial relations, unlike Descartes, who in so doing had thereby reduced them to mere passive states incapable of robust individuation. Jacobi faults Herder in this context for thinking that Spinoza had uncritically accepted Descartes's concept of extension. On the contrary, Jacobi claims, Spinoza's concept, just as much as Leibniz's, had been developed as a criticism of Descartes's. Extension, according to both Spinoza and Leibniz, is something inherently active, an expression of the actuosity of all things that drives each to try to usurp the space of others, and at the same time to resist a similar attempt on the part of

these others against it (368). The individuation of things is defined by
the measure of the resistance that each can muster in opposition to the
rest. Contrary to the standard view, Jacobi was claiming that Leibniz's
principle of individuation was directed against Descartes and not against
Spinoza.

Second, just as Leibniz had done, Spinoza had opposed Descartes's
dualism. The mind and the body constitute for him an indivisible whole,
to such an extent that one cannot think of one without thinking of the
other.[67] This is also Leibniz's position, according to Jacobi, despite some
texts that seem to indicate the contrary. With his usual scholarly attention
to detail, Jacobi argues at length that the disputed texts were meant by
Leibniz only as hypotheses contrary to fact, as arguments *per impossibile.*
There is no doubt, as he concludes, that for Leibniz mind and body are
coextensive. This, incidentally, was also the upshot of the theory of reason,
conceived as a more complex and refined form of sense, that, as we have
seen, Jacobi had developed in *David Hume* only two years before in opposition to Kant. However much the theory in the dialogue echoed themes
drawn from Thomas Reid, and though Jacobi had attributed it there to
Leibniz, it clearly bore the marks of Spinoza's influence. Yet, there is a
sense, as Jacobi recognizes, that Spinoza's monism is more unequivocal
than Leibniz's, at least inasmuch as, according to Spinoza, the attributes
of thought and extension are identical *in re,*[68] since each is identical with
God; and the 'thoughts' and 'desires' that are the finite modes of the
attribute thought are, again according to Spinoza, only the conscious
representations of bodily states. They are the reflections, that is, of the
finite modes of the attribute extension.

Third, from both Spinoza and Leibniz, Jacobi had learned where to
find, and how to define, human freedom. This might seem indeed a
strange thing to say after Jacobi's repeated claim that Spinoza's system
is the perfect example of a conceptual framework that leaves no room
for human agency. In Jacobi's complex mental universe, however, the
shift back and forth between endorsing and rejecting his two mentors,
Spinoza and Leibniz, comes quite naturally. At the moment, Jacobi's argument is that, if it is the case that the individuation of things, as one
learns from Spinoza and Leibniz, is constituted by the play of action
and reaction holding them together, or, to retrieve a theme of *David
Hume,* if it is the case that the finite I acquires identity only when confronted by a Thou, then, just as there could not be any such interplay
unless one assumes a source of 'passivity' in everyone engaged in it, so
one must equally assume in them a countervailing source of 'activity'.

This source is irreducible. It follows that activity and passivity must be assumed as running across every part of the world we know. In some parts, the one element might well display a greater degree of intensity than the other; nowhere, however, can either element crowd out the other totally. It also follows that, though mechanism is both possible and necessary, a totally mechanistic organization of things that would *eo ipso* allow no room for individual freedom, that is, one that would reduce all things to external relations, is an impossibility, for it would in fact reduce things to mere nothingness. It would make them totally passive. Passivity, however, has no meaning except in relation to activity. The conceptual basis for denying the reality of individually attributable human acts is thus removed.

As Jacobi says:

[Proposition] XXIV. It is undeniable that the existence of all finite things rests on coexistence, and that we are not in a position to form the representation of a being that subsists completely on its own. It is equally undeniable, however, that we are even less in a position to form the representation of an absolutely dependent being. Such a being would have to be entirely passive. Yet it **could** not be passive, since anything that is not already something cannot simply be **determined** to be something; in what has no property, none can be generated simply through relations; indeed, not even a relation is possible with respect to it. (xxxv)

XXV. But if a completely mediated existence or being is not conceivable but is a non-thing, then a completely mediated, i.e., wholly mechanistic, **action**, is equally a non-thing: hence mechanism is **in itself** only something accidental, and it must everywhere have a **purely autonomous activity** at its foundation. (xxxv–xxxvi)

XXVI. Since we recognize that in its existence, and consequently also in its action and passion, every finite thing is necessarily supported by other finite things to which it relates, we must equally recognize the subjugation of each and every individual being to mechanistic laws. For, to the extent that its being and action is **mediated**, to that extent it must absolutely rest on the laws of mechanics. (xxxvi)

Why, then, has Jacobi been relying on Spinoza for his account of a purely mechanistic organization, when it would seem that Spinoza's conception of bodies, which is contrary to Descartes's and in accordance with Jacobi's own, defies such an organization? Why the shift back against Spinoza? For this, we must return to the first reason that explains Jacobi's predilection for the otherwise much maligned philosopher. Of all the philosophers, Spinoza was the most consistent. More than any other, he had pressed to an extreme the philosopher's appetite for explanation. And that meant, in effect, that he had wanted to conceptualize everything with reference to something else; to 'mediate' everything, in other words, or to return to a thing always by way of an external medium, and to extend this process to a point at which nothing is left in the explanandum that has not been dissolved into external references. At that point, of course, all things are reduced to nothing. Thus, though Spinoza had well understood the nature of the vital forces that make for the individuation of things, his passion for explanation had led him to poise these things, so to speak, between two abstractions – 'abstractions', that is, from Jacobi's point of view. On the one hand, when taken in their immediate individuality (as 'real', according to Jacobi), these things are considered by Spinoza to be partial views ('abstractions', from *Spinoza's* point of view) of the one infinitely extended concatenation of causes that would explain them completely. On the other hand, when thus dissolved in this explanatory chain, they are rescued from nothingness by being recaptured, so to speak, by the other abstraction ('abstraction' according to *Jacobi*, this time), namely, by the one substance whose infinite actuosity is, according to Spinoza, the only true reality, and that explains all things in toto precisely by not explaining any of them in particular. The net result, in Jacobi's view, is that real things are made to hover between two abstractions – abstractions that Jacobi thinks, on the contrary, should rather be understood with reference to them.

This 'philosophical reason' that tries to conceptualize everything by way of mediation is itself, according to Jacobi, a conscious reflection of life. As Jacobi says:[69]

The principle of all cognition is living being; living being proceeds from itself, it is progressive and productive. The stirring of a worm, its sluggish pleasure or displeasure, could not arise without an imagination holding [such stirrings] together according to the laws of the worm's principle of life, and producing a representation of its state. The more manifold the felt existence that a being generates in this way, the more *alive* is such a being. (402)

The faculty of abstraction and language arouses the need for a more complete perception, a more manifold connection. A world of reason thus arises in which signs and words take the place of substances and forces. We appropriate the universe by tearing it apart and creating a world of *pictures*, ideas, and words that is proportionate to our powers but quite unlike the real one. We understand perfectly what we thus create to the extent that it is our creation. And whatever does not allow being created in this way, we do not understand. Our philosophical understanding does not reach beyond its own creation. All understanding comes about, however, by the fact that we *posit* distinctions and then *supersede* them. Even the most developed human reason is not capable *(explicite)* of any other operation than this, and all the rest refer back to it. *Perception, recognition, and conception* make up *in ascending order* the complete range of our intellectual faculty (403).

[Reason's] general occupation is the progressive making of combinations; its **speculative** occupation is the making of combinations according to recognized laws of necessity, that is to say laws of **identity**, for reason has no concept of any necessity except the one that it establishes itself by means of its progressive and unrelenting process of separating and reuniting, by alternately retaining and letting go and finally displaying this necessity in identical propositions. But the essential indeterminacy of human language and designation, and the mutability of sensible shapes, almost universally allows these propositions to acquire an external appearance of saying more than the mere *quidquid est, illud est;* of expressing more than a mere *factum* which was at some point perceived, observed, compared, recognized, and joined to other concepts. Everything that reason can produce through division, combination, judgement, inference, and reflection, is simply a natural thing. Reason too, as restricted being, belongs among these things. The whole of nature, however, the sum-concept of all conditional beings, cannot reveal more to the searching understanding than what is contained in it, namely, manifold existence, alterations, play of forms – never an **actual** beginning; never a **real** principle of some **objective** existence. (421)

I have cited Jacobi at length, because here we see him retrieving, but also transcending, the theme that he had already developed in *David Hume* but that, as we saw then, had landed him in the rather embarrassing position of flirting with naturalism. Jacobi now wards off this danger by using Spinoza to reaffirm the diagnosis of what is wrong with 'philosophical reason' that he had originally expounded in the first edition of the Spinoza-Letters. To be sure, human cognition is an extension of human life. This is the burden of the vitalism defended in *David Hume* and inspired by none other than Spinoza. But, life as reconstructed conceptually – in effect, mechanistically, as Spinoza wanted – falls short of the life that performs this conceptual reconstruction using reason as an instrument. As Jacobi argues, there is already something nonmechanistic in the very process of representation (429) – something that the reconstruction itself fails to capture precisely because it lies at its origin. This something is the unconditioned that everything conditioned presupposes, without which the very idea of calling something conditional would not arise. It is the irreducibly active, without which the sense of passive constriction would also not arise. It is what we constantly presuppose yet cannot comprehend, because, if made the object of a concept, it would be *eo ipso* falsified. As Jacobi says, "should the concept of what is thus unconditional and unconnected, hence **extra-natural**, ['extra-natural' since 'nature' is defined by the concatenation of things] ever become **possible**, then the unconditional would cease to be unconditional; it must itself receive conditions; and the **absolutely necessary** must begin turning into a **possibility**, so as to allow **construction**" (425–6).

That which escapes the concatenation of things as reconstructed in representation, but is presupposed by this reconstruction, is by that very fact incomprehensible. Though it is incomprehensible, however, it does not follow that we are not aware of it or that we do not have a broadly understood nonconceptual knowledge of it. Jacobi says that reason need not despair on this account (418). For we have immediate evidence of that which escapes this concatenation in everything we do. It is demonstrated in the very impulse that leads reason to search for a complete explanation of things, and thus to embark on the relentless regression from cause to cause in which human science consists and that, short of short-circuiting the whole process by means of empty abstractions, cannot in principle ever be brought to an end (417ff.). The human being, according to Jacobi, could not undertake this impossible task were he not to feel dissatisfied with the things of nature surrounding him, and were he not to seek futilely in them a reality that is in fact already in him and that transcends both him and the things of nature. This transcendent reality, Jacobi says, "cannot be apprehended by us in any way except as it is given to us, *as fact – IT IS.*" And he continues, "This Supernatural, this Being of all beings, all tongues proclaim *God*" (427).

What is said of God also applies, with due modifications, to human freedom. It too is incomprehensible, since it consists in that irreducible element of agency in the human individual that resists his being absorbed into the concatenation of natural events. If it were conceptualized, it would be *eo ipso* reduced to these latter and thereby falsified. But again, just as with God's presence in us, though freedom is not comprehensible, there is no lack of evidence for it. In the case of freedom, such evidence lies in conscience's efficacy to affect our conduct (xl) or, as Jacobi argues, drawing examples from classical antiquity, in the power that principles such as that of 'honor' equally have to motivate action. It is immediately evident, in both cases, that the human being can act autonomously, independently, and even in opposition to nature – that he cannot therefore be absorbed by the latter. To let Jacobi speak for himself:

XXXVIII. Absolutely autonomous activity excludes mediation; it is impossible that we should somehow cognize its inner being distinctly. (xxxvi)

XXIX. Hence the **possibility** of absolutely autonomous activity cannot be known; its **actuality** can be known, however, for it is immediately displayed in consciousness, and is demonstrated by the deed. (xxxvi–xxxvii)

XXX. This autonomous activity is called 'freedom' inasmuch as it can be opposed to, and can prevail over, the mechanism that constitutes the **sensible** existence of an individual being. (xxxvii)

XXXI. Among living beings we only know man to be endowed with the degree of self-conscious autonomous activity that brings the impetus and the calling to free actions with it. (xxxvii)

XXXII. So freedom does not consist in some absurd faculty to make decisions without grounds; even less does it consist in the choice of the most useful, or the choice of **rational desires**. For any such choice, even if it comes about according to the most abstract concepts, always still is a mere mechanistic event. On the contrary, this freedom consists essentially **in the independence of the will from desires**. (xxxviii)

By thus invoking the name of God and proclaiming human superiority over the mechanism of nature, Jacobi was rejoining the accepted tropes of German Enlightenment culture. It is important to note, however, that, unlike the many metaphysicians of the time who also accepted these tropes, Jacobi was not making himself vulnerable to critique of the Kantian type, for he refused to engage philosophers on their conceptual grounds. His strategy, as already suggested, was still the one he had used in his reported original encounter with Lessing, namely, to interrupt at some point the chain of philosophical argumentation, because it leads to conclusions contrary to the immediate evidence of one's own inner being. On the ground then of an unconceptualizable certainty that we call faith, one can perform that peculiar 'feet over head' jump, that *salto mortale*, that Jacobi had suggested to Lessing (a maneuver that should redress the typical position of a philosopher, since philosophers are given to walking on their heads) and thereby rejoin common sense on one's feet. In that new position, one was out of reach of any philosophical attack. In the second edition of the Spinoza-Letters, Jacobi portrays Lessing as actually agreeing to perform the maneuver, but only fictionally, since this portrayal appears at the conclusion of the imaginary dialogue between him and Herder on the subject of Spinozism (353).

That had been Jacobi's strategy in 1779 at the time of his conversation with Lessing,[70] and it was still his strategy in 1789, one decade later. In reaffirming it, Jacobi was in a way also redressing, as we have already suggested, his position in *David Hume*. For there, while defending in opposition to Kant what he took indeed to be the truth of Leibniz's and Spinoza's theory of mind, he had not known, so to speak, where and how to put an end to philosophical disquisition. In order to avoid the naturalism to which the theory, if unchecked, would have led him, he had to appeal to miracles, or the possibility of a divine revelation at the level of sensibility. It is now clear that the miracle, if one can call it that, is to be witnessed not externally in sensible objects, but internally in man's capacity in action to resist the tendencies of nature. But again, Jacobi was not thereby saying anything he had not said before. For, from the beginning in his reported conversation with Lessing, and even more explicitly in *David Hume*, the possibility of human agency had been his main preoccupation, and the supremacy of the witness of action over theoretical evidence his main point of doctrine. This is an aspect of Jacobi to be kept in mind, for it will appear again when Fichte comes on the scene.

4.5 JACOBI, REHBERG, AND REINHOLD VERSUS KANT

In much of the new text that was added to the second edition of the Spinoza-Letters, Jacobi has Herder in mind. He is annoyed by what he took to be the latter's half-baked Spinozism, just as, at the time of his encounter with Lessing, he had been annoyed by Goethe's new Spinoza-inspired poetic vision of reality. His particular point of attack is Herder's claim that one cannot attribute intelligence and personality to God – a claim possible, in Jacobi's mind, only if one has conceptualized both intelligence and personality naturalistically (read: philosophically). "The topic only deserves discussion," Jacobi says, "because the non-personal God is an absolute requirement of that poetical philosophy which likes to waver midway between theism and Spinozism, and which has found many followers amongst us" (338–9). To the end of his life, Jacobi was to wage a fight against this kind of 'poetical philosophy', whose chief proponent was eventually to be Schelling – though this is a subject that falls well outside the scope of the present study. Of more interest to us is that, in discussing Spinoza, Jacobi repeatedly introduces footnotes referring to Kant and pointing out the similarities between the two. He is implicitly elaborating on the point, already explicitly made in the

Appendix to *David Hume*, that, despite his claims of critical ignorance, Kant is still doing dogmatic metaphysics. In this respect, Jacobi and Rehberg, of course, agreed. But, to Kant's critical ignorance, Jacobi opposed his nonconceptual knowledge, a sort of knowing ignorance, while Rehberg opposed his skepticism. Reinhold, for his part, kept on adding determinations to the noumenal sphere that Kant had declared outside the bounds of human cognition while at the same time claiming ignorance of this sphere. It would appear, therefore, that the meaning of 'ignorance' or 'nonknowledge' was just as unsettled an issue in the debate on human freedom as was the meaning of 'knowledge'. We must now turn to this issue. As we shall see, it will lead to the question of the place of religion in human existence.

5

Kant's Moral System

[*The Critique of Pure Reason*] is a totally new science – one of which nobody has previously grasped even just the thought; of which even the mere idea was unknown; and to which nothing so far available is of any use.

Kant, *Prolegomena* (AK 4:262)

Accordingly, all metaphysicians are henceforth officially and legally re-lieved of their businesses, until they have satisfactorily answered the question: "*How are synthetic cognitions* a priori *possible?*"

Kant, *Prolegomena* (AK 4:278)

The debate on freedom did not stop where we left it in the previous chapter. The original Reinhold–Schmid controversy grew in scope with the publication of other books and reviews, and eventually acquired a new tone when Fichte entered on the scene. At one point, it degenerated into a nasty exchange of attacks and counterattacks between the new arrival and Schmid.[1] We shall resume the narrative in due time when introducing Fichte. First, however, we must consider the event of greatest intellectual significance that took place in the course of the debate. That was the publication in 1793 of Kant's *Religion within the Boundaries of Mere Reason*. The first part of the book, "Of the Radical Evil in Human Nature," had already been published the previous year in the *Berlin Monthly*. How it came to be published again, as the first part of a four-part volume, makes for an interesting story. In short, Kant found himself skirmishing against the Prussian censors. Since the story is well known, it need not detain us here.[2] Though the book was not deliberately intended by Kant to be a contribution to the ongoing debate but had been written, rather, as an effort on his part to add one more stone to his critical edifice,[3] it provided nonetheless a new rallying point for all the competing parties. We shall turn to it only at the end of this chapter. First, we must set the conceptual stage for the doctrine it propounds.

5.1 THE DOGMATISM OF THE CRITIQUE OF REASON

I spoke earlier of Kant's brilliant immodesty with reference to the innovative side of the Critique of Reason. But there is room to speak of an undue modesty as well, with reference this time to a conservative side that held the Critique hostage to the patterns of thought characteristic of *Popularphilosophie*. It was this side that exposed it to the misinterpretations and the criticism of friends and foes alike. We have already seen (Chapter 3) some effects of this conservativism in connection with the Transcendental Deduction. The Deduction ran into an impossible formalism that was in fact the consequence of Kant's acceptance of an empiricist concept of the senses. This formalism made the Deduction vulnerable to the same charges of skepticism that had already been a problem for classical empiricism. Any serious attempt, however, at overcoming this skepticism – in effect, at construing a model of the mind in which the distance between the formal I of reflection and the self of actual experience is successfully bridged – induced a slide into a more traditional (Leibnizian) conception of the senses and led as a consequence to a more naturalistic model of the mind. Jacobi and Reinhold, no less than the crowd of popular philosophers, were pulled in this direction. The problem is that on this model it was difficult to maintain the radical distinction between conceptualization and sensibility on which, on the contrary, the revolutionary character of the Critique of Reason depended. Kant's moral philosophy gave rise to a parallel problem – one that was at the heart of the debate regarding the nature of human freedom we have just detailed. How is one to conceive of the obligations imposed by the moral law if these obligations are to transcend the whole realm of sense-induced desires and yet are still to be effective in the shaping of actual human conduct? A suitable model of the 'moral individual' was now needed, and it was precisely in the construal of such a model that Kant's critics and commentators were at odds. How much Kant's own conceptual schemas stood in the way of satisfying this need, because of the still dogmatic modes of thought underlying them, can be seen, in the first instance at least, from the section of the *Critique of Pure Reason* that goes under the heading of "The Antimony of Pure Reason". This part of the *Critique* was likely one of the earliest composed by Kant, and one that helped him shape the rest of the work. It by no means contains his mature moral position. It was nonetheless the part from which his contemporaries derived their first clue regarding the critical theory of freedom by drawing upon the third of the four 'conflicts of reason' that Kant expounds in it. And, as we shall see, the logical difficulties affecting it will still be felt in his later, fully worked out treatment of this subject in the *Critique of Practical Reason*.

Kant's statement of his third alleged conflict of reason can be stated briefly as follows. It seems that as long as one restricts oneself (as one should indeed do in science) to the realm of temporal experiences, and considers causality in its schematized form as the necessary succession of events in time, there is no place in nature for a cause (call it 'transcendental', as Kant does), whose efficacy would not be dependent on an immediately prior cause but would rather originate with the assumed cause itself. The presence of this kind of transcendental causality, which we also call 'freedom', would disrupt the otherwise orderly sequence of events that we must presuppose in nature. Nature and freedom stand to one another as lawfulness to unlawfulness. The very idea of freedom must therefore be rejected (A445/B473–A451/B479). This is one possible and, within its limits, perfectly legitimate line of argument. According to Kant, however, another equally persuasive line is equally possible. Namely, unless there were at work in experience some principle such as freedom – that is, an absolutely spontaneous source of efficiency or, in other words, one whose efficacy originates with it immediately – there would be no end to the series of explanatory causes supporting any single event. But explanation requires completion. Without it, unity of experience would be unattainable. Freedom must therefore be presupposed (A444/B472–A450/B478).

On the face of it, the conflict as just defined is intractable, since both lines of argument start from well-established principles of explanation: the need to abide by the limitations of experience on the one hand, and the need for completeness of explanation on the other. Yet, as Kant continues to argue in great detail, the conflict can be resolved by relying on critical assumptions. One must keep in mind that spatiotemporal phenomena are not things in themselves but sense-representations and that, *in themselves*, things are neither spatial nor temporal but such as we cannot intuit and therefore cannot know. Kant had just resolved two other apparent conflicts of reason using precisely this critical distinction. Whether the cosmos is infinitely extended in space or has spatial limits, or, again, whether it has existed for an infinite period of time or has rather a beginning in time, are questions that Kant claims cannot be answered, not because we have no sufficient knowledge for dealing with them, but because they are in principle unanswerable. They are meaningless. Since they presuppose in phenomena the kind of full determination of being that only the things in themselves that we cannot intuit would have, they are misplaced. To be spatiotemporal means precisely *not* to have any intrinsic definite beginning or end, but to depend for such limits on an external observer. Spatiotemporal limits are by nature relative. Now, if one extends the consequences of this already invoked critical distinction between phenomena and thing in itself to the conflict presently at hand, and if one is also reminded that the schematized category of causality applies only to spatiotemporal events, a resolution can also be found to the conflict regarding freedom as well. This time, instead of denying the validity of the two opposing theses causing the conflict, one can grant instead that the two both have merit, provided, however, that the claim of each is limited so that the two do not intrude on one another. Strict determinism applies indeed to the realm of spatiotemporal phenomena, but, since these phenomena do not constitute the thing in itself, one can at least *think of* (without thereby presuming *to know*) a transcendental causality that is being exercised in the noumenal realm. One can thus think of an individual human agent whose actions, according to his character as a sense-determined being, are always explainable in accordance with the determinism of phenomena but who, inasmuch as he belongs according to his intelligible character to the world of the thing in itself, can nonetheless be deemed to cause his actions absolutely, and hence to be morally responsible for them. As Kant sums up his position:

In its empirical character, this subject, as appearance, would thus be subject to the causal connection, in accordance with all the laws of determination; and to this extent it would be nothing but a part of the world of sense, whose effects, like those of any other appearance, would flow inevitably from nature. [...] But in its intelligible character (even though we can have nothing more than merely the general concept of it), this subject would nevertheless have to be declared free of all influences of sensibility and determination by appearances. [...] Of it one would say quite correctly that it begins its effects in the sensible world **from itself**, without its action beginning **in it** itself (A540/B568–A541/B569).

On this ideal construal, one would have thus satisfied at one and the same time a number of conditions essential to experience:

(1) the theoretical interest of reason in completeness of explanation (the principle of causality is applied strictly to all realms of being,

whether phenomenal or noumenal, though in each with a different sense);

(2) the practical interest of reason in allowing for a line of causality that originates absolutely with an agent, and whose effects can thus be imputed to the agent unqualifiedly (as noumenal, causality is conceived as freedom of action);

(3) the critical interest of reason in retaining a connection between ideal constructions and actual experiences. Though these constructions do not add to our knowledge of the objects of experience, they are nonetheless of relevance in the process of explaining them. As Kant says, "As long as we, with our concepts of reason, have as our object merely the totality of the conditions of the world of sense, and what service reason can perform in respect to them, our ideas are transcendental but still **cosmological**" (A565/B593).

In brief, inasmuch as Kant had indeed resolved the otherwise intractable conflict between the scientific claims of determinism and the moral claims of freedom, and had achieved this feat by denying to each set of claims the standing they would have in dogmatic metaphysics, he would have fulfilled Rehberg's initial intention, as we remember, of insulating ethics from metaphysics ('dogmatic metaphysics', as Kant now calls it) in order to protect it from the vagaries of the latter while at the same time retaining the vital connection between ethics and experience. It is this result that from the start had appealed especially to the Jena theologians who were Kant's first followers. It was based on the denial of knowledge of things transcendent, coupled with the assertion that it is possible, indeed even existentially necessary, at least to *think of* such things without logical contradiction in order to attain theoretical as well as practical coherence of experience. But was Kant's strategy truly free of logical incoherence, and did it truly deliver the unity of experience that it promised? One could legitimately raise serious doubts.

5.1.1 Logical Issues: What Can I Know?

Kant's idea of a line of causality that originates absolutely with an agent free of spatiotemporal limitations, but that has effects subject to such limitations, is the one that Ulrich found particularly difficult to swallow.[4] Kant himself did not pretend to have demonstrated its real possibility. He claimed only that it was free from internal contradiction and that it had subjective validity as a principle of systematic unity. The idea permitted the unqualified attribution of an action to an agent by making the latter its direct and absolute source and thus allowed one to hold the agent responsible for the action. This sense of 'responsibility' is essential to morality. Kant believed that it could not be saved without assuming that the whole realm of moral action is autonomous with respect to nature, totally independent of spatiotemporally conditioned causality. In this he was taking a clear stand in opposition to the traditional metaphysics of which Ulrich was just one of the latest exponents. As Kant says:

> The **ought** expresses a species of necessity and a connection with grounds which does not occur anywhere else in the whole of nature. In nature the understanding can cognize only **what exists,** or has been, or will be, It is impossible that something in it **ought to be** other than what, in all these time–relations, it in fact is; indeed, the **ought,** if one has only the course of nature before one's eyes, has no significance whatever. We cannot ask at all what ought to happen in nature, any more than we can ask what properties a circle ought to have, but we must rather ask what happens in nature, or what properties the circle has. (A547/B575)

One can sympathize with Kant on this score. However gradually and imperceptibly one interpolates the full sense of an *ought* within a narrative that is otherwise about things that simply *are,* or events that simply *occur,* the interpolation is bound in the end to be surreptitious. The *ought* entails a break from the *is* that precludes any simple slide from this last back to it. Of course, some might dispute the claim. Ulrich did, and the modern compatibilists who are his conceptual descendants still do.[5] No matter. Important here is Kant's reason for advancing his claim. The force of an *ought* in directing action is, according to Kant, purely intelligible or ideal. It is based on a representation of reality not as the latter happens to be, but as it might possibly be according to requirements that reason itself dictates and that nature cannot deliver on its own. The *ought* does not derive the norm of conduct it proclaims from nature (as was claimed in traditional Leibnizian-style metaphysics) but instead subjects nature itself to a norm that transcends it. Whatever the influence Rousseau might have had on Kant at some point in his life,[6] Kantian morality (at least in its critical form) is definitely unnatural. The moral idea of humanity is a work of conceptual art rather than of nature. To cite Kant again:

> However many natural grounds or sensible stimuli there may be that impel me to **will,** they cannot produce the **ought** but only a willing that is yet far from necessary but rather always conditioned, over against which the ought that reason pronounces sets a measure and goal, indeed, a prohibition and authorization. Whether it is an object of mere sensibility (the agreeable) or even of pure reason

(the good), reason does not give in to those grounds that are empirically given, and it does not follow the order of things as they are presented in intuition, but with complete spontaneity it makes its own order according to ideas, to which it fits the empirical conditions and according to which it even declares actions to be necessary that yet **have not occurred** and perhaps will not occur, nevertheless presupposing of all such actions that reason could have causality in relation to them; for without that, it would not expect its ideas to have effects in experience. (A548/B576)

Kant's originality lies precisely here. To Spalding – if we can imagine him conversing with the theologian – to his question regarding the vocation of humankind, Kant would have replied that 'humanity' is not to be found ready-made in nature, but is rather an ideal to be construed according to norms dictated by the requirements of rationality in general. This is not to say that one should not engage in Spalding's kind of self-reflection, or not take stock of the inclinations that one finds within oneself, or not be mindful of the wisdom of the age. Any such self-reflection, however, is itself a product of reason from the start and is itself motivated by the interests of reason. It is not a matter of discovering one's human place in a given, God-created cosmos, as was was the case for Spalding, but rather of establishing the value of any such already existing cosmos insofar as humankind is concerned. Extant inclinations and past experiences are to be judged for their moral value precisely on the basis of their contribution to the human ideal.

Kant's break from the metaphysical tradition is, on this score, final.[7] Yet, it is when one takes the break seriously that Kant's inconsistencies in following through with its consequences show all the more strikingly. On his stated moral assumption, freedom loses whatever connotations of physical efficacy it might otherwise have. It has nothing to do, at least not in the first instance, with any capacity to alter one's given physical situation or to initiate a physical event absolutely. Certainly nobody is free to have not been born, and, at least so far as the technology in Kant's and still in our own age goes, nobody is free to not die at some point in the future. But one is nonetheless free to interpret the meaning that such events as 'being born' and 'dying' have in one's life. In a moral context, freedom consists essentially in a capacity derived from reason to establish values and meanings. The only norms limiting this capacity are the limits of meaning itself. To be sure, even within these boundaries there are limitations due to already established cultural settings and personal histories. Rehberg, for one, was keenly aware of these limitations. However, reason retains this capacity for reflection, and by extension a capacity to transcend such limitations by placing them intentionally in an ever-expanding context. Its effectiveness is 'ideal', which is exactly how Kant defines it. Its product is a new nature established ideally in the medium of intentionality; it establishes a new level of spontaneity and a consequent new sphere of intentional action. It is only by equivocating on the meaning of 'causality' that, in the resolution of the third alleged conflict of reason, Kant could maintain, on the strength of his distinction between appearances and thing in itself, that he had at one and the same time both allowed for the at least logical possibility of freedom – understood as some sort of hyperphysical cause capable of initiating a series of events absolutely – *and* provided a principle for the systematic unity of all experience.[8] Rather, the thing in itself became irrelevant as a principle of moral action as defined by Kant precisely to the extent that it was conceived in the manner of Spinoza's *causa sui*, as Kant was at times inclined to do, or in the manner of Leibniz's creator God. To the extent that it is, on the contrary, an effective principle of morality, it does not lie outside experience, for its effectiveness should be clearly recognizable in the difference that it makes in the day-to-day experience of things. In that case, the thing in itself is nothing but reason itself. In brief, Kant cannot have it both ways. The thing in itself cannot be at once principle "transcendental but still **cosmological**."

The issue here is one of conceptual coherence, not of knowledge. 'Critical ignorance' has no place here. Any claim to it is a show of undue modesty. On the one hand, Kant has already satisfied in principle any queries regarding the source of the norms that guide moral life. 'Reason', 'rational reflection', are at the origin of morality. An answer of this kind appears unsatisfactory only if one assumes a radically reductionist program and denies that such things as 'values' are definable on their own – that is, that these values are subject to an internal logic that is by itself sufficient to explain human conduct, since the latter, precisely *as human*, unfolds in the medium of idealizations. Such a denial would require that all moral language be translated into the language of physics before issues of truth or falsity can be raised with respect to it. Kant was, however, trying to resist precisely this kind of reductionism, and objected to the typical 'compatibilism' (as we would call it nowadays) of popular philosophy on the ground that, despite all good intentions, it was a slippery slope to reductionism. On the other hand, inasmuch as Kant did think of freedom, with reference to the thing in itself, as a cosmological principle that would both justify (but only hypothetically) the moral language of freedom and bring experiences (but only ideally) to systematic unity, he was himself engaging in a program of reductionism. It was a peculiar form of it (call it ideal, perhaps) but reductionism nonetheless. The message is that ideally, if one could just intuit the thing in itself, everything would be reduced to a system of ironclad hyperphysical determinism.[9] Kant was saying too much. Albeit only hypothetically, he still conceived of the thing in itself after the model of classical metaphysics and still used this conception for his own systematic purposes. He would, if he just could (but knows he cannot), consider things *sub specie æterni*.

Kant's strange ruminations, already cited in Chapter 1, can only be explained on the assumption that he still thought of the human individual as acting out, even when engaged in moral action, a preappointed hyperphysical order of which he, however, knows nothing determinate. The thought that, if we could just intuit things intellectually and see them as they truly are, that is caught up in an inescapable web of causal determinations – this thought, according to Kant, should bolster our hope that the order we are trying to achieve morally in the visible world is in fact being realized. Or again, ignorance about the true order of things is a blessed ignorance, for if we just knew how things truly are in themselves, there would be no point to the moral strivings that otherwise animate our earthly existence. Kant is still talking about 'morality' in these passages. Yet one has reason to wonder how, in the context of things that according to him might be intuited intellectually, the word has any meaning left at all – least of all the meaning on which Kant insists in order to retain the full sense of the ought. Perhaps Rehberg had a point. Kant had not sufficiently insulated ethics from metaphysics. As a result, he found himself justifying the human situation in a spirit that reminds one of the Venice of the doges, where accused criminals were tried in secret and kept in the dark regarding their decreed punishment, having been given the excuse that if they knew what they had been convicted of and the sentence meted out to them, they would despair at never seeing the light of day again. But despair is a sin deserving of eternal damnation.[10]

It might be objected that this is a misrepresentation of Kant – one that misses, moreover, the full meaning of his critical revolution. One must keep in mind – so it can be argued – that Kant's brilliant critical move was to conceive reason *formally*, that is, as a self-legislating faculty of intentional activities. Such activities can be conceived, on the one hand (i.e., practically), to be directed at establishing a nature according to the requirements of reason as stipulated by the ought; on the other hand (i.e., theoretically), at discovering this nature as already given. In this latter respect, precisely in order to recognize nature *as given*, reason must expect its events to be ordered according to strict mechanical causality. Finally, in order to retain its own formal requirement of explanation in general, reason also stipulates as an overarching principle its purely formal law of causality in general. There is no contradiction involved if one combines under this last principle reason's two other sets of norms, since reason's activities are purely intentional and its norms purely formal.[11] Contradiction arises only if these norms are understood dogmatically or as conveying a material determination of reality. Then there arises indeed the problem of reconciling freedom with determinism – a problem that is the philosophical counterpart of the tension generated in the Christian myth of creation by the juxtaposition of the image of God as the almighty and the image of the human creature as willfully disobeying his law. Classical metaphysics, whether in its more nuanced Leibnizian form or in the more transparent one we find in Ulrich and many others, played down the second side of the tension, in effect denying the irreducibility of moral evil. Now, Kant was by no means religious in any traditional sense. Indeed, according to his most recent biographer, he could be impatient with religion.[12] Yet he was the one who saved Christian belief in human freedom in its full sense, at least at the practical level where it counts most. And he did it, paradoxically, by expunging metaphysics of its still Christian imagery or, in other words, by demythologizing it. Kant's interest ultimately lay in the system of norms that govern the day-to-day conduct of human beings, as well as in the norms that regulate the praxis of scientific discovery. While not denying the value of speculation, he wanted at least to bracket metaphysics in a Tory spirit reminiscent of Rehberg's in order to prevent its domestic problems from interfering with our understanding of the process of experience. As he said in a footnote to the *Prolegomena*:

High towers and metaphysically-great men who resemble them, around both of which there is usually much wind, are not for me. My place is the fertile *bathos* of experience; and the word transcendental [...] does not signify something that surpasses all experience but something that indeed precedes experience *(a priori)*, but that, all the same, is destined to nothing more than solely to make cognition from experience possible.[13]

This is a strong and fair objection. It only helps, however, to restate in a more focused form the specifically critical problem that affects the Critique of Reason. Granted Kant's purely formal conception of reason, there is still a conceptual obligation to define how the two sets of intentional activities in which reason engages (the practical and the theoretical) relate to one another and respect each other's boundaries within the same mental universe. Kant's explicitly stated belief is that practical science determines the goal of theoretical science. Moral interests come first in the order of intention.[14] Fichte took this position to mean, as we shall see, that it is an individual human being's moral obligation to conceive of nature, his body included, as an organization of mechanically determined forces. This obligation, motivated by reason's interest to promote the cause of freedom, also provided Fichte with the justification for a political order in which the behavior of all its members, whether individual or collective, can be predicted with the same accuracy as the workings of a machine. Kant would not have wanted to tread this path. He is, however, still under the conceptual obligation to define, however formally, the relation of theoretical to practical norms. Whatever definition he might offer in this regard will have little pragmatic value for his desired fruitful immersion in the 'bathos of experience' unless it is translated into a concrete model of the moral individual who abides by moral norms in a supposed naturally conditioned world. Now, in matters of moral action, one cannot afford, as one might in a theoretical setting, to suspend judgment as to whether a certain situation is true or a certain line of action valid. Suspension of judgment itself constitutes a special kind of moral commitment. Reductionism or nonreductionism, or even a refusal to choose between the two, translate into different qualities of moral life. One can claim to be dealing in mere empty words – in which case there would be consequences indeed even for our understanding of scientific explanation, let alone moral praxis. But unless this is the case, it is disingenuous to think that one can attribute to a single transcendental idea of causality moral as well as cosmological significance, however formally one takes this idea, without thereby already implicating reference to actual moral praxis and actual physical explanation – without, therefore, running up against the incompatibility of meanings that we find in Kant's resolution of the alleged third conflict of reason.

These considerations raise the issue of Kant's implicit moral commitment regarding the vocation of humankind or, in other words, his moral idea of human nature. What form must this idea take in order for Kant to have attributed moral significance to the 'myth' (for that's what it is) of a hyperphysical causality that also brings moral intentions to realization? This line of investigation leads directly to Kant's anthropology. We shall follow it in the second part of this chapter. At that time, we shall also confront Kant with the critics and commentators we met earlier. Of more immediate importance, however, is Kant's critical model of a moral individual and the formalism that affects it.

5.1.2 Practical Issues: What Must I Do?

5.1.2.1 Of 'Law' and 'Duty'. The conceptual foundations of Kantian moral theory, though puzzling to Kant's contemporaries, were just as clear as they were brilliant. Their underlying basic intuition was that moral action, as contrasted with any other type of human conduct, is essentially *responsible* action, that is, action that originates with an agent absolutely and for which, therefore, the agent can be held responsible. This intuition is behind Kant's repeated claim that a subject is said to be morally good or bad not because of what he or she does materially (at least not primarily), but because of the spirit in which he or she performs the action in question. An action that appears according to its content to be virtuous, and would indeed be virtuous under different circumstances, can in fact be vicious when done for morally reprehensible motives. It is the moral character of an agent that determines the moral quality of his actions, not the other way around. If it were otherwise, the bond connecting agent and action would run the risk of being only accidental and the agent an 'agent' only in name.

On this particular point, Kant was not departing from long-standing scholastic moral theory that even antedated the German schools. In the *Summæ* of the theologians, in response to the question of whether the acquisition of virtue precedes virtuous action or whether, on the contrary, the performance of virtuous action institutes virtue in the first place, the commonly given reply was that the performance of actions that are morally good according to their effects precedes the acquisition of virtue materially (i.e., temporally); that formally virtue precedes virtuous action. A subject must indeed behave the right way, perhaps under the discipline of the rod, before he can interiorize the righteousness of the behavior in question. However, the subject's actions become *his* substantially and thus acquire the quality of virtue or vice formally only when righteous behavior has become habitual (a kind of second nature to him). As the moral adage went, one swallow does not make a spring; an action, by itself, is no indication of a subject's agency. Kant was still making this traditional point. The novelty of his theory (indeed, its revolutionary character) lay, however, in his further claim that what determines the moral righteousness of an agent, and of the agent's actions as a consequence, is the agent's commitment to upholding all the conditions that make for the maintenance of precisely this essential characteristic of moral conduct, namely, responsibility of action. This might sound like a purely formal, empty norm. And so it was indeed intended by Kant to be. Its formality, however, has wide-ranging material consequences, for it defines a new, very specific attitude on the part of the human being with respect to nature. According to traditional theory, nature sets the norm for right moral conduct. The task of moral action is therefore to take up intentions already at work in nature and to complete them in an agent's own life on the agent's own initiative. The agent's moral goal is to make his or her being conform to nature *responsibly*. Kant's point, on the contrary, is that there cannot be true responsibility of action unless the agent, rather than trying to conform to nature, distances himself from it instead by setting himself up as the one who legislates. In effect, he is the one who bestows moral meaning on it. The maintenance of the agent's autonomy (i.e., the agent's self-legislating capacity) is the overarching new value now being injected into an otherwise purely natural context. This value gives rise to a radically new, specifically moral system of ends to which any preexisting system of natural ends must be subordinated. Nature is now seen not as a source of morality but as a threat to it, since it is a possible source of heteronomy of action.

Many of Kant's contemporaries did not agree with this moral vision of Kant's. Many more, even when they claimed to agree with him, simply failed to understand it. In fairness to all, Kant himself, as we shall see in a moment, burdened his basic insight with extraneous claims that made the comprehension of it all the more difficult. The insight was nonetheless the one that governed his whole moral theory. In the *Groundwork of the Metaphysics of Morals* (1785), he tried to establish it analytically by demonstrating by way of a reflection on ordinary moral language that it in fact animates all moral experience. We say of an action that it is morally good only inasmuch as it proceeds from a 'good will', and a will is good absolutely only when it acts out of 'duty'.[15] Duty denotes an incontrovertible obligation to act in a certain way – 'incontrovertible' because, if the agent under its influence were not to abide by it, the agent's own sense of identity would be jeopardized. Duty is what one does because, all other factors considered, it is in the final analysis what is in one's character to do. In action motivated by duty, the agent's own agency is at issue. Upholding it is the ultimate determining motive of the action.

Kant was to make this same point again, but this time synthetically, in the *Critique of Practical Reason*, published shortly after the *Groundwork* (1788).[16] There, he proceeds, as if *more geometrico*, first by defining a number of key terms and then, on the basis of these definitions, by attempting to construct the concept of a law that, as law, would bind absolutely (i.e., without prior conditioning hypotheses). As is well known, and without having to rehearse the equally well known details of the argument, the concept that Kant comes up with is that of a law in which form and content coincide, or, as we might say by way of amplification, a law that sets up 'lawfulness' itself as the overriding value of moral life. Be lawful, for lawfulness is the value that defines your dignity as a rational being. This is the command that, according to Kant, gives rise to moral life. It expresses in formal terms the constant preoccupation with doing 'the right thing' that the concept of duty expresses in a more psychological mode. The right thing is defined by an imperative that trumps all more immediate interests even when its nature and origin remain subjectively obscure.

It might seem strange that, when developing an argument that was supposed to establish the first principle of his theory of morality, Kant applied a methodology that seemed to be borrowed from mathematics. This is all the more strange because of his repeated earlier warnings that the mathematical method has no place in philosophy.[17] Yet, Kant proceeds in the *Critique of Practical Reason* as if *more geometrico,* starting with the definition of what constitutes a 'principle' and then generating theorems and problems based on the given definition. And, on closer reflection, there is indeed a loose but nonetheless significant analogy between mathematics and morality as Kant conceives of both. In mathematics, one begins with the definition of an object construed on the basis of certain already assumed structural components. This definition, once set up and free of internal contradictions, establishes the intelligible boundaries within which certain problems can be raised about the object and valid solutions found for them (A713/B741ff.). Now, just as mathematical definitions establish a priori, by the very fact of being constructed, a sort of intelligible space that is the specialized domain for the exercise of certain conceptual activities, so the very conception of lawfulness in general establishes equally a priori the possibility of a new, qualitatively unique kind of human agency. The analogy between mathematical and moral argument lies precisely here, in the active engagement of thought in the production of the objects that both entail.

There are, however, crucial differences as well. Indeed, the disanalogy turns out to be even more instructive than the analogy. For one thing, mathematical thinking represents a very limited and specialized form of rationality, whereas practical reason, which is at the origin of morality, is reason operating in its most universal function as reason.[18] Moreover, however much a mathematical object might be in fact the product of thought itself, once constructed, it is taken as transcending thought, as if, in defining the object or in establishing its properties, thought were accessing a new level of *given* intelligibility and reading properties off a *given* object. As Kant puts it, in keeping with his critical model of experience, mathematics exhibits its objects in a priori sensible intuition (B16; B40–1). It is an essentially theoretical discipline. This is not the case with practical reason, in whose operations reason's rationality itself is at issue. Kant is making two claims here. The first is that reason is a faculty of reflective activity. It can make its own operations the objects of thought. As such, it can measure them, thereby establishing the possibility of normativity in general. This is an all-pervasive assumption in Kant, already transparent in the claim, pivotal to the *Critique of Pure Reason*, that every judgment is necessarily accompanied (potentially at least) by an 'I think that . . . ' Every judgment carries the measure of its own asserted truth. This is already true of theoretical reason, that is, reason that operates on the assumption of an already given reality. Kant's second claim is that, when reason operates in its full scope as a faculty of reflective activities, its one object, its unique contribution to experience, and the source of its special interest in all its operations is precisely its norm-setting capacity. Normativity is at once its product and, when reason functions precisely as reason, its overriding motivating interest in all its operations.[19]

When we understand Kant in this way, all the pieces of his moral theory fall into place (with one exception, as we shall see). There is, first, the question of Kant's much advertised 'deduction of the principle of pure practical reason'. Exactly where is this deduction? In the *Critique of Pure Reason*, Kant gave first a metaphysical deduction of the categories – in effect, an analytical exposition of the concept of an object in general – and then proceeded to justify ('deduce') this concept transcendentally by demonstrating that it is necessarily implicated in the experience of actual physical objects. As we remember, in this last enterprise Kant made himself vulnerable to a renewed attack by the skeptics. Now, in the *Critique of Practical Reason*, the construction (in quasi *more geometrico*) of the concept of lawfulness in general takes the place of the metaphysical deduction of the theoretical concept of an object in general. When we come, however, to the section that deals officially with the deduction of the law as the first principle of morality (AK V:42), we are referred back to the just completed construction,[20] with two added observations that Kant repeats in a variety of ways. The first is that the analytic of the Critique proves that pure reason can be practical (i.e., that the idea of the law is itself an effective principle of action) in virtue of 'a fact in which pure reason in us proves itself actually practical' (AK V:42). This 'fact of reason' is the law itself. "The moral law is given," Kant says, "as it were, as a fact of pure reason of which we are a priori conscious and which is apodictically certain, though it be granted that no example of exact observance of it can be found in experience" (AK V:47). It is significant that for fact, in this context, Kant uses the Latinate term *'Faktum'* rather than the more common German word *'Tatsache'*. *Factum* is in Latin a verbal noun, the past participle of the verb *'facere'*. For anyone in the know, the use of the Latin form would have brought out the verbal root of the term that is indeed also present in the German term *'Tatsache'* (and the English term 'fact', itself a Latinate word) but is likely to go unnoticed there. The law is a product of reason. It is a 'deed' that demonstrates its effectiveness precisely in being performed and thereby establishing a special mental universe (a *'Denkungsart'*, or a 'way of thinking') in which objects count as objects only as bearers of rationally recognizable values. Kant apparently believes that in principle, at least, being rational already constitutes this deed. Morality is therefore the natural condition (using 'natural' in a broad sense)[21] of humankind – witness the obsessive preoccupation (as I might gloss) with doing the right thing that affects every culture. The only task of philosophy is to bring this condition to explicit consciousness by construing the right concept of lawfulness. Only then are the foundations laid for a culture whose 'will' is not just rational but self-consciously rational.

The second observation is that the analytic part of the *Critique of Practical reason* has shown that "this fact [i.e., this *Faktum* of reason, or the Law, to be] is inseparably connected with, and indeed identical with, consciousness of freedom of the will" (AK V:42). Or again, it has shown that "the moral law, which itself has no need of justifying grounds, proves not only the possibility [of the faculty of freedom] but [its] reality in beings who cognize this law as binding upon them" (AK V:47). I leave aside for the moment the question of whether this concept of 'freedom' has any cosmological significance, as Kant seems to believe.[22] The important point now is that the language of freedom applies indeed to individuals inasmuch as they participate in that universe of meaning that is generated by the concept of lawfulness in general and within which otherwise merely physical things acquire new moral significance. To use a case that will be exploited by Kant himself for his conception of the juridical foundations of society, in this universe of meaning 'possession' is not just a matter of holding something in one's hand, but of holding it there 'legitimately'. Possession, in other words, acquires an intelligible character.[23] The language of freedom, rational choice, and responsibility has meaning only in the context of this presumed universe. Kant's deduction of the principle of morality simply consists in letting the law be its own witness to its efficacy (as *Faktum* or reason) in the generation of such a universe.

The form that the fundamental command of moral life assumes when it is based on the concept of Law is another piece of Kant's theory that falls into place. Kant actually gives different formulations of this command, which he thought, however, were equivalent. One formulation says, "*act only in accordance with that maxim through which you can at the same time will that it become a universal law,*"[24] or, in what is likely only a variant of the same, "*act as if the maxim of your action were to become by your will a* **universal law of nature**" (AK IV:421). Another, distinctly different formula is this: "*so act that you use humanity, whether in your person or in the person of any other, always as end, never merely as a means*" (AK IV:429). Now, a 'maxim', according to Kant, is a counsel of action that has been interiorized in a subject and therefore constitutes in the latter an immediate and compelling disposition to act in a certain way. Kant's point is that, inasmuch as the Law has been interiorized in an individual human being, it generates in him a radically new and compelling disposition to act with respect to both nature and other human beings. With respect to nature, the moral agent must consider himself as independent from it, as self-legislating; and hence under the added obligation of legislating for it as well in full recognition that he is re-creating it anew for moral purposes.[25] With respect to other human beings, since each is to be considered autonomous, any law issued by any of them would have to be such that any other would also legislate it. It is the interest of humanity in general, in other words, that must be the determining factor in any form of legislation. Whether with respect to nature or other human beings, the moral legislator must thus consider himself as instituting, and at the same time acting within, a Kingdom of Ends. Here another piece of Kant's moral theory falls into place. It is the idea of a Kingdom of Ends that Kant found especially fruitful (AK IV:433). The moral agent acts within the compass of an intelligible universe[26] – in effect, a rational culture that is the creation of the moral agent. Kant admits that the teleology of nature must be empirically determined and that nature can never be fully explained teleologically. Nevertheless, he believes that since "there are pure practical reasons that determine reason *a priori* and give ends to reason *a priori*,"[27] the moral agent must presume that this system of a priori ends, though uncomprehended by him, brings the otherwise incomplete teleology of nature to moral completion (AK V:445, 448).

The point to stress is that the force with which the fundamental law of morality (the 'categorical imperative') imposes itself on the human agent, or, in more psychological language, this agent's inescapable sense of being beholden to duty, is not, according to Kant, something that the agent can choose at will. The very idea of the Law or, if that idea is not yet at hand, the very fact of being rational gives rise to it. The Law is effective in originating moral disposition. And nowhere is Kant's claim about this efficacy of the Law as strong and incontrovertible as in his treatment of a moral agent's disposition with respect to the nature that is the closest to him, namely, his sensibility. The last, but by no means least, piece of Kant's moral theory that falls into place is precisely Kant's moral psychology. The key text in this respect is Chapter 3 of the *Critique of Practical Reason*, which deals with 'the incentives of pure practical reason'. And the first observation to be made regarding this chapter is that Kant's strategy there is to identify certain 'feelings', which he considers inextricably bound to moral conduct, and to show that reference to the Law (or to reason in general) is entailed in their very definition. They would never be identifiable on the basis of empirical observation alone. The recognition of these feelings presupposes that the Law is effective in generating a special kind of moral sensibility. Once again, Kant is simply bringing to explicit reflection what he takes to be a *Faktum* of reason.

What are these feelings? Kant operates with a number of concepts. There is the concept of will, the most fundamental of them all. All that it denotes in general is a capacity to act. Then there is that of maxim, which we have already seen. A maxim is a subjectively interiorized counsel to act in a certain way. 'Incentive' *(Triebfeder)* is a "subjective determining ground of the will whose reason does not by its nature necessarily conform with the objective law" (AK V:72). Incentives, in other words, are the particularizing factors that cause an otherwise still undetermined will to adopt certain maxims as immediately compelling directives for action. Though not all incentives are necessarily feelings, any feeling would be a kind of incentive. In origin at least, incentives are natural. Hence they have no place, according to Kant, in a will that is identical with reason – one that is devoid of sensibility (inasmuch as there is any such will) and that would therefore necessarily act in accordance with reason. Finally, an 'interest' "signifies an *incentive* of the will insofar as it is *presented by reason*"

(AK V:79). An interest is thus an incentive; to this extent, therefore, it is still a natural and sensible factor. Nevertheless, because an interest 'is presented by reason', it motivates the will (but, presumably, with the immediate subjective force that only sensibility carries) to adopt the kinds of maxims that make the law itself the overriding motive of action. The presence of moral interests, in other words, is testimony to the fact that reason has already modified sensibility; it has co-opted it, so to speak, in promoting the cause of lawfulness in general. Interest, however, as presented by Kant, denotes an already highly reflective state of mind. Can one identify more primitive instances of reason-modified incentives that would illustrate with even greater immediacy the influence of reason over sensibility?

Kant adduces two feelings as cases in point, or, as we might say, even though Kant himself does not use this language in the present context, two aspects of the one feeling of 'being fallen' or of 'guilt'.[28] As we have said, *Triebfeder* or incentives are originally products of nature. They work within the constitution *(Gemüth)* of an agent with the spontaneity of a natural mechanism. Yet, the moment the concept of the Law is introduced, this spontaneity is interfered with. It is 'constricted', as Kant put it, presumably by the realization that there is more at issue in action than just the satisfaction of already given natural predispositions, and that such predispositions necessarily fall short of the new measure now brought into play. Hence there arises in the agent a feeling of 'pain' (from his natural inclinations being thwarted) and at the same time a feeling of 'awe' inspired by a presence that the senses do not understand but that is for this reason all the more overwhelming. Kant's image is that the Law disrupts *(Abbruch tut)* natural inclinations (AK V:78); it makes them speechless or dumb (AK V:86). The Law, just like the word of God, is violent. If I may shift the focus of Kant's imagery while still retaining its biblical color, it is as if the Law preempted a space otherwise occupied by nature alone, thus making the senses strangers in what was once their own land. They now find themselves trespassing on a ground that is no longer theirs – a ground made holy, where their presence is in need of legitimation. The first effect that the Law has on nature, in other words, and the first witness to the Law's efficacy as a moral command, is precisely that it renders nature morally problematic.

Kant waxes eloquent on this point, using the well-worn tropes of edifying Christian discourse (AK V:86–7). However, two qualifications must be made. The first is that, although reason's influence on the senses is most invasive in the realm of morality, where the very legitimacy of sensibility comes into question, this influence, as Kant indeed knows, is by no means confined to that realm. It is already at work in aesthetic experience and in the theoretical domain where the understanding comes into play. The content of sensations needs objectification, and the latter requires in turn the synthesizing function of the 'I think', itself a reflective operation of reason. The second qualification concerns the well-known moral trope of a battle between nature and reason that Kant also uses. One must not be deceived by the surface imagery of the trope. The battle is not between strangers. On the contrary, it is from the start a family battle, so to speak, for the 'nature' engaged in it cannot be 'empirical nature', or a nature that the sciences would discover, or, even less so, a 'nature' of the kind that God himself would create as thing in itself.[29] Any such nature, how ever one conceives it, would be neither selfish nor unselfish, nor in need of either thwarting or promoting. It simply stands there innocently, the tacit but irreducible limit of human action. Only when already introduced within the realm of intentions generated by the idea of lawfulness in general, and measured against the requirements of the latter, does nature assume the character of a debilitating moral limitation. Only then, when it has been already idealized, does it appear as fallen – its heteronomy, there-fore, posing a threat to moral autonomy. Kant's moral rhetoric tends to hide this circumstance. Yet Kant knows (for he says so explicitly)[30] that na-ture is by itself neither morally good nor evil. Evil begins with humankind. As he says, "the history of *nature* begins with goodness, for it is the *work of God;* but the history of *freedom* begins with evil, for it is the *work of man.*"[31] Once more, the moral effectiveness of reason is revealed in its most radical form in the effectiveness that it imparts to nature itself as a new, morally significant quantity.

There is thus nothing formalistic or empty about Kantian morality; there is no incongruity in upholding the supremacy of the Law simply as idea, yet finding oneself in a particularized moral discourse that is nec-essarily involved in matters pertaining to nature. This nature is already qualified as moral nature, already part of the Kingdom of Ends estab-lished by moral legislation.[32] Yet Kant's moral theory was accused from the beginning of being impractical because it was formal, and the ac-cusation, though basically wrong-headed, was not altogether irrelevant. We are back to the issue already broached in our discussion of Kant's antinomy of freedom and necessity.

5.1.2.2 Critical Formalism Revisited. The image that the term 'formalism' normally conveys, and that motivated the criticism widely directed at

Kant by his contemporaries, is that of a material organized according to formulas imposed on it from outside. This is only an image, of course. In the contexts in which it prompted the accusation of formalism against Kant, it nonetheless carried some weighty conceptual assumptions. Notable among them was the assumption that sensibility reflects in its immediacy an order of meaningful intentions that are somehow embedded in reality itself and that might therefore stand in contradistinction ('in competition', one is tempted to say) to the order that the mind dictates. The assumption applied whether sensibility was understood as a matter of sensations or of feelings, and whether conceived in a more Leibnizian or empiricist form. On this assumption, the order defined by the categories would indeed be applied to sensations externally, just as the norm of the categorical imperative would be imposed on the affective life of feelings. In either case, whether it is a matter of applying categorical order or imposing categorical rule, the system is thus vulnerable to the charge of arbitrariness. The formalism of which Kant was being accused was of this kind. And this was unfair. For the formalism that Kant was endorsing on critical grounds was instead of a completely different nature. This typically critical formalism was intended to suspend precisely the assumption on which the other type of formalism was based. The operative new assumption was that the universe of meaningful intentions and moral values is exclusively the product of reason; that the categories, on the one hand, and the categorical imperative, on the other, say absolutely nothing about things in general (hence their formalism). But, because of this, they are in a position to define the new intelligible medium within which such things can, as it were, speak to us – that is, acquire meaning as the place where a rational individual is to establish his place rationally and realize himself as a rational being. This is not to say that things are not subject to necessitating factors of their own – factors that have been represented at different times in different explanatory idioms. The point is rather that these necessitating factors become meaningful objects of observation in the human domain of theoretical activities, or significant circumstances in the domain of moral praxis, only when they are represented in the medium of the concept (according to the specifically logical requirements that the Critique of Reason seeks to define). Just like the principle of contradiction that contributes nothing at all to the content of any discourse, but that formally pervades all discourse by making its discursiveness possible, the categories and the idea of the Law are totally empty of content yet make the presence and the value of immediate objects possible.

This, I take it, is the meaning of Kant's specifically critical brand of formalism. It is the substance of his claim that nature is a theoretical idea before it can become an object of observation, or a morally qualified quantity before it can stand as an obstacle to moral goals. This kind of formalism also bestows on Kant's subjectivism, I take it, its specifically critical character. But it is also the meaning that his contemporaries would not understand. The fault was not altogether their own, since Kant himself stood in the way.

For one thing, Kant himself repeatedly raised the issue of a desired *Übergang* (transition) to be performed a priori from the categories to the first laws of physics, as if the categories were forms to be externally applied to an independent sensible material in order to constitute 'physical objects'. Indeed, Kant's repeatedly stated project was to establish the foundations of a metaphysics of nature a priori.[33] Any such project, however, clearly transgressed the stipulations of his critical formalism. It is one thing to say that experience is conceptual, and to demonstrate this claim by actually exhibiting the structure of experience in paradigmatic form (as Kant does in the Analogies of Experience in the first Critique). It is one thing, therefore, to want to establish a logic of experience a priori. But it is quite another to want to derive from this logic a system of physical laws. Any such attempt would constitute, on Kant's own critical assumptions, a clear *metábasis eís állos génos* (category error). Yet Kant's preoccupation with the desired *Übergang* was enduring, and seems to have grown in his mind as the years went by.[34] As regards the concept of the Law, Kant gave at least the impression that he took the concept as a general formula for generating, with reference to a presupposed sensible content, particular yet universally applicable rules of conduct. This is especially true in the case of the first, and for Kant apparently the most fundamental, formulation of the Law as categorical command, that is, the universalization of maxims formula.[35] Just as Kant wanted to establish a metaphysics of nature on the basis of his Transcendental Logic, so he apparently thought of the Law as a first principle from which to derive a whole system of particularized yet universally valid laws. This is another project that he constantly had in mind and that he came the closest to realizing in the *Metaphysics of Morals* (1797).[36] But again, it is one thing to claim that the idea of the Law establishes by itself the possibility of a radically new type of conduct and to seek to define the boundaries of such a conduct accordingly. It is one thing to want to identify the basic values that would motivate this conduct and the most pervasive feelings that would accompany it. However, it is quite another to want to derive a priori a system of virtues characteristic of an individual historically engaged in it, as well as a system of laws governing this individual's society. Just as the theoretical determination of particularized objects of observation is to be done on the merit of actual experience alone (albeit within conceptual boundaries), so, in the practical domain, the moral appropriateness of a certain character and the validity of a social constitution are to be determined on the merit of given historical conditions (albeit on the assumption of lawfulness in general as the overriding value). To the extent that Kant at least tended to merge into a single system the two otherwise distinct domains of transcendental logic and actual experience, to that extent he was playing into the hands of the dogmatists. He was attributing a material function to what he intended to be logically pure forms of experience, in fact feeding the systematic expectations of the dogmatists. They were the ones whose presumed first principles of thought should have also provided the principles for a science of being. When measured against these expectations, Kant was exposing himself to the charge of 'external' formalism.

But there was another, much more serious ground for the charge. We remember, in connection with Schulze's exposition of the Transcendental Deduction, that the clinching argument for the justification of the objective validity of the categories called for the assumption, not just of an abstract I think in general of which the categories are the functions, but of an individualized self who is the actual subject of experience. This self acquires the sense of self-identity required for experience by constituting this identity a priori precisely in virtue of the I think and its categorial functions. But such an identity would have no real content without reference to a reality that is in fact the external object of experience. To the extent that the self thus constitutes through conceptualization his own immediate sense of identity, to that extent this self equally acquires (through the same process of conceptualization) a real sense of the order of the external objects on which it depends for the determination of that identity. This is in effect the main thrust of the argument of the Analogies of Experience, especially as expounded by Schultz. An individual's access in experience to external reality is limited by sensible conditions over which the individual himself has no original control. The determination of his 'here and now' is originally ambiguous. Because of this irreducible limitation, the individual can therefore make his way across that reality, and thereby determine his own real identity, only in virtue of conceptual signposts (the concept of an object in general) that make up intentionally for the otherwise still lacking determination. The net result is the progressive constitution – always reformable and vulnerable to illusions but not any the less valid for that – of a self's awareness of his identity across an equally progressively recognized order of external objects. An analogous argument can be construed to explain the constitution of a moral subject. The agency of any such subject is inherently dubious as long as his self-identity is bound up with an externally given nature, and his incentives for action are therefore subject to factors concerning which he does not have clear knowledge and over which he has no ultimate physical control. 'Who' it is that acts in any given situation is indeterminate. The subject becomes an agent in the strict sense only inasmuch as he distances himself from this given nature ideally and behaves with respect to it (his own immediate body included) as determined by values that he has himself thus introduced into it ideally. And since nature has now assumed a new moral significance for him and as such can be experienced as an obstacle to his agency, he is also in a position to limit his moral liabilities. He acquires a distinct moral personality. In other words, whether in the theoretical or the practical domain, the upshot of Kant's idealism is that nature can be progressively recognized for what it is as given, and at the same time also made the object of effective human agency, only in the medium of conceptualization. Only as idealized does nature acquire structure, and the human individual, in thus idealizing it, takes on his determinate identity as a subject of experience and a moral agent.

This is an idealism, however, that has no hope of gaining credibility unless it is pressed to an extreme, to the point of becoming the blueprint for a radical form of empirical realism. Such a realism would require that nature in itself is the object of experience. This is a nature that consists of real things standing in real spatial relations and undergoing real change, albeit *for us* always within theoretically definable limits. Conceptualization adds nothing to it except the medium within which it can meaningfully appear as given, including regulative ideal norms for its discovery. Ignorance of nature can only be comparative, that is, measured against possible, and always expected, future discoveries. Or again, it is nature in itself, driven as it is by unconscious forces and always a possible object of theoretical reflection, that becomes morally problematic (both as a whole and in its details) once the idea of lawfulness comes into play. Hence it also yields the apt physical medium in which the human individual erects his moral institutions and exercises his moral agency. Anything short of these two extreme yet supplementary claims – namely, that the concept outstrips and embraces with its intentional reach the whole of physical reality, and that this physical reality, however, appears as it is in itself, and becomes itself the medium of moral agency precisely in the medium of the concept – any more modest combination of claims would allow for the presence in experience of some extra conceptually intractable factor, some essentially opaque material ('essentially opaque', because only accessible in a light to which the human mind is constitutionally blind), against which the I think may indeed be suspected of construing an imaginary order where in fact there is none, and the idea of the Law may be suspected of generating only a mirage of effective motivation. Kant's idea of a thing in itself and his claim to critical ignorance allowed for precisely this extra opaque factor in experience. Kant was saying that from the standpoint of this thing in itself, the things of sense experience that are also the objects of the human sciences would be mere appearances, only the products of a specifically human sense apparatus. He was also saying that one can think of an absolutely spontaneous causality on the side of this thing in itself that would actually produce the kind of moral nature that the human moral agent must intend but never hope to realize on his own. This was a kind of false critical modesty that, by debasing the truth value of the senses, also withdrew the latter from the reach of conceptualization. The charge against Kant of skepticism in the theoretical domain, and of ineffective formalism in the practical, had their origin here.

It might be objected that this is a false reading of Kant, and that Kant's interest lay in the praxis of scientific research and in the daily discipline of moral life. Transcendentally, he was an idealist; empirically, he was as much of a realist as any ordinary human being. And his transcendental idealism was only intended to protect the robust realism of common experience from illegitimate philosophical extrapolations that in fact expose it to skepticism. Kant's distinction between thing in itself and appearances – the claim still goes – was purely conceptual. The only point it made is that access to reality in experience is always from some limited standpoint; that experience is therefore necessarily conceptual in order for any such standpoint to be recognized and accounted for; and that the conceptuality of experience does not, however, constitute a warrant for theoretical claims that transcend its limitations. Kant's denial of knowledge of the thing in itself was simply directed at the claims made by dogmatists of knowledge from an absolute standpoint. Only these claims were being denied.

Perhaps. In that case, the repeated criticisms of empty formalism made against Kant by his contemporaries would have been just a matter of failure in communication or, more likely, of sheer obtuseness on the part of the contemporaries. But the matter is not as simple as this. Take, for instance, the following well-known and not at all atypical passages:

[E]verything intuited in space and time, hence all objects of an experience possible for us, are nothing but appearances, i.e., mere representations, which, as they are represented, as extended beings or series of alterations, have outside our thoughts no existence grounded in itself. (A490–1/B518–19)

[T]he objects of experience are **never** given **in themselves**, but only in experience, and they do not exist at all outside it. (A492/B521)

The faculty of intuition is really only a receptivity for being affected in a certain way with representations, whose relation to one another is a pure intuition of space and time (pure forms of our sensibility), which, insofar as they are connected and determinable in these relations (in space and time) according to laws of the unity of experience, are called **objects**. The non-sensible cause of these representations is entirely unknown to us, and therefore we cannot intuit it as an object; for such an object would have to be represented neither in space nor in time (as mere conditions of our sensible representation), without which conditions we cannot think any intuition. Meanwhile we can call the merely intelligible cause of appearances in general the transcendental object, merely so that we may have something corresponding to sensibility as receptivity. To this transcendental object we can ascribe the whole extent and connection of our possible perceptions, and say that it is given in itself prior to all experience. But appearances are, in accordance with it, given not in themselves but only in this experience, because they are mere representations, which signify a real object only as perceptions, namely when this perception connects up with all others in accordance with the rules of the unity of experience. (A494–5/B522–3)

Now, one can read these passages as saying that the objects of experience are always *constituted* objects. Since they are given in experience in a typically human space and human time, one must always distinguish between such determinations that accrue to them in being thus given (i.e., in representations or as appearances) and such that belong to them as physical things existing in themselves but present in experience only in being given (i.e., in being represented or as appearing). But, just because these physical determinations are only given in representations or as appearances,[37] the things to which they belong must first be construed theoretically as objects of possible observation[38] in order to safeguard the distinction (inherent in them as objects of experience) between *what* is given in them and *how* it is given by virtue of being represented or of appearing. In this way the distinction between 'objective' and 'subjective' is maintained in experience. Of course, on these terms, it makes no sense to say that 'representations' or 'appearances' exist in themselves, or to say that, in construing an object theoretically, one thereby already knows it without its first being given in actual experience (under the limiting conditions of the latter). These are unimpeachable claims, and in the historical context in which Kant was advancing them, they were original as well as revolutionary. Philosophy has not been the same since. In the cited passages, however, Kant is saying more. He is not just saying that in experience we know things, indeed *in themselves* but only inasmuch as we de facto know them, that is, only within such limits as sensibility and conceptual constructs allow. Indeed, the perspicacity of sensibility admits of individual variations and cultural habituations, and with the exception of the categories that are totally formal, conceptual constructs evolve. Kant is also saying that the empirical object *is* the sum total of its representations or appearances and that we can indeed think of (though not know) a nonsensible, intelligible, cause of these representations or appearances that transcends experience. He is also saying that, when contrasted with this presumed cause, the phenomenal object that is its effect is nothing in itself. In fact, however, the only possible and the only theoretically required preconscious causes of sensible experience are the physical things that fall themselves within the purview of experience. And although the concept of a 'thing in general' prior to experience is indeed perfectly legitimate and even theoretically useful, to say that we know nothing of it is meaningless. As an abstract concept, it needs excogitation, not knowing; yet it contributes to knowledge by bringing to explicit reflection the distinction essential to any object of experience between this object as already known (*in itself*, albeit from a limited perspective) and as yet escaping the grasp of perception. Kant's extra claims transgress the warrant of his critical brief.

It might be objected again that we are giving too much importance to modes of expression conditioned by Kant's polemic against the metaphysicians of the day. Kant was simply granting the logical legitimacy of accepted metaphysical theoretical constructs while denying that, on their own, they yield real knowledge of anything. Perhaps – even though the very idea of an 'intelligible cause' of perceptions, however void of content, already bestows an independence on the part of sensibility vis-à-vis the concept that, as we have already argued, injects an element of irreducible opacity into the process of experience, and thereby makes the critical system vulnerable to the charges of skepticism and empty formalism.[39] Be that as it may, the problem is that this same idea of an intelligible cause appears again in Kant's system in the resolution of the dynamic antinomies, where it assumes the more fully developed meaning of a conceivable, though for us unknowable, absolutely original source of causality. And, as this same type of cause, it also finds a place in Kant's moral theory, where Kant prides himself on having found for it, though not a theoretical content, at least a practical content, inasmuch as it assumes the further connotation of absolutely spontaneous causality. It now stands for the freedom that is the necessary presupposition of morality. Though the idea might not make any material difference to scientific praxis when treated as a mere theoretical hypothesis, it does make a difference to the self-perception of a moral agent when elevated to the status of moral postulate. It marks the difference between an idealistically based moral theory in general and Kant's specific moral theory.

We are back to the issue of freedom as a supposed hyperphysical causality with which we began. How it affects moral self-perception can be gathered by considering two moral scenarios, quite different in their implications for ordinary life, yet both possible if one grants that the moral agent can (indeed must) consider himself as both *homo noumenon* and *homo phænomenon*. It is assumed, of course, that the one subject who thus considers himself from these two different standpoints is the historical human agent, and the one place where he assumes them is the context of daily human affairs. First, let us consider what Kant's moral theory involves if we do not assume that freedom is a hyperphysical source of causality. On this assumption, to be *homo noumenon* simply means to be engaged in a world of conceptually constituted entities, namely, the institutions that make up the immediate human environment within which the human individual (the *homo*) operates. It is these institutions that define the individual's specifically human identity formally. And for this individual to be free simply means to be capable of learning (by way of education, acculturalization, or what have you) to live and operate within them. Of course, historically speaking, such institutions are rarely established deliberately, as if de novo. They are normally found already established and even treated as if they were natural products. Nor, for that matter, are they ever established unless in response to some biologically determined need. Hence, it is possible, even imperative for human survival, that the individual agent abstract from his typically human world of ideally constituted objects and consider himself, as well as his moral world, with the kind of distance and theoretical freedom that the idea of an observer in general (itself a conceptual product) affords him. In other words, he must consider himself as *homo phænomenon* and his moral world as things of nature. From that point of view, he might well discover unconscious forces operating in him and sheer physical situations conditioning his culture of which he had no inkling before. None of this, however, detracts from the fact that such forces and such factors have made their presence felt from the beginning in his typically value-laden world of action as morally interpreted in the medium of concepts – indeed, have been all the more effective precisely to the extent that, as played out in the moral medium of the concept, they have caused moral interference. To come in the clear about them does not in any way limit the range of moral agency. On the contrary, doing so only adds extra complexity to problems that this agency must resolve and greater scope to the moral creativity it calls for. Suppose, finally, that in a given culture the human agent attains the kind of clarity about the Law as *Faktum* of reason that Kant made historically possible, and explicitly recognizes that the interests of reason have in fact been at work in shaping the typically human world from the beginning. This new awareness will indeed make a material difference to his culture and to the institutions in which such interests now find an explicit voice. This new circumstance does not, however, constitute a warrant for his hypostatizing the Law, as if the pursuit of lawfulness were anything over and above the establishment of a historically recognizable, and hence a historically conditioned and historically mutable, community of rational individuals.

Introduce the idea of a hyperphysical source of free causality and the whole moral scenario changes. In considering himself as *homo noumenon*, the moral subject now thinks of himself as a member of an intelligible Kingdom of Ends that is not to be identified with any historical system of social institutions. He holds as his moral ideal a Holy Will totally unaffected by physical factors – which alone, therefore, is 'free' in the strict sense of the word. And to consider himself as *homo phænomenon* means to be caught up in a web of heteronomous causal relations that are inherently intractable to moral determination. With respect to these, in order to preserve at least a semblance of moral agency, the subject must therefore maintain essentially conflicting attitudes. He must consider them as totally outside the pale of moral consideration, since they entail heteronomy. They stand in experience as a morally opaque material that resists rationalization. Precisely for this reason, however, since morality ought to prevail, he must equally consider them as nothing in themselves, as mere appearances of being rather than as anything substantial. Finally, for the same reason, he must also consider them as in fact reflecting, in ways unknown to him, the universal order that moral interests demand. And he would have to hold the same conflicting attitudes with respect to his own agency. For, on the one hand, the subject must consider himself as acting unconditionally – that is to say, according to a line of causality that totally transcends the limits of phenomenal nature. He must think of himself therefore in a way that escapes his actual comprehension. On the other hand, inasmuch as he actually knows himself as implicated in the play of heteronomous phenomenal causality, he must accept that he constantly lapses from the intended status of a moral agent. By the same token, he must consider his agency, on the one hand, as actually bearing results, although in ways that escape his comprehension; on the other hand, so far as he actually knows, as never reaching beyond the status of mere intention. Finally, the idea – to which he might resort in order to resolve this conflict of attitudes – of being only in a state of striving for actual moral efficacy cannot offer true relief. For a striving directed at a goal that escapes his comprehension, and executed on the strength of means equally incomprehensible to him, must remain just as opaque to his eyes as the agency that he is supposed to be exercising.

To the questions, therefore, "what am I?", and "where do I stand as a moral agent?", the subject in the second scenario has no clear answer. The problem is endemic. As a later critic of Kant was to say, the Kantian moral subject is essentially 'dumb'; he cannot speak because he does not know who he is.[40] His problem is not just a matter of ambiguity, as it would be for the subject in the first scenario. In that context, the same questions would also be problematic, since the moral character of a subject is always in formation, and so is the idea of humanity that governs the culture within which the subject operates. Any answers, therefore, would entail just as much of a creative commitment as the description of a given situation. Though reformable, the answers would not, however, be incomprehensible in principle, for they are determinable in the only context that counts morally, namely, in the context of publicly stated social norms of conduct and demonstrable rules of accepted evidence. In the second scenario, on the contrary, with the story of a cosmic freedom unfolding itself behind the human subject, so to speak, and without the latter being able to comprehend how he fits within it, the same norms and rules, though pragmatically necessary, would nonetheless have no ultimate moral value.[41] The moral standing of the subject remains not just always to some extent problematic, but inherently suspect, even to the subject himself. Who is this human subject? Does he really have a moral standing? God only knows.

5.1.3 Emotional Issues: What Must I Believe? What Can I Hope for?

The postulates of God, and of a life that one hopes will continue after death in order to allow for greater scope in one's striving after moral perfection, appear in Kant's system in various contexts. It is possible that the idea of God and of an afterlife, as they stand in the concluding part of the *Critique of Pure Reason,* do not play the same function that they do in the Dialectic of the later *Critique of Practical Reason.* Kant's position might well have changed in the interim.[42] At any rate, it is only the later, and presumably more mature position, that is of interest here. The main points of this position are well known. Conformity to the law constitutes the 'good', according to Kant. For a pure will, or a will unaffected by sensibility, such a conformity would also constitute its sole object, that is, its 'highest good'. So far as the human will is concerned, naturally associated with sensibility as it is, the highest good presents an ambiguity. On the one hand, highest can be taken as 'supreme' *(supremum),* that is, according to the Latin root of the word, 'above anything else', and hence 'original' *(originarium).* On the other hand, when the satisfaction of sensible desires is taken into consideration as well – a satisfaction that is essential to human nature – the term highest can also mean 'perfect', that is, again according to the Latin root of the word *(per-ficere),* 'brought to completion' (also *consummatum,* 'consummated'). In this last sense, highest good includes 'happiness' – a state that Kant always associates exclusively with the body.[43] This ambiguity, according to Kant, poses neither contradiction nor relaxation from the absolutely determining rule of the Law, provided that the right order is maintained between the two senses and the second is duly qualified by the first. One must take conformity to the Law, or the striving after the kind of purity of motivation that only a Holy Will (i.e., one free of sensibility) would possess, as the first and unconditional *(originarium)* condition of the highest good. In this sense, good is identical with 'virtuous'. In a second and derivative sense, highest good can also mean happiness, but one that is 'morally deserved' – that is to say, caused as a sensible by-product, so to speak, of the will's striving after virtue and proportionate to the degree of virtue achieved in the striving. But now, since it is clear that neither purity of moral intention (perfect virtue) nor due proportion between virtue and happiness is ever achieved in the world as we experience it, the moral individual must postulate that his life will extend (in ways unknown to him) beyond his visible death, so that he will be able to pursue his moral vocation effectively and continue indefinitely in his striving after virtue. He must also postulate, contrary to all empirical evidence and again in ways unknown to him, that an almighty cause (God) is bringing about a nature in which the due proportion of moral merit and happiness is realized. These postulates do not enlarge theoretical knowledge in any way. They are not, however, mere theoretical hypotheses. They constitute beliefs to which the moral individual commits himself spontaneously, out of sheer subjective practical necessity. One could not live without them. As Kant puts it most dramatically, one *wills* that there be God and life after death (AK V:143).

Beliefs are theoretical commitments. Kant seems uneasy about the idea that they can be commanded, uneasy enough at least to argue that reason is not being compelled externally by accepting these commitments, since reason has no theoretical grounds on which either to assert or deny them. Since it is in the interest of its rationality that it recommend them practically, its acceptance is spontaneous. After all, as Kant says, "every interest is ultimately practical and even that of speculative reason is only conditional and is complete in practical use alone" (AK V:121). Kant is also at pains to argue that, though the objects of these practically induced beliefs are transcendent, moral ideas as such are not transcendent. Their efficacy makes a difference to human conduct in this life. It is here, however, in this juxtaposition of immanent moral ideas and transcendent theoretical beliefs, that Kant made himself most vulnerable to criticism, and the already adumbrated difficulties that affected his system showed up all the more starkly.

Regarding the idea of a 'morally deserved happiness' and the beliefs it calls for, critics rightly objected from the beginning that Kant could not have it both ways. He could not claim at once that happiness consists exclusively in the gratification of drives and inclinations that are avowedly physical – therefore heteronomous and morally intractable – yet that this happiness is an essential component of the highest good and capable of being morally deserved. On the contrary, on Kant's own definition of it, happiness should be shunned by the virtuous man as his greatest temptation, because, to the extent that he were to enjoy it, he would have lapsed from the autonomy required for virtue.[44] Even more to the point, the idea that a due proportion between happiness (understood as the gratification of sensible drives and inclinations) and virtue is effectively being brought about in ways unknown to the moral subject by a transcendent cause constitutes a contradiction *in adjectis*. For happiness, on Kant's own definition of it, belongs to the realm of phenomena, and these, again on Kant's definition, are nothing *in themselves*. They are mere appearances due to the constitution of the human senses. As such, as Kant himself quite explicitly says with reference to the idea of creation, phenomena cannot be the object of a noumenally conceived cause (cf. AK V:102). The only cause relevant to them is the phenomenal human subject, and this subject, as phenomenal, is himself morally intractable because he is caught up in the play of heteronomous phenomenal causes.[45]

These are strong objections. And the cause of the embarrassment that they pose can again be traced back to the ambiguity in Kant's conception of freedom. Inasmuch as freedom is the product of reflection, the unique contribution of conceptualization to experience, moral ideas are indeed totally immanent to experience. In that case, however, though there are naturally predisposed drives and desires, there cannot be any such thing as a naturally preappointed happiness to which the attribute of morally deserved or undeserved has to come as if from outside. What counts as happiness or unhappiness in any given situation depends on historically made moral choices regarding human identity. The moment one declares that in a given situation the worldly state of an individual is deserved or undeserved, comforting or tragic, hopeful or despairing, delusionary or heroic, one has already transformed nature (the whole of it) into a moral quantity. The transformation is ideal, the contribution of conceptualization to experience. It does not follow that the concept of efficient causality has thereby lost moral meaning, or that the moral subject is absolved from the duty of taking effective action to promote or remedy the given situation. What follows, rather, is that any such efficiency, or any plan of action, has moral relevance only to the extent that it assumes visible historical shape.

Inasmuch as, on the contrary, one conceives of freedom as a type of efficient cause that originates outside the realm of sense experience and operates according to laws of its own, perhaps even in competition with the causality proper to the phenomenal domain of sensibility, to that extent one has withdrawn this presumed phenomenal domain from the reach of visible human moral action. An area of phenomenal existence is thus established where a morally neutral happiness finds its place – a happiness that must then be made morally relevant by the exercise of an external force; as if quantitatively (so much virtue, so much happiness), with all the formalism and the just detailed conceptual difficulties that this alleged process entails. This notion of freedom as *causa sui* with which Kant still operated had its ancestry in dogmatic metaphysics. Kant now treated it as a postulate of practical reason, indeed the most fundamental postulate of moral life, even more fundamental than the ideas of God and of life after death that actually derived their motivation from it. All these postulates, however much they are now posited as void of speculative value and dependent for their acceptance on moral interests, were nonetheless still consistent with a dogmatic vision of the universe. Kant, of course, knew that this vision undermined the possibility of effective human agency, and that it thus precluded the possibility of true morality. For this reason, he had inverted the logical order of dogmatic metaphysics by voiding the speculative claims of the theoretical constructs on which the metaphysicians based their moral theory and by making these claims rather depend on self-validating moral interests for credibility. This looked indeed like a promising strategy. The problem with it, however, was that, inasmuch as the vision of the universe that it evoked was still that of dogmatic metaphysics, and inasmuch as such a vision was inherently antithetical to morality, it still had the same general effect of undermining morality. It made no difference in this respect whether one accepted the vision on alleged speculative grounds or simply committed oneself to it on practical ones. In both cases, one still made the efficacy of human agency ultimately depend on morally extraneous factors. And so it is that Kant, after arguing for the primacy of practical reason throughout his revolutionary *Critique of Practical Reason,* was at the end to make the lame paradoxical claim, already noted in Chapter 1, that it is good that we are ignorant of the ways of God and the universe. For, if we knew them, we might discover that all our moral strivings are for nought.

When Kant died, he was honored at his funeral by the reading of a poem written for the occasion. Apparently, it was not much of a performance. The most recent biographer comments that a much more appropriate tribute would have been the reading of Alexander Pope's *An Essay of Man,* the passage where the poet depicts *man* as the 'riddle of the world', a being poised between two worlds, that of the mind and that of the body, and caught struggling between the two: "Plac'd on this isthmus of a middle state, / A being darkly wise and rudely great...."[46] This is no lapse into hagiography. Kant knew Pope's poem and loved it, and the poem reflected in fact his vision of humankind. Yet it should also be said that this image of a being struggling to hold two worlds together, the one above him and the other below, is by no means original with Pope, let alone Kant. It is as old as the tradition of Christian Platonism. Kant's originality (his brilliant immodesty) lay in the fact that, on his interpretation of this image, the being that is man does more than just hold the two worlds together. He contains them both within, for each is but his idea. And, to the extent that he is a riddle unto himself, this is because he has made himself such. In so doing, he has also made himself free. This is how close in spirit Kant's *Mensch* was to Goethe's Prometheus. The emotional tone that colors the human situation has also changed. There was once consolation to be had from the Christian belief that God had been made flesh and, by suffering in the flesh, had also redeemed the world below. In principle, the human being's struggle to hold the two worlds together had already been won. The cosmos was on his side. This belief was independent of reason, and reason fed on it. But now, in Kant's new vision of the human situation, since it is up to the human being to will that there be a God and a life after death, any consolation available to him in his formidable struggle for moral perfection must come from his own internal resources. Kant had not only inverted dogmatic metaphysics, he had inverted the spirit of Christianity as well.[47] And this move had far-reaching consequences even for the religion of humanity on which the Enlightenment set its store.

5.2 THE GOSPEL ACCORDING TO KANT

5.2.1 Radical Evil

In 1798 Kant published a book entitled *Anthropology from a Pragmatic Point of View*,[48] in which he collected the lectures that he had regularly given on the subject beginning in the fall semester of 1772–3.[49] There is much interesting material in these lectures. They reflect the psychology of the day that Kant also used in his *Critiques,* as well as views about human na-ture that were commonplace in the culture of the Enlightenment. Kant now rearranged this material into three parts, each corresponding to one of the *Critiques.*[50] In spite of this new arrangement, however, he still con-sidered the material to be empirical in nature. And since he also famously thought that the Critique of Reason, the practical part especially,[51] had to be conducted through pure reason a priori, one should not expect to find in it a *critically* derived concept of human nature. Kant's lectures expressed commonly accepted views and commonly held attitudes that Kant himself to all appearances shared, but that could hardly answer to, let alone remedy, conceptual difficulties caused by the Critique itself. Inasmuch as Kant did have a philosophical anthropology, it is rather to be found in the 1793 book, *Religion within the Boundaries of Mere Reason,* mentioned at the beginning of this chapter. It is in this book, where Kant turns his attention to the situation of a human individual seeking moral perfection in the context of a phenomenally given world, that we find an attempt at an a priori construction of human nature. As we shall see in a moment, the resulting concept conveys a somber view of humankind that stands in stark contrast with the typical optimism of the Enlightenment.

Religious practices deal with the individual in his naked individuality, when he is in need of comfort and consolation in his struggle for moral perfection. "Religion is the recognition of all duties as divine commands" (AK V:129), according to Kant. But God is imagined ideally as a real person; in some transcendent sense, therefore, as an infinite individual. The idea of a being who is at once 'individual' yet 'infinite' is, however, paradoxical and conceptually ultimately untenable. Nonetheless, inasmuch as the human agent *feels* that his duties issue from precisely this infinite individual – as he must, since his own actions engage him as an individual and hence necessarily evoke in him the feeling of an individualized command – he stands as an individual facing another individual that at the same time transcends him. He stands in opposition to this infinite Other because of his feeling of guilt in the recognition that he falls irreparably short of the Holy Will that the Other represents for him ideally. Evil individualizes absolutely. But evil is an inescapable fact of human existence. Religion ministers to precisely the needs that this circumstance creates for the human individual. It is no surprise, therefore, that the four essays that make up Kant's *Religion within the Boundaries of Mere Reason* all deal, in one way or another, with evil in human nature.

The first essay, subtitled "Of the Radical Evil in Human Nature," is the most puzzling and the most liable to misinterpretation. It starts off with the acknowledgment, apparently based on long-standing historical evidence, that the human race is affected by evil. That things have gone from bad to worse since the beginning is the wisdom of the ages – hardly counteracted by the more recent opinion, for which Kant does not appear to have much sympathy, that, on the contrary, the human race is constantly improving and is now even on the verge of a final outburst of rationality.[52] Granted this quasi-empirical moral premise, Kant turns his attention to the conceptual problem of how to represent the possibility and origin of the evil that thus vitiates human nature. Human agency and its requirements is still the governing issue in the discussion, just as it is for the whole of Kant's moral theory. The leading question that Kant must answer is how an evil act can be attributed to a moral subject in such a way that the latter can be deemed responsible for it.

Now, evil is attributed to human actions. These are evil when they fail to conform to the moral law. Any such lack of conformity cannot, however, be gauged in material terms alone, according to whether the visible results of an action agree externally with the law or not. Such results may well be connected to the action accidentally only and not as anything directly intended by it. External nonconformity to law is by itself no more certain evidence of moral evil than external conformity to it is of moral good. Hence, the test of whether an action is evil must depend on whether the action itself is the product of an individual already presumed to be morally evil – one who therefore has intended the nonlawful effects de facto resulting from it. According to Kant's argument, the line of moral attribution proceeds from agent to action to effects – not the other way around. This is his logical starting point.

What constitutes, however, a morally evil man? It is a general principle that every being behaves in accordance with its nature, that is, as predisposed to particular activities by its innate constitution. In the case of the human being, since his nature is a complex one, one should also expect in him a multiplicity of natural predispositions. Kant identifies three fundamental ones:

(1) the predisposition to the *animality* of the human being as a *living* being;
(2) the predisposition to the *humanity* in him as a living and at the same time *rational* being;
(3) the predisposition to *personality* as a rational and at the same time *responsible* being (26ff.).

It is this last predisposition, the one to *personality*, which is, of course, of interest here. For a human being is deemed to be morally good only inasmuch as he abides in his actions by the moral law *personally*, that is, according to a responsibly taken subjective decision. This is what happens when he takes as his own the command of the moral law by incorporating it into a maxim that binds him not just objectively (as the law does on its own universally), but subjectively as well – that is, in response to a particularized dictate such as 'Do this now'. Should a man be deemed to be morally evil, the assumption must then be that he has instead adopted, just as responsibly, a maxim that stands in opposition to the law. In that case, the subsequent action would be one that is at once significantly connected with the man in question (since it is undertaken responsibly) yet contrary to the law.

However, what might possibly induce a man to adopt a maxim contrary to law? Since adopting the maxim is itself an act, and since, as already argued, the quality of an act depends on the quality of the one responsible for it, in every man one should look for the cause in the first ground of his activities. Normally, this would be his nature or his innate predispositions. This cannot be the case, however, when evil is at issue. For one thing, just as one expects a man to be born physically healthy, so one should also expect him to be born morally innocent. However, quite apart from this consideration, none of the three dispositions that determine his nature, listed earlier, can be the direct cause of evil. Neither the predisposition to *animality* nor that to *humanity* qualifies as a candidate, since neither the sense-inclinations that define *animality* nor the rational self-love that defines *humanity* are per se either moral or immoral, though both are susceptible to misuse. The sense-inclinations and the self-love simply are what they are by nature. Inasmuch as they are misused, they already presuppose evil. As for the predisposition to *personality*, the objective rule of law that it presupposes is by definition infallible. Were a human being disposed by nature not to adopt it as his own subjective norm of action, he would thereby be evil by nature. He would be *diabolical* and therefore outside the pale of morality (26–8, 35ff.).

To resolve this difficulty, Kant suggests that the source of unlawful behavior should be sought not in any natural predisposition, but in what he calls a 'propensity' *(Hang)*, that is, an inclination that is accidental insofar as natural predispositions are concerned (this to avoid saying that human nature is evil per se) but that, once present, affects all such predispositions radically. The qualification 'radically' is important here for the following reason. Since there is no possible common ground between moral good and evil and the two thus exclude one another, the very presence of the presumed propensity would necessarily suspend in toto the positive inclinations of which the natural predispositions are the source. It is thus possible to say that man, though not naturally evil, is, however, corrupt by nature (31–2). What, however, could possibly be the source of this propensity to evil? It certainly cannot be, for the reasons just adduced, anything natural. It must be, therefore, itself the product of an act. Moreover, in order to ensure once more an essential connection between act and effect, the act in question must subjectively establish the very maxim of nonconformity to the law, in virtue of which an agent and all his subsequent actions become evil. Should one go on asking what might have been the cause of this adoption of the maxim of nonconformity, to avoid being forced into an endless regression of prior acts, one must conclude that the act is *original* – the product of *Willkür* or arbitrary choice. Of course, the term 'original' poses a conceptual difficulty, because, should the act in question be taken to be original in the sense of being *outside* time (hence something noumenal), one would be making a positive statement about something of which, according to critical principles, no knowledge is possible. Should it be taken instead as belonging to the world of temporal experiences and hence as original in the sense of being *first in time,* one is then faced by the impossibility of ever discovering it in time empirically. Now, Kant resolves the aporia simply by claiming that the act in question indeed belongs in time, but that it is original only in the negative sense that it is always presupposed at any given moment. In this negative sense, it can also be said to lie, *as it were,* at the beginning of time and to affect, therefore, the human species as a whole. So far as the individuals of the species are concerned, it can be generally presupposed both that the propensity to evil established by the act is innate to each and that each should therefore be deemed responsible for it. In like manner, an individual's nature is said to be innate to him, and since it thereby determines what he is essentially, this nature also defines the quality of his acts, thereby establishing the necessary condition for attributing such acts to him (39ff.).

It is in this sense that Kant thus asserts that there is a radical evil in human nature. I quote:

> Whenever we therefore say, 'The human being is by nature good', or, 'He is by nature evil', this only means that he holds within himself a first ground (to us inscrutable) for the adoption of good or evil (unlawful) maxims, and that he holds this ground qua human, universally – in such a way, therefore, that by his maxims he expresses at the same time the character of his species. (21)

The ground of good maxims is a natural predisposition, while the ground of evil maxims is a propensity that, though derived, has for all practical purposes acquired the force of a second nature. Obviously, Kant has throughout been using 'nature' in a special sense. I quote again:

> But lest anyone be immediately scandalized by the expression *nature,* which would stand in direct contradiction to the predicates *morally* good or *morally* evil if taken to mean (as it usually does) the opposite of the ground of actions [arising] from *freedom,* let it be noted that by 'the nature of a human being' we only understand here the subjective ground – wherever it may lie – of the exercise of the human being's freedom in general (under objective moral laws) antecedent to every deed that falls within the scope of the senses. But this subjective ground must, in turn, itself always be a deed [*Actus*] of freedom (for otherwise the use or abuse of the human being's power of choice [*Willkür*] with respect to the moral law could not be imputed to him, nor could the good or evil in him be called 'moral'). (20–1)

Though his analysis has been carried out a priori, Kant insists that there is plenty of historical experience to demonstrate that moral evil is indeed a pervasive principle of human conduct. As proof, he cites for the benefit of the reader a long list of depressing anthropological data drawn from recent reports of voyages to distant parts of the globe (32ff.). The Scriptures also have canonized this universal experience in the form of a story about an original fall from an otherwise unspoiled state of nature. Humans are all born in original sin, and all share in its guilt (41ff.).

Thus Kant. What can one make of this doctrine of radical evil? At one level of interpretation, Kant is simply performing an exercise in language analysis, one that spells out all that is entailed in the language of evil, thereby bringing back into circulation, but under reflective control, otherwise ordinary modes of speech. There would be nothing problematic in this but also nothing of particular philosophical interest. Kant is, however, doing much more. The idea of an acquired yet original propensity to evil is an explanatory theoretical construct, a synthetic one at that, the critical status of which is not at all obvious. It is easy enough to say that it constitutes yet another practical postulate. Indeed it does. It makes a theoretical statement about human nature without thereby conveying any knowledge, yet demands acceptance on the ground that it renders at least pragmatically tractable certain otherwise alleged unintelligible facts of human experience. Though it is not a postulate in the sense in which Kant at times treats freedom as a postulate, that is, as a necessary precondition of morality, it is one at least in the sense in which God and life after death are also postulates. While it does not stand at the foundation of morality, it is required nonetheless for the practice of it. The difficult issue that it raises, however, is why the need for it should have arisen in the first place. What element of the practice of morality or the human situation makes such constructs pragmatically necessary?

The postulate of God suffers from the juxtaposition of a presumably noumenal cause (God) and an expected phenomenal effect (happiness). The postulate of life after death, it should be added, also suffers from a similar juxtaposition of irreducibly incongruous elements, in this case a noumenal goal (purity of intention) and an assumed infinitely protracted phenomenal approximation to it. 'Approximation' has no place here, for, by definition, not even the beginning of a move toward purity of intention can be made starting from the heteronomy of phenomenal nature. In both postulates, the juxtaposition of the noumenal and the phenomenal constitutes a contradiction *in adjectis*, the conceptual equivalent of a *generatio æquivoca*. Now, in the idea of a power of arbitrary choice *(Willkühr)* that corrupts human nature without, however, irreparably vitiating it, there is also an internal difficulty. And this time also, the difficulty is caused by the impossible juxtaposition of incompatible claims. *Willkühr,* or arbitrary choice, is a power that belongs to the phenomenal world but that is not part of it; it does not belong to the realm of freedom proper (the realm that is the product of reason and that is hence not liable to errors or exceptions), yet it effects the economy of human freedom. The radical evil that is its product is a condition for which all human beings are deemed responsible. Yet, no single action of any of them can be singled out as being at the origin of it. 'Indeterminate temporality', 'phenomenal agency', 'anonymous responsibility' – these are all paradoxical ideas, their internal contradictions only masked by the images in which they are phrased. Nor does Kant's insistence that they do not convey any knowledge at all, or that they are incomprehensible by definition, do anything to attenuate the conceptual difficulty they pose. For, short of claiming that they are just a play of words devoid of meaning (in which case, there would be no point in introducing them at all), they *are* contradictory, and, to this extent, though not wanting to make metaphysical claims, they do make a difference to a moral individual's perception of himself. Indeed, their very incomprehensibility says a lot about this individual's situation. It says, in effect, that his position in the universe is inherently ambiguous or incomprehensible and is therefore fundamentally irrational. The situation of the individual vis-à-vis the moral righteousness that it is his duty to attain is that of one who is indeed relevantly related to it (he is not just a thing of nature), but related to it only negatively, that is, that of one who starts off on his moral vocation by finding himself already fallen from it, in virtue of an event that, though predating him, nonetheless affects him personally and irreparably impairs him in the pursuit of that vocation.[53] His situation is existentially impossible. Yet that is where he has to work out his moral salvation. In essence, this is what Kant's postulate of radical evil says.

It would be a mistake to dismiss it as just a rationalization of a long-standing myth, a sort of bow made by Kant in the direction of pious beliefs. The echoes of the story of the Adamic fall are unmistakable in it. But such biblical allusions should not distract from the fact that the story, now reintroduced as an exercise in a priori idealization of human history, and still a myth even in this new rationally controlled form, is not just an accidental accretion to Kant's moral theory. It plays a definite systematic role. It brings the theory to a conclusion by identifying the mark that finally individualizes the moral subject, that is, the singularly human shape under which the obligation of the Law is subjectively interiorized. The human individual begins his moral life by standing, precisely as individual, condemned under it.[54] Whatever the psychological motivation behind the biblical story, or other similar stories, and whatever the peculiar vision of the cosmos that these stories bring in train, Kant's version of it has the specific systematic function of investing with some sort of moral significance that area of experience that, according to the architectonics of his system, remains otherwise morally intractable. This is the area occupied by phenomenal nature – at once nothing in itself, yet resistant to autonomous action; outside the scope of moral motivation, yet the area where the individual moral agent necessarily seeks his happiness by relying on a transcendent form of causality. This area is incomprehensible, a surd in the system. Yet, it is where the individual agent is subject to his most radically individualizing conditions. Who is he, finally? One born in sin. This is a story, of course. But storytelling is the only way of dealing with what is, fundamentally, an irrational quantity. The remarkable feature of *Religion within the Boundaries of Mere Reason* is that there Kant deliberately adopts this mystifying strategy with respect to his own system. He methodically spins out (even 'cynically', one is tempted to say) his version of an ancient story quite explicitly *as a story* – in full awareness, moreover, that the story might well be used as a moral opiate.[55]

One can sympathize with both Ulrich and Reinhold if the one felt unable to judge whether Kant was a determinist or not and the other thought, on the contrary, that Kant's concept of *Willkühr* injected human agency with an element of radical indeterminacy. So long as one superimposed traditional modes of thought on Kant, his text indeed remained ambiguous. But in fact, in the matter of Kant's handling of moral evil, both were wrong. Unlike Ulrich, and contrary to some cherished beliefs of the religion of the *Aufklärung*, Kant was not saying that moral evil is only a variation of the physical, the product of limitations necessary to a universe of finite beings. He was not saying that, from the standpoint of the whole, this alleged evil is in fact a good, part of the perfection of the universe. On the contrary, the presence of evil is for Kant an irreducible quantum of human experience. But neither is its presence the product of some noumenal source of indeterminate causality, as Reinhold thought. It is, rather, simply there – an irreducible yet incomprehensible factor of moral existence, the one that individualizes the moral subject absolutely. In the dogmatic schemas of both Ulrich and Reinhold, evil posed a problem that threatened to break out into sheer irrationality, and had therefore to be conceptually resolved at all cost. Kant now takes it precisely as something irrational, at best to be contained conceptually *in abstracto* or dealt with pragmatically *in concreto*. In either case, as anything irrational would have to be, evil is simply to be accepted. And it is as standing in a world colored by precisely this experience of evil that, according to Kant, the moral individual tries to comprehend himself, now assuming the standpoint of pure reason, now that of phenomenal nature. Unable to put the two together conceptually without contradiction, he must finally resort, as individual, to myth and prayer. But again, to put the case in this fashion is already to have gone along with Kant – to have accepted his schema of things and thus to be the victim (as the Kantian-styled moral individual necessarily is), so to speak, of an optical illusion. For 'responsible human agency' turns out to be a problem per se (rather than just the source of endless individual problems, as it no doubt has always been in every society) only inasmuch as one has already conceptualized experience in terms of the noumenal and the phenomenal, and has already conceived freedom, not just as the product of reflective rationality, but as some sort of hyperphysical cause. In brief, the irrationality of the human situation that Kant's rational myths are supposed to contain pragmatically is in fact a product of the Kantian system of experience, that is, of experience already interpreted according to Kant's historically conditioned moral judgment. It is an irrationality caused by the system, not one of moral experience as such. The optical illusion consists in confusing the one with the other.

5.2.2 Redemption and Salvation

Although it is doubtful, it might be possible, if one concentrates exclusively on the theoretical side of Kant's Critique of Reason, to read out of it any hint of a 'transcendental story'. So far as science is concerned, the only subject of experience who really counts is the ubiquitous observer in general. Whatever difficulties the latter might experience in his research because of the individual human being he happens to be can be easily bracketed out from the objective report of his final results. Things are not, however, as simple in moral theory. Not that the latter necessarily has to deal with individual cases. There is always a well-recognized distinction to be drawn between foundational theory and casuistry. But the point here is that a moral theory cannot afford to set up its premises in such a way that the very individuality of the human agent, as contrasted with the various historical circumstances that always affect it, becomes problematic. The individual human agent constitutes the subject matter of moral theory. To render his individuality ultimately incomprehensible is to cast doubt on the viability of moral theory itself. This is, however, what happens in the case of Kant's moral doctrine, not indeed because

of the conception of Law on which it is based (that conception constitutes, on the contrary, Kant's great discovery), but because the doctrine
conceives of the freedom that it associates with the conception of Law,
rather than just as the product of rationality in human affairs, as *causa sui*
instead, that is, as a transcendent form of causality that has its source on
the side of the thing in itself. The net result is that the individual human
agent, while meaning to act as the individual that he is, must at the same
time assume that his action, to the extent that it is successful, initiates
outside him. And while it is in this world that his agency should make a
difference if it were ever completely successful it would actually bring this
world (morality included) to an end. Thus he acts, yet he does not; he
lives in this world, yet does not belong to it. But this notion of freedom as
pure spontaneity is one that Kant borrows from dogmatic metaphysics.
It represents his still unsevered bond to the classical tradition. It makes
little, if any, difference, that it now reappears in his system in the form of
a practical postulate rather than a metaphysical claim. So far as a moral
agent's perception of himself is concerned, it gives rise to the same intractable difficulties that the metaphysical ideas of divine omniscience
and divine predestination did in the systems of the dogmatists. The extent of the presence of a transcendental story in Kant's critical system can
be measured by precisely the difference that separates his critical conception of Law and the particular moral theory that he develops on its
basis. This last does not necessarily follow from the other but is the product, rather, of historically conditioned assumptions, uncritical as well as
uncriticized, that affect Kant's moral judgment.

Now, the story that Kant spins out in his 1793 book is the anthropological counterpart of the transcendental story. In the first essay, the issue
is how the individual human agent must think of himself as he starts off
on his moral vocation, granted the conflicting demands that morality
in general imposes on him. As we have just seen, he is a sinner.[56] The
three essays that follow expound the added beliefs that this original acknowledgment of sin brings in its train in the course of the individual's
earthly travails. The ideal that informs him is that of a *"humanity... in
its full moral perfection,* from which happiness follows in the will of the
Highest Being directly as from its supreme condition" (60). This is the
principle that governs the second essay. But now, as sinner, the individual
cannot even begin to fathom how such an ideal might possibly have ever
arisen from within him in the first place. Yet, he is duty bound to act in
conformity to it. Hence, he must assume that the ideal has descended
from God unto him. And, since what *should* be must *effectively* also be,[57]

he can also presume that it has indeed been realized in a person who has come from God (the 'Son of God') – one in whom God has, so to speak, 'debased himself' for the sake of humankind and who, though God-like, is nonetheless human. As such, this God-like man stands as the prototype of humanity, and hence also as a proportionate example for every human individual to emulate. Because of his sinfulness, the human individual must think of himself as the cause of all the physical evils for which the God-like man suffers. He stands in the way of the latter. Yet, by taking him as his prototype that he at least intends to emulate, he can at the same time in virtue of this intention also hope that he shares in his state of a humanity well-pleasing to God (61–2).

This is, of course, an imaginary construction fraught with internal difficulties. Kant himself raises the most obvious ones. The first is this. Since the distance between a fallen (sinful) humanity and a humanity well-pleasing to God is infinite, how can any individual human being ever traverse it, especially in view of the fact that, because of his sinfulness, each and every one of his deeds must be deemed to be defective? Kant's answer is that, from God's transcendent point of view, granted at least the intention on the part of the individual sinner to emulate the Son of God, this intention covers over, so to speak, all his single deeds, with the result that, though still a sinner according to each deed, he "can still expect to be *generally* well-pleasing to God" (66–7). Can this human individual therefore presume from the start that he already belongs to the Kingdom of God? This presumption can be a recipe for enthusiasm, as could its opposite, namely, the assumption that he must work for his salvation always in fear and trembling. This is the second difficulty. Kant's resolution is that one can avoid both these extremes of presumptuous assurance or morbid doubt and have reasonable confidence that one will enter into the Kingdom of God, on the one hand by reflecting on the difference that the adoption of the right moral attitude has made in one's life, and on the other by counting on this newly acquired disposition to be constantly reinforced in view of what the future might hold for one, that is, eternal bliss if one perseveres steadfastly in this disposition and eternal damnation if one falls away from it (67–71).

On Kant's own reckoning, the third difficulty is the most formidable. Granted a sinner's change of attitude (his change of heart or moral conversion, which must be presupposed by the whole discussion) (76), such a change does not annul the debt that the sinner has incurred prior to it. This debt is infinite, for sin constitutes an offense against God, and since God is infinite, so is the caused offense and the liability or the expected punishment thereby incurred. No amount of merit accumulated after the conversion can possibly make up for the debt. Nor can somebody else (the Son of God) atone for it, as when a third party pays the money one owes to a creditor. For, unlike money, sin and the liability incurred through it are something personal and can therefore only be absolved personally (72). Kant's more than tortuous resolution of this problem consists in taking the moment of moral conversion (the adoption of the right moral disposition) as marking the 'death of the old man' and the birth of 'the new'. Now, since these two 'men' are radically different in disposition, the second (i.e., the 'reborn man') cannot be deemed as deserving the punishment to which the first (the sinner) is liable. To be sure, this liability is in no way thereby absolved. Punishment is still due. But, since the two men, though intelligibly quite distinct (before God), are nonetheless empirically continuous; and, since in the moment of conversion all the ills that so far have empirically afflicted the now new man, and will afflict him in the future, are taken by this new man as the crucifixion of the old one (the punishment due to him), these thus newly interpreted ills can be taken by God as discharging vicariously the other-wise still owing debt (but not as if by a third party, since there is empirical continuity between the two men). This process of expiation extends, of course, across the whole life of the new man, perhaps also across another life after death. However, if one figuratively represents the intended re-sult as accomplished once and for all by the Son of God dying on the cross, then one can take consolation in the thought of an already extant surplus of merit from which everyone can draw as one would from a gift benevolently put at one's disposal (grace) (72–6).

These are indeed problematic and ultimately mystifying constructions. They are called for, as Kant points out, only as answers to speculative ques-tions that one might (but need not) pose. According to Kant, they are of no practical use to a man who, already in the right moral disposition, is intent simply on living in accordance with it (76). Yet, the ideal of a humanity well-pleasing to God, though itself defying comprehension, has 'real objectivity' according to Kant, because it is required by the idea of the Law (62–3). And, inasmuch as it is itself fundamentally incomprehen-sible and *can* therefore give rise to problematic speculative questions, the constructions have at least the negative value of preempting the possibil-ity of answers that are the mere products of unbridled fantasy and would be the cause of fanaticism (76). This is what Kant claims. Yet, however arbitrary the constructions are, and however they obviously depend on a Christian cultural context, they do convey a definite moral psychological model. The picture conveyed is that of an individual agent who must act always by proxy, so to speak – in terms of a self whose effective presence within the agent is itself a mystery for him; before whom his own individuality is a scandal for which he must constantly make amends; in whom he must find nonetheless his true identity. In the second essay of *Religion*, this model is played out in individual terms, as we have just seen. In the third and fourth essays, Kant adds a sociohistorical dimension to it.

Already at the beginning of the second essay, Kant has represented the incomprehensible factor in the human constitution that is at the origin of its moral fall in the figure of an evil principle – one that can be indifferently imagined as residing either within or outside the human individual but that has traditionally been personified as a being all by itself (57–60). This evil principle stands in opposition to the good principle also at work in human nature, this last personified in the figure of the Son of God. This good principle is the one that rightfully holds claim to dominion over humankind and has in fact already successfully asserted this claim. Yet, because of the radical evil that affects human nature and that, however atoned for, cannot ever be simply expunged, the dominion of the Son of God must be figured as being wrested by him from the evil principle in a battle in which he has indeed already shown himself to be victorious but that will not be concluded except at the end of time (78ff.). This battle, as Kant portrays it in the third essay, has social implications.

The premise of his construction is that, just as in a political (or 'juridico-civil') state human beings stand joined under public juridical laws (laws that are essentially coercive), so one can conceive of an 'ethico-civil' state in which the same beings stand united under the noncoercive laws of virtue (95). Kant begins by playing at length on the analogy between the two states. Prior to contracting their political bond, individual human beings enjoy infinite freedom in the juridical state of nature in which they find themselves. And, although in contracting the political bond they thereby limit that freedom, they do so freely. Moreover, they do so for the sake of freedom itself, because, by thus putting an end to the state of universal warfare that is the inevitable result of their necessarily conflicting infinite desires, they have an opportunity of promoting their freedom under regulated conditions, to the ultimate advantage of each. By analogy, one can also think of a 'natural ethical state' – one in which every individual is free under the Law of virtue. In this case as well one must assume warfare ('moral' warfare, that is) as the de facto universal condition of humankind, both because of the battle in which every individual is engaged against the evil principle in him and because of the corrupting influence that individuals have on one another in giving rise, when grouped together, to special social needs. Here too, therefore, one can think of humankind as stepping out of its natural ethical state in order to constitute a society of individuals dedicated to the promotion of virtue (95–100).

Here, however, is where the analogy breaks down and the disanalogy between the two states becomes more important. In the case of the ethico-civil union, the step out of the natural state does not entail the limiting of anyone's freedom, as is the case in a juridico-civil context. Nor does it involve the promotion, through the discipline of limitation, of what still are essentially selfish interests. As Kant says, the issue here is "a duty *sui generis*, not of human beings towards human beings [as is the case in the juridico–civil state], but of the human race towards itself. For every species of rational beings," Kant further claims, "is objectively – in the idea of reason – destined to a common end, namely the promotion of the highest good common to all" (97). Like-minded and morally well-intentioned people are motivated to step out of mere ethical nature in order to join together their individual efforts (without thereby limiting them) into a single, well-organized striving toward a common good (97–8). The result is a society whose members, bound to a Law that they recognize as transcending them all, accept this Law as divinely imposed rather than as the product of mutual agreement. They will thus consider themselves as ruled by God himself, not indeed as the author of that Law, but as governing for all in accordance with it. This society, according to Kant, constitutes a veritable People of God, that is, a people under divine governance in accordance with the moral law (98–100). It will be essentially universal in scope, for it encompasses in principle all those bound to the Law, that is, the whole of humanity. In this it will also differ essentially from any juridico-civil society. For the latter is by nature always *some particular society,* one visibly identifiable with some historical group of individuals. On the contrary, whatever shape the communion of the People of God might visibly assume at different places and at different times (as indeed it must, since individuals can associate in their effort to promote virtue only under given historical circumstances), this communion must always be thought as distinct from it – this visible shape, which is only a limited and essentially contingent manifestation of it (100–2).

Kant's construction is long, tortuous, and driven by different motivations. First, Kant wants to establish a clear distinction between the political

state and any morally inspired association of individuals within it. Though
he admits that the state has a political interest in promoting such associations within its legal framework, he also wants to safeguard the autonomy
of the latter within this framework (95–6). The most that the state can
do on their behalf is to establish the proper external conditions for their
existence (113). It has no authority in matters internal to them, such as
the authentication of beliefs or the enforcement of discipline. Second,
Kant wants to legitimize the existence of historically constituted churches
(ecclesiastical political bodies); at the same time, however, he also wants
to distinguish them clearly from the Church Universal, that is, the congregation made up by the People of God. Insofar as this last congregation
is concerned, the pursuit of virtue under the Law is its one motivation as
well as its one determining principle of governance under God. Its only
faith is the certainty that such a pursuit will bear results, not just in the
realm of intentions but in the real world. This is a strictly 'moral faith',
one induced by pure reason alone. And its only religion is the practice of
a virtuous life itself under the moral rule of God (i.e., in accordance with
the Law considered as commanded by God himself). Its religion, in other
words, is one of pure reason. However, since virtue cannot be pursued in
general, but always within certain contingent historical conditions, the
otherwise Church Universal will de facto always assume the visible shape
of a particular ecclesiastical body, complete with a governing body, an
internal discipline, and a set of beliefs normally based on some ancient
Scripture upon which canonical status has been bestowed with the passing
of time. These ecclesiastical bodies, and all the hierarchical and doctrinal
trappings that go along with them, enjoy a type of legitimacy precisely
by virtue of being de facto necessary. Yet they are to be distinguished
from the Church Universal.[58] Indeed, their eventual transition that is to
be hoped for into the one People of God will mark, according to Kant,
the final establishment of the Kingdom of God on earth (115). Third,
granted the historical reality of ecclesiastical beliefs associated with
ecclesiastical bodies, Kant wants to clarify the issue of who has the ultimate
authority to interpret the meaning of such beliefs.[59] The juridical body
politic has no say in the matter. This is clear (113). As for the governments
internal to the ecclesiastical bodies, these have a right to explore the
historical sources of the texts on which their ecclesiastical beliefs are based
in an ultimately futile effort at recovering their presumed original purity.
In the process, all sorts of perfectly legitimate historical and scriptural dis-
ciplines will be spawned (112–13). According to Kant, however, the only
individuals who are capable of adjudicating the legitimacy of ecclesiastical

beliefs according to the absolute criteria of pure moral religion, and even of reinterpreting them in order to make them conform to such criteria (however forced the reinterpretation will have to be) (110–11), are those individuals in society at large whose specialized discipline is reason itself. In any society, in other words, the supreme authorities in matters moral and religious, according to Kant, are none other than the philosophers.[60]

From the beginning of *Religion,* Kant has himself been presenting a lesson in this process of reinterpretation. His constructions, always tortuous, become even more so in this third essay, where the project is to retrieve conceptually what are, in fact, items of belief of the Christian catechism. At one point, an alleged 'antinomy of reason' also appears, complete with a proposed resolution. The antinomy is created by the question of whether salvation is through faith alone or through good works (116ff.). In a final section of the essay, Kant then turns to the history of what he refers to as 'the gradual establishment of the good principle on earth'.[61] A history is, however, impossible, Kant points out, without some a priori principle defining its field of research. In this case, the required principle would have to be the visible appearance of the good principle on earth. And since we have a reliable case of such an appearance only in the Christian dispensation, in the form of an influential moral teacher (Jesus), the history in question must coincide with the history of the Christian church (124–5, 128). Kant is especially keen to disqualify Judaism as a suitable subject on the ground that, strictly speaking, the Israelite community founded by Moses at God's command was a political rather than a moral body, charged with the mission of a specific nation here on earth (125–6). Of course, the Christian church, of which a history is possible, is itself a recognizable earthly community, that is, an ecclesiastical entity. No history is possible of the People of God considered strictly as a community of virtue. But, even in its ecclesiastical shape, the Christian church is at least in intention *universal,* encompassing in principle all of humanity, and also internally cognizant of the distinction between its ecclesiastical faith and the faith of pure reason. Though temporal (hence a visible subject of historical research), it also points beyond its temporality (hence its history can be taken as a reflection of the spread of virtue among God's subjects).

In the final essay (Book IV, "Concerning service and counterfeit service under the dominion of the good principle, or, Of religion and priestcraft"), starting with the fundamental assumption that "*religion* (subjectively considered) is the recognition of all our duties as divine commands" (154), Kant proceeds to distinguish between 'natural' and 'revealed' commands. This distinction is determined according to whether, in its practices, the obligation of a duty is taken to depend on the duty's being divinely revealed ('revealed religion') or whether, on the contrary, the divinely revealed duty is taken to depend on its being a duty ('natural religion'). An individual is a 'rationalist,' 'naturalist' 'pure rationalist', or 'supernaturalist' according to the different stands that he takes on the relation of 'duty' to 'divine revelation' (154–5). Having stated these distinctions, Kant is then in a position in the rest of the long essay to examine the different shapes that the service of God can assume in the Christian church and indeed has historically assumed. These shapes will more or less approximate, or deviate from, the plain practice of a virtuous life, depending on the extent to which the faith held in the church more or less approximates, or deviates from, the plain moral faith of pure reason. This fourth essay is Kant's rendition of the traditional treatise *de ecclesia* that at the time came at the conclusion of every textbook on dogmatics. Here is where Kant gives his inventory of what he takes to be the many spurious, essentially superstitious, ritual practices of the established churches, and, more explicitly than anywhere else, gives vent to his irrepressible anticlericalism.

5.3 KANT'S WAY

This is then the result of *Religion* for Kant's anthropology. The moral character of a human individual, and his consequent status as agent, are inherently ambiguous. The character is constitutionally good yet historically affected by a radical evil. Though as agent he is a historical being, the individual must conduct himself in the name of a transcendent pure self by whose standards his historical actions cannot be but morally adulterated. This is the result of the first and second essays. From the third and fourth, it further transpires that the moral status of the communion of such individuals equally suffers from ambiguity. The People of God transcends history yet, as a communion of real individuals, necessarily assumes visible shape here on earth as an ecclesiastical society. And this society, even when it knows that its truth transcends its historical shape, indeed, especially when it knows this, must admit that whatever historical content its religious rituals exhibit over and above the plain practice of virtue is inherently corrupt – a counterfeit service of God rather than true service. But, according to the result of the first two essays, there is no such thing as a historical practice of virtue on the part of any individual agent that is not morally suspect. The moral ambiguity, in other words, is all pervasive.

One must be careful when judging the level of importance that Kant attributed to the anthropological constructions in *Religion*. They all have the marks of ad hoc responses to long-standing Christian beliefs – a sort of rational apology on their behalf in the style of traditional Apologetics, though on a completely new note, since the apology now consists in deflating rather than solidifying their claims to a supernaturally revealed origin. According to the most recent biographer, Kant himself was remarkably indifferent to religion.[62] Perhaps as a reaction to his early harsh pietistic education, he neither practiced religion as an adult nor, to all appearances, did he feel any need for it. Though not a declared atheist, for all practical purposes Kant was one. His attitude toward the postulate of God, life after death and, all the more so presumably, also toward his many constructions in *Religion*, was that they are important only if one needs them subjectively. For his part, he did not need them. His moral resources were directed instead to leading a life governed by well-thought-out, subjectively firmly established maxims of actions.[63] That was his way.

This sounds like a reliable image of Kant the real man. The image does not, however, detract from the fact that religion – an individual's subjective response to the encounter in moral praxis of the 'holy' or the 'divine' – is an essential component of the system of Kant the philosopher. As he says in the "General remark" appended to Book 3 of *Religion*:

It is impossible to determine, a priori and objectively, whether there are such mysteries or not.[...]Freedom – a property which is made manifest to the human being through the determination of his power of choice by the unconditional moral law – is no mystery, since cognition of it can be *communicated* to everyone; the ground of this property, which is inscrutable to us, is however a mystery, since it is *not given* to us in cognition. This very freedom, however, when applied to the final object of practical reason (the realization of the final moral end), is alone what *inevitably leads us to holy mysteries*. (138)[64]

Or again, as Kant had argued earlier in the same essay, conflicts regarding the right way of working out one's salvation "cannot be mediated through insight into the causal determination of the freedom of a human being, i.e. into the causes that make a human being become good or bad. [... They] cannot be resolved theoretically, for this question totally surpasses the speculative capacities of our reason" (117–18). In other words, the ground of the freedom that we know is essential to moral praxis is for us a *natural* mystery. Precisely for that reason, however, in the course of the same praxis we run up against *holy* mysteries that call for the subjective responses, the subjective idealizations of experience, in which religion consists. And the fact that Kant could defend the validity of such traditional responses (provided that they were properly reinterpreted), while at the same time ignoring them completely in his private life, neither abrogated the necessary place of these responses in his system of experience nor made his own personal response (apparently one of righteous self-assurance)[65] any less subjective, any less dependent on an ultimately arbitrary attitude toward the universe at large. Kant's attitude only gave further testimony to the presence in experience – as interpreted by him theoretically and, presumably, also personally apprehended in praxis – of a surd, an irreducible element of irrationality, a 'holy mystery', that necessarily summons a purely private response.

This is how far Kant's notion of rationality differed from that of the popular philosophers or diverged from the optimism of the mainstream Enlightenment of his day. To be sure, Kant's intention was to contain the sacred within the boundaries of reason – reason, that is, as he understood it. But again, this effort on his part does not detract from the fact that it was precisely Kant's understanding of reason, because still beholden to the notion of freeedom as *causa sui* of dogmatic metaphysics, that gave rise in the first place to the natural mystery in his system that, in turn, produced the holy as he understood it. Jacobi had been the one on record regarding the irrationalistic consequences of Enlightenment philosophy. In a sense, Kant was only rationalizing these consequences – giving them official status, so to speak, within reason itself. To this extent, he was himself a product of the rationalism of the Enlightenment, as Jacobi was again to argue. Still, one can understand why, for his contemporaries, he would have been the source of much misunderstanding.

6

The Difference That Fichte Made

6.1 THE DEBATE ON FREEDOM, CONTINUED

Coming on the scene when it did, Kant's book on religion, and especially the original essay on radical evil incorporated within it, seemed to strike a blow against Schmid in support of Reinhold. Kant was now playing on the distinction between *Wille* and *Willkühr*, the faculty of will and that of arbitrary choice, on which Reinhold's position was based. Of course, *Willkühr* had merely anthropological meaning for Kant. The concept did not commit him to any transcendent claim. This is not, however, how Reinhold, quite understandably, read the essay in a self-congratulatory review of Kant's book.[1] He took Kant to have seconded his position. As it happened, contrary to what he might have expected, Kant went out of his way only a few years later, in the *Metaphysics of Morals* of 1797,[2] to deny that freedom can ever be defined as the faculty to choose indifferently between either conforming or not conforming to the moral law. In this denial, he was tacitly, but not any less obviously, taking aim at Reinhold. Confronted by this authoritative rebuff, there was nothing that the latter could do but vent his exasperation at what he took to be Kant's inconsistencies in a response he published that same year.[3] By that time, Fichte already loomed large on the scene and had already captured more than a modicum of Reinhold's attention. In his response to Kant, Reinhold had borrowed concepts from the *Wissenschaftslehre*.[4]

We shall return to Fichte in a moment. Two other publications should be mentioned first, both of which were reviewed by Fichte.[5] In 1793,[6] a certain Leonhard Creuzer published a long essay in which, arguing from the standpoint of a skeptic, he had reviewed the whole history of the debate on free choice and had concluded that Kant's critical distinctions had not helped to resolve the issue at all. They had rather added new difficulties of their own. The essay was riddled with references to Jacobi, and was in effect a skeptical defense of Jacobi's original position that all metaphysics leads to a denial of freedom. The defense was skeptical because it was mounted on a methodical exposition of all the sophisms of which traditional scholastic defenses of freedom were guilty[7] (Ulrich's defense included).[8] At the end, Creuzer had tentatively come down (against Reinhold and, as he thought, Kant as well) in favor of determinism, though not of the type advocated by Schmid. One can appreciate Creuzer's position. Having exposed the sophistry of the traditional scholastic justification of the concept of freedom, he thought that the Kantian camp was offering him what he took to be a choice between the determinism of Schmid and the indeterminism of Reinhold (of Kant as well, because he understood Kant's just published essay on radical evil to be an endorsement of Reinhold). And since he did not believe that Reinhold had succeeded in safeguarding the principle of sufficient reason, and since he thought that the principle was synonymous with rationality (as just about everyone did, Reinhold included), he had no choice but to opt for determinism. Yet he wondered how the alleged critical modifications that Schmid had brought to the older statement of this position were any improvement on it. In Creuzer's opinion, a transcendent I totally subject to laws that are presumed intelligible but are unknown is no less exempt from fatalism than a phenomenal I subject to natural laws for which there is experiential knowledge. In the humanistic tradition of Abicht, Rehberg, and many others, Creuzer therefore concluded by accepting a skeptically mitigated form of natural determinism. For practical purposes, so far as morality is concerned, all that is required is *some* freedom from the necessitating impulses of the senses, however conscious one is that, if one were to investigate far enough and long enough, one would discover that, though free of these immediate constraints, one nonetheless acts under the influence of other, more far-reaching ones. These constraints can at least be investigated, whereas those that Schmid had postulated, and were the basis of his so-called intelligible determinism, must remain a mystery for us. In the words with which Creuzer brought his long investigation to an end:

The difference between the two fatalisms [the intelligible and the empirical] appears to be just this: that the empirical forges visible fetters for us, whereas the intelligible [forges] invisible ones. The first type of fetters have at least the advantage that, [with respect to them,][9] the honest seeker of truth, for whom their burden might become too oppressive, can conjure the higher genius of his pure practical reason, and derive some intimation of freedom; whereas with respect to the other fetters – under which not only the phenomenal 'I' sighs, but that higher genius as well – there never appears any hope of liberation. What is there left for one labouring under such fetters but for its giddy reason to let itself be lulled by phantasy, this sorrowful comforter, into the wild dream of a *Providence?* And this Providence would drive all rational beings – some later, by way of a detour into the so-called vices; others sooner, along the straight path of the so-called virtues – to the one common final goal of unhindered moral efficacy and of the happiness bound to it. And it would drive them mechanically, on the iron chains of necessity (a necessity which, in virtue of a charitable illusion, appears to most to be freedom), in the manner of mere automata. Together with Voltaire, one must cry out to any man engrossed in the proud illusion of his freedom:

> You vile and imperfect atom, who believes, doubts, disputes,
> Creeps up, rises, falls, yet denies his fall,
> Who tells us, *I am free!*, while showing us his chains.[10]

The other publication, entitled *Concerning the Moral Good as Derived from a Disinterested Will for the Good* [*Wohlwollen*], was by a certain Friedrich Heinrich Gebhard.[11] Unlike Creuzer, Gebhard professed to be a Kantian, but, popular philosopher that he was as if by nature, he had defended Kant's moral theory on grounds still consistent with traditional eudaimonism. His argument, in brief, was that morality depends on a feeling of sympathy (*Wohlwollen*) for the whole of humankind. Such a feeling, however, cannot be effective unless it is based on the 'pure' satisfaction that follows from abiding by the rule of reason. This rule, derived a priori, is the only reliable guide for determining what should count as the good of humankind. Anything else, especially when dependent on the senses, might well lead to harmful results. But only practical reason as understood by Kant can provide the kind of 'rule' that gives rise to genuine pure satisfaction in following it – a pure satisfaction that is in turn the basis for effective 'sympathy'.[12] Now, despite the differences in tone and intention separating the two, Creuzer's and Gebhard's essays were both connected with Schmid. The latter had produced a Preface for Creuzer's essay in which he had tried to distance himself (indeed, not very successfully) from the 'intelligible fatalism' that Creuzer had attributed to him. Gebhard had deferred in his essay to Schmid for the right solution to the problem of how to reconcile duty and the desire for happiness in moral life. When Fichte therefore reviewed the two essays (Creuzer's in issue No. 303, 1793, of the *ALZ*;[13] Gebhard's in the following issue, No. 304[14]), his reviews turned out to be attacks on Schmid himself. It is at this point that the already mentioned Fichte–Schmid dispute broke out.[15]

What happened, in brief, is that Fichte sided in his review of Creuzer's essay with the author's rejection of Schmid's intelligible fatalism. However, whereas Creuzer had made his point civilly, as an issue of debate, without in any way impugning the good intentions of Schmid, Fichte charged the latter with undermining even the possibility of moral life.[16] In the review of the other essay, Fichte had ridiculed Gebhard. Fichte had tried in vain, so he says, to find in the essay the slightest indication that the author had even an inkling of what reason in general, and practical reason in particular, mean in critical philosophy.[17] Gebhard had, however, deferred to Schmid for the right solution to the problem of how to reconcile duty and the desire for happiness in moral life. In ridiculing him, Fichte had by implication ridiculed Schmid himself. The latter did not fail to rise to the occasion. He replied in the same tone, and Fichte replied to the reply. In 1796, he lampooned Schmid's psychological Kantianism in an article in which he compared his own philosophy with Schmid's.[18] This is the notorious piece in which Fichte accused Schmid of exhibiting "facts of consciousness" as if pickled in alcohol and declared him "nonexistent as philosopher."[19] At that point, in 1796, the dispute was finally quieted, though it was not resolved.

In the whole affair, Fichte did not cut an attractive figure. The new inflammatory language he was bringing to philosophical discussion was both noted and widely condemned.[20] Yet the philosophical claims he was making were not only valid but also profound. Regarding the Gebhard review, the piece is so polemical in tone, and so convoluted in execution, as to risk making no sense at all. Its knotted arguments apart, the one clear, and clearly valid, complaint that emerges from it is that, according to Fichte, the author of the essay might have defended Kant against his opponents more satisfactorily if he had limited himself to explaining that it was pointless for these opponents to request a material for the otherwise merely formal moral imperative, since the posing of the request presupposes that the request has already been satisfied.[21] That is, there is no point in trying to lay out (*vorlegen*) a material for the moral law ahead of it, for to seek such a material is to seek the law that makes it a *moral* material in the first place. The ultimate content of the law is thus the law itself. In the Creuzer review, if one ignores the broad salvo directed at Schmid, Fichte's behavior is much more diplomatic and constructive. Since he thought that Kant had come out on the side of Reinhold, and since he himself had a high regard for the latter, his first concern was to defend both Reinhold and Kant from the charge that the two had violated the principle of sufficient reason. As he says, a product of freedom carries its own explanation (its own sufficient reason), since freedom is its own cause. Reinhold had explicitly said this much.[22] However, as Fichte proceeds to elaborate on the point, he diplomatically criticizes Reinhold. There cannot be a direct line of causality between freedom understood as its own source of causality and the realm of appearances, since the two belong to totally different levels of conceptualization. Appearances must be explained within their own realm according to laws of nature. The most that one can do, therefore, is to postulate a *tertium quid* (middle term) that accounts for the harmony (but not a direct causal relation) between the two. This is what Kant had done. He had provided the required *tertium quid* with his postulate of God without thereby compromising the distance separating the noumenal and the phenomenal.[23] By postulating a transcendent source of causality with direct results in the phenomenal realm (namely, the faculty of arbitrary choice), Reinhold had compromised this distance.[24]

This is Fichte's criticism of Reinhold. There is more, however, to his commentary than this. Fichte also argues that, as the source of intelligible causality, the will does not appear in experience 'as determining', that is, precisely as act. It does, however, assume an appearance there, ex post facto as it were – that is, 'as determinate' or as objectified in its results,[25] notably in the form of the law but also in the appearance of free choice. And how this last appearance arises, that is, how we come to believe that we have arbitrary choice, needs explaining – though not in Reinhold's fashion. Inasmuch as there is in Fichte's review also an implied criticism of Kant, it is that the latter had equally failed on this count. He had failed to explain the *appearance* in experience of arbitrary choice. This is a criticism that would have easily been lost on the unwary reader of the review or, if noticed, would have sounded cryptic indeed. It was couched in a language that already presupposed conceptual moves that were systematically expounded by Fichte only later. Yet, though not altogether innocent of obscurantism, Fichte could also not be totally blamed for expecting at least some comprehension from his readers. For, as a matter of fact, he had already at least adumbrated his moves publicly in his first publication ever, a book-length essay published in 1792 under the title of *Critique of All Revelation*. This is the publication that, by a play of circumstances, had propelled him to notoriety overnight.[26] And he had further refined the same moves in a paragraph (§2) added in 1793 to the second edition of the essay. The paragraph contained the sketch of a theory of the will and was Fichte's contribution to this ongoing debate. The following year (1794), Fichte was to publish his well-known review of Aenesidemus's skeptical attack on Kant and Reinhold in which he introduced the notorious distinction between *Tatsache* and *Tathandlung* ('matter of fact' and 'matter of action').[27] This distinction is normally taken to mark the beginning of the *Wissenschaftslehre*. But in fact, the strategy that Fichte was to adopt for clarifying Kant to his satisfaction had already been mapped out in his first treatise on revelation in the two editions of 1792 and 1793.

6.2 THE GOSPEL ACCORDING TO FICHTE

6.2.1 Theory of 'Revelation'[28]

Fichte's *Versuch einer Critik aller Offenbarung (Attempt at a Critique of All Revelation)*[29] was written in the transcendental style inaugurated by Kant. Its project is the a priori deduction of the idea of revelation – such as can be derived from the principles of practical reason in abstraction from the content of any historical religion.[30] Presupposed is a distinction between 'theology' and 'religion'. Theology becomes religion when its theoretical propositions about God, the soul, and the world bear practical results in the determination of the will. As theoretical instruments the propositions have no practical consequence, for as such they only express assumptions made for conceptual purposes alone, without reference to the require-ments of moral existence. Before being capable of determining our will in any respect, the propositions must be subjected to the influence of a moral interest in general for which the will alone is responsible. Once this interest has been established, the propositions can then be used as instruments for generating particular attitudes in us such as the 'fear of the Lord', 'reverence', and the like, all of which have moral significance. At this point theology becomes religion.[31]

The influence, however, that theological ideas have on our will varies, depending on how they relate to the two sides of our moral constitu-tion – namely, the sensuous and the intellectual.[32] We can revere God as the creator of nature and as the one who guarantees that the natural happiness of each individual will be commensurate with the individual's moral righteousness. Or we can revere God as the one who through his Will has authored the very natural laws that allow nature to con-form to our transcendent moral ends. Now, religion in its most proper sense arises when the moral law brings with it the added weight of being accepted as God's Commandment. "Or finally [theological ideas] have immediate effect upon our will because of the added weight that the [moral] Commandment has by being God's Commandment; it is then that religion in its *most proper* sense arises."[33] The concept of revelation is directly connected with this sense of religion. God, as the creator of nature, can also manifest himself to us as the author of the moral law inasmuch as he proclaims himself as such through his causality in the world of the senses. "The concept of revelation is the concept of an effect produced by God in the world of the senses through supernatural causality, in virtue of which he announces himself as the Giver of the Law."[34]

Now, there is nothing in all of this that cannot be found at least implicitly in Kant's doctrine on religion, except for one point that has to do precisely with the relation between the two senses of freedom that in Kant remained problematic, namely, freedom as a source of purely spontaneous agency *(causa sui)* and as the function of rational reflection or freedom as 'pure will' and as 'practical reason'.[35] In Fichte's discussion of the possibility of revelation, it is now clear that in the genesis of morality it is the power of the will (whether it be God's will or the pure will in us humans) that comes first. However, this otherwise unconstrained power needs the reflection of reason, and the limits that such a reflection entails, in order to become conscious of itself. The will produces 'rationality', thereby limiting itself in order to know itself, that is, it acquires determinate being or determinateness.

Insofar as Fichte's immediate concern in *Critique of All Revelation* was concerned, one consequence of this inversion in the relation of reason to will is that, since the will's spontaneity transcends the distinctions of moral reason (for morality is only a product of it), one can legitimately ask why we should attribute the law to God and not to the will itself. Fichte's answer is that, materially speaking, that is, so far as the content of moral obligation is concerned, the law is to be attributed to the will in general. All agency flows from it. But, so understood, this will is equally present in every moral being (God included, to the extent that he too is a moral being). Whether the law is therefore presented as the product of man's moral agency or God's is a purely formal question. It really has to do with *how* the law is promulgated.[36] And since it is clear that the human individual is first motivated by the law because of the will in him, and would not be able to recognize the same law as promulgated by God without this original motivation, it follows that God (the supposed author of the law and the object of religious worship) has significance for him only because he (God) is an objective projection of the individual's own subjective commitment to morality.

The idea of God (the Giver of Law through the moral law in us) is based on an externalization [*Entäusserung*] of our moral law, by the projection [*Übertragung*] of something subjective in us into a Being outside us; and this projection is the specific principle of a religion instrumental in the determination of the will.[37]

A second consequence emerges in response to a further question. Why should a moral individual ever want to project the source of morality that lies within him outside onto a God who is first conceived only as the creator of nature? Or, in other words, if the moral law is already within us, and must be there in order for any of its external manifestations to be recognized by us, why should we ever believe in a divine revelation of the same law? Why should we ever need any such revelation in the first place? Fichte's answer is that revelation has to do with *consciousness* of the law. To *be* a moral being, and to *know* oneself to be one, is for practical purposes one and the same thing. Whatever is required for our knowledge of the law is therefore also required for our moral existence. But since we are not just pure will, but beings of nature as well, the process by which we acquire moral self-consciousness must also be part of nature. And since God is the creator of nature, he must also be responsible for constituting it in such a way that in it we acquire the self-consciousness required for moral life. In this sense God can be said to reveal the law, and the concept of revelation is thereby justified.[38]

These two consequences alone are already significant. In the century that followed, the notion of religion as an objective projection of a subjective state became canonical for the Young Hegelians (who actually were much more Fichtean than Hegelian). Here we have it explicitly and unequivocally formulated in Fichte's earliest publication. Even more significant for our purposes, however, are the moral consequences of Fichte's move. It might appear at first that, in privileging will over reason, Fichte has thereby given a new *practical* importance to 'freedom' understood as *causa sui*. According to Kant, this kind of causality is indeed a theoretically necessary presupposition of moral life. As such, it must be postulated. It remains nonetheless a mystery for us, and, once postulated for systematic purposes, it takes second place in moral praxis to what, practically, should be the primary interest of moral life, namely, the formal exigencies that the law, the product of reason, places on human conduct. By making the law flow from the will, Fichte seems to have made the voluntary aspect of an action – such as must remain inherently transcendent – the central consideration of moral life. In an important sense that we shall note in a moment, this is indeed the case. In another equally important sense, the opposite is, however, also true. For, whatever the freedom in question might amount to, if there is to be any consciousness of it, it must become, according to Fichte, the object of reflective conceptualization; hence it must acquire determinate being in the form of some particularized action. This is a defining move on Fichte's part, since it stipulates a necessary condition of knowledge in general. There is no knowledge without reflection, hence without conceptualization, hence without objectification. But an object is always a determinate 'somewhat', since it cannot be object without being such *for someone* with respect to whom it necessarily stands determinate. Finitude, such as is entailed by determination, is therefore essential to all knowledge. It follows that the idea of an intellectual intuition of the type that God might have – one that, as Kant thought, would know its object by creating it and would therefore in effect be identical to the absolute spontaneity of free agency – such an idea, on Fichte's assumption, is self-contradictory. For any such intuition, in order to know itself as the intuition of anything at all, itself included, would need conceptualization and would thus cease to be intuition.[39] To be sure, Fichte does not deny intellectual intuition. On the contrary, at a later point he will claim that intellectual intuition is an essential moment of all experience. In this, he could easily have been taken as granting what Kant had denied. In fact, in the spirit in which he was making it, Fichte's claim had the effect of deflating whatever theoretical importance Kant's purely hypothetical idea of a possible intellectual intuition might have had. Any such intuition, even if entertained by God, would be in no better position to know anything about freedom than the immediate but empty awareness of oneself that, even according to Kant, accompanies all experience. This empty awareness is what Fichte now calls 'intellectual intuition'.[40] Kant's hypothetical 'intuition' could not amount to any more than this awareness. Hence, just like it, it would have to find determinate content only by means of conceptualization. Even if there were God, and this God had intellectual intuition, he would still have to discover in finite existence *what* this intuition is the intuition of. Revelation through nature, inasmuch as there is any, is just as much *for* God as *for* humans.

Therefore, there is nothing intrinsically mysterious about freedom. Freedom *appears* in the sense that it assumes determinate forms ('determinateness'). On the one hand, it assumes the form of categorical imperative; on the other hand, it assumes that of law of nature; and, in the interface between the two, freedom assumes the form of arbitrary choice. The theoretical problem that freedom poses is to recognize reflectively how these different appearances that it presents fit together. The practical one is to conceive of a humanity, complete with appropriate legal and political institutions, that would make its realization here on earth just as necessary as any mechanism of nature. This last task was, of course, one that Kant also had in mind in his idea of history. The crucial difference brought about by Fichte is that this process of reconciling the natural and the intelligible is not to be conceived as involving two radically different spheres of existence (i.e., the noumenal and the phenomenal), since both nature and the moral law are appearances of freedom. Nor would the process have to entail a line of efficient causality running directly from the noumenal to the phenomenal – on Kant's own assumptions a contradiction in terms. Nor, again, would it have to be conceived in terms of a *tertium quid* mysteriously reconciling the two. The realization of freedom is strictly a worldly affair. In this respect, moral life in Fichte's conceptual framework loses the semblance that it has in Kant of seeking its consummation in a transcendent beyond. Any such consummation, inasmuch as it is possible, would have to be immanent to experience.[41]

This is only one aspect of the story, however. The moment of transcendence is still very much present in Fichte's system, but in a different sense than in Kant's. Though freedom *appears* indeed, and is therefore realized as well as known in its appearance, it is nonetheless thus realized and known *exclusively* as appearance, that is, in a necessarily objectified and hence limited form. Freedom, therefore, can only be striven for – not, however, in the sense that it calls for a realization that would bring the striving to an end (except, of course, when one talks and thinks in the medium of imagery), but in the sense that the striving *is* its realization, to the point that it would have to be institutionalized precisely as striving in any adequate moral or sociopolitical structure. Moreover, since freedom thus transcends any of its objectifications, it must be taken on faith that freedom is the primary determining factor of experience. The assumption of a 'system of freedom' in which the mechanism of nature is the necessary condition for freedom's realization can only be the result of a commitment freely made because of moral interest. Conceptually, as well as socially, it would be just as possible to assume that the mechanism of nature is the primary determining factor, and that the otherwise postulated system of freedom follows from it only as its epiphenomenon. Fichte will concede this much in due time.[42] Indeed, he will even argue that the presence of an original, albeit still unspoken, intuition of freedom, or of such an event that deserves the name of 'freedom' rather than of 'blind nature', is itself an object of belief, albeit a practically necessary belief.[43] This is where Fichte officially states the position that, as we have been arguing, is the conceptually unavoidable consequence of Kant's critical system. In so doing, Fichte completes the breach from the Enlightenment already initiated by Kant. When it takes a commitment of faith in order to accept one conceptual position as contrasted with another, faith is no longer contained within the bounds of reason. It rather contains reason.

Fichte considered himself just as much a disciple of Jacobi as of Kant. One can understand why. But we are way ahead of ourselves. We are well past the limits of Fichte's essay on revelation and already deeply involved in his system. For a more detailed exposition of the latter (the *Wissenschaftslehre*), we shall recruit Reinhold's aid in just a moment. As for Fichte's vision of humankind, we shall return to it only in the concluding chapter. Rather, the most pressing object of consideration at the moment is Fichte's phenomenological account of how freedom appears. For this, we must turn to the 'Theory of the Will' that he sketched in §2 of the second edition of *Critique of All Revelation* "as preparation of a deduction of religion in general."

6.2.2 Theory of the 'Will'

"To determine oneself to the production of a representation, with consciousness of one's own activity, is called *volition* [*Wollen*]; the capacity to determine oneself, with consciousness of this self-induced activity [*Selbsttätigkeit*], is called *faculty of desire*. [. . .] Volition differs from faculty of desire as the actual differs from the potential" (GA I.1, 135:4–8).[44]

Thus begins Fichte's theory. The definitions are borrowed from Reinhold, from a nine-page section entitled "Outlines of the Theory of the Faculty of Desire" that he had added, as if as an afterthought, to his essay of 1789.[45] To the modern ear, they will sound strange. They make sense, however, in the neoscholastic, Kantian, conceptual context within which both Reinhold and Fichte operated. Assume that consciousness is the product that results from the representation or active apprehension of a sense-material that is originally simply *found* in the mind.[46] This material is given to representation in 'affection' or *Empfindung*, and when taken on its own is blind. Inasmuch as this material is assumed as simply given to representation, even the a priori forms of sense-intuition and the equally a priori forms of conceptual recognition that constitute it as the material of a representation, must also be *given* in affection – in their case, in 'inner affection', or inner sensibility. Any desire whose object is conditioned by a representation whose content is thus given to it is deemed 'sensuous'. It is an empirical desire, one that cannot be determined a priori but depends rather on affectivity (135:16–29).

The matter does not end here, however. For, however passively a subject might stand in representation to a given material, the question still remains as to why it would make that material an object of desire (135:30–136:1). If I may gloss on Fichte's text, no matter how passive a modification of the mind is, it still becomes implicated in the mind's active process of self-representation. And it is of the essence of desire that, even when going after a *given* object, it nonetheless actively represents this object to itself as the kind of thing it would go after (or actively avoid). This active representation on the part of a subject of an otherwise passive state, together with the consciousness that it generates, constitutes, according to Fichte, the basic structure of 'desire'. In desire, a subject of experience productively takes hold of its own affected state as subject – it takes a stand with respect to it.[47] The problem that Fichte must resolve in his theory is whether this active process of self-determination, already at work in desire, can occur in abstraction from the sense content that conditions it in the latter; or, in other words, whether a subject's stand with respect to its own affectivity can be assumed a priori, without any dependence on the affectivity itself. If this is possible, we would then have a purely self-induced, and self-determined activity – a volition, in other words, that determines its own capacity to desire. Such a purely self-determined activity is what we call freedom, the reality of which would thereby be established.

Fichte's strategy is to begin by further developing the already outlined structure of desire. As just analyzed, desire is a synthesis of active production and passive reception. But any such synthesis of opposites requires a medium that would induce it. Can we think of a state of mind even more primitive than desire in which this opposition between active production and passive reception has already been overcome or, more accurately, has yet to arise? Such a state, according to Fichte, is 'impulse' (*Trieb*, also translated as 'drive') (136:1–5). This term conveys the idea of a movement on the part of the mind that is spontaneous but that has no choice as to its direction. The important point about it is that it occurs on the side of *Empfindung*, that is, 'sensation' understood in the sense of 'affection' or 'sensibility' (136:6–9). The implication is that in the genesis of experience, 'passion' and 'action' are originally inextricably bound together. There is no passive reception without an active resistance on the part of the receiver (a sort of preprogrammed 'reaction', so to speak) that, by contrast, gives the reception the character of being 'passive'. This is a point that Fichte does not develop in the present context, but it will become all-important in his system. It undercuts from the start any absolute distinction between a priori and a posteriori. Now, this original impulse, which is part of *Empfindung* itself, qualifies the content of the latter. It makes it either 'pleasant' or 'unpleasant' (136:10:14). And, to the extent that it gives rise to a sense of 'pleasure' or 'displeasure', *if left unchecked*, it provides the *tertium quid* required for inducing desire or repulsion, or the active determination that allows one to be passively affected in a certain way.

As it happens, impulses *can* and *are* checked by the intervention of reason (138:10ff). Without such an intervention, they would only induce desire for immediate satisfaction (*Glück*). By means of conceptualization, reason brings into play the possibility of maximizing this satisfaction by postponing it in view of future, more advantageous conditions. It can also introduce the idea of a greatest possible satisfaction or an idea of unqualified happiness (*Glückseligkeit*) (138:29ff.). It thus sets in motion a process of deliberation that finally results in a practical judgment regarding what should be desired and willed. And this process is effective in modifying both the degree of strength and the direction of the drive on which desire is based. What would have been desire for limited satisfaction (*Glück*) is transformed into desire for happiness (*Glückseligkeit*). Here Fichte goes into great detail in explaining the origin of the traditional eudeimonism of popular philosophy, even though he does not mention it as such. (138:10ff.; 29ff.). His main concern throughout is to stress that in all instances – regardless of the extent to which an impulse is rationally modified – what counts as pleasant *for* an individual subject does not ultimately depend on him but on laws over which he has no control. Such laws are experienced as necessary and, when expressed in conceptual form by theoretical reason, are equally recognized as necessary (139:10–15). Moreover, since there is no such thing as a unit of sensation (*Empfindung*) determinable a priori (sensation understood here again as a subjective modification of the mind, in contrast to its meaning as content of immediate intuitions subject to space and time determination), the subject is totally at the mercy of the vagaries of the senses for what constitutes for him an irreducible quantum of pleasure (*Lust*) (136:20–30).

It follows, for all the reasons just stated, that if one acted only on the basis of pleasant sensations (however modified by rational deliberation), one would not be deemed capable of moral responsibility (139:16ff.). In all cases (as Kant and Reinhold had already argued, though Fichte does not mention them by name), one would be acting simply on the strength of the strongest impulse as determined by necessary laws. The question of whether 'free volition' is possible – or again, whether it is possible to bring oneself to a certain determination spontaneously in an absolute sense, without presupposing the content of the determination a posteriori – this question still remains unanswered. To be sure, as Fichte points out, there is already evidence of the reality, and hence of the possibility, of this spontaneous self-determination in the development of desire as it has been explained so far. For it is clear that it is possible to suspend an otherwise natural impulse by means of deliberation and thus to modify it rationally, thereupon releasing it, so to speak, and allowing it to follow its still natural, though now rationally modified, course. A subject of experience must engage in some sort of spontaneous self-determination in order to make that suspension effective. Yet, lest one accuse him of making things too easy for himself by relying on this evidence alone – as if he were introducing 'absolute freedom' by a sleight of hand – Fichte raises his question again, namely, whether there is such a thing as a totally self-induced representation.[48]

The problem is not whether the concept of absolute freedom is logically possible. The concept can quite easily be derived by thinking of a faculty of desire that, in volition, would have nothing but its own form as object of realization – or again, one for which the material of the representation that it wants realized is the form of the representation itself[49] (140:20–9). In this way, by attending to the internal requirements of such a self-directed act, we arrive at the notion of a law that has only its own lawfulness as content, and hence that defines what constitutes right absolutely (141:16ff.). Kant had already trodden that path. The problem, rather, is to demonstrate that this form of desire is a *fact of consciousness* – one that would force universal acceptance and therefore constitute the ultimate principle of philosophy (140:33–5). *'Tatsache des Bewußtseins'* ('fact of consciousness') and *'allgemeine geltende Prinzip aller Philosophie'* ('universally accepted principle of all philosophy') belong, of course, to Reinhold's terminology. At this early stage, Fichte is still bound to it. It soon becomes clear, however, that, though still abiding by it, Fichte has already transcended its original conceptual framework. He has already abandoned Reinhold's or Schmid's conception of an immediate fact of consciousness for the very good reason that freedom, in any relevant sense, requires consciousness of being free, while consciousness (self-consciousness included) is bound to the passivity of the senses (141:28–142:1). The totally self-contained faculty of desire that is required, however, would have to be a pure act of spontaneity – one that therefore transcends the internal distinctions on which its stated concept is based. Because it transcends these distinctions, there is no immediate consciousness of this faculty of desire, nor could there ever be any in principle. It cannot be picked out of consciousness, so to speak, as a fact that is immediately apprehended. The danger of illusion to which any supposed consciousness of being free is susceptible is due precisely to this juxtaposition of opposite requirements, that is, to the disproportion between alleged consciousness and intended object. For the required evidence, Fichte has no choice, therefore, but to turn to impulse again, in order to see whether there is enough scope in the synthesis of activity and passivity that it entails for a meaning of spontaneity that, though sense-qualified (hence within the scope of consciousness), is nonetheless still absolute (142:1–19). Can impulse be developed to fit the bill?

Once restated in this way, Fichte's problem is in principle already resolved. Impulse indeed yields the required evidence once it acquires the form of a 'feeling of self-respect'. Three conceptual moves are required here, starting from impulse, namely, the moves (1) to feeling (*Gefühl*), (2) to feeling of self-respect, and (3) to consciousness of freedom, as follows.[50]

(1) Given Fichte's definition of impulse, rooted as it is in *Empfindung*, there is already in this *Empfindung* an incipient moment of active reflection. In impulse, the content of a sensation is subjectively determined as either pleasant or unpleasant. A stand is being actively taken with respect to it. One need only raise this moment of reflection to a higher level, thereby turning *it* into an object of reflection, to obtain the type of mental configuration that, though not necessarily what 'feeling' ordinarily explicitly denotes in English (or, for that matter, *Gefühl* ordinarily denotes in German), still falls within the general range of meaning of the word. At issue in feeling is not simply how one spontaneously stands with respect to a sense-given material (as is the case with impulse), but how one stands with respect to one's original stand before that material. Or again, at issue is not whether one finds some sense material pleasant or unpleasant, but how one *finds oneself* in thus finding that material, that is, how *one feels* about one's otherwise purely impulsive reaction to it. One can feel good or bad about it, elated or depressed, guilty or innocent. In other words, in feeling, though this feeling still is very much part of the sense economy of the mind, and is therefore a suitable object of consciousness, a first abstraction has already been made from the given

content of sensations. Feeling presupposes a norm that is not necessarily derived from the senses. In principle, therefore, it already constitutes a self-directed experience. As such, it exhibits in inchoate form the reflective properties that define reason.[51] All this is in line with Fichte's general intention of establishing a gradation between rationality and sensibility.

(2) One cannot, however, ignore, even in feeling, the passive aspect of sensibility. This passivity must still be present there, in some modified form, for otherwise feeling would turn into plain rational activity. Can we think of a special type of feeling that would most clearly satisfy the two conditions that define it as feeling, namely, freedom from mere sense impulse coupled with external constraint (hence affection) in the exercise of this freedom? Feeling of respect, according to Fichte, fits this bill. Respect is, in the first instance, 'respect for another'. Now, in respecting another, one stands before this other as *checked* by it, that is, as affected by its presence. This check (*Affektion*) denotes a moment of passivity on the part of the one feeling respect – not, however, a passivity due to any external or positive action exercised by the other. If that were the case, respect would be merely a matter of impulsive reaction. Rather, for respect to be aroused, the other to which it is directed need do nothing more than just be there. The detachment from original *Empfindung* required by feeling is thus retained. The passivity is self-induced in the sense that it stands witness to the fact that one has actively interiorized the presence of that other, has made it part of him, as something, however, that is greater than him and that, therefore, will necessarily act as some sort of constraint on anything he does. This constraint takes the form of an *interest* in promoting in all things the cause of the other.[52]

What constitutes, however, this other originally? Fichte's answer is that it is none other than reason itself.[53] Fichte does not elaborate on the answer. He has, however, already established, in his first analysis of impulse, that it is possible for reason to force a subject in experience to transcend the immediacy of sensations. His task, now, is only to define the most primordial form that reason's presence to the senses can assume – a presence that can make the transcendence possible in the first place. And he finds this primordial form precisely in the feeling of respect. Within the economy of truly human experience, this feeling therefore comes first; it constitutes humanity. In brief, on the basis of the feeling of respect, one must assume that there is a primordial relationship between the senses and reason, in virtue of which the senses are indeed affected by reason – not, however, as if by a thing in itself, under the positive influence of an external cause, but internally and negatively, as if, when confronted by it, the senses were stepping on a territory already occupied. Fichte points out, moreover, that respect is by nature always 'self-respect, since it is a product of reflection, and hence instrumental in the establishment of a self.[54] With an obvious though tacit reference to Reinhold, he adds that the distinction between selfish and nonselfish impulses, though perhaps useful in certain contexts, is ultimately pointless.[55] All impulses are self-centered. The question is how rational they are in thus being self-centered.[56]

(3) Here we have the notion of a volition that respects both the requirements of freedom and of consciousness, and therefore renders the experience of being free credible. We can think of a uniquely human form of freedom that consists indeed (as it must, according to the purely abstract concept of freedom) in the capacity for the self-induced production of a representation that has nothing but its own form as content. This capacity, however, demonstrates its effectiveness in imposing its own norms of representation as a determination of sense-affectivity (i.e., in actively informing this affectivity) only by way of interfering with the impulses of the senses (in virtue of its mere presence, which presence thereby makes its first appearance in consciousness). It is a fact that there are feelings that would have no meaning except on the assumption of rationality – that reason, in other words, necessarily stands in the way of one's sensibility even if one were deliberately trying to operate exclusively at the level of the latter. In virtue of these feelings, a subject of experience recognizes that he is bound in volition to a transcendent and unimpeachable moral necessity. Yet, since this necessity is present in him only negatively (by way of interference with his senses), insofar as his experience is concerned, the execution of that volition is qualified by the vagaries of the senses. Volition thus becomes part of his conscious life, and in this way – in this sensible though rationally qualified context – it also assumes *for him* the form, not just of freedom, but of 'arbitrary choice' as well (*liberum arbitrium*).[57] This is the deduction that Fichte had found wanting in both Kant and Reinhold.

Fichte will eventually fail to exploit all the conceptual potentials of this original analysis of desire, and because of this failure he will make himself vulnerable to the criticism of Hegel. This is not a point that we can develop in the present study, but we shall see in the concluding chapter that Fichte will at the end promote an ideal of humankind that few would find acceptable nowadays. Nevertheless, one must still pause here to admire Fichte's skills in reconstructing the complexities of affective experience conceptually. Much of the phenomenological literature of the nineteenth and twentieth centuries is indebted (albeit more often than not by way of Hegel) to the descriptions of mental phenomena condensed in §2 of Fichte's first published book. Fichte has already gone a long way in defining his philosophical position. While relying on Reinhold's theory of representation and borrowing many of its definitions, he is in fact recasting the theory on a completely new basis. The distinction between *Tatsache* and *Tathandlung* was yet to come. It is already clear, however, that Fichte's model of the mind is no longer intended, as Reinhold's was, as a sort of anatomical diagram of an entity that we call the mind, one that we cannot know directly, and will never know, but that we must nonetheless *think* in order to explain, according to some physical or hyperphysical mechanics, certain facts *(Tatsachen)* allegedly apprehended in consciousness directly. Rather, Fichte's model is a conceptual construct, the whole point of which is to bring to explicit awareness the complexities and the quality of what Fichte takes to be typically human behavior – a behavior of which one becomes aware in the act of performing it (i.e., as *Tathandlung*), quite apart from any consideration of physical or hyperphysical causality. Fichte, in other words, is abandoning the older explanatory models of rational psychology, even those that, like Reinhold's, are reintroduced with alleged critical restrictions, and in their place he is providing a purely analytical account of distinctions and relations that have no meaning apart from the behavior that the account is supposed to bring to explicit awareness in the first place. As Fichte was later to say, though not a journalist of the mind, he was nonetheless providing a pragmatic history of it.[58] In this way, on this new functional or pragmatic basis, Fichte was thus satisfying the popular philosophers' demand (Reinhold among them) for an account of the genesis of experience – one that overcame Kant's all too rigid distinctions between a priori and a posteriori, form and content of experience. Reinhold had indeed already overcome these distinctions in his essay, as we have seen, but seemed to do so by accident. Fichte was now doing it quite deliberately.[59]

This is not to say that Fichte was thereby joining the ranks of the popular philosophers. On the contrary, he was defining his idealism in opposition to their various forms of subjectivism. The fundamental lesson to be gathered from his theory of volition, even in this earliest formulation of 1793, is that experience is from the start conceptual in nature. On that theory, the mistake of all popular philosophers was to think that one can somehow abstract a purely natural content of experience all by itself; examine how a human being would act when exclusively determined by it; and then add to it rational determinations as a final complement. Their mistake lay in failing to recognize that the presence of reason modifies the content of experience even before one begins to look for a would-be natural content in it, and that the natural is a normative concept from the beginning. Fichte's claim is so strong in this respect, and so important, that it deserves to be cited in full. I quote:

> Everyone is doubtless justified in living; yet it may nevertheless become a duty to sacrifice one's life. This revoking of justification would be a formal contradiction of the law with itself. Now the law cannot contradict itself without losing its lawful character, ceasing to be a law, and being forced to surrender itself completely. – The foregoing would lead us for the moment to conclude that all objects of sensuous impulse, in accordance with the requirement of the moral law that it not contradict itself, could only be appearances, not things in themselves, and that such a contradiction is therefore grounded in the objects insofar as they are appearances, and is thus illusory. So this proposition is just as surely a postulate of practical reason as a theorem of theoretical reason. There would accordingly be no death, no suffering, no sacrifice for duty in themselves; rather, the illusion of these things would be based merely on that which makes the things into appearances.[60]

'Life' is doubtless a concept amenable to empirical and even scientific definition. Yet, in the context of action, it is not this life thus empirically defined that is the object of desire, but the 'life that is right for me' or 'life as it ought to be'.[61] As thus defined, life is no longer empirically determinable but demands, rather, that it be injected into a world of cultural and social meanings. When contrasted with this new life, any hypothetically prior, empirically determinable life loses whatever appearance it might otherwise have of setting the norm for what counts as real. And that would be the case even if certain individuals, or even a whole culture, made it its deliberately chosen goal to live a life strictly according to the requirements of an empirically defined 'health'. For in that case too, health would have acquired a new meaning – itself a work of art rather than anything natural in a straightforward sense. In brief, it is ideality that ultimately defines what constitutes the thing in itself or the 'real unqualifiedly'. This is the thesis of idealism and the thesis that Fichte was defending from his earliest published texts.

One can understand, therefore (though not necessarily excuse), Fichte's condescending tone toward Creuzer or his contempt for Gebhard and Schmid. Fichte could well appreciate Creuzer's skepticism. It was the inevitable result of the confusion caused by Creuzer's treating freedom, as Reinhold did, as a sort of hyperphysical efficient causality. The effectiveness of reason is instead merely formal. It consists in its capacity to establish through representation a world of meaning, within which alone one can then speak of volition meaningfully. To speak of actual volition, of deliberation or choice, is to consider how this world, once established in principle, works itself out in detail with reference to a material that has already been conceptually interpreted. Reinhold had reverted to scholastic speculation in order to explain a human phenomenon, whereas he ought to have dwelled within the phenomenon itself – describing and analyzing it rather than invoking noumenal explanatory causes on its behalf. This was Reinhold's mistake, and Creuzer had not been perceptive enough to recognize it. A more illuminating strategy would have been, rather, to treat 'choice' as a specifically human phenomenon, as an operation conditioned by such factors as education, culture, individual judgment, and individual circumstances, and as falling, therefore, within a world that has indeed no reality apart from the intervention of reason. As a result, this sort of choice is not susceptible to purely empirical tests, but is one in which 'efficiency' still carries recognizable references to physical phenomena. In this context, one can meaningfully speak of human agency, yet recognize that it is conditioned by physical causes over which one might, in certain circumstances, have no control at all. The important consideration is that one *should* have control and that, in a proper human world, all the social conditions should therefore be in place that make the exercise of such control possible.

With respect to Gebhard,[62] the issue that the latter had raised – namely, whether desire for happiness is formally constitutive of moral motivation, or whether (as Gebhard was arguing in defense of Kant) it should rather be taken as subordinate to the quest of duty for duty's sake – this issue, according to Fichte, begs the more fundamental question of what constitutes 'happiness' in the first place. Gebhard, in the manner of all popular philosophers, had based his discussion on supposed facts of consciousness without realizing that any such fact, inasmuch as it falls within consciousness, is already a conceptually interpreted fact – in effect, a deed of reason or the product of a *Tathandlung*. The point was dramatically made in Fichte's parting shot at Schmid in 1796 at the end of the dispute that the review had caused. At that point, the shot was directed not just at Schmid's pseudo-Kantian moral doctrine, but at his whole idea of philosophy. Ultimately (Fichte says), the difference between idealism and dogmatism (Schmid's theory of facts of consciousness included) is that the latter assumes that the world is ready-made, "without any assistance from reason,"[63] and immediately sets out to demonstrate the harmony between the mind's representations and this presupposed world. How representations arise in the first place, why we should presume that they correspond to anything, or, for that matter, how and why we should come up with the idea itself of a 'world' – these are questions that are simply begged. Idealism, on the contrary, is concerned with precisely these questions. And it answers them by reenacting the reflective operation by which the mind, in turning to itself, thereby establishes the logical space within which things become objects for it. It is not the existence of things, in other words, that motivates idealism, but the meaning they have for us or the place they occupy within a world that is the mind's own contribution to reality. Whereas Schmid (or any other dogmatic philosopher) thus treated philosophy as a continuation of the physical sciences – as if, to the facts that the latter offer to our gaze, philosophy were simply to add some more, the mind itself among them, pickled in alcohol, as it were[64] – idealism distances itself from these facts totally, restricting itself rather to the genetic reproduction of the acts that are constitutive of the world of meaning (that of the physical sciences included).

6.3 REINHOLD ON FICHTE AND KANT

Fichte published the first systematic exposition of his new science of experience in 1794[65] at Jena, where he had just arrived to take over the chair of Kantian philosophy recently vacated by Reinhold. He published it piecemeal at first, in the form of successive student handouts for his first series of university lectures.[66] He repeatedly modified its exposition until his departure from Jena in 1800 and presented it again in even more modified forms later in Berlin. He himself considered his system as a project in progress, and explicitly cited later versions as improvements over earlier ones.[67] So far as we are concerned, just as we turned to Reinhold for an entry point into *Popularphilosophie*, so we can now do the same for the *Wissenschaftslehre*. Reinhold published a review of Fichte's first cycle of writings in January 1798 in the *ALZ*.[68] The review was long and detailed, and also honest in its attempt to represent Fichte's position accurately. It was not, however, necessarily insightful. As we shall see, Reinhold missed the true significance of the *Wissenschaftslehre*, just as he had missed the significance of popular philosophy or the fact that he was himself part of it. Despite his misunderstanding, and maybe even because of it, the review nonetheless helps to bring into focus precisely what was important about Fichte's new science. The review is all the more interesting, even curious, because of two circumstances. The first is that, only a few months earlier, namely, in a text dated March 1797, Reinhold had declared that he finally understood what Fichte meant by the I. He understood that Fichte had not meant by it the individual self. He was therefore ready to accept this I as the highest principle of all philosophical science.[69] Reinhold, in other words, had become a convert to Fichte's science, or, at least, this is the appearance that he conveyed. The second circumstance is that, at the same time, Reinhold was also undertaking a project of social reform that still called to mind the social program of the recently proscribed Illuminati and still presupposed the general philosophical outlook of their founder, Weishaupt. We shall return to these circumstances in due time. We can abstract from them for the time being and concentrate instead on the *Wissenschaftslehre.*

The review is a grandiose tour de force. At one level of discussion, Reinhold grants that Fichte has succeeded in abstracting the highest principle of experience and thereby has made possible the a priori reconstruction of its genesis. At the same time, however, he also wants to maintain that Kant's science of experience (especially in Reinhold's own systematized form) is still valid in its own right. This apologetic tone is already struck in the first part of the review, where Reinhold offers a lengthy historical recapitulation of the situation of philosophy prior to the appearance of Kant's Critique of Reason on the scene. His clear intent is to demonstrate that this Critique and Reinhold's restatement of it were the only logically possible resolution of the otherwise impossible problems hitherto incurred by all the major systems of philosophy. Fichte's own abstract reconstruction of experience, as Reinhold argues in the rest of the review, is in fact dependent, not just historically but also insofar as the structure of experience is concerned, on Kant's transcendental science.[70]

History gives evidence, according to Reinhold, that "the strivings of philosophical reason were always directed to *pure,* unconditional knowledge, independent of experience" (Col. 33). If this knowledge were ever achieved, it "would have to be one which is certain because of [*durch*] its truth, and true because of its certainty, [...] i.e. one that presupposes nothing except what it contains by itself and through itself" (Col. 36) – one, in other words, in which subjectivity and objectivity somehow coincide. Now, Kant had shown that "knowledge independent of experience is indeed *possible,*" but only inasmuch as it has "as object only the possibility of experience *as such.*" Reason, in other words, "is active exclusively *for itself* and *through* itself [as unconditional knowledge requires] only as *pure* reason," that is, only in its practical function, with reference to a moral world brought into existence through free agency alone. "*Objectively real* knowledge is possible [on the contrary] only *by means* of the senses, and of an *understanding* bound to the latter" (Col. 34). According to Kant, therefore, human knowledge is either the result of theoretical reason, that is, is *objective* knowledge without, however, being *pure* knowledge or is the product of a practical reason guided by the moral law. In this latter case, however, there is no question of 'knowledge' in any strict sense (Col. 37). Kant reached this conclusion on the basis of certain facts of consciousness, notably the original unity of apperception on the theoretical side and the moral law on the practical (Cols. 35–6). And, to the extent that he stayed by these factual presuppositions alone, he had kept (so Reinhold now says) within the boundaries of the method that philosophy had hitherto always followed. He had based himself on a theoretical as well as a practical use of reason that are *natural.* His only great contribution was to have led philosophy back to the sources of its otherwise natural convictions – such convictions, however, that dogmatism and skepticism had "desecrated" over the centuries through their conceptual artifices. "The discoverer of *synthetic judgments a priori,*" Reinhold proclaims, "could not have gone about his work except as the mere *analyst* of the thoughts of his predecessors," even though, in the situation in which he had found philosophy, "his *return* to the *natural* conceptions of *experience* and of *moral law,* and the development of these in their *original* [...] purity [...], would not have been possible without a *degree of healthy common sense* perhaps never before exhibited by any philosopher since Socrates" (Cols. 35–6).

It followed that for Kant philosophy had to remain an eternal striving toward pure knowledge, a never-ending external approximation to it. Reinhold, however, now argues that, though philosophy must indeed always be a striving, even as such a striving it need not be conceived with the restrictions that Kant had imposed upon it. And this freedom from restrictions is possible only if one engages reason in a use that is not just *natural* (whether theoretical or practical), but *pure* though *artificial.* The term 'artificial' (*künstlich*) is one that Reinhold borrows from Fichte but that, as we shall see in a moment, he actually understands quite differently from him. This allegedly artificial use allows reason to transcend its other natural use, thereby defining the one principle from which the concepts of experience and of moral law that the natural use simply presupposes both derive (Col. 38). The derivation of these two concepts in turn makes possible the comprehension of the relation between nature as it appears in experience de facto and as it should appear according to moral law, a relation that in Kant must remain unknown (Cols. 38–41). Pure knowledge, of the type that Reinhold has defined from the beginning, is then realized. As a further consequence, philosophical striving acquires a different meaning than it has in Kant. It finally ceases to be a mere external approximation to pure knowledge and becomes rather a progression internal to pure knowledge itself – one that presupposes that such knowledge has already been attained, and only seeks to comprehend within it, in its artificial ways, the whole content of experience (Cols. 36–7).

Here is where Fichte comes in, because he, according to Reinhold, had gone beyond Kant by engaging reason in its artificial use, thereby succeeding in the project, which for Kant had to remain only an impossible ideal, of reconstruing the whole system of experience on the basis of a single principle. Animating the project is the belief that the necessity encountered in nature has its origin in moral necessity, that is, that it is originally self-induced. In common experience, however, any such necessity is felt subjectively as externally imposed. The justification of the belief therefore depends on whether Fichte succeeds in reducing this subjective experience of externality to a moral source. Of course, it is possible to undertake a directly opposite project. It is possible to assume that natural necessity is primordial, and to try to derive the sphere of moral action from sources presumably external to a moral agent. This was the thrust of Weishaupt's cosmology, as we remember (though Reinhold does not mention the name here), and of much of popular philosophy as well. Fichte is, on the contrary, committed to turning the naturalism entailed in this position upside down. Nature must be understood as the product of freedom. But how is this to be done? More specifically, what is the nature of this artificial use of reason in virtue of which, according to Reinhold, Fichte was able to do the job?

The notion of *Tathandlung* is key to the answer. Reinhold knows at least this much. In contemporary philosophical jargon (which neither Fichte nor Reinhold, of course, had at their disposal), *Tathandlung* can quite easily and accurately be defined as an activity of which one becomes aware in the very act of performing it. This is what Fichte fundamentally means by it. A *Tathandlung* is 'a matter of doing', so to speak. 'Agency' and 'awareness' are inextricably bound together in it.[71] Fichte tries to abstract it in its most generalized form as a still indeterminate yet already intelligent activity, as the capacity for a thought performance in general. In this respect, he quite rightly connects it with the I think that, according to Kant, accompanies all representation and constitutes the principle of any synthesis of apprehension. The I is appropriately introduced in this context, since any self-awareness, of the kind that is attained in experience, depends in some way on intelligent activity. Yet, as Kant argued well and as Fichte now repeats, though the generalized awareness that accompanies all experience is indeed the necessary condition for any actual conception of one's self, inasmuch as the I of the I think is based on this awareness alone, it remains itself an empty thought, a reflective placeholder rather than the concrete self that actual experience requires. For the latter, the presupposed capacity for a thought performance in general must be realized in the thought of something determinate. Only then is the generalized awareness that otherwise accompanies it turned into the awareness of someone in particular, that is, a real, determinate self engaged in a world of real objects.

So far, there is nothing that separates Fichte from Kant. The difference comes at this point, and can be stated in two different yet complementary forms – one with more phenomenological, the other with more systematic, repercussions. Kant had drawn upon a supposed given sense content of experience, relying on the passivity of the sense organs for the material content that would determine both the object and the subject of experience. For Fichte, on the contrary, this move on Kant's part constituted an unwarranted excursion outside the boundaries of the prescribed problem of accounting for the possibility of experience from the standpoint of one actually engaged in it, that is, according to the conditions that make for meaningful existence. Kant had taken the passivity of the senses to be a physical fact without first exploring the conceptual context within which passivity acquires meaning for a subject in the first place. According to Fichte, on the contrary, the assumed *Tathandlung* is at the origin of experience. This capacity for a thought performance in general that carries in its train an equally generalized awareness of itself constitutes in principle the realm of intelligibility in general – a still empty intelligible space, so to speak, or a mere possibility for thought, within which recognizable objects can, however, appear. And the first among such objects to appear is precisely the original *Tathandlung* itself, which, in order to complete itself and thereby become actually *conscious of* itself, finally assumes a certain determination. From an act in general, it becomes a determinate mind or a self. But since there is no determining of a thing except with reference to something else, the appearance of this determinate mind must occur pari passu with the appearance of an object external to it (call it 'nature') to which it stands nonetheless in relation. This is not to say that nature, in a physical sense, is created by the mind according to Fichte. There is no question of physical 'causality' here. It is rather to say that the resistance that natural things pose to human actions, their opacity or the experience of passive externality that they induce in the mind, is in fact the product of a necessarily frustrated attempt at objectifying the act that gives rise to intelligibility in the first place and can therefore be grasped only ex post facto in an already particularized form that does not quite fully express the possibilities that it generates. Fichte's point is still the one that he had made in §2 of the second edition of his *Critique of Revelation,* with reference to the structure of feeling, but that he now expands as part of a general theory of experience. Just as in feeling it is how one stands with respect to oneself (ultimately, to reason within oneself) that gives rise to the special emotional color that qualifies otherwise external objects, in experience in general it is likewise the interest in promoting the intelligibility originally generated by the assumed *Tathandlung* that motivates the whole process of experience. It is this interest, in other words, that first delineates the opposition between oneself and a yet to be intellectualized 'other', and then leads to the various attempts at turning this other into 'another self', that is, into a humanized world.

The difference between Kant's and Fichte's systems follows accordingly. This is the other difference that separates the two men. In Kant's system, the assumed thing in itself provides the moment of transcendence that gives the objects of experience their character of mere appearances, but at the same time also stands as the term of reference in virtue of which these appearances are categorized according to a specific type – whether as 'things of nature', or 'moral obstacles', or 'aesthetically pleasing objects', or 'organic instruments', or, finally, 'historical witnesses'. These are objectifying forms all held together in a unity of tension that constantly risks running into contradiction. The contradiction is, however, held in abeyance in the name of critical ignorance. Fichte's system is, on the contrary, linear in construction. It starts with the explicit recognition that the first intelligible form that otherwise merely physical things acquire for us (in the medium of the concept, of course) is that of an other in general, with reference to which (indeed, in opposition to which) the task is thereby defined that motivates the rest of experience. This is the mind's task of determining a self for itself – of assuming, in other words, a deliberate position with respect to this other. And this the mind will do, first, by trying to define the other as if it existed in itself, on the assumption (which the dogmatists adopt unreflectively) that it has a meaning in itself quite apart from the mind's still nonthematic attempts at constituting a self. Here the mind's efforts result in the establishment of the theoretical sciences. But the objectivity of these sciences fails to live up to the norms of intelligibility in fact being sought by the mind in its self-constituting efforts. It fails because it is based on the assumption that the other is meaningful in itself (as if there were Platonic forms or

Aristotelian essences). As a result, these very efforts become the explicit object of the mind's reflection. The mind now posits that the other is such only for a self intent on establishing its own distance with respect to it. The other acquires moral significance, in other words, and so also do the theoretical sciences of which it has hitherto been the object.

As Fichte's system unfolds, the other thus assumes all the shapes that the object of experience also exhibits in Kant's system. In Fichte's, however, these same shapes emerge in a definite order of priority, and are all genetically deduced as episodes in the mind's single effort at constituting its self-identity. The thing in itself also makes its appearance, but only as an idea that is repeatedly excogitated precisely as part of that effort. This is not to say that the thing in itself was not an idea for Kant. In the context of Fichte's system, however, to either assert or deny knowledge of what this idea is allegedly the representation of is neither right nor wrong. It is just plain nonsensical. There is nothing to the idea except the speculative constructs that either the theoretical or the moral sciences supply for it, all of them as parts of the one effort to define the vocation of humankind that motivates the whole of experience. According to Fichte, practical interests ultimately motivate theoretical activity. The kind of humanity a culture makes its own also determines the types of sciences that it will promote. And in this respect at least, on this pragmatic bias, Fichte and Kant are of one mind.

That is, in its barest outlines, the *Wissenschaftslehre* that Fichte presented in several versions, always with an eye to its improvement. I have long since abandoned in this presentation Reinhold's review, even though an honest exposition of the nuts and bolts of the science can be found there.[72] I have tried to reassemble the same nuts and bolts in a more recognizably spirited body. We now return to the review in order to resolve the still unanswered question of what artificial meant for the two men. Fichte himself characterized his science as *künstlich* on the obvious ground that, as a science, it is the product of a specialized, indeed even contrived, abstractive reflection that philosophers alone practice because of the especially deliberate interest in promoting self-awareness that historically motivates them. This is the interest that also colors an especially philosophically inclined culture. Fichte sets his science in motion with a request (a 'postulate') directed at anyone willing to listen. The request is simply 'to think', in abstraction from anything in particular one might be tempted to think about, while at the same time reflecting on this intended thought in general. This act is the *Tathandlung* that constitutes the opening move of the *Wissenschaftslehre*, the performance that one performs just for the sake of performing it and of which one becomes aware in its very performance. Of course, the attempt at this act fails. One cannot think without thinking something determinate, whereby the thought itself becomes a determinate thought. The important lesson that the philosopher nonetheless learns from this failure is the one already stated. Mere physical things acquire meaning by becoming implicated in a kind of activity for which the mind is first of all responsible. And the first meaning that they acquire is precisely that of an other of this activity – a limit to it, a sort of distraction from the activity's original intention of exhibiting just itself. In virtue of this limit alone, however, the activity begins to assume the determinate shape of personalized conduct. This original meaning of other is the one that the philosopher assumes as the prototype of all determination and then develops in his systematic reproduction of experience.

But, of course, the philosopher's act that sets the *Wissenschaftslehre* in motion is an artificial construct, a thought experiment that might indeed personally affect the philosopher himself but has little to do with everyday life. At a later date, addressing himself to Reinhold, Fichte will acknowledge that life has its own immediate exigencies, its own commitments made on faith; and these are the factors that color common experience and motivate people's actions. One need not become a philosopher to discover one's conscience.[73] Yet, it does not follow that for Fichte the *Wissenschaftslehre* was just a game of no relevance for actual existence. The model of experience that the science offered explained why the ordinary human being is spontaneously a realist in a dogmatic sense. However true it might be that the search for a self or for the determination of the human vocation is the motivating force behind all experience, on that model the self will necessarily appear at the dawn of explicit consciousness as a ready-made thing of nature, since this self has no content except with reference to its other. Any individual's deliberate search for it always begins ex post facto, on the already (culturally) made assumption of what constitutes a self. The request that elicits the *Wissenschaftslehre*, that is, Fichte's call to think just for the sake of thinking, was therefore also a call to the historical individual to remember what he has forgotten about himself, namely, that he is the one who gave rise to the problem of meaning in the first place. The request also explained why the call might go unheeded. It might fall on distracted ears, all too attuned to a humanity simply accepted as given or ready-made by nature. And even if one were to heed the call, it does not follow that one would necessarily have to answer it in the way the *Wissenschaftslehre* prescribed. One might grant to Fichte that man's intelligent agency generates, in the first place, the realm of meaning, yet maintain that the questions raised within this realm must be answered in natural terms on the assumption that what constitutes a self is ultimately determined by nature rather than prescribed by the interests of reason. This, in essence, was the position of the popular philosophers. With his usual clarity of mind, Fichte saw this possibility. As we have seen, he recognized that naturalism is a conceptually consistent position. And while he expected everyone to be able to engage in the thought experiment of the *Wissenschaftslehre*, he knew that to accept the consequences that he drew from it required a commitment to a special view of humankind. This view, at the beginning at least, had to be taken on faith. What a human being already is, or the kind of prereflective commitment he has already made to his humanity, is what ultimately determines the kind of philosopher he becomes.[74] Cognizance of this circumstance explained, perhaps, the immoderate animosity that Fichte displayed toward Schmid and, in general, toward the philosophers of the facts of consciousness. His objection to them was moral just as much, if not more, than it was intellectual.

I shall return to this last consideration in just a moment. The point now is that Reinhold's use of artificial with reference to the *Wissenschaftslehre* could not have been the same as Fichte's. Evidence of the difference is to be found in one crucial criticism of Fichte that Reinhold felt obliged to advance in his review. At issue is the nature of sense-intuition and its place within experience. Fichte, of course, took Kant's claim that sensations without thought are blind in the strongest sense possible. From his standpoint, he could hardly do otherwise. Sensations, as physical events, might belong indeed to the prehistory of experience, but they have no place, *as such events*, within the history of experience itself. They enter the latter only as already conceptually interpreted.[75] In his review, however, Reinhold denies precisely this interpretation of Kant. As he says:

Mr Fichte asserts . . . : "According to Kant intuition is possible only *through its being* thought and conceptualized; according to him, *intuition without concept is blind,* i.e. *is nothing at all.*" To say *that thought is the condition of intuition in and for itself* contradicts, however, not only many explicit declarations of the Critique, but the latter's whole teaching. In the place where Kant calls an intuition without concept *blind* and a concept without intuition *empty,* it is not intuition which is being declared impossible without the concept, but *cognition.* It never occurred to Kant to hold, or to give to understand, that *pure,* but at the same time *empirical intuition as such,* is to be explained from the *original synthesis of apperception.* So much so that Kant does not even derive the *synthesis of the understanding* from that original synthesis exclusively, but has this very original synthesis no less conditioned by the categories than these by it. (Cols 64–5)

Now, quite apart from Kant's own mind on the matter, Reinhold was being inconsistent in his criticism of Fichte. He could not maintain at once such incompatible positions as the following:

(1) Kant's system was independently valid; indeed, Fichte was wrong in thinking that his own system was the same as Kant's (Col. 65).

(2) Fichte's science had finally succeeded in abstracting the highest principle of experience, and thereby had made possible the a priori reconstruction of its genesis. This is a feat that Fichte had accomplished precisely by denying that sensations constitute a so-called objective material prior to the activity of the subject. The year before the review, in a letter to Fichte announcing the light that had finally dawned on him regarding the *Wissenschaftslehre*, Reinhold had conceded that the defect of his hitherto held position lay precisely in having assumed this so-called objective sense material.[76]

(3) According to Kant, sense-intuition has some experientially relevant meaning quite apart from conceptualization, that is, quite apart from 'its being thought'.

From Fichte's point of view, to the extent that (3) was true, (1) could not be the case. Either Kant's system was reformed according to his or it was not valid. Moreover, to the extent that (2) accurately reflected Reinhold's mind, Reinhold could not maintain (1) and (3) at once.[77] To Fichte himself, therefore, the harmonization of Kant's Critique with his own *Wissenschaftslehre* that Reinhold was proposing in his review, on the basis of precisely those three claims, had to appear a hopeless pastiche. According to Reinhold, the two sciences were independent. Nonetheless, as he says,

by allowing to the Critique as well as to the *Wissenschaftslehre* their typical standpoints, true *agreement* can be demonstrated [between the two]. Whereas the *Wissenschaftslehre* proceeds by way of *abstraction* from experience, Critique does the same by way of *reflection* on it. The two are thus *essentially different perspectives of one and the same* matter [*Sache*], namely the *possibility of experience;* they are *essentially different systems* that can be called *philosophy* in totally *opposite meanings.* (Col. 67)[78]

For Fichte, however, there could not possibly be any such meeting of alleged symmetrically opposed systems. For it would have presupposed a norm-setting subject matter (a sort of *tertium quid*), with respect to which both the alleged reflection of the Critique and the equally alleged abstraction of the *Wissenschaftslehre* would remain external thought processes. Reinhold, on the contrary, was assuming this *tertium quid* throughout his review, and also clearly asserting both its priority in experience and its

nature. It consisted of none other than the alleged naturally given facts of
consciousness that had been the foundation of popular philosophy and
that Fichte had of late derided in his attacks on Schmid. Reinhold was
now saying that these facts were prior to Fichte's *Tathandlung;* that the
Critique conceptualized them in a still natural mode; and that, without
them and the still natural conceptualization of the Critique, Fichte's own
artificially abstractive reconstruction of experience would not be possible
(Col. 38).

Of course, on this assumption, artificial could only mean 'cleverly
concocted' (*Erdichtung*) – of significance for the specialized interests of
the philosophers but ultimately irrelevant so far as real experience is
concerned.[79] Here is what Reinhold says:

> The *presuppositions* from which Critique derives its results can only be mere *facts*,
> not at all pure *principles*. Indeed, the task of Critique is to establish whether, and
> to what extent, *pure knowledge in general* is possible. But, in fact, in the *Critique of
> Pure Reason*, it posits **as ground** the natural concept of *outer and inner experience
> in general;* in the *Critique of Practical Reason*, the *immediate consciousness of the moral
> law*. And it never goes *beyond* these absolutely [*schlechthin*], but only inasmuch as it
> takes its start *from them*. [...] Its proper task thus consists in the analysis of the *two
> principal concepts* of the mere *natural* employment of reason (of sound common
> sense), and in the application of the results thereby attained to the judgement of
> the extant *systems of metaphysics and morals*. The new doctrine of *suprasensible objects
> (freedom, God, and immortality)* that Critique derives as the result of the *principle* it
> assumes as ground, does not in any way supercede the convictions of mere *natural*
> reason. It owes nothing to *philosophical* reason except clarity and completeness of
> *form.* (Cols 34–5)[80]

This is an important text. It shows not only how distant Reinhold was
from Fichte, but also how far he had gone in reintegrating Kant within
the thought patterns of popular philosophy. To be sure, for Kant and
Fichte, not any less than for Reinhold, common sense (which includes
the voice of conscience) precedes philosophical reflection, and the latter,
if it is to have any relevance for real life, must be somehow continuous
with it. Reinhold, however, despite his excursions into the Critique of
Reason and into the *Wissenschaftslehre*, was obviously still operating on
the assumption of a God-created human nature permeated by innate
tendencies that reflect the order of the universe of which it is a part. On
this view, common sense is what a man knows because of what he is by
nature. The task of philosophical science is to clarify the content of this
naturally endowed certainty, to bring it to objective representation as far
as possible; that of moral education is to refine and enhance the natural feelings that are its source through right choice so that, at the end,
heart and mind, subjective certainty and reflective conceptualization,

can agree. Reason is the capacity in general to bring about this reconciliation. For Kant and Fichte, on the contrary, reason is a capacity for setting norms by which to judge nature, and its creator as well just in case there is one. Philosophical reflection is continuous with common experience only in the sense that it institutes one more organ in the task, which motivates the whole of experience, of setting up an authoritatively norm-bearing subjectivity.[81] Fichte actually defined quite well the difference that divided his philosophy from Reinhold's. The latter's Philosophy of the Elements retained throughout the character of theoretical science.[82] It was an account of 'what is' or must be postulated 'as being'. The *Wissenschaftslehre*, on the contrary, was from beginning to end a philosophy of freedom – the determination of what 'ought to be'. The differences separating Kant and Fichte notwithstanding, the two stood together in this pragmatic position.[83] Whatever Kant might have meant by 'freedom, God, and immortality', he could not therefore have meant the same as what was implied by the alleged 'natural reason' (read: the 'Christian reason of the theologians') that Reinhold still attributed to him.

We are back to Fichte's moral brief against the popular philosophers. There is still one more point to be made regarding it. The message clearly conveyed by Fichte at the beginning of his new science was this: Either with me and for freedom or against me and for subservience to nature. This was a moral disjunction, however, that one need not have accepted. We have been saying that Kant's system was held hostage to classical metaphysics because it assumed the existence of a thing in itself that might be the object of intellectual intuition. As such, it would have revealed itself to be not unlike the *causa sui* of dogmatic metaphysics. Before it, therefore, both the realms of nature and morality would have been reduced to mere epiphenomena. Fichte saw this last consequence and took the thing in itself to be not only a myth, but a morally harmful myth. He replaced it, however, with another myth of his own – one that, to Fichte's merit, he knew was a myth. He took the *Tathandlung* that set his science in motion not just as the reflective reenactment (the abstract paradigm, so to speak) of an intelligent performance in general, as we have so far portrayed it, but as the would-be conscious reenactment of a supposed infinite, more than human freedom, of which the whole of experience is an expression. This was just a myth. Nonetheless, it gave both Fichte's moral faith and the moral sociopolitical, system based on it an added, typically Fichtean character. And, even if one sided with both Fichte and Kant in their rejection of naturalism, one need not have accepted either that peculiarly Fichtean moral faith or the system based on it. Alternatives were possible that were still consistent with idealism. As a matter of fact, an enfant terrible by the name of Schelling was precisely at that time proposing one with a distinctly Romantic flavor. Some of the precisions that Fichte was bringing to his restatements of the *Wissenschaftslehre* were intended with this Schelling in mind, to meet his objections and to fend off his special brand of idealism. It is doubtful that anyone who found Fichte's idealism objectionable would have thought that Schelling's was an improvement. The formula for yet another alternative, however, was soon to be suggested by none other than Reinhold again – as if by accident, without Reinhold's himself realizing all that he was saying, just as, in his essay of 1789, he had failed to recognize how much he had in fact undermined Kant's critical distinctions (and had thereby framed a first genetic model of experience for Fichte) while trying, on the contrary, to establish these distinctions on a demonstrative basis. Reinhold did not take up his own suggestion. Instead, he was soon to turn against all idealism, Kant's included. But someone else eventually did take up this suggestion and thereby defined the program for another type of idealism – one more nature-friendly, so to speak. This someone was a friend of Schelling, older than he was but, unlike him, still an unknown literary quantity at the time. His name was Hegel.

Schelling and Hegel must remain only mentioned here. Their names alone already take us well beyond the scope not just of this chapter, but of the present study. We shall, however, return to Reinhold one final time for his suggested formula in the following chapter. The point now is that, however much one might have disagreed with Fichte's transformation of the Kantian Critique, in the Fichtean form in which the latter was being presented its truly revolutionary character (the true nature of its idealism) was finally being brought to light. The *Wissenschaftslehre* precipitated a moment of crisis in its reception. After it, the kinds of compromises with older modes of thought to which *Popularphilosophie* had hitherto subjected the Critique of Reason were no longer possible – not, at least, to anyone aware of the new situation.[84]

6.4 THE SCANDAL THAT FICHTE WAS

Jacobi's name came up earlier. Fichte never tired of declaring himself his disciple, and Jacobi, for his part, never tired of distancing himself from Fichte. One can understand Jacobi's discomfort. Fichte was saying that philosophical reflection necessarily elicits an act of faith at its inception. And this might well have sounded the same as Jacobi's claim that faith is the matrix of reason. But, in fact, 'faith' meant something quite different in the two cases. For Fichte, it meant a commitment to interpret an otherwise given nature as a work of man, or, more precisely, to interpret it as assuming through human work the shape of a product of transcendent freedom. For Jacobi, faith meant quite the opposite – the acceptance, that is, of God's creation. It meant the same as it still did for Reinhold, despite the latter's excursions into idealism, and as such was still consistent with the religiosity of the commonsense philosophers.

Actually, the situation was more complex than this. On the one hand, Fichte was being disingenuous. He proclaimed that what he held reflectively as a philosopher was the same as what Jacobi already lived in actual experience and held on faith without any need of philosophizing. Existentially speaking, so Fichte said, there is no need of philosophy. That was the case for Jacobi just as much as for 'everyman'. Indeed, according to Fichte (still existentially speaking), philosophy posed a special problem for the one afflicted by it. For, since it begins with an act of reflective pride, it opens up the ditch that separates the philosopher from common experience, and that it is then the philosopher's task to overcome with yet more philosophy in an effort at recovering the immediacy of the latter. As Fichte once put it in a letter to Jacobi, "Presumption led us to philosophize, and this cost us our innocence. We caught sight of our nakedness, and since then we have had to philosophize for our own salvation."[85] Fichte was being disingenuous because he failed to acknowledge that, on his own principles, there is no a priori guarantee that whatever immediacy the philosopher might recover through his reflection is the same as the type in which everyman can be assumed already to be immersed. That new immediacy, the product of reflection, would be necessarily qualified by the philosopher's original moral commitment, and this commitment, on Fichte's own principles, is not necessarily the one that animates everyman – unless, of course, the latter's common sense has already been Fictheanized through the right kind of social indoctrination.

On the other hand, Jacobi was being disingenuous as well, for he could not run away from the fact that there was at least some justification for Fichte's claim that he was his disciple. It is not just the language of faith that was at issue. More than that, the paradigm of experience that Jacobi had advanced in *David Hume* in opposition to Kant's was the same as the one that now governed Fichte's *Wissenschaftslehre*. The idea of a feeling of power that carries with it a representation of itself, but in representation becomes aware of itself only upon being checked by an obstacle that therefore assumes for it the meaning of an other – this idea, which Fichte was now developing phenomenologically, was already in the *David Hume*. Jacobi had derived it from Spinoza, as he said. In 1789, in one of the appendices added to the second edition of the *Spinoza-Letters*, Jacobi used the trope of an infinite blind power in which thought implants eyes with reference to Herder's claim that God has no personality, since he surpasses consciousness. He was using the trope disparagingly in order to stigmatize what he believed to be Herder's half-baked pantheism.[86] Fichte entered this trope *("Es werden* Augen *eingesetzt dem Einem"* ['Eyes are implanted in the One']) in a gloss to his copy of his *System of Ethics* of 1798.[87] It did indeed portray in figurative terms his idea of an absolute but indeterminate activity (an 'actuosity') that acquires determination in consciousness (i.e., by 'seeing' itself). As we shall see in the following chapter, Jacobi was also to accuse Fichte of inverted Spinozism. In all this, Jacobi was forgetting that he had been the one responsible for bringing Spinoza to the center of philosophical discussion. While rejecting Spinoza's rationalism, he had nonetheless praised him for his sense of actuosity, for giving existence primacy over thought. In his idealistic ways, Fichte was following in his footsteps.[88] And Jacobi should have been able to recognize that much. Again, he had been the one to declare, "No I without a Thou." For Jacobi, this Thou was the Christian God, whose transcendent presence alone is capable, according to him, of radically individualizing the otherwise abstract I. In God's presence, the I is revealed to be just a sinner. This is the trait that ultimately marks him, in opposition to God, as the irreducible individual he is. Fichte was now saying the same thing, except that for him the Thou is first and foremost reason, and the form that this reason finally assumes in individualizing the I is that of a social community mechanistically organized according to law. In this community, the I first acquires the character of a legally defined persona. In itself, this is still an abstract determination. Yet, when measured against it, any extant natural self finally finds the source of his radical individualization. He finds it, namely, in the natural eccentricity that makes him necessarily fall short of his moral obligations. There was cause again for Fichte to think that he was following in Jacobi's footsteps. For him just as much as for Jacobi, the human individual is, as such, essentially a sinner.

Jacobi had indeed reason to feel discomfort. If, at the time of *David Hume*, he had found himself driven in his criticism of Kant in the direction of a naturalism that he wanted at all cost to avoid, he now saw himself as having inspired an idealism even more radical than Kant's. He just seemed unable to steer away from the two extremes of naturalism and idealism. Hamann had once faulted him for flirting with the philosophers too much.[89] Perhaps he had been right. The time had perhaps come for Jacobi to give up on philosophy altogether.

Issues of religious beliefs invariably tend to become implicated in issues of political practice. This was especially true in Europe at the end of the eighteenth century, when the French Revolution was upsetting long-standing religious as well as political establishments. Now, so far as religion was concerned, anyone with any philosophical perspicacity should have been able to see that Kant's religion had nothing in common with traditional Christianity, despite some imagery that the two still had in common. In Kant's system, the idea of God, quite apart from its being just an idea, was an instrument of human moral agency. This was a remarkable reversal of the Christian view of a creature's relation to his creator God. In Fichte, as it became clear even in his *Critique of All Revelation*, this aspect of Kant became all the more explicit. It also assumed extra political overtones that were not difficult to discern. We remember Rehberg.[90] Rehberg had granted to Kant that the idea of the Law has moral value in itself, independently of natural considerations. He did not think, however, that by itself it can be an effective determining force of human action, and had therefore accepted it only as a sort of moral principle of contradiction, a negative test of the moral legitimacy of rational but still naturally motivated rules of human conduct. Rehberg had also advanced some very trenchant criticisms of what he took to be Kant's illegitimate mingling of noumenal causality and phenomenal effects in the realm of moral action. With respect to religion, Rehberg thought that it was an irreducible dimension of human existence motivated by the human being's natural desire for order in the universe. This order, however, is to be conceived in phenomenal terms. The God or gods guaranteeing it fall on the side of the phenomenal realm. Good Tory that he was, Rehberg took it for granted that religious beliefs are grounded in the historically accepted practices of a society. Religion is always the religion *of* a given society. Fichte, for his part, was definitely no Tory. From beginning to end he was a committed Jacobin. No two individuals could have been as divergent in temperament, metaphysical inclinations, and political convictions as the two of them. Within his system, Fichte had indeed met Rehberg's criticisms of Kant, but hardly in a way that Rehberg would have found acceptable.[91] Yet, despite these differences, on the issue of religion the two men agreed in at least one respect, though again with differences that brought into view all the more strikingly the political implications of Fichte's idealism. It was clear from the *Critique of All Revelation* that revelation was for Fichte a phenomenal event. It followed that the interpretation of it, and any religion based on this interpretation, had to be a social affair. For Fichte, no less than for Rehberg, religion was therefore always the religion *of* a society. On this point, the two men agreed. But note the difference in attitude toward accepted social religious practices that arose from the opposing mind sets conditioning the two men. For Rehberg, these practices were the repository of long-standing moral judgments that govern social conduct and that were originally made unreflectively in response to natural and historical pressures. They constituted, therefore, a sort of natural wisdom that was not to be tampered with by political action except in extreme cases. For Fichte, on the contrary, since the whole point of moral life is to overcome the immediacy of natural or historical events, it was the duty of political action to shape (or reshape, as the case might be) accepted practices for the sake of bringing about an explicitly free society. Fichte was in spirit a social engineer. Religion had become for him social ideology – exactly what it was to be in the revolutionary currents of the nineteenth century.

The political overtones of the process that finally led to the expulsion of Fichte from the university in 1799 on the charge of atheism, and his departure from Jena in 1800, were not altogether unjustified. Fichte stood as a scandal to many. But that was precisely one of his great merits. With him on the scene, the kinds of compromises between the old naturalism and the new idealism that *Popularphilosophie* had attempted were no longer possible.

7

The Parting of the Ways

> But the philosopher would *necessarily become atheist,* if he could be nothing *but* philosopher.
>
> Reinhold[1]

7.1 ANNO DOMINI 1799

By all accounts, 1799 was not a peaceful year. It certainly was not peaceful for the German lands, threatened as they were by the revolutionary armies of France. But neither was it peaceful for the more recondite circles of academic affairs. In this case, the center of turmoil was at Jena. Fichte was finally losing his battle against the charge of atheism that he had been waging for over a year. His legal case with the university administration had spawned a dispute that, just like the earlier Spinoza dispute, had engaged intellectual as well as political figures from far and wide. In the literature, it is known as the 'atheism dispute' *(der Atheismusstreit).* It all began with the claim made by a certain Forberg, and published in a journal of which Fichte was the editor, that religious faith in God is but a pious wish.[2] But the circumstances that had led to the charge against Fichte need not concern us here, nor are we concerned with the details of the surrounding controversy. They are all well documented in the literature.[3] Of interest to us is rather the role that Jacobi and Reinhold played in it. The two men had also figured prominently in the earlier dispute. There was much that differentiated the two controversies. In the earlier one, Lessing's reputation was at stake – the reputation of a man who still was in spirit a dominant literary figure in the German intellectual world, but one who had already departed from it physically. In the present one, the person under attack was still very much alive, and at stake was not just his reputation but his livelihood and political welfare as well. Yet, despite these obvious differences, there still was a remarkable unity of philosophical theme running across them. In both, whether in the figure of the deceased Lessing or the still living Fichte, the idea of reason was on trial. In the earlier controversy, Jacobi had accused this reason of necessarily leading to atheism. It undermined the possibility of a transcendent God, and hence ended up denying both human individuality and human freedom. In the present controversy, Jacobi was now arguing that Kant's critique, though it intended to curb the claims of reason and thus make room for faith, had not really broken free of its reflective mold. Like the dogmatic reason it criticized, Kantian reason was still given to mistaking conditions of explanation for conditions of existence. It therefore led, just as Jacobi had been predicting all along, to equally antihumanistic consequences. The case of Fichte, a self-proclaimed disciple of Kant, was proof of Jacobi's point.

The presence of Reinhold in both controversies was another element of continuity. On the face of it, Reinhold was offering in this second controversy an encore of his previous performance. In the first, still a marginal figure in the literary world and only a recent convert to Kantian critique, Reinhold had cast Kant in the role of one who could mediate the opposing claims that were being advanced by Jacobi in defense of faith, and, in lieu of Lessing, by Moses Mendelssohn on reason's behalf. In this second controversy, now an apparent convert to Fichte's idealism, Reinhold was exploiting some of Fichte's statements on the relation of philosophical reason to religious faith in an effort to find a middle ground between Jacobi's position, on the one side, and the Kantian reason Jacobi was attacking in the person of Fichte, on the other. In this case also, just as he had done in the earlier one, Reinhold was thus casting himself in the role of an honest broker of opposing parties.

But in fact, whatever reconciliation in the first controversy might perhaps have been possible between the conflicting parties on their own terms, none was really possible on Kant's terms. Kant had shifted the whole issue of the relation of reason to faith to a different level of conceptualization. At that time, he had already been reinterpreted and appropriated by the theologians for their apologetic purposes. The illusion of a critical resolution to otherwise conflicting tendencies of the Enlightenment was therefore understandable. Kant himself had played into it. In this second controversy, no such illusion was, however, possible. Fichte was there to make the difference. He had now brought to light the truly

revolutionary implications of the Critique of Reason. There was therefore something overly ingenuous in Reinhold's attempt at a mediation
between Jacobi and Fichte. The latter, for his part, had unambiguously
disavowed the possibility of any such mediation,[4] and Jacobi would have
found it ridiculous indeed. Reinhold himself declared that he was not
attempting to mediate between the two philosophers,[5] but in fact he was
doing just that. And, if he could honestly believe in his own denial, that
only showed how much he misunderstood Fichte; how much, in fact, he
had also misunderstood Kant from the beginning. In brief, whatever conversion to Fichte Reinhold might have recently undergone, in the course
of the atheism dispute he had been quick to undergo another, this time
to Jacobi. But again, this last conversion would have had to be of a special
kind, a 'return' rather than a 'turn' (if I may play on the Latin root of
'conversion'), for Reinhold had in fact always been on the side of Jacobi.
From the beginning he had shared with him the view of reason that was
typical of Enlightenment *Popularphilosohie.* Signs of the dubious quality of
his recently declared allegiance to Fichte were already abundantly clear,
as we have seen, in his just published review of the latter's works. In a more
practical context, even more abundant signs could have been gathered
from the social activities in which Reinhold was engaging at the time.
Clarification was soon to come. Reinhold finally declared himself against
all forms of idealism.

There was to be clarification of Jacobi's true position as well. The tone
of his 1799 open letter to Fichte conveyed all the emotional intensity, and
the uncompromising quality, of his earlier attack on the philosophers in
the Spinoza-Letters. There was no longer the dillydallying with Hume,
Spinoza, or Kant, that one could witness in *David Hume.* Jacobi was now
unequivocally declaring himself against philosophy. In his letter, however, there was no hint of the recent excursions he had himself made in
speculative thought. And, in this, he was being disingenuous. Soon he
was to return to philosophy, but under auspices that no longer left any
doubt about his *Popularphilosophie* heritage.

There was clarification in 1799 coming from Kant as well – about
which, however, more in due time. Right now, Reinhold and Jacobi are
our subject of discussion.

7.2 REINHOLD CONVERTS AGAIN[6]

Our texts are two works of Reinhold, both published in 1799, though the
first, entitled *Concerning the Paradoxes of the Most Recent Philosophy*, carries a

Preface dated March 28, 1798.[7] The second is entitled *Open Letter to I. C. Lavater and J. G. Fichte Regarding Faith in God.*[8] We learn from an introductory editorial note (3–4) that this second essay had been composed by Reinhold in response to a request made to him by Lavater and Fichte to make public his views regarding "the most recent philosophy" (i.e., Fichte's *Wissenschaftslehre*) now being declared atheist by some. The work is accordingly made up of two parts. In the first, addressed to Lavater, dated May 1, 1999, Reinhold defends Fichte's science before a targeted public of religious yet learned believers; in the second, addressed to Fichte himself, Reinhold defends for the benefit of the "friends" of the new philosophy the autonomy of faith vis-à-vis all speculative philosophy. Internal evidence, introduced by Reinhold himself, shows that this second letter was penned at two different locations. An early part (one-third approximately) bears the dateline of "Euten, 27 March" (76–88), while the rest that of "Kiel, 6 April" (89–113). This circumstance is important. Kiel was Reinhold's place of residence, while Euten was where Jacobi lived at the time and where, in the same year, he had composed his own open letter to Fichte.[9] Reinhold was at Euten when he began writing his letter, a guest of Jacobi and obviously under the spell of his host. Jacobi's physical proximity is almost palpable throughout the letter.

This is not to say that the earlier publication, *Paradoxes*, did not already bear the marks of Jacobi's influence. The two writings are both animated by the belief that the individual who is the subject of common experience – the one we denote in common speech by the pronoun I and have no difficulty identifying among the many objects that make up the world – that this individual must be the beginning as well as the end point of any process of reflection. This was a belief dear to Jacobi. It was the one for which he had stepped into the polemical arena in 1785. Reinhold was now making it the theme of both of his essays.[10]

7.2.1 The Paradoxes of the New Philosophy

Reinhold had declared himself for Fichte in 1797. At the time of the composition of *Paradoxes*, he was still a Fichtean officially. It is no surprise, therefore, that throughout the essay he would rely heavily on both the language and the conceptual apparatus of the *Wissenschaftslehre*, however much Jacobi was obviously on his mind. Reinhold's leading question is why this latest scientific product should confront ordinary consciousness with a paradox. 'Paradox' is generated, according to Reinhold, whenever claims are made "with respect to which one is left oscillating between having to think what their author might have thought, yet being unable to do it" (43). The *Wissenschaftslehre* is paradoxical because, whereas ordinary consciousness is necessarily led to it, the same consciousness is ultimately unable to abide by its results. This is then the delicate balancing act Reinhold is trying to perform. On the one hand, he wants to grant the validity of the *Wissenschaftslehre* as a science of experience. (Thesis 1: One must think in terms of the *Wissenschaftslehre*.) On the other hand, he also wants to justify Jacobi's inability, and that of ordinary consciousness in general, to accept it as such a science. (Thesis 2: Ultimately one cannot think in those terms.) While standing by Fichte with the first claim, Reinhold is also trying to make moves in the direction of Jacobi with the second. And the ground he takes upon which to perform this balancing act is the belief that individuals are capable of moral action.[11] The belief is a common one. But how is it to be justified speculatively?

Now, according to Reinhold, the move from belief to speculative justification presupposes two features of experience. The first is that all experience is by nature reflective.[12] It is important to keep in mind the imagery that conditions Reinhold's claim here. In experience, immediately apprehended objects are transposed into a broader conceptual context, from which they are 're-viewed' (so to speak) and judged accordingly. Objects of experience, in other words, always appear as reflected from (or 'mirrored in', as in a *speculum*) a presupposed transcendental background. To say that experience is 'reflective' in this sense is also to say that experience is by nature 'abstractive', since its objects, by being thus reflectively represented, are removed from the conditions under which they are immediately given to apprehension in the first place.

The second feature is that a subject of experience enjoys an irreducible freedom with respect to his objects. This second feature is the direct consequence of the first. For, since the subject in question can in principle always treat his objects in terms of possibilities only accessible to conceptual reflection (i.e., as reflected from a broader background), he is not obliged to accept them as they happen to appear to him in the first instance on any given occasion. He can treat them, in other words, not just as they 'are' but as they 'might be' or 'might have been', and hence, under certain circumstances, as they 'ought to be'. Moral life begins precisely with the recognition of these possibilities.[13]

These two features of experience are assumed by Reinhold to be facts of consciousness, *"Tatsachen des Bewußtseins."*[14] They define experience itself. Now, according to Reinhold, the move from common experience to philosophical speculation is made in virtue of an abstractive reflection that, though unique in its results, still falls nonetheless within the economy of experience as just defined. Originally at least, *that* such a reflection occurs, and that it therefore *can* occur, must be taken as itself a plain fact of consciousness. It consists in a subject's freely undertaken resolution to abstract from all the historical circumstances under which reflection takes place, that is to say, from all the circumstances that qualify the subject's day-to-day experiences, in order to take reflection as an object by itself. In effect, since it is reflection that frees the subject from the immediacy of his perceptions in the first place, this abstractive move is an attempt at objectifying freedom itself. The upshot is that, though the move begins (as just said) as a fact of natural consciousness, it concludes as an act that is self-justifying, since it has only itself as its intended object. It supplies the object through its very attempt at conceiving it – in this way testifying to its own possibility as act. As Reinhold puts it, though freedom is originally a *Tatsache* of natural consciousness or an act that in consciousness is always presupposed as already established (*factum*), it becomes with this move a *Tathandlung*, or an act that freely establishes itself (*agere*).[15]

This is a historically significant transition from 'fact' to 'act' that Reinhold posits here. It will have Hegelian consequences, as we shall see in a moment. Fichte is, however, now at issue, and *Tathandlung* is his technical term.[16] Reinhold is borrowing it, as he is also the notion of 'speculative concept'. The latter is a representation that results from the mirroring effect of reflection. Reinhold's next move is equally Fichtean in inspiration. Repeating Fichte, Reinhold also claims that the products of speculative thought are necessarily 'artificial' or 'artful' (*künstlich*), since they abstract from the conditions of real life.[17] And, since the execution of the original abstractive reflection on which these products depend may be flawed, the resulting artificial systems of thought based on the reflection might equally be flawed. In the scholastic, pedantic style that is the hallmark of all his writings, Reinhold proceeds to explain how the one-sided philosophical systems of the past all originated in their failure, when defining first principles, to abstract completely from the internal or external content of the historical experience that occasioned each. Subjective idealism, dogmatism, skepticism – all came to be in this way (50ff.).

In these Fichtean considerations there is a critique tacitly being leveled against Jacobi. In effect, Reinhold is saying that Jacobi had been wrong on two counts. First, Jacobi had failed to draw a distinction that Reinhold now simply assumes along with Fichte. The distinction is one between theoretical and speculative concepts and the abstraction typical to each. Theoretical abstraction is directed at a material apprehended in experience as given externally, hence explainable only by being referred to something 'other than it'. This material thus becomes the object of representations that necessarily seek to reduce it always to something else precisely in order to explain it. The infinite regression of explanatory concepts to which the things of nature must be subjected is the product of this kind of abstraction. The other kind is, on the contrary, one that directs thought away from any presumably given content of experience for the sake of avoiding precisely the infinite regression that reflection on it would otherwise bring into play. This is the kind of abstraction that results in the speculative concept with which philosophy proper begins. It is the product of a reflection that turns back upon itself in order to detect there, in the circular movement of its thought, the foundation of all experience.

Jacobi had failed to recognize this last function of reflection. That had been his first failure. The second was that he had also failed to recognize that the abstractive reflection of speculative thought is at the origin of the very freedom that he quite rightly, wanted to defend for the sake of saving moral responsibility. It is not the case that philosophical reason is essentially antithetical to human freedom and moral action, as Jacobi had contended. On the contrary, when properly abstracted on its own, the principle of philosophy is the same as the principle of freedom – exactly as Fichte had argued. Jacobi's stricture against reflection only applied to a thought that is bound to external nature.

This was a powerful criticism that Reinhold, albeit tacitly, was directing at Jacobi. The criticism was already implicit in the first part of the paradox he had defined at the beginning. Ordinary consciousness is inexorably driven to think in the terms stipulated by "the most recent philosophy," precisely because, in structure as well as in interest, the two are continuous. Both ordinary consciousness and philosophical speculation are reflective in nature. Philosophical speculation only seeks to satisfy the need of ordinary consciousness to objectify the origin of its certainty, a need that this consciousness naturally has since it too is in principle reflective (36–7, 42ff., 52ff.). There should be no point, therefore, to the charge often raised against Jacobi that, by relying on faith as he did, one is thereby exposing oneself to the excesses of fanaticism. Faith is in principle rational. Jacobi's antagonism toward philosophy obscured precisely this point and also made his own position open to attack.

This result amounted to an implicit criticism of Jacobi. But it also did not leave Fichte untouched. At issue now is the artificiality of the products of the reflection that, according to Reinhold's Fichtean analysis, gives rise to typically philosophical speculation. This artificiality is unavoidable, as Fichte had admitted and Reinhold now confirms. As Reinhold has been arguing, philosophical reflection seeks to represent, by means of a concept, the freedom that a moral agent derives in virtue of self-generating acts of thought. This task is accomplished when reflection – an arbitrarily initiated performance and one undertaken under perfectly abstractive, and hence perfectly controllable, conditions – takes itself as a typical case of such self-generating acts. Reflection thus produces a concept of freedom and demonstrates its validity at one and the same time, since it provides an object for the concept by the very act of producing the concept. Now, implicit in this analysis of reflection is that its operation should be at once intuitive *(selbst-anschauend)* yet discursive. It must be intuitive because, unless subject and object were identical in it, it would not be self-validating. Its intended object *is* its own subjective performance as reflection. But it must be discursive as well, that is, it must issue in a concept that, as a subjective product, remains distinct from its intended object. For unless this distinction were retained, the reflection would not produce the explicit consciousness of itself as object for which it is intended. These two requirements are, however, mutually exclusive, since they entail at once both identity and non-identity of subject and object. The only way they can therefore be satisfied is in the form of an attempt, that is, as a reflective performance that, on the verge of completing itself (thus running the risk of degenerating into either an intuition that is not conscious of itself for lack of distance between subject and object or a conceptually explicit self-consciousness that, however, misses its intended object), simply starts all over again and goes on repeating itself *in infinitum* (74–6, 76–8).

This constantly self-repeating abstractive reflection is what gives rise, according to Reinhold, to the system of speculative determinations of the concept of freedom that constitutes the domain of philosophy. Now, the series of these determinations, though circular, so to speak, is just as never-ending as the linear series of theoretical concepts produced by the sciences of nature. Hence, just as the theoretical concept transforms the natural individual into an individual in general, so the speculative concept transforms the highly personal actions of moral individuals into freedom in general. And just as the one thereby misses the reality of its intended object, so does the other. The philosopher refers indeed to the *Tathandlung* in which freedom consists as an I, in order to denote the subject–object identity that it entails. But, Reinhold adds, the philosopher must be careful to distinguish this abstract I from the moral self of actual experience – a self to which Reinhold now refers as person, precisely in order to distinguish it from the abstract I of the philosophers.[18] Whatever reflective awareness this I in general might produce, it still falls short of the immediate experience of personal freedom that the other self carries as its exclusive property (71–3). In contrast with the latter, therefore, the I and all its reflective determinations are mere idealizations – artificial products, in other words, that at best only approximate the reality they intend to express.[19] Even for the philosopher, therefore, no less than for ordinary man, the certainty that his acts are freely performed are a form of faith rather than cognition proper. It is a faith because, though necessarily committed to comprehending itself in a concept (hence, nothing per se irrational), it just as necessarily fails in the attempt. Philosophical speculation issues in faith just as much as it originates in it.[20]

Here then is how Reinhold has made his move to the second part of his paradox – to the claim, namely, that ordinary consciousness cannot ultimately be satisfied with the recently declared philosophical positions, even though it is inexorably driven to them. On the face of it, Reinhold appears again to be only repeating an item of Fichtean doctrine, though rehearsing it in a form that would also explain Jacobi's antagonism toward philosophy. Notice, however, how much, appearances apart, Reinhold has in fact slanted his argument in favor of Jacobi. So far as Fichte was concerned, the artificiality of philosophical reflection is what guarantees both its freedom and the validity of its conceptual products. Once established, such products play a normative role with respect to ordinary experience. Accordingly, the philosopher is committed to reconstructing a priori, in terms of his own free reflection, the natural content of the experience from which his thought has severed itself in virtue of its original abstractive leap. Reinhold is, however, inverting this order of priority. In his account, it is the natural matrix in which speculation originates (i.e., ethical feeling or moral faith) that retains priority throughout. Philosophical reflection would indeed set itself up as an absolute starting point. In actuality, however, it always remains existentially dependent on that matrix and must constantly be steered back to it when issues are at stake that affect the moral agent personally (87–8, 90).

The fact is, in other words, that the concept of faith did not mean the same thing for Fichte and Jacobi, and that, although its presence in *Paradoxes* might have seemed to provide a point of contact between the two,

Reinhold was using it in a spirit that was much more consistent with Jacobi's meaning. That faith has to be moral in character, that is, that it has to do with certainty of one's freedom of action, was, of course, a position common to all three. So too was the supposition that faith naturally leads to religion, that is, to belief in God. Neither Fichte nor Reinhold nor Jacobi, moreover, would have accepted the assumption, common at the time among the epigones of Kant, that such a belief is required in order to guarantee the happiness that should be the lot of a morally deserving human being. Reinhold explicitly rejects this doctrine at the beginning of Paradoxies (28). Belief in God originates, rather, in the awareness of the limits of one's freedom that takes hold of the moral agent in the moment of action. This is again a position that the three shared equally. This, however, is as far as their common ground extended. The parting point came at the issue of the nature of freedom's limits. So far as Fichte was concerned, human freedom generates its own limits because of the inherently self-defeating structure of a would-be self-positing as well as self-comprehending act of perfect reflection. Faith consists in the commitment to persevere in the attempt at such a reflection in spite of its impossibility, and God stands for the ideal perfection of being that the moral agent would achieve if the reflection were ever to succeed. God is an ideal yet impossible goal, in other words – one that an agent nonetheless accepts as the material norm of moral perfection. For Jacobi, on the contrary, faith is witness to a possession already at hand, albeit darkly, in a feeling. It is a certainty about God being already present in the moral agent – indeed as a limit to his freedom, but only in the positive sense that, by thus confronting the agent's I in the form of an irreducibly transcendent Thou, God thereby ensures the agent's individuality and, along with his individuality, his freedom as well. Without this divine presence, the reality of the agent would necessarily tend to dissipate into the mere appearance to which philosophical reflection inevitably reduces it. For Fichte, in other words, faith is the necessary product of a paradox created by reflection. For Jacobi, it is rather the avoidance of all paradox.

It is in this latter sense, however, that Reinhold uses faith in *Paradoxes*. As he explicitly declares, speculative reflection is at the source of the paradoxes that recent philosophy poses to natural consciousness, however talented the latter might be (94). For the sake of moral action, therefore, natural consciousness must ultimately make its way from speculation back to its own more primitive faith. It is this faith that serves as the ultimate norm of what should count as true philosophical reflection, and as the judge of whether and how such a reflection is in any way relevant to actual life. This is Reinhold's conclusion. But he could not have reached it without thereby having also taken a position on the side of Jacobi. The common sense of Jacobi, not Fichte's speculation, is what ultimately gives a true account of moral action.

Yet, at the time of writing, Reinhold was still officially a Fichtean. How deliberate he was in siding with Jacobi, or how explicitly aware he was of what he was doing, is therefore still open to question. This question is resolved, however, when we come to his next writing.

7.2.2 Fichte Explained to Pious Lavater

Paradox comes into play again in Reinhold's letter to Lavater, but not quite in the same way as we have just seen. The point now is that the current conflict between religion and philosophy is driven by a paradox that has its origin not just in speculation, but within the consciousness itself of the believer. It is due, ultimately, to the limitations of being a creature. As Reinhold explains to Lavater in conspicuously religious rhetoric, faith is 'supernatural' in the sense that the believer is in possession of it even as he begins to reflect or act (17, 20–2). He must assume it, therefore, as a gift from God to him, just as he assumes his existence to be such a gift. However, were he not to act on this faith through deeds in which he freely engages and that are, therefore, 'natural' in the sense of being totally his own, his faith would be nothing to him. It is of the nature of faith, in other words, that the believer should both presuppose it as a gift from above and yet appropriate it through natural action. It presents a paradox to the believer in that it requires of him both dependence on God for the faith that should inspire his action and independence of action for the deeds that should give concrete meaning to the faith. He cannot act without believing, yet cannot believe without acting – and he is aware of both requirements by thus believing and thus acting. This is indeed a paradox, but one that should be expected because (as every Christian knows from his catechism and as Reinhold is now rehearsing for the benefit of Lavater) created existence consists precisely in a state of tension between the natural and the supernatural. This is where all the paradoxes of the believer's experience have their origin (24, 36–7).

But then, as Lavater asked, why speculate (34)? Why muddle with useless doubts the believer's certain consciousness of where he stands with respect to both God and nature? To this Reinhold replies that, as a matter of fact, speculation is not the cause of uncertainty. Speculative thought, as such, can never entertain doubts regarding the validity of its conclusions, since its operations are strictly under its own control. Speculation rather presupposes doubt, for it emerges precisely in an effort at quelling it (34). And Reinhold adds:

God is the immediate object of faith; nature is the immedite object of knowledge [*Wissen*.] God becomes object only to our living faith – to be sure, not through our *mere* knowledge of *nature*, and yet through loyal and honest use of *nature as stipulated by knowledge*. A faith which scorns and rejects knowledge is for that reason certainly *not from God*. It is *superstition*. . . . (36–7)

The key note here is 'living faith', that is, a faith that indeed presupposes union with God as its immediate object, but that does not know itself for what it is except in the context of nature, through actions governed by the knowledge of nature. Doubt is the by-product of this already recognized tension in the believer's experience between received faith and self-induced action. It is part and parcel of the economy of faith. Speculative thought is therefore called into play by faith itself in response to a need that is internal to it.

Having made this point, Reinhold proceeds to explain to Lavater how, once speculation has set in, it follows a course of its own independent of faith. Reason's independence had already been defended in *Paradoxes*. But Reinhold now defends it again, still on the basis of the supposed absolute reflective abstraction with which speculation begins.[21] In an appendix Reinhold also repeats his claim – now with explicit reference to Fichte – that failure to perform the abstraction properly, leaving a natural residue behind, leads to false systems of philosophy.[22] He now adds that Fichte's philosophy is indeed based on an adequate abstraction. Hence it is neither idealist nor realist, but consists rather in an endless process of self-explanation on the part of reflective thought that never achieves its purported aim of objectifying itself.[23] However, Reinhold drops hints in a second appendix that, though based on the right kind of abstraction, there might yet be something wrong with the *Wissenschaftslehre*. We shall return to these hints in just a moment.

The place of speculation in the believer's consciousness is not, however, the main point of interest in Reinhold's address to Lavater. Just as in the preceding *Paradoxes*, the stress falls rather on the role that conscience (*Gewissen*) plays as the ultimate guide to human actions. Even by itself, conscience harbors a kind of knowledge (*Wissen*) that makes for infallible judgment. To be sure, this reflective dimension of conscience is what makes the faith based on it a 'human faith', that is, one that justifies itself by its efficacy in bearing visible results in the world of nature. It is therefore also the source of possible doubts and of the consequent motivation for speculation. But, Reinhold insists, in the conscience of the morally upright man this human faith is constantly sliding into 'divine faith' – that faith that comes from God and makes the creature at one with him (24). Hence the authority of conscience (*Gewissen*) is both primordial and unimpeachable. Should any conflict ever arise between belief based on it and would-be knowledge (*Wissen*) based on speculation, it is faith that must have the last word (40). After all, the certainty that speculative reflection has about its truth derives solely from the control it has over its own performance in actually being performed. It is an empty certainty, in other words, one in no way based on the ability to reach conclusions. On the contrary, speculative reflection must suspend any conclusion it might be on the verge of achieving, at the very moment of achieving it, precisely in order to retain its purely speculative standpoint and, therefore, its self-certainty. If conscience makes a demand, the moral man within the philosopher must therefore force the philosopher to interrupt his speculation and quietly make his return to what is ultimately the source of all knowledge (82–4). In the words that Reinhold will later address directly to Fichte, the philosopher "tears himself loose from that [reflective] knowledge through his own strength [*Kraft*]; he raises the *man* above the *philosopher*" (83).

It is this last feature of speculation, its ultimate emptiness unless it is connected to faith, that Reinhold stresses in the accompanying letter to Fichte. The letter, as we said, was penned under Jacobi's direct influence, even under the influence of his physical proximity, and one can detect the Jacobian shadow throughout. We are now told, in a language reminiscent of Jacobi's, that the "absolutely real" (*das Reelle schlechtin*) that the philosopher tries to conceptualize is none other than God (84). It announces itself in conscience through a feeling that is at the origin of conscience itself and also of human reason. The latter originally consists of a tendency "within the infinite towards the infinite" (*Tendenz ins Unendliche zum Unendliche*), (84–6), that is, the movement by which the moral individual, taking his start from the divine infinity present to his conscience through feeling, tries to circle back to it, so to speak, by way of finite actions that testify to the infinite by objectifying it in its products. At its origin reason is a practical, natural activity oriented by a divinely inspired feeling. And it must remain so oriented if it is not to turn into 'empty reason'.

But how is this empty reason ever instituted? It comes to be, according to Reinhold, because of the philosopher's attempt to isolate reason by itself in order to observe how it functions and how far it can reach in its operations. Through this isolating, however, the philosopher suspends it as *natural* reason and establishes it instead as *artificial* reason (84–5). He reenacts its movement. However, since he has abstracted it from the divine feeling that inspires it originally, this reenactment is not performed within the infinite – that is, as the movement from the infinite and back to it that it naturally is and naturally knows itself to be. He reenacts it, rather, as an operation that tries to comprehend the finite precisely as it transcends itself (qua finite) toward the infinite. In this attempt, the operation also seeks to comprehend the infinite, but as a transcendent reality that it constantly falls short of, thus falling back to the finite (85–6, 90).

As thus conceptually isolated by the philosopher, reason thus necessarily fails to comprehend the absolutely *real (das Reelle schlechtin)*. It never reaches past an empty idealization. And Reinhold rehearses its failure in different ways. It fails because it is born of an abstraction that, by trying to comprehend reason all by itself, in fact removes it from the conditions under which it operates naturally and where it *in fact* already is in union with that infinite. The abstraction thus destroys the union of finite and infinite that it wants to conceptualize (90ff.). It objectifies the two as terms external to one another, hence both as finite; and thereby, in an attempt to bring them together, it sets in motion the speculative process of reflection from one back to the other. In the words of Reinhold, "What the philosopher *constantly abolishes* through free abstraction, he *constantly restores* through free reflection" (91). But the attempt necessarily fails, and the process runs the risk of extending *in infinitum* unless the man interrupts it for the sake of action.

It also fails for another and even more profound reason. Real freedom – that is, the kind of freedom in virtue of which one partakes of God's infinity – is radically individual. It is what constitutes the individual as a person vis-à-vis a personal God. In trying to objectify freedom reflectively, speculative thought, however, necessarily abstracts from individuality and hence from real freedom. It only achieves a 'freedom in general', such as is, at best, a mere *Erdichtung* – not just an artificial but a fictional product. As Reinhold reminds Fichte:

I am *myself* partaker of *infinity* only through my *freedom*. But I *originally* find my freedom *only* from the *standpoint of conscience*. And it is from this standpoint *alone* that I *can retrieve* it as my individual freedom when, by philosophizing for the sake of pure knowledge, I have abstracted from my individuality and thereby have forever given up *my* freedom as such. (87)[24]

One ends up annihilating freedom, in other words, when one abstracts it from its individual carrier, just as one also annihilates reason when one thinks of it in itself or, as Reinhold puts it, independently of its being "someone's own" (87).

With this, however, we find one more way of explaining speculative thought's impotence with respect to its intended object. The fact is that real freedom is in itself a divine product, one of which we can only have an intimation in conscience through divinely inspired feeling. Freedom, as the product of abstraction, is, on the contrary, a human product – one that is therefore bound to nature. But nature is phenomenal. As such, it lacks depth and hence contradicts even the possibility of freedom (93.ff.). The works of the philosopher must be quite different, therefore, from those of a moral agent. Since the latter acts on the strength of his moral conscience, his works are such that, even within the limits of nature, they attest to the divine or supernatural origin of the faith that informs them. The philosopher's works are, on the contrary, speculative concepts. But these are possible, as we have seen, only as the products of an abstraction from that very intimate union of finite and infinite that one finds in the highly individualized person of the moral agent – a union that alone makes true freedom possible. It follows that, however much speculation is in itself an exercise of freedom, it is nonetheless a kind of freedom that directs itself away from its sources. It is bound to finite nature, in other words. And here Reinhold repeats a point he had already adumbrated in *Paradoxes*. The endless reflection of speculation is the counterpart of the endless linear determination to which natural phenomena are subject. The most that philosophical reflection achieves through its freedom is the production a priori of a concept of nature, the reality of which needs then to be verified through experience a posteriori by stepping outside the circle of philosophical reflection. Speculative thought is only the counterpart of theoretical science (93–4).

The upshot is, of course, that the philosopher as such knows only finite nature. He cannot know God and, to this extent, he is an atheist. "He would *necessarily become atheist,*" Reinhold says, "if he could be nothing *but* philosopher" (93). These are important words, for they are a measure of how far Reinhold has come in identifying his position with Jacobi's. Reinhold is in fact reaching back to the claim that Jacobi had made to Lessing roughly two decades earlier – the claim, namely, that philosophy ultimately equals atheism. To be sure, Reinhold does not want to pass any such judgment unqualifiedly. It might even have appeared that, by claiming in his letter to Lavater that faith itself harbors a paradox, Reinhold had actually gone an extra length in justifying philosophical reflection – at least inasmuch as he had thereby provided a motivation for it in the felt need of resolving faith's own paradox. But in fact Reinhold was simply preparing the stage for the central thesis of his writing – namely, that philosophy is totally dependent on faith for motivation no less than for content, even though, in an effort to take hold of faith conceptually, it suspends its immediate certainty and tries to transform it into what turns out to be an endless progression of abstract representations. These representations are uniquely the property of the philosopher – devised exclusively for the sake of explanation. Should the philosopher forget this limitation, they would then indeed become a mere fiction *(Erdichtung)*. And since the philosopher would then be confusing his philosophizing with his being a *Mensch*, he would thereby also become atheist.

In a letter in which Fichte gave Reinhold permission to publish the explanation of the position that the latter had just sent to him, Fichte had warned Reinhold against trying to carve out a middle position between himself and Jacobi. Fichte claimed that no such middle ground was possible. And he pointed out that Jacobi would have said the same.[25] In the introductory note to his *Sendschreiben,* in which he was obviously reacting to Fichte's warning, Reinhold declared that his position was neither Fichte's nor Jacobi's but that "of a human being *(einer Menschen)* who, after having recognized the mutual independence of speculative knowledge and living faith, compares the two, and for the sake of this comparison holds himself above both in a state of oscillation. In so doing, this human being must therefore make assertions which those who are fixed to either the one or the other standpoint can neither understand nor find to be true."[26] Reinhold was being overingenuous. The act of oscillation he alleged was, however peculiar, still a way of taking up a position between Jacobi and Fichte. And if the sought middle ground eluded him, that was because, as a matter of fact, there was no oscillation. Reinhold had not risen above both Fichte and Jacobi. He definitely stood, rather, on Jacobi's side. To the extent that he was still carving a role for himself as an independent philosopher, it was in keeping faith and speculative thought together without allowing either to interfere with the other. He kept faith practically independent of philosophy without, however, allowing it to encroach on the speculative independence of the latter.[27] It was the role of what Reinhold now calls practical, as contrasted with merely scientific, philosophy. In Reinhold's mind, Lavater apparently needed the aid of such a philosophy. But so did Fichte. In the context of the current dispute regarding Fichte's alleged atheism, his defense of Fichte on the ground that the *Wissenschaftslehre* was per se neither theistic nor atheistic was not altogether unqualified. In the second of the two appendixes to his letter to Lavater, the one to which we alluded earlier, Reinhold points out that the nonatheism of Fichte's philosophy cannot be derived from its author's own words directly – that, when speaking in his own defense, Fichte failed to distance himself sufficiently from the claim that religious faith in God is just a pious wish (114–19). This was the claim that had occasioned the whole current dispute. Hence, Reinhold says to Lavater that he must accept Reinhold's defense of Fichte relying on Reinhold's conscientiousness and philosophical expertise.

7.2.3 Hegelian Intimations and Masonic Efforts

It was to be Reinhold's fate that he would hit upon penetrating statements of how things stood philosophically, and also make potentially brilliant philosophical moves, without himself appreciating, however, all that he was in fact saying or doing. It would be up to others to profit from it. We have already seen an example in his essay on a theory of representation. There, while thinking that he was establishing Kant's critical distinctions on a solid systematic basis, he was in fact relativizing them and, in the process, also providing the genetic model for a phenomenology of the mind that Fichte then exploited. Now, in his discourse to Lavater, couched in religious language, he hit upon the real difference that separated him from Fichte, but without appreciating its full significance. On hearing Reinhold, one would think that the abstractive thinking in which the philosopher engages is essentially a game – a serious game, perhaps, but still a game that must be given up in the face of the more pressing affairs of real life. This game view is especially prominent in *Paradoxes*. It recedes in the letter to Lavater, perhaps because, since he is addressing a man for whom philosophy as such is suspect, Reinhold wants to stress that the questions the philosopher raises are motivated by difficulties encountered in real life. Nonetheless, the point is still being made that, by branching out on his own in his quest for answers, the philosopher is forging a purely human way of resolving the original difficulties. He is therefore doomed to failure from the start unless he knows when to abort his reflective project and return to the matrix of natural intuitions where alone God's presence is felt immediately. On Reinhold's description of the philosopher's vocation, when ultimately taken as more than just a game, philosophy is the product of pride. On its being a product of pride, Fichte would have agreed. Philosophical reflection constitutes a break from nature, because it is in the first place an effort to forge nature anew according to the demands of reason. It is equally, therefore, a break from God, its creator, or a rebellion against him. For Fichte, there was, however, no return from reflection back to the immediacy of nature because, on his view of the human situation, the turn against God, the beginning of freedom, has its origin in the exercise of reason itself. Philosophy is there from the beginning. Where rationality has had its effect, unspoiled nature is no longer possible. Even less possible is an alleged common sense that serves as the repository, so to speak, of nature's supposed pristine inclinations. Human history begins in sin. There is no return from the path of reflection. Philosophy might have indeed begun naturally enough as playful curiosity. Once begun, however, as Fichte said to Jacobi, we philosophize for our own salvation, or, as one might put it, we do so in quest of a new nature. Reinhold's innate piety did not allow him this view of things. The irony, however, that he failed to perceive was that, of the two – the officially Christian crowd that was accusing Fichte of atheism and Fichte, who was defending himself against the accusation – the one closer in spirit to Christianity, at least as represented by Luther, was undoubtedly Fichte.

Hegel was to notice the irony. He does not belong to this study. It is not unfair, however, to drag him in momentarily as a way of bringing out the full complexity of the conceptual situation at hand. 'Original sin' was a myth for Kant – a necessary myth nonetheless, one that Kant had to bring into play as a way of rationalizing the irreducible presence in moral experience of *Willkühr*, of 'arbitrariness' or 'the irrational'. We have argued that Kant had to fall back on myth because of the still dogmatic encumbrances in his system that made the individuation of the I a problem. In Fichte's system, these encumbrances are gone. Sin is now a philosophical quantity. According to Fichte, as we have seen, thought becomes aware of its own lawfulness in virtue of the freedom or the spontaneity of action that it enjoys. Though free to exercise its activity, it is not free to exercise it at will. In the exercise, it feels constrained by necessities that the idealist philosopher recognizes as internal to thought itself. In other words, thought is by nature normative. However, in the recognition of this normativity, there is also the recognition of the possibility of not abiding by it, that is, of thought exercising its spontaneity arbitrarily.[28] In a theoretical context, this arbitrariness gives rise to error; in a moral context, to sin. But now, awareness of thought's freedom comes on the scene only ex post facto, that is, only when thought, as an aptitude in general, has been actualized in the thought of something particular and has thereby become

itself a particular thought. Normativity is experienced, therefore, equally
ex post facto, as having already had its effect.[29] It appears that norms bind
externally, in other words, as the first 'Other' before which the already
particularized thought appears to itself (this is the first effect of a norm)
as contingent or arbitrary, as falling short of all that a norm requires and
as that which could only be realized in a would-be pure thought. We are
born in sin. The Law binds externally, and the task is therefore set for the
individual human being of revealing this apparently external Law as 'his
own Law'. Kant, of course, had already said that much. But he attributed
this state of affairs to the de facto, and unexplainable, presence of sensibility in human thought. Fichte was now saying that the phenomenon
of individuality, the contingency and arbitrariness that affect all experiences, are first and foremost a necessary by-product of rationality itself.
To this extent, they are also the most primordial witness to reason's power
to shape experience. As Hegel will say, playing on the ancient Christian
liturgical theme of '*felix culpa*', Adam's disobedience was indeed a fall, but
a fall upward, since it marked the beginning of self-consciousness. This
was still mythological language. But it did not hide the great philosophical insight it harbored. Error, no less than truth, is internal to reason. It
is not just a surd affecting the latter accidentally. And the same applies
to sin.

I am saying that Fichte had demythologized the language of sin. I am
not saying, however, that he was free of myth. On the contrary, he was
still bound to it. And that was because he still interpreted the freedom
of thought, of which we become aware in experience only ex post facto,
in metaphysical imagery. He still portrayed it as, at its origin, a would-be
causa sui that would realize itself in a form free of all determination if it
only could (though de facto it cannot). It is this move that gave Fichte's
moral theory its special Promethean character, since it necessarily led to
accepting failure as itself a sign of success in moral striving. As a result,
any positive program of social action based on Fichte's moral premises is
necessarily reduced to the status of ideology, the kind promoted through
manipulation of propaganda rather than rational suasion. For, on those
premises, the program would have to remain only an ideal and would
gain its moral value precisely because it is only an ideal. Fichte's move
had the effect as well of projecting the starting point of reflective thought
to a mythical past already left behind as experience begins. The genesis
of the structure of experience, which Fichte brilliantly reconstructs on
the basis of the complexities of actual experience, then finds its place
projected into an equally mythical time interlude between that past and

the present of experience. It is this repeated erruption of myth that unfortunately makes Fichte's system susceptible to the charge of metaphysical mystification – whereas, in fact, Fichte was putting an end, once and for all, to metaphysics.

Fichte did not, however, have to make the move he made. As a matter of fact, Reinhold was to offer, as if incidentally, a perfectly viable, naturalistic alternative to it. We are back to the place in *Paradoxes* that we earmarked earlier for later attention.[30] Reflective thought originates as a fact of consciousness – a natural event, in other words, that can presumably be observed and explained (though Reinhold himself does not press this implication) within the parameters of a theory of nature. However, once this novel kind of activity, this *Tathandlung*, de facto occurs, a new universe is thereby constituted – a universe of meaning in which nature is made to reexist in the medium of the concept and acquires there meaning and value determinations it would not otherwise have. This is the typically human universe of theoretical and moral endeavors that, according to the idealistic thesis, sets itself up as a priori with respect to nature. But, on this paradigm of Reinhold, this universe never escapes continuity with nature. Naturally, it still is a product of it. Reinhold himself did not see how much he was in fact reformulating Fichte on a more humanistic, less heroic, basis. He was much too concerned with showing that the world of philosophical reflection is just a game – frightened perhaps, as indeed he should have been, of the atheistic implications of all idealism. But Hegel was to see the point. In his version of idealism, reflective thought originates not in any mythical time, but in the midst of nature itself – indeed, in the first instance, in the course of an animallike battle of prestige. Gone is any idea of a transcendent *causa sui* making its appearance in experience or otherwise conditioning the latter. Man's upward fall from nature occurs within nature itself. And the task is thus set for the human spirit to retrieve his natural past through his cultural creations. The retrieval is done in real time, with actual history as its record – a record that the human spirit must reinterpret over and over again in an effort to understand how he stands with respect to nature. With Hegel's idealism, Transcendental Logic will acquire a historical dimension. It truly becomes the 'phenomenology' that Fichte himself wanted it to be, that is, a science of experience, but in Hegel's sense as a logic of the appearances of spirit in nature in the shape of history.

The mention of history leads to one final consideration and one more episode in Reinhold's multifarious activities. In *Paradoxes*, by juxtaposing facts of consciousness with reflective acts, Reinhold was in fact trying to vindicate his own earlier systematization of Kant while at the same time reconciling it with Fichte's idealism. That systematization, despite Reinhold's vocal criticisms of *Popularphilosophie*, was still very much in the spirit of the latter. The primacy that it accorded to the supposed facts of consciousness clearly gave it away in this regard. Now, the *Popularphilosophen* were not very creative thinkers as a group. However, we have already noted the resilience of their tradition. Quite apart from their impeccable intellectual pedigree (the traditions of Leibniz/Wolff and of British empiricism), their interest in the sociohistorical dimension of human activities held a special attraction of its own.[31] And so did a philosophical program, such as theirs, that stressed the social vocation of philosophical reflection. These interests, incidentally, were not to be foreign to Hegel, whose historical and intellectual affinities with the tradition of popular philosophy are well known. It is not insignificant that his first public philosophical confrontation (1802) was with Traugott Krug, at the time an eminent philosopher of common sense. But, in the execution of their intellectual program, the popular philosophers constantly ran into a naturalism that ultimately undermined their still basically Christian intuitions. We have seen repeated examples of this. Kant's idealism, and even more dramatically Fichte's, kept naturalism at bay, but at the price of taking reflective thought (of which morality is the most significant product) as involving a radical break with nature. Hence, the popular philosophers' suspicion of what they took to be (as indeed it was from their point of view) the 'abstract formalism' of Kant and their various attempts to bring the Critique of Reason back into the mold of their naturalistic ways of thinking. They did not see the possibility that Hegel was to exploit, namely, that of taking seriously the break that reflective thought marks in nature while still keeping the product of the break within the compass of the latter. The product is a *new* nature, motivated and determined by interests unique to the life of spirit; yet, as new, it still has a memory of original nature. None of this was also in Reinhold's mind when he advanced his formula in *Paradoxes*. To the extent that philosophical reflection indeed constituted a new universe, to that extent, in his opinion, it became a game that flirts dangerously with atheism. The true vocation of reflection, according to him, was the conceptual clarification of tendencies innate to nature and put there in the first place by God. Nature, as God's given, is the ultimate norm of truth and virtue. This was the conviction that stood at the foundation of the naturalism of popular philosophy. In the spin he gave to his formula of reconciliation between facts of consciousness and product of reflection, Reinhold was now giving irrefutable evidence of how much he still belonged to that tradition.

This aspect of Reinhold explains an otherwise curious project in which he was engaged at the same time as he was reflecting on Fichte's *Wissenschaftslehre*. The project brings us back to Weishaupt. In 1798, the same year in which he had begun penning his *Paradoxes*, Reinhold published a hefty volume entitled *Negotiations Regarding the Fundamental Concepts and First Principles of Morality; from the standpoint of healthy common sense.*[32] The volume has an interesting history. Reinhold's association with the Masonry, and the propaganda activities he conducted on its behalf even when still a priest in Vienna, are well documented. More precisely, Reinhold belonged to the Illuminati, a sect that had secretly infiltrated the already secret Masonry and used it as a front, while also taking advantage of its considerable social influence, for promoting its particular agenda of social reform. The sect had been founded by Weishaupt, who ruled it despotically. Its activities were governed by his belief that, if unhindered in its operations, reason would eventually shape a society that reflects in its institutions the mechanical harmony of the universe. The potentially revolutionary implications of the Illuminati's agenda were obvious. There is reason to believe that the sect had had a hand in fomenting the French Revolution. Its existence and its activities were, however, quickly unmasked. In Bavaria it was dissolved by two edicts, the first of June 22, 1784, and the second of March 2, 1785. In Austria, all secret societies were disbanded in 1785. Weishaupt himself was publicly denounced for aspects of his private life deemed immoral at the time.

It is possible that Reinhold's flight to Protestant Leipzig in 1783 was motivated by fears that his Illuminati association would be discovered. As it happened, he was quick to distance himself from the sect, and also to condemn Weishaupt, whom he at one point declared "morally dead." He was also to object to the latter's strident attacks on Kant. It is far from clear, however, that he ever rejected the ideology that had motivated Weishaupt. His well-documented activities at the time among fellow Masons show that he had not lost hope that the social ideals of the Illuminati, though impractical in southern Catholic Germany, might take root in Protestant Germany. In 1794, together with three trusted Masonic friends, he struck an accord *(Bund)* that, after a number of vicissitudes that need not concern us here, led to this program of action. It was agreed that an original number of prominent intellectuals would declare, in an original exchange of letters, certain basic beliefs that they held on the strength of their common sense. A list of these beliefs in proposition form would then be sent by the original contributors to chosen friends, with the request that they comment on the list, suggest modifications and additions, and send it in turn to their chosen friends with a similar request. Periodically, all the responses would be reviewed by the initiators of the project (Reinhold, in fact); a new list would be drawn that took into consideration any objections or suggestions of additions; and the process would be repeated. The idea was that, in this way, openly but still from the bottom up (so to speak), a universal consensus regarding fundamental beliefs based on common sense would be achieved in society, on the basis of which proper authorities could then institute suitable social reforms. This was Reinhold's idea of a nonrevolutionary social revolution, the German counterpart of the French Revolution.

The 1798 volume *Negotiations* was the published record of the results of the first round of communications. It was not followed by any other. Its contents do not concern us. They are uniformly uninteresting. If anything, they show how much healthy common sense curiously reflected the mores of the more affluent German bourgeoisie of the time. The idea that inspired the project behind it is, however, significant. It opens a special window into Reinhold's mind. Reinhold was still operating on the assumption that there is such a thing as an already given harmonious universe; that the reason that informs such a universe is a light that cannot be resisted once allowed to shine; and indeed, that it has already exercised its power in each of us, by virtue of our being part of the universe, in the form of common sense.[33] This was the view that had inspired Reinhold even when still a priest in Vienna.[34] It also happened to be Weishaupt's view and the basis for his social program, of which Reinhold's project still was a reflection. Reinhold had never abandoned that view, but had rather reinterpreted the new idealism of Kant in light of it. For Reinhold, rationality was a given quantity; reason itself, still a contemplative faculty. In this sense, despite his Jacobin sympathies and his social activities, he was a quietist. The reason of the idealists was, on the contrary, a constitutive faculty; rationality, its product. And Fichte had been the one to press this aspect of idealism to an extreme, perhaps even absurd, limit. Reinhold had good reasons to be hesitant before him. Fichte was indeed the true philosopher of revolution.

7.3 JACOBI'S *CRI DE CŒUR*

In the Preface to his own 1799 open letter to Fichte, Jacobi had given Reinhold the task of defending him in the current fray in case he should come under attack. "To the *Rein* and *Holden*," he had said punning on Reinhold's name,

to the pure and the gracious one, who for the sake of truth courageously forsakes himself and all else – to him I defer in advance, in case I should somehow come under attack because of this writing. – You, dear friend and brother, will have to step into the fray if that happens, and carry the *older* companion away from the heat of battle upon your shoulders, just as Socrates once carried the *younger* one. (ix)

Reinhold was graciously to accept the challenge in the concluding words of the Preface to his own open letter to Lavater and Fichte by publicly extending his hand to Jacobi. "With gratitude, respect and love," he said, "do I reach out my hand to him, the philosopher and the believer" (8).

In fact, Jacobi had never liked Reinhold. We hear in a letter to a friend, describing his first meeting with the then recent exile from Catholic Austria, how much Reinhold's nonstop philosophical talk had exasperated him. It was as if from his pockets Reinhold could draw on demand, now a metaphysical proposition from this pocket here, now an ethical one from that there.[35] Later Jacobi was to express annoyance at Reinhold's insistent attempts at drawing his attention to Bardili's thought – at the time the latest in Reinhold's philosophical discoveries.[36] And indeed, the two men were the products of totally different backgrounds. Jacobi was the scion of a patrician merchant family, Protestant to the core and with strong pietistic leanings. Reinhold, a sometime priest who had fled his cloister and his native Catholic Austria with the help of the Masonry, had converted to Protestantism and, an upstart in Protestant lands, had climbed his way up the social and academic ladders by dint of much industrious writing.[37] Yet, in their different styles, the two were now forming a common front in the face of Fichte. Reinhold had reacted to the atheism crisis with a new attempt at philosophical mediation. Jacobi was now returning to the intuitions that had originally motivated him in the Spinoza-Letters, and that the Fichte phenomenon, as he now claimed, had vindicated.

In his opening shot, Jacobi grants that Fichte is the philosopher without qualification – the one who has finally brought the strivings of philosophical reason to a conclusion. Fichte is the Messiah of reason, reason's incarnation on earth. Kant was only his precursor. Jacobi agrees with Fichte that the subject–object distinction runs across the whole of experience and that the philosopher, in order to satisfy his need for complete systematic explanation, has no choice but to take as his principle one of the two terms in the distinction, and to then endeavor to reduce the other to it. Here Jacobi presents the two images that were to become famous in the literature, and that probably did more to discredit Fichte rhetorically than any argument could have done discursively. Imagine a cube, and think of two parallel sides of it as representing extension and thought, respectively. Now, Spinoza gave precedence to being in his system. Hence, he took the two, extension and thought, as attributes of the one principle he called 'substance'. Imagine this substance as a third side of the cube, spanning the other two parallel sides on the top and thus uniting them from above. Spinoza called 'objective' the intuitive thought that rises up to this one substance, and therefore recognizes extension and thought as mere abstract aspects of it. He called 'formal' that kind of thinking that, on the contrary, trades in abstractions and thereby falls victim to the illusion of believing that individual things, which are really the products of the imagination, have standing on their own. Imagine reality, as represented through this kind of abstract thinking, as a fourth side of the cube spanning the two parallel sides at the bottom. Think of this cube as the 'speculative cube'. Fichte, according to Jacobi, had only to invert it in order to arrive at his system. Once inverted, abstractive thought stands at the top as the principle of all reality. Being is only its product, whereas substance, or anything putatively standing on its own independently of thought, is reduced to a fiction of the imagination. Invert Spinoza's cube, in other words, and, as Jacobi now says (4), "in exchange a pure flame will flare up, burning all by itself, with no need of *place* or *material to nourish it*. **Transcendental Idealism!**" It had never occurred to Spinoza to make that move. Nor had its possibility occurred to Jacobi at the time of his *Spinoza-Letters*. Now that Fichte had, however, made it, it appeared obvious. It also retroactively explained to Jacobi why, from the beginning, he had not been able to find access into Kant's system (the precursor of Fichte's) except by way of Spinoza.

Jacobi offers his other image to represent what the product of Fichte's abstractive thought would truly amount to. It is an image that, as he says, he conceived in a mischievous moment. Imagine someone knitting a stocking with thread and a hooked needle. The texture of the stocking progressively emerges as the needle repeatedly turns the thread upon itself into a series, and then a series of series, of conjoined knots – as if the thread were constantly reflecting upon itself. In the process, using ever more complex techniques of knotting, all kinds of pictures can be incorporated into the surface of the texture – flowers, animals, or what have you – until, with sufficient thread, all the things that populate the

world are represented and the stocking itself is made to appear a 'world'
unto itself. But, if one simply pulls the thread, everything disappears, and
the supposed world of the stocking thus reverts to the one-dimensional
thread it has in fact never ceased to be. Fichte's *Wissenschaftslehre*, Jacobi
now says, is like the knotting of this stocking. It is the repeated reflection
upon itself of an abstract thought that mistakes its own emptiness for
infinity and, through its complex internal contortions, is deluded into
believing that it is thereby producing being. Fichte paraded himself as
the champion of subjectivity. His claim was, however, only a sham, for
individuality (which is the essential condition of subjectivity) is no more
possible in the emptiness of his reflective thought than it was possible
in the emptiness of Spinoza's substance. "Taken *simply as such*," Jacobi
proclaims, "our sciences are games that the human spirit devises to pass
the time. In devising these games, *it only organizes its non-knowledge* without
coming a single hair's breadth closer to a cognition of *the true*" (24). Jacobi
was to regret this outburst and tried to soften it in a later edition of his
Letter.[38] In the context in which he uttered it, however, there is no doubt
that he meant what he said. Nor is there any doubt regarding whose lesson
Reinhold had taken to heart when he himself called philosophy a game.

Sensitive to Fichte's possible rebuttal that he had not understood the
Wissenschaftslehre, Jacobi preempts it by pointing out that there is nothing particularly difficult about Fichte's science or, for that matter, about
Kant's moral theory that had inspired it. Kantian morality boils down to
a demand for consistency of action – a consistency that requires, in turn,
the application of universal law. Jacobi has, of course, no objection to
the demand; nor does he object to the idea of universal law. His point,
however, is that neither the law nor the consistency that it makes possible
amounts to anything real unless the law is of a self that antedates it and
to which it is itself ultimately subservient, and unless the required consistency is that of a self not constituted by just this consistency. Jacobi can
hardly restrain his anger at the thought of the 'impersonal personality'
that, as he claims, is the only possible subject of Kant's or Fichte's morality. In one more outburst (32–3) that he later tried to soften,[39] Jacobi
proclaims himself the champion of individuality, the defender of the individual's privilege to stand above the law. Full of righteous indignation,
he thunders:

Yea, I am the atheist and the Godless one, who, against the *will that wills nothing*,
will tell lies, just as Desdemona did when she lay dying; the one that will lie and
defraud, just as Pylades did when he passed himself off for Orestes; will murder,

as Timoleon did; or break law and oath, like Epaminondas, or John de Witt; commit suicide like Otho, perpetrate sacrilege like David – yea, I would pluck ears of wheat *on the sabbath* just because I *have hunger, and the law is made for man, not man for the law.*[40] I am this godless man, and I scoff at the philosophy that calls me godless on this account. I scoff at it and at its highest Being, for I know, with the most sacred certainty that I have in me, that the *privilegium aggratiandi*[41] for such crimes against the pure letter of the absolutely universal law of reason is man's true *right of majesty*, the seal of his worth, of his divine nature.

To Fichte all this would indeed count as madness. But Jacobi is not to be unnerved. Against the philosophers' definition of sanity, he, for his part, has no hesitation making his stand on the ground of madness.

Throughout the Letter, Jacobi proceeds unsystematically, "rhapsodically" as he says, in a deliberately preachy tone. Despite his brimming indignation, he repeatedly addresses Fichte as "his dear one" in the manner of a father tutoring a wayward son. Yet, despite all this rambling and sanctimoniousness, Jacobi does not fail to define exactly the distance that separates him from Fichte. It boils down to a difference in conceptions of reason. For Fichte, reason is a would-be creative faculty. For Jacobi, it is an essentially 'perceptive' faculty – one that apprehends given objects and for which, therefore, sensibility is primary and irreducible. To abandon the senses is, literally, to lose one's senses or to go out of one's mind. Though Jacobi does not mention his *David Hume*, the reference to it is unmistakable. The other that checks the activities of the I, and in virtue of which alone, as Jacobi had said in that dialogue, the I is individualized – that other, as Jacobi now stresses, must be understood as in origin an independent, given entity. Jacobi is, of course, mindful of the objection that Fichte, who had exploited his own model of experience, could have raised. Without the I generating through reflection the intelligible space within which the other significantly offers resistance to it and thereby acquires the meaning of a Thou, no meeting between the two would ever be possible. Jacobi is aware of the difficulty. But he also has an answer for it. God is the required meeting ground. His presence within the creature is the source of the intimations of truth that allow the creature to recognize this truth when revealed in the presence of the other.

This statement, however clichéd it might sound, is important. It shows the extent to which Jacobi still lived in the mental and emotional world of a Spalding; how much, despite his many fulminations against the *Herren Aufklärer*, he still drew inspiration from the same vision of a harmonious universe governed by an all-present God that was the heritage of popular philosophy. It is no surprise that he would soon gravitate toward

Schleiermacher and Fries, both of whom he influenced in turn. Fries's apparently Kantian distinction between reason and understanding was but a sclerotized version of commonsense philosophy. On the one hand, the understanding was to provide concepts for construing theories on the basis of materials yielded by the senses. This was the realm of the physical sciences. On the other hand, reason (also associated with a higher form of feeling) provided through its alleged intuitive apprehension of eternal truths the basis for religion, morality, and the fine arts. Jacobi relied on this distinction in the final stage of his public career, even when he was attacking Schelling. Reinhold, for his part, was to tread a more cerebral path, but still along the line of the mixture of rationalism and empiricism that was the hallmark of *Popularphilosophie*.[42] He became an adept of Bardili's so-called logical realism, which he tried to improve and promote through an endless stream of publications. This position – again, a mixture of rationalism and empiricism – was based on the idea of thought as a sort of activity of self-reference that, not unlike a counting (an *idem per idem*), slowly absorbs all content of experience, including its subject. This activity unfolds on its own, as if anonymously, and thus provides the element of transcendence in experience. Eventually Reinhold produced some entertaining parodies of the genesis of Idealism from Kant to Schelling – brilliant pieces in their kind, but all based on the assumption that Idealism is psychological theory.[43] The point being missed on all sides was that, from the beginning, the question of Idealism had been one regarding the origin and the legitimization of meaning.

7.4 KANT'S ANATHEMA

I hereby declare that I regard Fichte's *Wissenschaftslehre* as a totally indefensible system. For pure theory of science is nothing more or less than mere logic, and the principles of logic cannot lead to any material knowledge. [...] Since [a] reviewer finally maintains that the *Critique* is not to be taken *literally* in what it says about sensibility and that anyone who wants to understand the *Critique* must first master the requisite 'standpoint' (of Beck or of Fichte), because *Kant's* precise words, like Aristotle's, will destroy the spirit, I therefore declare again that the *Critique* is to be understood by considering exactly what it says.[44]

This was Kant's declaration in 1799. A decade earlier, Kant had exchanged letters with Sigismund Beck, hoping to find in him the faithful disciple that Reinhold was already proving not to be. At the time of the declaration, he might still have had some recollection of what Beck had been up to. So far as Fichte is concerned, however, it is highly unlikely that Kant's acquaintance with the *Wissenschaftslehre* was more than just by hearsay. As a matter of fact, for some years Kant had ceased to produce creative new work. He had only reassembled materials from early lectures, and was at the time of the declaration engaged in a project of transition from Transcendental Logic to Physics that was of doubtful critical credentials. There is something sad about the declaration. It is not just that Kant was no longer in touch with the public he was addressing. The public itself was no longer in touch with him. Kant might have indeed become, by that time, an icon in the German lands. The care that Jacobi had taken, in the Preface to his Letter to Fichte, to profess his highest esteem for the great philosopher of Königsberg was witness to the fact. It is as if Jacobi wanted to spare Kant the full brunt of the blow he was striking against Fichte while still associating him with Fichte in the body of the Letter. Kant's eminence did not, however, detract from the fact that he no longer was at the center of discussion. The world of the late Enlightenment, in whose terms he had originally still defined his own critical problematic, was at an end. Interests had shifted. Ironically enough, Jacobi and Fichte were perhaps the only ones at the time who were in a position to remember how much Kant had himself contributed to that end. The Critique of Reason continued, but in the dogmatic form that the Jena theologians had given to it from the beginning and in which the popular philosophers had striven to make it their own. So it was that the one to replace Kant at his chair in Königsberg, after his official retirement, was to be none other than the already mentioned Traugott Krug, the same eminent philosopher of common sense who was the first to arouse Hegel's ire in public.

8

The Vocation of Humankind Revisited, 1800

Conclusion

"Your vocation is not merely to *know,* but to *act* according to your knowledge": this *is* loudly proclaimed in the innermost depths of my soul, as soon as I recollect myself for a moment and turn my observation inward upon my self. "You are here, not for idle contemplation of yourself, or for brooding over devout sensations – no, you are here for action; your action, and your action alone, determines your worth."[1]

Fichte

The practical reason is the root of all reason.[2] [...] I am hungry, not because food is before me, but a thing becomes food for me because I am hungry; similarly, I act as I do not because a certain end is to be attained, but the end becomes an end to me because I am bound to act in the manner by which it may be attained.[3]

Fichte

Everything that *is* is good and absolutely legitimate. There is but one world possible – a thoroughly good world.[4]

Fichte

Voltaire's procedure is an authentic example of sane sound sense which Voltaire possessed in such high measure, while others babble about it all the time in order to pass off their insanities as sound sense.[5]

Hegel

8.1 NEW BOOK, OLD THEMES

In January 5, 1795, writing from his Tübingen seminary, Schelling bitterly complained to his friend Hegel:

Here there are Kantians in droves. [...] All imaginable dogmas have been stamped as postulates of practical reason, and wherever theoretical and historical proofs are lacking, the practical Tübingian reason cuts the knot. [...] Before you know it, the *deus ex machina* pops up, the personal individual *being who sits up there in heaven!*[6]

This is how far some theologians had gone in reintegrating Kant into the mental universe of a Spalding without apparently recognizing the drastic changes brought to that universe by the transition from faith understood as still unclarified reason (as vision still "in a glass darkly") to faith based on practical postulation. Schelling himself, *Wunderkind* that he was, was soon to publish treatises apparently siding with Fichte.[7] But he quickly became one of Fichte's most stubborn critics. The monism that he eventually developed is more reminiscent of Goethe's Spinozistic naturalism than of anything connected with Transcendental Idealism.[8] He does not belong to this study. His name, however, raises the interesting question (also not part of this study) of whether Romantic Idealism, though historically continuous with the idealism of Kant and Fichte, was in fact yet another product of the same late Enlightenment naturalism that both Kant and Fichte had opposed on moral grounds.[9] Schelling's older friend, Hegel, was not to publish for some years. He also does not belong to this study. He shall, however, make a brief appearance later in this chapter in connection with Fichte. His first published essay included a criticism of the latter that, while pointing to the main flaw of his idealism and Kant's as well, gave intimations of how Fichte's idealism might be developed in ways that remedied the flaw without, however, moving in the direction of Schelling's. For the purposes of this study, the criticism is all the more significant because it was specifically directed at the latest of Fichte's publications. And this latest publication, as it happens, brings us back to the theme with which we began.

It bore exactly the same title as Spalding's essay written over half a century earlier, namely, *Die Bestimmung des Menschen*, or *The Vocation of Humankind*.[10] Fichte had begun to work on it in 1799, immediately after his expulsion from the University at Jena, and published it the following year in Berlin, his place of retreat after the expulsion. This little book was in fact the fulfillment of a plan to present his thoughts in popular form, a plan that he had entertained as early as 1797.[11] It falls into three parts, or books. The first is entitled "Doubt." It consists of a monologue by someone identified simply as 'I'. The second, entitled "Knowledge," is a dialogue between this I and a supernatural Spirit that now addresses him in a vision. The third reverts to the form of a monologue. It carries the title of "Faith." This last is by far the longest of the three parts and the one that, as we shall see, was to be the object of the sharpest criticism.

As Fichte stresses in the Preface, the I who speaks his mind aloud throughout the work should not be identified with Fichte himself but stands, rather, for everyman. "It is at least [Fichte's] wish that the reader would himself be this 'I'" (vi, 3). The someone for whom this I stands finds himself in a predicament not unlike, as we remember, that of the speaker in Spalding's much earlier essay. Having already accumulated a great deal of knowledge about the world around him, he now realizes that on one point he has been delinquent. He has not asked himself what he himself is or what his vocation is. To be sure, he has long been instructed on these matters, and has always acted on the assumption that he has full knowledge about them. In fact, however, the instruction on which he has relied has come to him from external sources. His supposed knowledge was never the result of personally undertaken inquiry; to this extent, therefore, this knowledge is not now truly *his* knowledge. And the point has finally come in his life when he should make it truly his by seeking truth independently. "I will *know*," he declares. "With certainty [...] will I know what I am and what I shall be. And should it prove impossible for me to know this, then I will know at least that I cannot know" (7–8, 7). On this note of willfulness – a note that actually contrasts him with the speaker in Spalding's essay, since the latter primarily sought peace rather than independence of mind – he nonetheless embarks on the same project of reexamining what he knows about nature.

The results, spelled out in the following pages of Book I, are remarkably also the same as those in Spalding's essay. They add up to a vision of the universe that a Weishaupt could have endorsed. As actually developed by Weishaupt, this vision, however, carried explicit pantheistic consequences that were indeed logically consistent with the assumptions of Spalding's speaker, but from which the latter, whether consciously or not, had shied away. In Fichte's work, they are now being reiterated, almost with a vengeance. We should let the I speak for himself:

In every moment of her duration, Nature is one connected whole; in every moment *each individual part* must be what it is, because *all the others* are what they are; and you could not remove a single grain of sand from its place without thereby (although perhaps imperceptibly to you) changing something throughout all parts of the immeasurable whole. But *every moment of this duration* is determined by *all past moments,* and will determine every *future moment;* and you cannot conceive even the position of a grain of sand other than as it is in the *present,* without being compelled to conceive the whole indefinite *past* to have been other than what it has been, and the whole indefinite *future* to be other than what it will be. (24–5, 13–14)

There is only one power, call it Nature, that manifests itself in a manifold of forms, all necessarily connected with one another and constituting together a single harmonious system of being. Moreover, upon further reflection, the I discovers that there is nothing about his conscious, and presumably active, life that cannot be interpreted as falling within this system. He is free in the sense that, like any other living being, through his many activities, he spontaneously brings to completion predispositions innate to him by nature, thereby satisfying Nature's general tendency to express its power. His only difference is that, unlike other living beings, he is conscious of these activities. He performs them while at the same time representing them. If a tree were conscious of its growth, it would think of itself as free, just as the I thinks of itself in this way. Indeed, instead of saying that the I is conscious of his activities, it would be more accurate to say that in him, in his activities, Nature becomes conscious of itself. Moreover, in thus becoming conscious of his activities, the I also becomes immediately conscious of his own limitations, and thereby is also led to assume the existence of other things and other thinking beings, in virtue of which alone, from the different perspectives that each affords, Nature is in a position of surveying itself exhaustively (38–44, 20–2).

In this system, "the known phenomenon in our consciousness called *Will* also becomes just as intelligible" (45, 23). 'Volition' is the immediate consciousness of the power of any of the activities of Nature within us. Inasmuch as this power is being hemmed in by the conflicting power of other activities, it is called 'desire'. The more successful a power is in asserting itself, the nobler is its standing within Nature. The notions of 'moral law', 'virtue', and 'crime' all follow from this basic conception. As the I now recognizes:

If the striving power [in us that we call desire] be the whole undivided force of humanity, then the desire is worthy of our nature and may be called one which is higher. The latter effort, considered absolutely, may be called a moral law. The effect of this latter is a virtuous Will, and the course of action resulting from it is virtue. The triumph of the former not in harmony with the latter is vice; such a triumph *over* the latter, and despite its opposition, is crime. (45–6, 23)

One thing is clear: Whether a striving is successful or not, whether it results in virtuous action or crime, depends in all cases on the place of a given power within the overall system of Nature. The net result is that "the power, which in each individual occasion proves triumphant, triumphs of necessity; its superiority is determined by the whole connection of the universe; and hence by this connection the vice or crime of each individual is irrevocably determined" (46, 23–4). It also follows that "'repentance' is the consciousness of the continued effort of humanity within me, even after it has been overwhelmed, associated with the disagreeable sense of having been subdued – a disquieting but still precious pledge of our nobler nature" from which there arises the further "sense which has been called 'conscience'" (47, 24). Finally, "the ideas of guilt and accountability have no meaning outside of external legislation. Man incurs guilt, and must render account of his crime only if he compels society to use artificial, external, force to restrain those of his impulses that are injurious to the general welfare" (48, 24).

This consideration brings the inquiry of the I to a close. The I finally knows what he is. "I know what I am. [...] I am a manifestation, determined by the whole system of the universe, of a power of Nature which is determined by itself alone" (48, 24–5). This is exactly the same consideration that brought peace of mind to Weishaupt and, though not stated in such a stark form, had also brought peace of mind to Spalding's *Mensch*. For Fichte's I, however, it now turns out to be a new source of consternation. For reasons at first unknown, the I finds it disturbing. And, upon reflection, he discovers why. The fact is that the immediate consciousness he has of himself irresistibly leads him to believe that he, the individual that he is, is the direct source of his actions, and that such actions are irreducibly *his* because, in performing them, he realizes intentions that are the product of his own intelligence. These intentions define his identity, so that, in realizing them, he realizes himself. As if by way of paradox, he becomes in action what he already is. His becoming is an internalized process. Quite the opposite is the case with the things of nature. The modifications to which these are subject are brought about *on them* (as contrasted with *in them*) by external factors. Therefore, the things themselves can only be said to *be* what they are at any given moment – never that they have *become* it. The modifications to which they are subject realize possibilities that are originally *in them* only in the sense that their constitution allows for them. They are never, however, *for them* in the sense that the things strive for them, so that, once realized, these things come back to themselves. His body apart, which he is ready to relinquish to the mechanism of nature, the I is instinctively led to believe that he stands above Nature, at least insofar as his intelligent life is concerned, precisely because of his capacity to govern his actions internally. In principle, he is therefore also capable of imposing his intentions on Nature as well and of thereby becoming its Lord. As the I now discovers upon reflection, it was this belief, based on his immediate consciousness, that had led him to inquire about his vocation in the first place (52–6, 26–30).

This is the quandary in which Fichte's I thus finds himself. On the one hand, immediate consciousness tells him that he stands in the universe as an agent, individually responsible for his feelings and actions. His heart bids him listen to this voice. On the other hand, he has no logical ground on which to challenge the view of the universe that reflection holds out – one in which he is just a cog in a greater organization. And his intellect bids him in the direction of the latter. This was indeed the quandary in which the *Aufklärung* had found itself – because of its trust in both the universality of science and the individuality of the human being. Spalding's *Mensch,* still relying as he did on the intuitions of Christian piety, might not have appreciated the contradiction that was at the root of this dilemma. Fichte's I now knew better. Jacobi and Kant, let alone a host of others, would have sufficed to sensitize him to it. The same line of reflection that had brought peace of mind to Spalding's character now sinks Fichte's I into a state of despair.[12]

But the despair does not last for long. A Spirit *(Geist)* appears to the I at the beginning of Book II and engages him in conversation. Why Fichte would have now presented in dialogue form what was in effect still a monologue is a question that some early reviewers raised. One reviewer suggested that the shift was required because, according to Fichte, the I could not have performed the leap in self-awareness that Book II requires without the help of proper education.[13] That might be true. The suddenly materialized Spirit is, however, also clearly reminiscent of Descartes's evil genius, and it is indeed instructive to consider him in that role. The Spirit's function, just like that of the evil genius, is to sow a seed of doubt regarding the reliability of the view of the universe generated by reflection. Both Fichte's Spirit and Descartes's Demon disappear as soon as they have done their work. This work, though destructive on the surface, has, however, in the end the effect of revalidating beliefs originally held on a completely different basis. In the case of Descartes, the original belief that clear and distinct ideas correspond to reality, previously based on intellectual instinct alone, is now buttressed by the newly acquired confidence that God, who is the author of that instinct, would not use it as a means of deception. In the case of Fichte's I, as we shall see in a moment, it is the same view of the universe as expounded in Book I that is finally reintroduced, but with an altogether different meaning. This will happen only by the end of Book III. And, though the name of God is invoked and a gesture is made in the direction of immortality, this is done again on the strength of a faith and a consequent trust that are of a totally different nature than was possible in the mental universe of Book I or, for that matter, in the mental universe of a Descartes.

The difference was due to Kant. The analogy between Descartes's Demon and Fichte's Spirit is indeed so strong that Kant's presence in Book II might go unnoticed. Yet, Kant is there. In the case of Descartes, the Demon succeeded in sowing his seed of doubt in him because he was addressing him in his own language of subjectivity, thus exploiting a weakness in that very language. Fichte's Spirit also speaks the language of subjectivity. And it would seem that, at first at least, the doubt he sows is directed at the kind of scholastic Aristotelian realism that lay just below the surface of Spalding's ruminations but that was also the object of Descartes's own original doubt (let alone that of his evil genius). The doubt is based on the recognition, one that is actually common to both Descartes and Kant, that, since knowledge is representational, there is no direct consciousness of an object without self-consciousness being implicated at least in principle.[14] Therefore, the picture of the universe that the I has conceived in Book I, mostly on the basis of reflectively refined common sense, is legitimate only on the condition that it be indexed throughout by an 'I think'. Hence, as thus directed to Spalding's picture of the universe, the doubt has indeed the apparent first saving effect of reenabling the subjectivity that Fichte's I feared to have lost by the end of Book I. But this is all only an appearance. For the 'subjectivity' the Spirit now brings into play is in fact the transcendental subjectivity of Kant. It is the subjectivity of a thinker in general, just as the objectivity of the universe excogitated through it (the possible presence within this universe of particular thinking beings included) is only one that would satisfy the requirements of this thinker's abstract thought. And, as Fichte's I is quick to realize, his own individual self, his own reality as he believes he grasps it in immediate consciousness, the subjectivity he is trying to save, have nothing to do with the I of this I think. The latter is but the possibility of a thought in general – one from the point of view of which the individualized self that Fichte's I presumes to possess is dissolved into a flux of transient intuitions or mere appearances. These appearances, once reflectively granted, require in turn the fiction of the I think in general (of an anonymous subjectivity, so to speak) precisely in order to reassemble the presumed self, otherwise dissolved into a flux of vanishing determinations, into some sort of presumably stable being. Such a reconstituted being is avowedly only a product, itself a conceptual figment based on the other figment of the I think in general. Thus, as Fichte's I despairingly recognizes, by following the path painstakingly set out for him by the Spirit with whom he has been in dialogue, he would have to conclude that what he believed to be his self, the core of his immediately apprehended subjectivity, is in fact a contrived product of his thought. Or more precisely, since there is no longer any obvious sense in which he can even say "I," he must conclude that it is the product of an anonymous thought that unfolds in general and gives rise to the illusion of an immediately apprehended individuality.[15] In his words:

> Strictly speaking, I may then indeed say, *"It is thought that . . ."* but no, I can hardly say even that; more accurately, I may say, *"the thought appears* that I feel, perceive, think"; in no way, however, may I say *"I feel, perceive, think."* The first alone is a fact; the second is a fictional addition to the fact. (172, 80)

As the Spirit makes a move to leave, Fichte's I holds him back. "Stay, deceitful Spirit!" he cries out, and asks:

> Is this all the wisdom towards which you have directed my hopes, and do you boast that you have set me free? You have set me free, it is true; you have absolved me from all dependence, for you have transformed me, and everything around me on which I could possibly be dependent, into nothing. You have abolished necessity by annihilating all existence. (162–3, 76)

The noble Spirit, as he appeared at first, has now turned into a 'deceitful Spirit'. I have said that Descartes's evil genius sowed his doubt by relying on a weakness of Descartes's language of subjectivity. On his own understanding of the mind, Descartes ran the risk of finding himself totally shut up within the mind. Fichte's Spirit has now exploited the weakness of Kant's language of transcendental subjectivity. It is a language that does not ultimately clarify how the flesh-and-bone individual whom we normally have in mind when we say "I" can identify with the I of the I think. It leaves unclarified how, from the standpoint of the latter, that is, from the standpoint of an observer in general or a legislator in general, the full sense of the other I can ever be retrieved. It is not by chance that, as the Spirit puts Fichte's I through his reflective paces, he repeatedly evokes Spinoza's language, thereby silently, but not any less clearly, conveying the warning that, by following Kant, one is still being held hostage to Spinoza.[16] It is as if the Spirit were playing along with Jacobi, pressing

Kant to the conclusions Jacobi had extracted from his Idealism. At the end of Book II, Fichte's I indeed has good cause to despair. He discovers that he has never abandoned the universe of abstractions where he had found himself at the end of Book I. The only difference is that he now knows how such abstractions were produced and how they could indeed generate – once their standpoint has been assumed – only an illusion of immediacy. The despair is now all the more intense for being an informed one.

A temptation is, however, only as strong as its victim is subjectively vulnerable to it. To cast either Descartes's Demon or Fichte's Spirit exclusively in the role of the villain is not, therefore, altogether fair. Descartes was vulnerable to the deceit of his evil genius only because he had forgotten that the idea of God was within him. The presence of this idea in him had him outside the bounds of his subjectivity from the beginning, regardless of how methodically he might have tried to withdraw within them. Once Descartes remembers this truth, the language of subjectivity that the Demon was exploiting is no longer a cause of temptation. And the Demon, in fact, disappears. The situation of Fichte's I is more complex but still analogous to Descartes's. Historically speaking, this I differs from Descartes's by the very fact that he, no less than Spalding's *Mensch,* is a character of the *Aufklärung.* He has not deliberately bracketed all consideration about human conduct and resolved to abide in his life by traditionally sanctioned practices, as Descartes had done. On the contrary, his main interest is in how he should act; his leading question, the destiny to which humankind has been called. There is a point to the reviewer's suggestion, already mentioned earlier, that the Spirit in Book II stands for the external factors that raise Fichte's I to a new level of self-awareness, thereby also leading him to his new bout of despair at the end of the book. Together these factors amount to the experience of the late *Aufklärung.* Psychologically speaking, that is, in terms of the character of the I as portrayed in Fichte's book, the defining aspect of this I lies precisely in the fact that he is motivated from the start not by any skeptical doubt that he wishes to resolve (as had been the case for Descartes), but by a desire to validate through knowledge certain beliefs that he harbors about himself – notably the belief that he is a free being responsible for achieving his vocation in the universe. His despair is caused by the conclusion, to which he is forced first at the end of Book I and then again at the end of Book II, that, far from validating his beliefs, knowledge in fact undermines them. However, granted his original state of mind, another option was open to him – namely, to explore whether, rather than knowledge validating belief, it is belief that validates knowledge, granted that one commits oneself to satisfying belief's requirements. This is the option that Fichte's I has failed to consider. He has therefore entertained false expectations regarding what the Noble Spirit might offer him. And this Spirit, in turn, assumes before him the figure of a deceitful tempter.

As it happens, it is the Spirit who, at the end of Book II, in defending himself against the charge of deceit, reminds Fichte's I of the real cause of the I's present conflict and the exact onus of his original promise. As he says:

> You wanted to *know*, and you took a wrong road. You looked for knowledge where no knowledge can reach, and you even persuaded yourself that you had obtained an insight into something which is opposed to the very nature of your insight. I found you in this condition. I wished to free you from your false knowledge; but by no means to bring you the true.
>
> You wanted to know of your knowledge. [...] But all knowledge is only re-production [*Abbildung*]; and there is always something wanting in it – that which corresponds to the production [*Bilde*]. [...]
>
> Knowledge is not reality – just because it is knowledge. You have seen through the illusion; and without belying your better insight, you can never again give yourself up to it. This is the sole merit which I claim for the system which we have together discovered; it destroys and annihilates error. It cannot give us truth, for in itself it is absolutely empty. You now seek, and with good right as I well know, something real lying behind mere appearance, another reality than that which has been thus annihilated, as I also well know. But in vain would you labour to create this reality by means of your knowledge, or out of your knowledge; or to embrace it by your recognition. If you have no other organ by which to apprehend it, you will never find it. (175–8, 82)

The other organ is, of course, the faith that has motivated Fichte's I from the beginning. The Spirit's task (again, not unlike the task of Descartes' Demon) was to force this I back to his subjective resources.[17] And now that he has done his work, he can retreat to his ethereal abode. "But you have such an organ," are his parting words. "Give it life and fire, and you will attain to perfect tranquility. I leave you alone with yourself" (178, 82).

Thus in Book III ("Faith") the I begins the arduous task of examining his own longings and discovering the commitments that he already held in virtue of them. This is the longest Book, as I have said, but also the easiest one to rehearse, since it simply recapitulates, in popular language, the core lesson of the *Wissenschaftslehre*. It makes its start in the name of Jacobi, so to speak – a circumstance that might have indeed surprised Jacobi himself, though one that is not surprising in itself, since faith is the theme now and Jacobi was the self–declared philosopher of faith. His name is not mentioned, but his presence is unmistakably evoked. "We are all born in faith," the I says. "He who is blind, follows blindly the secret and irresistible impulse [that fuels such a faith]; he who sees, follows by sight, and believes because he resolves to believe" (197, 90–1). These words are practically a paraphrase of Jacobi's challenge to Mendelssohn just fifteen years earlier.[18] But now, upon reflection, this is the message that Fichte's I distills from them.

There is within me an impulse to absolute, independent self-activity. Nothing is more insupportable to me than to exist merely by another, for another, and through another; I must be something for myself and by myself alone. This impulse I feel along with the perception of my own existence, it inseparably united to my consciousness of myself. (184, 85)

This is a fact about the I of which the latter is indubitably certain in action; of which, therefore, he can say he has an immediate intuition. But he can claim to have knowledge of it only to the extent that it is expressed reflectively in the medium of representation.[19] This process of representation is necessary for action as well, for it translates the sense of purposiveness that otherwise animates the I only in general (the I's certainty, that is, that all things acquire meaning only to the extent that they are made part of the economy of his actions)[20] into a system of particularized purposes. One cannot act in general, but only in determinate situations and with determinate intentions. However, inasmuch as the I is made the subject of particular purposes, he is particularized as well. And, as thus objectified in representation, he enters into a system of other particular objects of representation with which he unavoidably comes to stand in relations of dependency. He depends on them at least for his particular determination. A distance is thereby created between the original but still indeterminate sense of absolute freedom that animates him and the system of representations that should have given particular content to that sense. This distance, this disconnection between subjective certainty and reflective validation, though necessary for consciousness as well as real action, is what makes the I vulnerable to the doubt that perhaps the certainty he instinctively has about his freedom is only a mirage. This was the unspoken doubt that at the beginning of Book I had set Fichte's I on his journey of reflection.

His mistake was to think that he could resolve the doubt theoretically by developing his system of representations. Spirit's contribution was to demonstrate to him that representations are, however, *only* representations – never the real thing they claim (or perhaps only pretend) to

represent. By itself, however, this contribution leads only to one more
doubt. Whereas by the end of Book I the I is in despair about his freedom, by the end of Book II he has cause to despair about his knowledge
as well – unless, of course, he heeds the other lesson that Spirit has indirectly conveyed to him as well, and restarts his meditation (as he does)
taking his belief in being free as the determining norm of truth. And
behold, all things that seemed lost are given back to him – a hundred-
fold, so to speak, because invested with a new meaning. The I had lost
confidence in his power to know. He now regains it because he is finally
in possession of the link connecting representations to their intended
objects (187, 86). Things acquire meaning only to the extent that they
satisfy his purposes, the first among these purposes being that of establishing his autonomy as the norm governing all things (215–18, 99–100).
What we call 'things of nature' are in fact products of moral art. Hence,
the ultimate test of whether a theory is valid or not rests on whether,
on that theory, the interests of freedom are satisfied. The I was given to
despair because of the conflict that reflection created in him between a
conception of reality unassailable on logical grounds and the demands
of his desire for freedom that that conception apparently undermined.
He now discovers that that same logically unassailable picture of the universe that had just been the cause of his despair is in fact also required to
satisfy his moral interests. The ultimate question is not whether nature
is mechanistically organized but whether it *ought to be* thus organized.
And indeed, so it should be, for otherwise it would be impossible for the
I to exercise the control over it required for the exercise of his autonomy. "Nature must gradually be resolved into a condition," the I says, "in
which her regular actions bear a fixed and definite relation to that which
is destined to govern it – that of man. [. . .] Thus shall Nature ever become more and more intelligible and transparent" (224–6, 103–4). Or
again, the question is not whether all things *are* as they should be, but
whether they *should be presumed* to be thus – as they should indeed, since
the truly real is ultimately a product of freedom. "Everything that *is* is
good and absolutely legitimate. There is but one world possible – a thoroughly good world" (311–12, 142). The universe as envisaged in Book I
thus reemerges exactly as it was conceived then. The only thing lost is
the belief, under which Fichte's I originally labored, that a free self is a
given individual operating within nature arbitrarily rather than, as the I
now knows, a reflectively constituted individual – one that sees himself
as reshaping his own being, and that of nature around him, according
to the requirements of a freedom in general that he can ultimately only

feel but that he can give witness to through his determinate actions. That belief, however, was only a mirage, nothing that truly belonged to the reality of things.

Spalding's Enlightenment universe thus seemed saved, but it had been revolutionized from the inside out. Kant had posited a *homo phaenomenon* and a *homo noumenon,* depending on whether one views human actions from an empirical or a transcendental point of view. At the beginning of this study, the question was posed regarding the identity of the I who can thus view himself from these two points of views and the place of this 'where' from which the two points of view are to be assumed. The question might not be important to us nowadays, since we instinctively identify the I with the historical self (as we should indeed) and then pragmatically shift between treating the latter sometimes as a thing of nature, at other times as a product of culture, and often as a mixture of the two as the situation demands. But the question was important in the Enlightenment, when people still longed for the unity of experience that Christian faith had once provided and, in some form, still provided. It must have been important to Kant, since he built a whole critical system around it. Insofar as the popular philosophers were concerned, they also identified the I with the historical self, and they too were keenly aware, no less than we are nowadays, of the complexity of this self. But they tried to define, and at the same time also to reconcile, all the strands of this complexity by assuming the place of a cosmic observer, from whose unrestricted standpoint all the conflicting views to which individual humans are bound in experience are resolved in the single vision of one harmonious whole. The problem with which they were, however, faced was that, in this vision, the individuality of the historical self that they were trying to comprehend, and hence the possibility of true human agency, dissolved into the whole. Exceptions such as Adam Weishaupt aside, this is a conclusion that nobody really wished. Kant, for his part, denied precisely the possibility of making any claims about the thing in itself except in terms of its appearances in experience, that is, always as conditioned by a historical point of view. His Critique of Reason was nonetheless still based on the possibility of transcending actual experience – albeit only ideally. Moreover, for systematic purposes, that is, in order to attain unity of experience, he still held on to the at least empty logical possibility of assuming a universal, intuitive view of things in the light of which all the modal distinctions that make for moral life would dissolve into a simple '*is*'. Kant had indeed succeeded in undermining the metaphysics of the scholastic theologians and in rendering their many disputed questions irrelevant. In effect, however, he still retained (though now only ideally) their vision of the universe. And, as I have repeatedly argued, except for the new element of self-deception that is thereby being introduced, it makes little difference to the tenor of one's moral life whether one claims *to know* that one's belief in personal agency is only an illusion, or whether one is forced to hold (because of the internal logic of one's adopted ideal system) that, if one could just know the thing in itself (but fortunately one neither does nor can know), all moral strivings would appear pointless, since all that can be already is. It is no surprise that the popular philosophers, whose interests lay especially in the system, either thought that Kant's Critique of Reason could be reclaimed for their modes of thinking or argued that it added nothing to accepted metaphysics except new problems.

Insofar as Fichte is concerned, his answer to the question is clear. The I might very well be, in a chronologically first instance, just a natural individual. But he becomes morally significant only inasmuch as (through an act that can be comprehended only retroactively, since it sets up the conditions of intelligibility in the first place) he generates the idea of an I in general, from whose point of view (indeed, *in virtue of it*) he sees his originally presumed natural being reduced to unsubstantial appearances. The difference between *homo phœnomenon* and *homo noumenon* is thus generated by the human individual himself, who is now reconstituted through his reflective activities into a moral self. And the task is thereby posed for the latter to reclaim the *homo phœnomenon* morally – on the one hand, by developing the idea of an I in general into the idea of a Holy Will, and on the other hand, by establishing sociopolitical structures, in virtue of which his otherwise morally intractable natural individuality is absorbed into a mechanism of well-regulated performances. Existentially speaking, that is, insofar as an individual's irreducibly subjective sense of himself is concerned, this whole process is motivated by a belief in one's own freedom. The individual cannot, however, give objective expression to this belief (as he well recognizes) except by talking of himself always in the third person, that is, in terms of a self that is admittedly only the product of moral art. It is this disconnection between subjective feeling and objective expression that makes, of course, for the stresses and agonies of an individual's private life. However, there is nothing arbitrary in all this. For, whatever is at the end irretrievably left out of an individual's objective self-expression is incomprehensible per se. This is not just a matter of the human intellect being incapable of having access to a thing in itself that would explain it, but of this subjective left over falling short of the norms of intelligibility that the will itself generates in an act that is at once an expression of freedom and an attempt at representing it. As was the case for Kant, religious language and religious imagery have their place in experience for Fichte precisely in order to cope existentially with this subjective residue.

One might not approve of this answer that Fichte gives; no one can dispute its internal consistency. Fichte had methodically refashioned Kant's system on the belief, which Kant himself had at least suggested, that "practical reason is the root of all reason."[21] Shortly after the publication of his *Bestimmung des Menschen* in 1802, Fichte resolved that he would henceforth communicate his thought no longer in writing but only orally.[22] He also began at the time to direct more and more of his energies to the practical problem of education.[23] His vision of the human vocation would not, after all, be credible unless human individuals were first induced, through nonspeculative means, to the moral choice that makes idealism, ex post facto, the only acceptable philosophical position. These were personal moves on Fichte's part that gave proof that his consistency extended beyond his mental universe to his lifestyle.[24] Was his answer, however, even within the resources of idealism, the only possible one? On the whole, the critics of the book, whether in principle idealist or anti-idealist, did not think so.

8.2 THE CRITICS, OLD AND NEW

Many were those who reacted to Fichte's latest publication, whether in private communication or publicly. With the odd face missing and a few new ones added, together they make up a parade, so to speak, of all the characters encountered so far.[25] Jacobi found it distasteful, as he confided to Jean Paul Richter, with the expressed wish that his words would not find their way past Richter himself. He wrote:

In the 3rd Book, where this cold Spirit warms up, glows, preaches, sings and prays, and even preaches the Gospel – there I could not hold my laughter; I was angered and hurt, and could hardly resist putting the book aside. [...] Just there, the beautiful passages are about to start, and one begins to philosophize with timpani and trumpets, and the sound of all bells is added, while the organ pitches in with full registers, in between the thundering of canons, and psalms and hymns, and trombones, cornets and harps, drums and whistles.[26]

Fichte, according to Jacobi, had been transmuting genuine human speech into idealistic cant and idealistic cant back into human speech.[27]

Apparently, Jacobi had forgotten how much he himself had been responsible, with his Spinoza-Letters, for introducing the bombastic language of
the preacher into the philosophical discourse of the Enlightenment and
for sealing his work "with a word from [the] pious and angelically pure
lips" of Lavater.[28] Indeed, one reader, dismayed by what he took to be the
lack of philosophical precision in Fichte's language, compared it to that
of Jacobi's early book.[29] Jacobi had apparently also forgotten that he had
been the one who said that a man's philosophy is a reflection of his moral
being, and that it was also he who had provided a paradigm of experience
in which conceptualization is a reflective activity that accompanies (in an
effort at comprehension) the feeling of constraint that is elicited in the
course of action. In censuring Fichte, Jacobi was perhaps exorcising his
own past.

Reinhold, for his part, objected to what he considered a pretentious
display of popularity in Fichte's book. So far as he was concerned, Fichte
was all the more caught up in his speculative mode of thought precisely
when he believed himself to have soared above it. Indeed, Reinhold
thought the book to be "idealist by profession," as speculative a production and as given to dry formulas as any speculative philosopher had
ever written. And he concluded: "So little is this otherwise so eloquent
man familiar in the ways of thought and expression of the natural understanding, and just as little is he capable of abstracting from his artificial
abstractions! For myself, I take it as a warning example."[30] Reinhold need
not have worried. He had been solidly ensconced in the tradition of popular philosophy from the beginning, and as his latest Masonic activities
demonstrated, he had never really diverged from it. It is not just that
Reinhold disagreed with Fichte. One might sympathize with him on that
score. Rather, he did not understand him. Of course, together with Kant
and Fichte, Reinhold did grant that there is a logic to experience, or,
as we can also say, that judgment is essentially normative. He had gone
so far as to develop, in great detail, a whole theory of the development
of thought on that assumption, arguing that, in the past, philosophical
theories emerged each time in an attempt to remedy the one-sidedness
of an earlier one, until finally, as one should hope, all sides of the one
truth underlying them find expression, and truth is therefore ready to
be revealed in its full light.[31] The difference (which Reinhold did not
perceive) lay in the very notion of 'logic' or 'normativity'. For Reinhold,
to abide by this logic meant to recognize an order established by God in
the universe and already reflected in principle in everyman's conscience.
The task of philosophy is to bring this implicit awareness of order to full

conceptual fruition. For Fichte, on the contrary, one abided by this logic insofar as one generated such constraints as are required for autonomous action. It involved establishing order in the first place, in other words – on the understanding, of course, that truly personal agency necessarily entails autonomy or freedom, and that the certainty of one's freedom, therefore, ineluctably comes with action but receives its first objective expression in the definition of a norm. One first finds determination, and thereby also a first and most universal norm of objectivity, in the self-awareness that accompanies action (and that Fichte normally calls, perhaps unfortunately, 'intellectual intuition').[32] 'Abstraction' thus meant for Fichte something quite different than Reinhold reproved him for. For Fichte, all experience is abstractive inasmuch as it is normative, since, as such, it entails action. The philosopher's reflection is only a conceptually purified and, in this sense artificial reenactment of the first moment of experience that everyman has already acted out. Common sense should therefore always be expected to be the result of decisions already taken and possibly misconstrued. On his theory of the historical progression of thought, Reinhold would have had to grant that much himself. But for Fichte the decisions would have to be moral in the first place – 'moral', moreover, not in the sense of being the responses (at times misguided) of tendencies that reflect a rational order, but in the sense of constituting such an order in the first place, along with the tendencies dependent upon it. In all cases, they would constitute the choice of a 'human vocation'.

Reinhold was therefore wrong to accuse Fichte, as he also did, of subjectivism and arbitrariness. His point was that Fichte had tried to justify the faith of natural consciousness in a real Absolute by deducing it from his ideal construction of primordial truth (*das Urwahre*). In this, however, he had restricted the true (*das Wahre*), that is, the truly real, to the sphere of subjectivity – thereby not abolishing it, but driving it away from the sphere of knowledge and making it instead the object of a consequently arbitrary faith.[33] This is an objection that made sense on the assumption that subjectivity is the counterpart of an objective being to which it stands externally and that faith has (in principle at least) theoretical value. For Fichte, on the contrary, subjectivity is identical with the autonomous activity that, by generating norms, constitutes objectivity in the first place; and faith is the subjective response ('subjective' understood here more in line with Reinhold's sense) to the kinds of highly individualized situations and states of mind that are forced outside the pale of rationality precisely by the introduction of universal norms. This faith has no theoretical content, only pragmatic value, since its object is per se unknowable – even though, as one should add in all fairness to Reinhold and other readers of *The Vocation of Humankind*, Fichte is misleading because of his habit of appealing to God, whose Will is allegedly not like ours, whose ways are not our ways, and of whose Will and whose ways we cannot therefore presume to know anything at all. And he is also misleading because of the trust he put in a humanity in which there are no individual men.[34] Fichte still gave the impression throughout that he presupposed a thing in itself that we *would* know if we just *could.* On this presupposition, his whole doctrine did, of course, fall into the realm of subjectivity and arbitrariness as defined by Reinhold.

Reinhold was writing from the standpoint of one who, at one point, had made a foray into idealism (or at least thought he had done so) and had mastered its language. In reaction to Fichte's book, however, there also was the chorus of those who had rejected idealism from the beginning or who, at most, had adapted it to their naively realistic views. Their objections against Fichte's book, already once made against Kant's system, were prosaically, but also most typically, expressed in the *Neue allgemeine deutsche Bibliothek*.[35] Against Fichte's theory of freedom as ideally informed action, the reviewer restated the traditional Leibnizian claim that anyone can be said to be free who acts according to innate tendencies without external constraints. In effect, he reasserted the eudaimonistic theory of morality. In an eclectic spirit, he argued that there is to date no such thing as a system free of difficulties, and likely none will ever be found. Idealism has its fair share of problems, and, before rejecting opposing systems in its favor, one would do best to compare it with the others and assess the relative freedom from difficulties of each concerned.[36] He also accused Fichte's faith of arbitrariness, warning that, on Fichte's principle, namely, "I believe it, because I will to believe it," one is necessarily led to seek an authority that would resolve conflicting wills, and this would in turn lead to the establishment of a philosophical popery.[37] On the assumption, moreover, that Fichte's idealism really represents a form of Berkeleyism (an assumption also already commonly made by the popular philosophers with respect to Kant), the reviewer goes to great lengths to produce arguments in support of the belief in the existence of an external world. These are arguments, of course, that make sense only if one presupposes the reviewer's conception of subject and subjectivity but are totally out of place on Fichte's or, for that matter, Kant's.[38]

These objections were to be expected coming from the side of common sense. Still in the same vein, but more focused, were the reactions of Abicht and Schmid, both (as we remember) self-declared Kantians of a sort. The review of the first appeared in the *ALZ* of Erlangen.[39] Abicht grants that the consciousness of an object is the product of our self, and that we have no knowledge of a thing except what we posit about it in consciousness. This Abicht takes as a given. His point, however, is that there is no evidence in consciousness of an activity of the I that is not in some respect or other qualified by passivity; that the consciousness of the presence of an object external to consciousness itself is just as immediate as the consciousness of the consciousness of this presence; and finally, that, although perception requires active engagement in consciousness on the part of an I, the sensation that is at the basis of any perception is not itself the product of the activity of the I. In short, however much in individual cases the perception of an object is conditioned by determinations that the I posits on its own, if one is not to fall into an endless regression or opt for arbitrariness, knowledge ultimately requires the theoretical apprehension of an object. Faith cannot just be willed; it presupposes theoretical knowledge.[40] These are objections that again would make sense in the context of Abicht's project of a descriptive account of the genesis of individual self-consciousness – a project in which the main problem, as we remember,[41] was how to arrive at the consciousness of an external world on the basis of an originally subjective material and for which Abicht had borrowed elements from Kant's transcendental method. But that was not Fichte's project. From a psychological standpoint, there is nothing that Abicht was saying that Fichte might not have been able to agree with.[42] His problem was rather a conceptual one, namely, how the meaning of otherness (on which 'objectivity' and the possibility of 'consciousness' depend) is constituted in the first place, and why this otherness should necessarily come with a sense of 'immediacy' (itself a phenomenon of consciousness) attached to it.

According to Schmid, Fichte's book was testimony to the fact that the author, far from being an atheist, should be considered rather a mystical theist.[43] This was a compliment of sorts, but the only one that Schmid had for Fichte. He strongly objected to the latter's claim, developed in the first part of his book, that past metaphysics logically leads to a pantheistic naturalism; most of all, that, on the premises of that metaphysics, both the individuality and the freedom of the human being are denied.[44] Schmid was obviously defending himself. Together with Abicht and other reviewers as well,[45] he also thought that there was a contradiction between

Fichte's doctrine of theoretical and practical reason. If it is the case – so it was argued – that I *know* theoretically, on the strength of demonstration, that external reality is a nothing, how can I then act practically on the *belief* that that reality actually exists and is offering resistance to my actions?[46] This was, of course, an objection based on a misunderstanding of idealism, one that made sense only on a psychological or subjectivistic reading of Fichte's idealism. In fact, Fichte was saying that meaning first arises as a product of action, and that ideas hypothetically introduced for theoretical purposes therefore receive their final validation only on practical grounds. Nature is to be interpreted as phenomenal and as mechanistically determined, because, in the final analysis, it must be such in the system of freedom that Fichte required. Fichte was certainly modifying, but still working in the spirit of, Kant's claim that his system found confirmation in the fact that ideas required for theoretical purposes gained a practical content in the context of moral action.

In one respect Schmid's objections did hit the mark. Repeating an objection that Rehberg had also raised with respect to Kant, Schmid objected to the idea of a pure will that is the first member of a chain of causes and consequences running across an invisible suprasensible world. According to Schmid, this will was a fiction for which, for one thing, there is no evidence, and, for another, has the deleterious moral effect of distracting from the real business of moral action here on earth. The Law is a formal idea that should have its effects in the visible world. In Fichte's fiction, Schmid argued, any "moral teaching [otherwise] suited to the actual human life of the senses is distorted into mystical, arcane, enthusiasm [*Schwärmerei*]," as must indeed be the case "if one lays at its foundation a forever unknown and unintelligible goal in a foreign and unknown world, to the realization of which I am [allegedly] being constantly driven by a dark, unintelligible drive of conscience."[47] Schmid's original compliment to Fichte was not, after all, altogether unqualified. And, to the extent that his objection was directed at the tenor of moral life as defined by Fichte, and at the mythology that it brought in its train (neither of which was necessary to idealism), Schmid had a point. The problem, however, was that, to the extent that the objection was being raised from Schmid's point of view, to accept it meant falling into a naturalism that, on idealistic principles, undermined morality completely. Again, like the rest of the reviewers, Schmid was not addressing Fichte at all.

These were all old voices, so to speak. But there were new ones as well, and it is interesting to note what, if anything new, they added to the debate. As we have already seen, Jean Paul Richter was in correspondence with Jacobi and shared the latter's repulsion at Fichte's moral message. He famously produced a parody of Fichte's philosophy of the 'I–ness' *(Ichheit)* that was just as philosophically unilluminating as it was entertaining.[48] More to the point was the lengthy review that Schleiermacher published in the *Athenaeum* at the request of August Wilhelm Schlegel.[49] The review was divided into three parts – the first in monologue form; the second, a dialogue; the third, a monologue again – each a reflection on the corresponding part of Fichte's book and, taken together, a critical reworking of it as a whole. The speaker in the first monologue is a recent reader of the book – one who, at first, seems satisfied with its conclusion, even reconfirmed in his original belief in personal freedom; but, on reflection, begins to wonder why he should have been led through the circuitous route of an alleged opposition between 'materialism' and 'idealism' when, at the end, he must still fall back for the certainty of his freedom on the immediacy of his original feeling. When all is said and done, nothing has really been learned by the whole exercise. At this point the reviewer enters into the picture, and in his dialogue with the speaker enlightens him about the pedagogical devices deployed by Spirit in the second part of Fichte's book and the purposes they serve. Thereupon the reader can resume his monologue in the third part of the review – now wondering, however, whether there are other venues of thought that Fichte's I might have explored before reaching his conclusion. At any rate, he now knows what this I has learned through the three parts of Fichte's book, namely, that "nowhere is there merit or guilt in an individual, but only in one's being what one is." Hence the I is at the end glad to be whatever he is only with respect to, and for, some other.[50]

One must acknowledge Schleiermacher's literary skills. A. W. Schlegel called his review a masterpiece of fine irony and parody, one of deferential archdevilry.[51] Schleiermacher himself thought of it (perhaps overingenuously) as an example of Christian irony, the only way of criticizing Fichte while respecting him personally.[52] Schelling was another who joined in these congratulatory exchanges. However, apart from the style that certainly made for a pleasant change from the dry scholasticism of the popular philosophers, nothing was in fact being added to what the other critics, all representatives of *Popularphilosophie*, were also saying. In sum, Fichte was being criticized by Schleiermacher on two points. The first was for giving primacy to practical reason – the implication being that, in this, Fichte gave reign to immediacy of feeling and arbitrariness. This was an objection, however, that the other, more prosaic critics were also raising.

In the case of Schelling, inasmuch as the latter was joining his voice to
Schleiermacher's on this score, the objection sounded particularly disingenuous, since he, as recently as 1800 and even after the publication of
Fichte's book, was still asserting that the Absolute is to be assumed in
action, that is, as an object of faith.[53] Of course, Fichte *did* give primacy
to practical reason. But that did not mean that he endorsed arbitrariness, since agency carries with it its own requirements. It only means that
rationality assumes a new character. As for 'feelings', Schelling at least,
if not Schleiermacher as well, should have known from Fichte's earliest
publication that, according to him, feeling is a complex phenomenon
that already displays the structure of reason *in nuce*.

The second objection was directed at Fichte's vision of humanity on
the ground that, as the other critics also argued, it ends up absorbing
the human individual into some sort of mystical union with a Will in
general. This was a fair criticism. There was something definitely unap-
pealing about Fichte's ethical conclusions. Coming from Schleiermacher,
however, the criticism sounded strangely disingenuous. One must not
forget that, since his student days, Schleiermacher had been under the
influence of his Halle teacher and mentor Johann August Eberhard,[54]
unequivocal defender of typical Enlightenment scholastic ideas and, as
we remember, strident critic of Kant.[55] Now, after Dilthey's discovery of
his early manuscripts,[56] we learned that, although Schleiermacher might
have been said to be from his earliest days a Kantian of a sort, since he
granted Kant's idea of law (indeed, even criticized Kant's idea of the *sum-
mum bonum* on the ground that it granted too much to eudaimonism),[57]
he nonetheless accepted the idea only in the spirit of Schmid, that is, by
integrating it into a natural system of human tendencies and desires.[58]
The same young Schleiermacher, moreover, was a staunch defender of
determinism in the metaphysical tradition of Ulrich or Weishaupt. As
of 1792, and as his immediately subsequent reflections on Spinoza and
Jacobi also bear out,[59] he was already well on the way to pressing Kant
back into metaphysical disquisitions about nature. Under the influence
of classical metaphysical themes, he was already advocating a form of
naturalistic pantheism. And this raises the question, first, of whether the
human individual fares any better in this pantheism than he does in the
moral system of Fichte that Schleiermacher was decrying ironically in his
review; and, second, of how much Schleiermacher's romantic pantheism,
and that of his colluding friends, while often operating with idealistic
language and idealistic distinctions, still found its intellectual home in
the popular metaphysics of the late *Aufklärung*.

The "new" voices were not that new after all. Though all sides were quick to criticize Fichte, none was ready to provide a fresh alternative solution to his position. Times had changed, and so had literary and philosophical styles. Yet, short of opting for Fichte's radical solution or Kant's compromise of critical ignorance, as of 1800 Spalding's original quest for a determination of the human vocation was still caught up in old patterns of thought. Were there at least some intimations of new things to come?

8.3 BACK TO THE BEGINNING

One new voice that Fichte's *Die Bestimmung des Menschen* elicited was Hegel's. It came only in 1802, in the form of an anonymously published lengthy article that carried the title *Faith and Knowledge*[60] at a time when Hegel was still an unknown quantity and his position (such as could be gleaned from this early text) was still indeterminate. It was part of a larger study on the philosophies of Kant, Fichte, and Jacobi. The last, taken aback by being portrayed in the article as representing a position substantially identical with Fichte's, found it altogether comic that he should be treated as if he were an idea making up with Kant and Fichte (also treated as ideas) a system of thought.[61] Indeed, Hegel was treading roughshod over many fine distinctions. The article nonetheless deserves a hearing at this point by way of conclusion, because, as we shall see in a moment, despite its new language it brings us back to the beginning.

Hegel's case against Fichte is quite simple. Inasmuch as one takes as the norm of moral action the kind of purity of intention, of autonomy of will, that can be defined only by way of abstraction from anything natural, 'nature' necessarily assumes from the start the moral character of something unredeemably fallen. It is evil by definition. Action is, however, necessarily particularized both in goals and in effects. And, since this particularity is not possible without reference to nature, and since any reference to the latter entails a moral lapse, nature ends up being reintroduced (by way of subterfuge, so to speak) under two rubrics that are ad hoc. First, it is reintroduced as still sensuous nature, but without the traits that make it such – in effect, therefore, as a sort of unnatural nature. If one were to listen to Fichte, the human agent should strive for an earth free of earthquakes, droughts, swamps, diseases, hunger, enmities, barbarisms, and what have you. These, according to Hegel, are circumstances that belong to the natural course of events; as such, they have no moral significance in themselves but should be accepted instead with equanimity, as plain limitations of human action. In being reintroduced by Fichte into the moral sphere with a negative sign, under the rubric of 'what ought not to be', they are in fact being invested with a moral importance they should not have, in contradiction to the original moral intention of deflating nature of all value. It is as if the moral agent ought to feel guilty for there being earthquakes, floods, or the like. Second, nature is reintroduced in spiritualized form, as a kingdom of ends that only autonomous agents can aspire to – such, therefore, that cannot be seen as realized, or even hoped ever to be seen as realized, but that the moral agent must nonetheless believe will be realized in an infinitely distant future. However, as Hegel argues, such a spiritual kingdom of ends still has particularized nature for its content – projected indeed into a realm beyond, with its sensuous content now conceded only under protest (with a negative sign attached to it, as Hegel puts it), but still nature in spite of this. The original moral intention is again being contradicted without, moreover, the required effective norm of action being thereby provided. For, since the assumed supersensuous nature stands related to real nature only externally, the teleology that it establishes fails to affect the latter except formally. By default, real nature is left to the realm of mere pragmatics.[62]

The net result is that faith, rather than being based on a genuine intuition of the union in experience of concept and nature,[63] is invoked instead as a means for asserting the practically necessary, yet theoretically impossible, union of the two. It is there for covering up a contradiction inherent in the originally assumed moral standpoint.[64] Insofar as action itself is concerned, the distance between the ideal and the real is bridged by means of an ought – more precisely, in the form of an agency for which the commitment to the attainment of a morally mandated object is the morally determining factor rather than the actual realization of that object (which is in fact impossible). The net result is that an agent, while avowedly engaged in the process of realizing a given intention, must in fact make the intention itself *as subjective* the point of interest of his action instead of the intended *objective* effect. But this attitude, according to Hegel, smacks of hypocrisy.[65] It is like giving alms for the sake of being an almsgiver rather than for the welfare of those receiving the alms – a welfare that in Fichte's system would fall under the amoral mechanism of nature anyway. These criticisms, incidentally, apply in Hegel's view to Kant as well because of the opposition that the latter assumes at the basis of his system between freedom and being. To be sure, in Kant's particular case, the effects are not as patently disastrous, because the system is not as single–mindedly deduced from the I think as Fichte's is, and because in his *Critique of Judgment* Kant made a serious effort at bridging the distance between freedom and being by construing the idea of a teleology internal to nature. In this, as Hegel acknowledges, Kant has an advantage over Fichte. But the advantage is only an apparent one, since his idea of teleology is still introduced as merely subjective, and hence without the formalism common to the systems of both being thereby overcome.[66]

These criticisms of Hegel have now become commonplace. The point of interest, however, is that they are all directed at the systems of Kant and Fichte, not at their idealism.[67] Hegel accepts the premise that idealization is the source of meaning and value. He also does not deny that, once reflection sets in and experience becomes normative as a consequence, nature with respect to its idea, that is, as caught up in the web of rational expectations, might indeed appear as merely 'given', as 'contingent', or, from a moral standpoint, as 'fallen'. Hegel does not deny this much. His objection is to fixating it at this negative result of idealization. The opposite is just as true. One can just as well say that, precisely in being invested with moral significance, nature is also re-born. It is humanized, in other words. It acquires in the medium of reflective conceptualization, and as object of human actions, a positive value that it does not otherwise have. In principle, moreover, it acquires this new character as a whole. In being totally fallen, it is by the same token also totally redeemed. And the task is thereby posed for the human agent to realize this positive value in the particulars of nature thus reborn, distinguishing between what is appropriate and what is not – all this in view of how the human vocation is defined ideally and in view of the social institutions established accordingly. Materially speaking, that is, according to the chronological unfolding of events, this task stretches out, of course, into an indefinite future. It constitutes the substance of spiritual life. Hegel's point, however, is that, essentially, it is already realized at the very inception of moral life – the moment the moral community is visibly constituted and nature acquires its new noumenal significance in the contexts of its institutions. It is a mistake, therefore, to deny that the effects of moral agency are not visibly recognizable in this world or, as a corollary, to believe that they only occur in an invisible world beyond us, or that the moral ideal is to be realized only in an infinitely distant future. For Hegel, either nature is spiritually transformed *now*, and totally transformed, or it never will be.[68]

In this, inasmuch as Hegel criticizes his predecessors from their own point of view, his voice is indeed a new one. It is new, moreover, in a peculiar sense, for it strangely sounds notes reminiscent of the old voices of common sense. Hegel does not mention Reinhold in the present context. Indeed, he had vehemently attacked his facts of consciousness in a recently published essay.[69] Yet, he is in fact operating with Reinhold's explanation of the genesis of the idealistic model of experience – the model, at least, that Reinhold had construed in his effort to explain what he took to be Fichte's philosophical gamesmanship. Reflective praxis (*Tathandlung*), however much it might itself be originally the product of organic nature (*Tatsache*), once at work generates a universe of meanings and values that retroactively constitute themselves as norms of the truth of nature itself. In this universe, the very presence of the latter becomes problematic. This is the fundamental thesis of Fichte's idealism at least. Reinhold himself, as we remember, had taken it as indeed a possible reflective standpoint, one that the philosopher necessarily assumes because of his passion for explanation. But he had also denounced it as philosophical hubris if taken to mean that, albeit formulated in the artificial language of reflection, it defines nonetheless the essence of experience. This is because Reinhold, naive realist that he still was at heart – a realist, moreover, with religious preoccupations – still thought of nature as fully determined in itself, and as carrying intentions that are reflections of God's creative ideas and are therefore the source of meaning for us. Hegel's argument is the direct opposite. Kant's and Fichte's idealism did not go far enough. This idealism was not true to its own logical resources, and, for that reason, it had to assume that formalism with respect to nature for which the commonsense philosophers rightly reproached it.

It made this mistake, however (here is where Hegel's argument turns against the whole tradition of *Popularphilosophie*), precisely because it did not free itself completely from the standpoint of common sense to which Reinhold still adhered. In the culture of Locke and Hume, subject and object were conceived as finite natural things that are only externally connected. This, according to Hegel, was the assumption on which common sense was based, and which also dominated the culture of the *Aufklärung*. Kant made a difference by shifting the problem of truth from the question of how to mediate these two things called subject and object to the question of how in experience, by means of conceptualization, an object is constituted in the first place, and how the distinction between subjective and objective is thereby also established. This shift from a 'physiology' of knowledge to a phenomenology of experience indeed marked the beginning of idealism. But, according to Hegel, Kant, and, even more clearly, Fichte after him moved too quickly, so to speak. Instead of pursuing this constitution of an object and of its respective subject step by step in the context of actual nature – in effect, instead of pursuing it historically, in terms of social and political structures, albeit always according to conditions set by the concept itself – they came up with an abstract I think and its objective counterpart, that is, the abstract conception of an object in general, all at once. Both of these ideas, though perhaps defining the conditions of intelligibility in general, have no direct connections with actual experience. And the task was thereby posed of bringing this abstract construction to bear upon the content of the latter – a task that proved just as intractable as the task of establishing, in Locke's and Hume's model of the mind, the supposed conformity of a subject to its intended object.[70]

Hegel, in other words, accepts the charges of formalism raised against Kant and Fichte by common sense. According to his diagnosis of the situation, however, his two predecessors had made themselves vulnerable to these charges because, in distinguishing by way of abstractive reflection between form and content while defining *in principle* the structure of the whole of experience, they had allowed the two, form and content, to fall side by side as two finite externally related quantities. They thus allowed the content to escape the comprehension of the concept, thereby abandoning it to the realm of empirical abstractions and pragmatic rules.[71] In this, they were still conforming, paradoxically, to commonsense modes of thought.[72] And according to Hegel, it was on the issue of 'happiness' that one could most clearly see the ambiguous relation that connected the idealism of Kant and Fichte with these modes of thought typical of the *Aufklärung*. The culture of the *Aufklärung* manifested its Protestant spirit because of the importance that it placed on subjectivity. But it conceived this subjectivity positively, in the context of an assumed objective order of things that can be apprehended empirically. Accordingly, personal happiness was identified with natural perfection attained through reason. Because of the optimism that characterized the culture, the evils that de facto affect the human situation were glossed over in a metaphysical theory that made this world the best of all possible worlds. It idealized reality in fact, without recognizing that what it deemed real was in fact the product of abstraction and bore no visible connection with actual experience. In other words, it unwittingly absolutized the finite. Faith (Spalding's kind, we should gloss, fueled by natural optimism) was brought in for the precise purpose of bridging the gap between abstraction and reality.[73] This did not prevent wags such as Voltaire from ridiculing both the metaphysical theory and the faith summoned on its

behalf. Now, in Kant's and Fichte's type of abstraction, the optimism of
the metaphysicians gives place to a somber moral view in which anything
that has to do with nature, happiness included, becomes in principle suspect. In Fichte's book, the litanies of evils afflicting the human race that
were only good sense when coming from Voltaire – *ad hominem* attacks
directed at the abstract optimism of the philosophers – such litanies become instead universal statements about 'fallen nature'. "It is just what
the Germans generally boast about," Hegel comments ironically. "They
take a French *aperçu* and develop it; then they return it improved, put in
its proper light, thoroughly worked out and scientifically formulated."[74]
Even in this more somber view of things, however, happiness is still required, and faith is again brought in to do the job. This is quite a different
faith than that of the *Aufklärung*. Whatever the difference separating the
two, Hegel's point is that in both cases it is brought in to make up for a
deficiency created by bad abstraction, that is, for not having taken the detailed work of idealizing nature seriously enough.[75] Jacobi was essentially
no different. He too, no less than Kant or Fichte, had made subjectivity his principle. Unlike the other two, however, he had stressed (quite
rightly) the individuality of the subject. But since he had only the empirical content of experience (what the *Aufklärer* also relied on) for defining
this individuality, and lacked the conceptual means for mediating this
content with the ideal of subjectivity that actually inspired him, faith (understood now simply as feeling) had again to make up for the deficiency.
According to Hegel, this was indeed still typically Protestant faith, but unwittingly sullied by the empiricism of the *Aufklärer*. Jacobi (not Spinoza,
as Jacobi himself thought) was the inverse of Fichte.[76]

Thus Hegel. Whether his own version of idealism eventually met the
objections that he was then raising against both the metaphysical tradition of the *Aufklärung* and the idealism of his immediate predecessors is
not the issue here. At the time, nothing definitive could have been said
on the basis of this early article. With respect to Fichte, it must be added
that the charge of formalism was certainly unfair if directed at his early
phenomenological analyses, such as that of feeling in §2 of his *Critique of
All Revelation*. Hegel's criticism was, however, directed at Fichte's system.
At any rate, Hegel is being introduced here only to bring us back to the beginning. In the debate regarding freedom and religion that we have been
exploring, the last word belongs to the common sense of *Popularphilosophie*. It is not just that, historically speaking, the popular philosophers had
the last word in the politics of academia. Hegel was well aware of the fact.
Traugott Krug, the commonsense philosopher who was to replace Kant at

Königsberg, was the object of his scathing first review in the first issue of the *Kritisches Journal der Philosophie*.[77] Hegel's first battle for philosophical recognition was with *Popularphilosophie*. More to the point, however, is that Spalding's vision of the universe, and the faith it begat, had dominated, whether directly or indirectly, the debate from beginning to end. That vision had translated the Christian belief in Divine Providence – a belief that relied on the highly personalized stories of the Fall, the Incarnation, and Redemption – into a system of forces and counterforces, all governed by a hypostatized Reason. This Reason assured the proper place of every individual within the system, since the place was prepared for him in the order of things from the beginning. The human vocation consisted in recognizing, and actively appropriating, this place for oneself. However, in the abstract interplay of these forces (such as the metaphysicians conceived them), it was precisely the individuality of the individual human being that was lost. Metaphysical reason made for irrationality insofar as the an individual's perception of himself was concerned. Jacobi was right to protest on this score. Now, Hegel also says in his article that Kant, Jacobi, and Fichte represented the true Spirit of the North against the optimism of the Enlightenment.[78] This claim is not to be taken any more seriously than his other remark about the pedantry of the Germans in contrast to the wit of the French. However, leaving Jacobi aside (whose notions of reason and faith remained obscure to the end), it is nonetheless true that, with Kant, the question of the vocation of humankind assumed a radically different form, one more in tune with the tradition of Protestant Christianity than the optimism of the *Aufklärer* was.[79] The issue is no longer one of discovering humankind's proper place in the order of nature, but rather one of forging such a nature (in itself otherwise voided of value) in a shape that is demanded by the formal interests of reason. This was indeed a revolutionary move. The kind of nature, however, that, if ever attained, would have satisfied such interests was still being conceived as the metaphysicians of the Enlightenment expected it. And in this nature, however much now reintroduced explicitly as a construct of reason, the individual still had no place. Jacobi was again right on this score. Fichte modified Kant's system, but he did not change the result. Throughout, it was still Spalding's vision of a well-ordered universe that caused the problem.

Common sense had the last word also in one last, and more positive, respect. Reinhold has his place here. One must not forget that the popular philosophers pursued, first and foremost, a social educational agenda in which the individual was indeed all-important. They were the ones who

had brought the issue of the historical vocation of this individual to center stage in the Enlightenment. Their interest in a genetic model of the
human mind, as contrasted with Kant's a priori transcendental model,
had its speculative merit indeed. Hegel himself, still a young man and
before his Jena association with Schelling, had thought of himself as an
educator of humankind. This was a vocation that animated his philosophical speculations to the end.[80] And even at Jena, while still associated with
Schelling, he had already in effect deserted the intuitionism of the latter's
Identity Philosophy by seeking the basic conditions of experience in the
form of a community of potentially rational, conscious individuals.[81] All
this was still in keeping with the social vocation of his youth and with the
general cultural agenda of *Popularphilosophie*. Reinhold's Masonic activities were intended to contribute to this same agenda. True *Aufklärer* that
he was, Reinhold still conceived reason on a cosmic scale, as if it were
a force inexorably working itself out across the vicissitudes of historical
events. He had, however, at least hit upon the idea that there is a necessity
internal to historical experience dependent on the logic of human discourse – on positions being advanced, developed, and collapsing under
the strain of their internal limitations. One had only to drop the myth
of cosmic reason, the secularized and sclerotized remnant of Christian
Providence, for attention to be directed to the logic internal to typically
historical agency. And it is only in the context of the human universes
generated by discourse, quite apart from physical or alleged hyperphysical considerations, that the question of individual human freedom and
individual human identity can be intelligibly raised and perhaps even
answered. The nineteenth century was to concentrate precisely on the
historicity of human existence. Whether it dealt with the issue with any
success is not a question here. One thing is, however, clear. As of 1800,
the outlook was not very promising.

Notes

Chapter 1

1. For J. F. Fries's brand of positivism, see di Giovanni (1997a), pp. 212–41. Nietzsche was acquainted with Fries's work. At the end of a collection of notes for his planned PhD thesis, *Die Teleologie seit Kant*, under the heading of *zu lesen sind* ("to be read"), Nietzsche made a list of works he thought crucial to his research. The list includes the entry "*Fries, Mathematische Naturphilosophie.*" Cf. Friedrich Nietzsche, *Gesammelte Werke, Erster Band, Jugendschriften 1858– 1868* (München: Musarium Verlag, 1922), p. 428.
2. "Kritik der Vernunft" (Critique of Reason) was the title normally attributed by Kant's contemporaries to Kant's critical work as a whole. It refers to Kant's special mode of philosophizing. I capitalize the expression to indicate that it carries a specialized meaning.
3. I am borrowing this formulation from a well-known novelist: Naguib Mahfouz, *Sugar Street* (1992), p. 198. But see note 8. The formula is already in Kant.
4. This is the poem that Friedrich Heinrich Jacobi prefaced to his tract on Spinoza. I have argued elsewhere that this poem, rather than either Lessing's or Mendelssohn's views, was the principal though indirect object of Jacobi's polemic. *Jacobi*, pp. 73, 75. For the text of the poem in English (tr. Jeremy Walker), see *Jacobi*, pp. 185–6.
5. See, for instance, the theologian Spalding's statement of the purpose of his treatise, *Die Bestimmung des Menschen*. See note 15 and p. 44 of Spalding's text.
6. '*Organization*' was comparable to a password in German intellectual circles at the time.
7. Here sit I, shaping Men / In my likeness: / A race that is to be as I am, / To suffer / and weep, / To relish and delight in things, / And to pay you no regard – / Like me! Tr. Jeremy Walker. *Jacobi*, p. 186.
8. K. L. Reinhold, *Über die Paradoxien der neuesten Philosophie* (1799b), p. 34. Cf. KrV Bxvi.
9. The literal translation of the Latin *entia rationis* is 'entities of reason'.

10. Cf. *The Metaphysics of Morals*, AK VI:371.
11. Cf. *The Metaphysics of Morals*, AK VI:354.
12. Korsgaard (1996), pp. x–xi.
13. Cf. *The Metaphysics of Morals*, VI:418.
14. I have made this point in di Giovanni (2003b), pp. 365–8.
15. *Die Bestimmung des Menschen* (1800). The German *Bestimmung* conveys both meanings of 'determination' and of 'vocation'.
16. 1714–1804, of Scottish ancestry. On Spalding's influence, especially with reference to Mendelssohn's and Kant's anthropology, see Hinske (1994).
17. New improved ed. (Leipzig: Weidman, 1794), p. v.
18. *Die Bestimmung des Menschen*, p. vi.
19. I am using the edition of 1774 (Leipzig: Erben und Reich).
20. More about common sense and its British sources in Chapters 2 and 3.
21. Kant says that the physico-theological proof of God's existence, though not theoretically conclusive, is nonetheless the oldest and the noblest and, for this reason, deserving of respect. (KrV A623/B651). This proof from the order and the beauty of the universe is, however, precisely the one that Spalding takes to be at the basis of humankind's natural religiosity.
22. Cf. Chapter 7, Section 7.4.
23. *Über die Lehre des Spinoza in Briefen an den Herrn Moses Mendelssohn*. English tr., *Jacobi*, pp. 173–251.
24. For an account of the events and an analysis of Jacobi's work, see di Giovanni (1994), pp. 68–90 and di Giovanni (2001a).
25. *Dichtung und Wahrheit*, V, *Sämmtliche Werke*, XVI, p. 681.
26. Moses Mendelssohn, in the Preface to his *Morning Hours, or Lectures on the Existence of God, Gesammelte Schriften*, vol. 3.2 (1974), p. 3. The expression was put in circulation by one of Kant's earliest biographers. Borowski (1804), p. 149. In the same place, Mendelssohn acknowledges that, because of his health, his acquaintance with Kant's Critique is only secondhand. See also his Letter to Kant, 10 April 1783, AK X:307–8. See also Mendelssohn's letter to Elise Reimarus of 5 January 1784, in which Mendelssohn expresses some pleasure in knowing that Elise's brother did not think much of the Critique. He confessed that he had not been able to understand it, and it was reassuring to know that he had not missed much. For a translation of the relevant passage, see Zweig's Cambridge edition of Kant's *Correspondence*, p. 182, note 3. Kant was disappointed on hearing that Mendelssohn had put the Critique aside. Letter to Markus Herz, after 11 May 1781, AK X:270.
27. These are not to be confused with the much enlarged version of the same letters published in 1790–2. See rather *Der Teutsche Merkur* 3 (1786), 99–127; 127–41; 1 (1787), 3–39, 117–42; 2 (1787), 167–85; 3 (1787), 67–88, 142–65, 247–78.
28. Spinoza-Letters, p. 18. *Jacobi*, p. 189.
29. Spinoza-Letters, p. 17. *Jacobi*, p. 189. I am deliberately avoiding the word 'leap', normally used in this context, because it conveys the false impression that, by means of Jacobi's 'jump', one would leave reason behind. According to Jacobi, the whole point of the jump is to redress one's present false position in order to land on one's feet – that is to say, on the ground provided by true

reason. According to Jacobi, the philosophers walked on their heads. The Italian *salto mortale* belongs to circus idiom.

30. See note 4. Jacobi's relation with his younger contemporary, Goethe, was both passionate and uneven. It saw a peak of exhilarating intimacy but later depths of bitter enmity. For a short account, see *Jacobi*, pp. 51–4.

31. Moses Mendelssohn, *Jerusalem* (1983), pp. 95–6: "I, for my part, cannot conceive of the education of the human race as my late friend Lessing imagined it under the influence of I don't-know which historian of mankind. One pictures the collective entity of the human race as an individual person and believes that Providence sent it to school here on earth, in order to raise it from childhood to manhood. In reality, the human race is – if the metaphor is appropriate – in almost every century, child, adult, and old man at the same time, though in different places and regions of the world. [...] Progress is for the individual man, who is destined by Providence to spend part of his eternity here on earth. Everyone goes through his life in his own way. [...] It does not seem to me to have been the purpose of Providence that mankind as a whole advance steadily here below and perfect itself in the course of time. This, at least, is not so well settled nor by any means so necessary for the vindication of God's providence as one is in the habit of thinking." Mendelssohn rejected Kant's view of history for the same reasons. For an account of the historically as well as conceptually interesting circumstances in which this rejection occurred, see Hinske, (1994), pp. 135–56, especially pp. 152ff.

32. Cf. *David Hume* (1787), pp. 84–7. English tr., *Jacobi*, pp. 284–5 and notes.

33. *David Hume.*

34. He did this in the Introduction to the second edition of *David Hume* (1815) that was also to serve as the Preface to his *Collected Works*, p. 40, note 11. *Jacobi*, p. 554.

35. I take it that this is the essence of Kant's claim that, whereas all things in nature work according to laws, "only a rational being has the capacity to act *in accordance with the representation* of laws, that is, in accordance with principles, or has a *will*." *Groundwork of the Metaphysics of Morals*, AK IV:412, tr. Mary J. Gregor.

36. *David Hume* (1787), Supplement, p. 223, *Jacobi*, p. 336.

37. Cf., for instance, H. A. Pistorius's review of Johann Schultze's Kant commentary in *Allgemeine deutsche Bibliothek*, 66 (1786), 92–123, pp. 107–8 for the relevant passages. (For Schultze, see Chapter 3.) Also see Christian Garve's review of Kant's *Critique of Pure Reason* in *Allgemeine deutsche Bibliothek*, supplements 37–52 (1783), 838–62, p. 845 for the relevant passages. An English translation of both (only excerpts of Pistorius's) can be found in Sassen (2000).

38. Schulze assumes that the mind, according to Kant, is like a thing in itself that is responsible for causing the necessity of judgments. G. E. Schulze [anonymous], *Ænesidemus* (1792), pp. 154–7; for a more generalized claim, see pp. 176–7.

39. As we shall see, this is the move that Fichte, quite consistently, will make. See Chapter 6, Section 6.6.4.

40. *Critique of Judgement*, §176 (P. Guyer, E. Matthews, trs.), AK V:401–2.
41. "The action which is morally absolutely necessary can be regarded physically as entirely contingent (i.e. what necessarily *should* happen often does not...)," *Critique of Judgement*, §76, AK V:403. What Kant should have said is that nothing ever happens physically as it *ought* (i.e., according to moral norms), since a physical event is by nature heteronomous. Physical nature eschews, as such, moral meaning.
42. So far as I know, in two instances, A808/B836; *The Metaphysics of Morals*, AK VI:367.
43. K. H. Heydenreich, an influential author at the time, objected to Kant's cosmological concept of freedom, if defined as the capacity to *initiate* a situation starting from oneself *(aus sich)*, as self-contradictory, since the idea of 'initiating' necessarily carries mechanistic overtones antithetical to the concept of freedom. *Betrachtungen über die Philosophie der natürlichen Religion*, vol. 2, p. 59. See also Nuzzo (1994), p. 498, note 47. But Heydenreich still accepted Kant's main thesis that, though we are certain of being free because of the moral law, we cannot know how this freedom is possible. We know that we cannot know. Cf. pp. 65, 68–9.
44. The Enlightenment was a complex cultural phenomenon, as Hunter (2001) has forcefully argued of late. Crusius and Thomasius already shared views that, as I am now arguing, are consequences of Kant's position.
45. I am not in any way trying to rehabilitate dogmatic metaphysics or denying that what Kant says about the modal categories is not in fact true. I am denying Kant's estimate of what he was doing. I am denying the myth of critical modesty that commentators have construed around him.
46. *Critique of Judgement*, §76, AK V:403–4.
47. *Critique of Judgement*, §73, AK V:394.
48. Cf. the theses in "Idea for a Universal History from a Cosmopolitan Point of View" (1784) (AIT VIII). Mendelssohn objected to Kant's idea of history on the same ground as he had objected to Lessing's. It failed to make the individual the real subject of history. See Hinske (1994), pp. 152ff., and note 31.
49. Cf. *Groundwork of the Metaphysic of Morals*, AK IV:450–53. See also ibid., AK IV:448, note. Kant says that he assumes "freedom" as laid down by rational beings merely "*in idea* as a ground for their actions" – this in order to relieve the pressure of having to prove the reality of freedom theoretically. The idea of freedom (of lawfulness as itself a motivating value) is *all* that one needs for moral life. But Kant still thought that, if we just could, we would have to provide some other explanation for moral life as well, i.e., a conception of freedom as some sort of physical cause.
50. *Causa sui* is much more relevant than any reference to theological antecedents. In orthodox Christian theology, God creates through his Word. The latter constitutes within the Trinity a personality irreducibly distinct from that of both the Father and the Spirit. The distinction was necessary precisely in order to retain, within God's substance, the conditions necessary for knowledge.

51. "What Real Progress Has Metaphysics Made in Germany Since the Time of Leibniz and Wolff?" (1793), AK XX:267, tr. Henry Allison. See also note 49.
52. *The Metaphysics of Morals*, AK VI:218, tr. Mary J. Gregor. Cf. "For if the world proceeded in accordance with the precept of the law, we would say that everything occurred according to the order of nature, and nobody would think even of enquiring after the cause." *Religion within the Boundaries of Mere Reason*, AK VI:59, note.
53. *Critique of Practical Reason*, AK V:147, tr. Mary J. Gregor.
54. *Critique of Practical Reason*, AK V:147.
55. Cf. *Critique of Practical Reason*, AK V:146.
56. *Critique of Practical Reason*, AK V:147–148.
57. *Jacobi an Fichte* (Hamburg: Perthes, 1799), pp. 32–3. *Jacobi*, p. 516.
58. In the second edition of his *Wörterbuch zum leichtern Gebrauch der Kantischen Schriften*, §384.
59. I have developed this theme by way of a contrast between Kant and Hegel in di Giovanni (2003b).
60. Cf. his play, *Nathan the Wise*.
61. Johann Friedrich Flatt, *Briefe über den moralischen Erkenntnisgrund der Religion überhaupt, und besonders in Beziehung auf die Kantische Philosophie* (1789), p. 72. Flatt was Hegel's professor of logic and metaphysics at the Tübingen Seminary. Cf. Henrich (1965); Pozzo (1989), pp. 70ff.
62. According to the Apostle Paul.
63. Hinske (1994), pp. 152ff., and notes 31, 48. On the issue, Mendelssohn cast a *votum* against Kant at a meeting of the Berlin Mittwoch society (a Berlin discussion group that met on Wednesdays).
64. For the early Jena reception of Kant, see Hinske (1995a), pp. 15ff.; also Hinske (1995b), pp. 231–43, especially pp. 241ff.
65. The expression "alles zermalmenden Kant" is famously Mendelssohn's. See note 26.
66. "I doubt that many have tried to formulate and carry out an entirely new conceptual science. [. . .] Nevertheless, [this project] inspires me with the hope that, without fear of being suspected of the greatest vanity, I reveal to no one but you: the hope that by means of this work philosophy will be given durable form, a different and – for religion and morality – more favorable turn." Letter to Markus Herz toward the end of 1773, AK X:145, tr. Arnulf Zweig. "In spite of that, I boldly allow myself to believe that this book will lead every treatment of this subject in a new direction and that the doctrines propounded in it can hope for an endurance which until now one has been accustomed to deny to all metaphysical endeavors." Letter to J. E. Biester, 8 June 1781, AK X:272, tr. Arnulf Zweig. "Yet these *Prolegomena* will bring [the readers] to understand that there exists a completely new science, of which no one had previously formed so much as the thought, of which even the bare idea was unknown, and for which nothing from all that has been provided before now could be used except the hint that *Hume's* doubts had been able to give." *Prolegomena*, AK IV:262, tr. Gary Hatfield. "All metaphysicians are therefore solemnly and lawfully suspended from their occupations until such a time as they shall have satisfactorily answered

the question: *How are synthetic cognitions* a priori *possible?" Prolegomena*, AK IV:278.

Chapter 2

1. Karl Ameriks is certainly right on this point. But it is at least confusing to say that, though Kant is still doing metaphysics, this metaphysics is, however, modest as contrasted with absolute. This would imply that Kant is still engaged in the project of dogmatic metaphysics, but on a reduced scale. My point, rather, is that Kant changed the nature of metaphysics altogether. He was thoroughly immodest. Cf. Ameriks (2000), pp. 13ff.

2. See what Reinhold has to say on the matter in *Fundament* (full reference in note 12), pp. 67–8. As he points out, a recently published textbook in metaphysics had replaced the traditional sections on psychology, cosmology, and theology, with excerpts of the Critique demonstrating the impossibility of such sciences.

3. Here is where the issue of Kant's relation to the voluntarist/nominalist tradition of the jurists could be broached. (Cf. Hunter, 2001) My suggestion is that Kant's idealism transcends, and even renders obsolete, the traditional realism-versus-nominalism debate. Kant is a nominalist in the sense that, according to him, essences are the products of conceptualization. But they are not arbitrary products, since they must abide by the rules of meaning that govern the universe of mental intentions. These intentions define *the real* so far as the human being is concerned. In this sense, Kant is a nominalist only *sui generis*. And, inasmuch as he identifies will and practical reason, he is equally a voluntarist *sui generis*. The validity of the law depends, not on the good that it might prescribe, but on the weight of the authority that stands behind it. This authority, however, is ultimately reason itself, and reason, far from being an arbitrary power, is a norm-generating faculty. Reason is self-legislating. It sets up its own tribunal. Nominalism and voluntarism were not, however, issues in the culture of the popular philosophers, which is primarily the object of the present study. This culture was dominated by Leibniz and Wolff rather than by Thomasius and Crusius.

4. *Phenomenology of Spirit, Gesammelte Werke,* IX:295.8–296.7.

5. Ameriks (2000), pp. 3ff., writes of Kant's 'modest system'; of his 'modest science'.

6. Hegel was especially annoyed by him. He attacked him at length in one of his first publications and repeatedly returned to his challenge even much later in his career. "How the Ordinary Human Understanding Takes Philosophy (as Displayed in the Works of Mr. Krug)," in di Giovanni and Harris (2000), pp. 292–310.

7. For an account of the episode, see di Giovanni (1995).

8. Cf. his polemical piece, *Etwas das Leßing gesagt hat. Ein Commentar zu den Reisen der Päpste nebst Betrachtungen von einem Dritten* (1782).

9. For details and references, see di Giovanni (1995). Hegel's portrayal of the confrontation between *Aufklärer* and believer in Chapter 6 of the

Phenomenology of Spirit reflects a type of literature popular at the close of the eighteenth century.

10. *Verhandlungen über die Grundbegriffe und Grundsätze der Moralität* (1798), p. 272. This work is "late" only with reference to the time frame of this study. For Reinhold's connection with the *Illuminati*, see Lauth (1979).

11. Chapter 7, Section 7.2.3.

12. Both in *Versuch einer neuen Theorie des menschlichen Vorstellungsvermögens* (1789), e.g., pp. 24ff., 133, 154–8, 188, and in *Über das Fundament des philosophischen Wissens* (1791), pp. 50ff., 88ff., 97ff. An English translation of a substantial excerpt of this last work is available in di Giovanni and Harris (2000). It includes the pagination of the original German text.

13. For an example of the cultural breadth of popular philosophy in Germany, see Chapter 7, note 31.

14. The story is detailed in *Fundament* (see note 12), pp. 44ff.

15. *Fundament*, pp. 34ff.

16. *Fundament*, pp. 19–20. The text that Reinhold very likely has in mind is Book II, Chapter 2, of Leibniz's *New Essays Concerning Human Understanding* (1949), p. 120.

17. See Chapter 3, note 78.

18. *Fundament*, pp. 51–2.

19. Here as elsewhere, Reinhold uses the more common (German) expression 'human common understanding'.

20. *Fundament*, pp. 52–3. Cf. my translation in di Giovanni and Harris (2000), which I have modified somewhat.

21. *Fundament*, p. 53.

22. *Fundament*, p. 50.

23. *Theorie*, 155–6.

24. *Theorie*, 154. My translation is rather loose for the sake of conveying in English the rhetorical force of the German.

25. It must be said that Reinhold was a passionate reader of English literature.

26. One cannot help but note Hegel's indebtedness to this vision.

27. Kuehn rightly criticizes nationalistic interpretations of the history of German philosophy. Kuehn (1987), p. 253. I am not in any way disagreeing with this view. One need not, however, engage in such a dubious form of historiography to grant that there was a home-grown tradition of German eclecticism.

28. See, on this point, Albrecht's essay (1989).

29. But Crusius was also under British influence. Kuehn (1987), p. 264.

30. *Briefe, die neueste Literatur betreffend* I (1 March 1759), 129–34. Cited after Kuehn (1987), p. 36.

31. Reinhold's polemical writings of this period have been collected and edited in *Karl Leonhard Reinhold. Schriften zur Religionskritik und Aufklärung, 1782–1784* (1977). The Introduction by the editor is especially instructive.

32. Cf. *Theorie*, pp. 66, 71 (§I), 120 (§II). Reinhold endlessly belabors the point throughout Part I of *Theorie*.

33. In Chapter 7.

34. This is how Weishaupt described his philosophical program: "My whole striving is directed [. . .] to making myself understood [as philosopher], not just
by some, but by very many men. If I just possessed the right degree of popularity, I would want to demonstrate to as many human beings as possible
that they have no cause to mistrust the first principles of their thinking; that
the hitherto recognized supreme principles of which every man, perhaps
unwittingly, makes use in practice, are all contained as part of their healthy
common sense [*gesunder Menschenverstand*], and are perfectly sufficient to
provide for us, if not with respect to all objects, yet surely with respect at
least to the most important ones, the kind of certainty indispensable to action as well as to peace of mind. For I believe that whatever human beings
necessarily need to know, they must all be capable of knowing – without
privilege of person. I believe that in this matter all depends on duly order-
ing, developing, determining, and bringing closer together, principles and
concepts that are already known – thus, through proper combination, on
producing the kind of conviction which we in vain expect from the discovery
of totally new, supposedly still unknown truths." Adam Weishaupt, *Über die
Gründe und Gewisheit* [*sic*] *der Menschlichen Erkenntnis. Zur Prüfung der Kantishen Kritik* (1788), pp. xxv–xxvii. I have somewhat streamlined the prose.
Here is another statement of popular philosophy, included in the first ever
review of the *Critique of Pure Reason* (*Zugabe zu den Göttingischen Anzeigen von
gelehrten Sachen*, 19 January, 1782; anonymous but very likely by Feder and
Garve): "The right use of understanding must accord with the most universal
concept of right action, with the basic law of our moral nature, and hence
with the furtherance of blessedness. As becomes quickly clear, understanding has to be applied in accord with its basic laws. These find contradictions unacceptable and necessitate grounds for assent – indeed, prevailing
and enduring grounds if there are contrary indications. It similarly follows
from this that we have to adhere to our stronger and most enduring **sensations** or the strongest and most enduring semblance [*Schein*] as our reality. This is what common sense does" p. 47. Translation in Sassen (2000),
pp. 57–8.
35. For details, see Lauth (1979). Reinhold came to consider Weishaupt a moral
reprobate and an intellectual charlatan who unscrupulously attacked Kant
without understanding him.
36. Nürnberg: Grattenhauer, 1787. Idealism should be understood in this context in its pre-Kantian meaning, i.e., to use Kant's language, as psychological
subjectivism.
37. The image is my own.
38. Pp. 94ff., 185ff. It is interesting to note that Weishaupt denies the validity of
the notion of a gradation of perfections, or of classes of beings of different
perfections. He takes the very idea of a class to be a function of our ignorance.
Perfection is always individual. It is to be measured within a given world on
terms specific to just that world. All concepts ought eventually to refer to
individuals. Pp. 153–7, 159.
39. The belief that one can infer on the basis of experience the possibilities of
other future worlds was an Enlightenment scientific commonplace. See, for

instance, Charles Bonnet, *La Palingénésie philosophique, ou Idées sur l'état passé et sur l'état futur des êtres vivants* (1769). Peculiar to Weishaupt is that he denies that the transition from world to world entails a gradation of perfections, and that he applies this principle also to the variety of moral systems found in human history (pp. 204ff.).

40. For instance, in the already cited *Über die Gründe und Gewisheit* [*sic*] *der Menschlichen Erkenntnis. Zür Prüfung der Kantishen Kritik*, pp. 208, in §46 and also repeatedly in his voluminous *Über Wahrheit und sittliche Vollkommenheit* (1797). The last part includes a very interesting Appendix, 'Concerning the Origin of the Doctrine of Ideas' ("Über den Ursprung der Lehre von der Ideen"). Here Weishaupt insists again that all knowledge is of individuals, and that all philosophical errors can be traced to the beliefs in 'universal ideas.' See also note 38.

41. "Der Grund meiner Vorstellungen liegt sodann *in der jedesmaligen Lage der Seele unter den übrigen Theilen der Welt, in der nach dieser sich verschiedentlich äussernden Einwirkung der Gegenstände, mit welchen sie coexistirt*" §39, p. 162.

42. Appendix to Part 3 of *Über Wahrheit und sittliche Vollkommenheit.* See note 39. Also, see pp. 324–34.

43. This is not Weishaupt's word.

44. "If the physical elements are the supersensible grounds of the appearances, the ground and the content (corresponding to these dark representations) of all our cognition, then, all higher and derivative cognition is nothing more than clarification, development, and contrast, of the simultaneous effect, of the sensible impressions, of these darkly known supersensible forces. And so Leibniz made a great discovery in claiming that our sensibility is confused cognition, such that contains, in the heap of traits which we are unable to dissect consciously, what befits the things in themselves; that, therefore, only the understanding, by means of attention, is capable of dissipating this obscurity up to a determinate degree possible to us here. He rightly claimed that only the understanding affords distinct cognition and concepts; that its whole performance consists in raising to distinctness what we already know through the sense indistinctly." *Über Wahrheit und sittliche Vollkommenheit,* Part 2, pp. 111–12.

45. *Über Wahrheit und sittliche Vollkommenheit,* Part 2, pp. 109, 198ff., 307–21, 324–34. *Über die Gründe und Gewisheit* [*sic*] *der Menschlichen Erkenntnis,* pp. 79–83.

46. Lauth (1979), pp. 608ff.; Le Forestier (1914), pp. 15–29, 198; Van Dülmen (1975), pp. 47ff., 127ff.

47. According to Reinhold's own reading of Locke. In *Theorie* (pp. 310–11) he quotes the "acute" Plattner as saying that "Locke grants to the soul fundamental dispositions that make it capable of *sensing (empfinden)* necessary truths [. . .]; Leibniz would have ideas without images *(Ideenbilder)* [. . .] Leibniz's ideas, without images, are perhaps nothing more than Locke's fundamental dispositions." Reinhold agrees in principle with this suggestion, and wonders why Plattner dropped it in the new edition of his *Aphorismen.* The two, i.e., Leibniz and Locke, had each seen a common truth from their opposite points of view. Yet they both failed inasmuch as they failed either to distinguish in a representation sufficiently between form and

content (Leibniz) or to distinguish between the content *in* a representation that belongs to its object and the content *of* the representation itself (Locke).

48. *Fundament*, p. 22.
49. *Fundament*, pp. 52–3.
50. Spinoza-Letters, pp. 84 (very bottom)–85, 85 (very bottom)–86.
51. 'Was heißt sich im Denken Orientiren?' See Chapter 3, Section 3.2.3.
52. Anonymous, but Feder and Garve, "Review of KrV," *Zugabe zu den Göttingschen Anzeigen von gelehrten Sachen* (1782). 40–8.

    Christian Garve, "Review of Kant's KrV" (1783).

    Anonymous, but H. A. Pistorius, "Review of Schultz's Kant commentary" (see Chapter 3) (1786).

    Anonymous, but J. G. H. Feder, *Über Raum und Causalität: zur Prüfung der Kantischen Philosophie* (1787).

    Anonymous, but H. A. Pistorius, "Review of KrV," (1788).

    Translation of excerpts of all the preceding works, and other sources as well (some of which we shall cite in due course), can be found in Sassen (2000).

    J. A. H. Ulrich, to whom we shall return in Chapter 4, was a professor of philosophy at Jena, where he had a long and successful teaching career. In 1785 he published *Institutiones Logicae et Metaphysicae*, a text book on which his lectures were based. The book was divided into two parts, Logic and Metaphysics, and was accompanied by another text on rational theology. The whole book was a compendium of basic philosophical terms and definitions; of philosophical problems normally associated with such terms; and of positions traditionally taken regarding these problems. In each case, in typical textbook format, the relevant authorities were cited and a list of relevant readings was suggested. What is especially significant about the book is the way in which it treats Kant. The latter is cited as just one more authority. His definition of phenomena, for instance, is listed as one more possible position regarding the nature of the objects of experience (Chapter 2 of the Metaphysics); his moral proof of the existence of God, as one more possible rational demonstration of the universally accepted belief in a supreme cause of the universe (§49 of the Rational Theology). Whatever Ulrich's intentions – whether that was his way of accommodating Kant or of opposing him by denying him any special originality – the net effect was that the Critique of Reason lost the effect it would otherwise have of forcing hard decisions regarding the nature of rationality itself.

53. On the subject, see Allison (1973), pp. 8ff. Eberhard was Schleiermacher's much revered teacher at Halle. This is another indication of how much the tradition of popular philosophy carried on in the nineteenth century. Schleiermacher's criticism of Kant, though already an expression of Romanticism, reflected that of his teacher.

54. See Chapter 1, note 61.

55. Anonymous, but Gottlieb Ernst Schulze, *Aenesidemus, oder über die Fundamente der von Herrn Prof. Reinhold in Jena gelieferten Elementarphilosophie*

(1792). Schulze is known mostly because of this *Aenesidemus* connection. But he continued to play an unintended, yet important, role in the development of post-Kantian Idealism. He did this with three later publications, namely:

(1) *Kritik der theoretischen Philosophie* (1801).

(2) Anonymous, "Aphorismen über das Absolute, als das alleinige Prinzip der wahren Philosophie, über die einzige mögliche Art es zu erkennen, wie auch über das Verähltniß aller Dinge in der Welt zu demselben" (1803).

(3) "Die Hauptmomente der skeptischen Denkart über die menschliche Erkenntnis" (1805).

The early Hegel disparagingly reviewed the 1801 book from Schelling's standpoint of 'intuition' that he still endorsed at the time. *Kritiches Journal der Philosophie* 1.2 (1802), 1–74. Schulze replied in strict anonymity with the 1803 essay ("Aphorismen"). There he feigned to be a disciple of Schelling, and he quite consequentially argued that, when in the grip of intuition, the mind must be unconscious, since the distinction between its self and the Absolute that it presumably intuits is superseded. As if in a night of the spirit, the mind falls into a dreamlike state. This implicit criticism of intuitionism was at least one important factor in precipitating Hegel's rejection of Schelling's idealism. Hegel's famous phrase in the Preface to the *Phenomenology of Spirit*, "the dark night in which all cows are black," is ostensibly a criticism of the author of *Aphorismen* (whom Hegel knew to be Schulze parading as a disciple of Schelling), but is just as much a criticism of Schelling and of his own earlier self (GW IX:17.27–9; also 14.20–2). In the 1805 work, Schulze produced a systematic interpretation of the place of skepticism in the history of philosophy. This interpretation, together with Reinhold's systematic reading of the development of philosophical thought, might very well have been for Hegel a blueprint of his own phenomenological method. The *Phenomenology* is a historically marked pathway of skeptical doubt and even despair that, unlike Schulze's, leads to positive results.

For a detailed history of the episode, see the instructive but unfortunately seldom cited essay by Meist (1993).

56. One of the most repeated and most strident objections leveled against Kant was precisely that his theory of knowledge abstracted from the data of empirical psychology. J. F. Abel (professor of philosophy at Tübingen and, like Weishaupt, also a spokesman of Feder) argued the point in perhaps the most naive but for that reason all the more revealing fashion. He agreed with what he took to be Kant's main critical thesis, namely, that we do not have objects unless we first synthesize them out of subjective appearances. We thereby transform the subjective into the objective. But this process is governed by certain fundamental laws of the mind that determine the formation of representations. The task of science is to examine the soul in detail in order to discover these laws – not to appeal to pure reason, as Kant did. There is no discontinuity between psychological and logical laws. Even the law of contradiction must be based on psychological necessity. Now, this was indeed a

naive claim, just as naive as Weishaupt's charge that critical philosophy was a crass form of solipsism. There was nothing naive, however, either in the desire to save the organic unity that binds the many elements of experience together or in the suspicion that Kant's Critique of Reason might have disturbed this unity, that inspired both the claim and the charge. And there was enough intellectual rigor to the model of experience on which these were based to give at least prima facie validity to any doubt regarding the validity, let alone the usefulness, of the thought revolution that Kant now demanded. Abel's relevant works on the subject are *Einleitung in die Seelenlehre* (1786; see pp. 620–45 for an example of how subjective experiences can be turned into the picture of an objective world); *Plan einer systematischen Metaphysik* (1787); and *Versuch über die Natur der speculativen Vernunft. Zur Prüfung des Kantischen Systems* (1787), especially pp. 7ff. for a criticism of Kant and pp. 56ff. for Abel's own program. The last two books were both widely reviewed at the time. While there were good things said about them, in general Abel was criticized for accepting Kant's 'subjectivism,' and for thinking that he could derive Kant's would-be a priori results on the basis of empirical psychology. Abel was the teacher of Hegel at Tübingen.

57. C. C. E. Schmid, *Wörterbuch zum leichtern Gebrauch der Kantischen Schriften* (1788). See Chapter 1, note 69.

58. "Einige Bemerkungen über den Empirismus und Purismus in der Philosophie; durch die *Grundsätze der reinen Philosophie* von Herrn Selle veranlaßt," 52 pp., appended to *Wörterbuch zum leichtern Gebrauch der Kantischen Schriften*, 2nd augmented ed. (1788). Christian Gottlieb Selle was best known in his day as a practicing physician and the author of many medical treatises. But he also wrote the occasional philosophical piece. The *Grundsätze der reinen Philosophie* (1788) is an example. The Lexicon sold out in no time, and there were repeated editions.

59. J. A. H. Reimarus was another author who interpreted Kant in this way, i.e., as if, according to Kant, one would have to infer the existence and the characteristics of things in themselves inductively, on the basis of the purely subjective and passive experiences that the senses provide. This interpretation of Kant brought the Critique of Reason more in line with the commonsense empiricism of Mendelssohn, with whom Reimarus was closely connected personally as well as intellectually. See, for instance, *Über die Gründe der menschlichen Erkenntnis und der natürlichen Religion* (1787), §20, for a brief statement. (The first 15§§ of this book are a debunking of Jacobi's Spinoza-Letters and of the idea of faith advanced by Jacobi's friend Wizenmann.) F. G. Born, who coedited with Abicht the *Neues philosophisches Magazin* in an effort to diffuse Kant's ideas, is yet another example of a similar 'empirical' interpretation of Kant. There could hardly be a more naive, a more physiological reading of Kant, than one finds in his essay "Über den transcendentalen Idealismus," published in the third issue of the *Magazin* in Leipzig (1790).

60. *Über die Gründe und Gewisheit* [*sic*] *der menschlichen Erkenntnis. Zür Prüfung der Kantishen Kritik*, especially §§17, 18, 22, and *Über Wahrheit und sittliche Vollkommenheit*, Part I, pp. 275–6 and Conclusion. What Weishaupt says about skepticism would apply in his mind also to Kant.

61. *Über Wahrheit und sittliche Vollkommenheit*, Part I, pp. 27–8, 275–6. Note that what I call 'solipsism' is called by Weishaupt 'egotism'. Cf. *Über die Gründe und Gewisheitß*, §41; *Über Wahrheit und sittliche Vollkommenheit*, Appendix to Part III, p. 8.

62. This point is argued for in a great variety of ways in Weishaupt's "Presentation of Kant's System" in *Über die Gründe und Gewisheit* [*sic*] *der menschlichen Erkenntnis*, from §11 to the end.

63. *Über die Gründe und Gewisheit*, §22, p. 91.

64. Cf. *Über die Gründe und Gewisheit*, §§19–23, especially pp. 91–8.

65. Cf. *Über die Gründe und Gewisheit*, §39.

66. *Über Wahrheit und sittliche Vollkommenheit*, Part II, pp. 307–21, 390–1. Weishaupt held the strange belief that one cannot be happy unless one learns that everything that happens, whether to one's individual advantage or disadvantage, is determined to happen according to a wise plan and contributes to the perfection of the whole.

67. As we shall see in Chapter 4, Schmid was as much of a determinist as Weishaupt.

68. These are the texts on which I base my account, in chronological order: *De philosophiæ Kantinanæ habitu ad theologiam. Dissertiatio philosophica pro gradu doctoris* (1788); "Über die Freiheit des Willens" (1789); *Philosophie der Erkenntnisse* (1791); *Kritische Briefe über die Möglichkeit einer wahren wissenschaftlichen Moral, Theologie, Rechtslehre, empirischen Psychologie und Geschmakslehre, mit prüfender Hinsicht auf die Kantische Begründung dieser Lehre* (1793); *System der Elementarphilosophie oder vollständige Naturlehre der Erkentniss-Gefühl und Willenskraft* (1795).

69. In the dissertation (1788), Abicht follows the line of interpretation of the Jena theologians and of Reinhold's first Kantian Letters. All the basic Christian beliefs are reintroduced on the basis of interests of reason.

70. "Eine vollständige innere Tatsache, d.h. Etwas das sich mir unmittelbar zu erkennen gibt." *System der Elementarphilosophie*, p. 5. An early influence of Reinhold's *Elementarphilosophie* (see Chapter 3) is obvious. Cf. *Philosophie der Erkenntnisse*, §§8off. But Abicht also severely criticizes Reinhold's theory of freedom (see Chapter 4). Cf. *Kritische Briefe* (1793; there is an obvious reference here to the Kantian Letters in which Reinhold had developed his theory), pp. 255ff.

71. See Chapter 3, Section 3.2.2.

72. *System der Elementarphilosophie*, p. 6.

73. They are mostly derived from the rational psychology of the day. One possible exception might be the concept of *Besonnenheit* – apparently a generalized faculty of reflection that, according to Abicht, is uniquely responsible for the activity of judgment that Kant and Reinhold had instead attributed to the understanding and reason. *System der Elementarphilosophie*, pp. 90–7.

74. *System der Elementarphilosophie*, pp. 137–8.

75. *System der Elementarphilosophie*, pp. 140–9.

76. *System der Elementarphilosophie*, pp. 209ff., 258ff. Especially p. 258: "*Thus we possess a moral nature*, and this consists in general in the *faculty of our soul*,

which is its original characteristic, *to display to itself, in the process of realizing its powers* [*in dem erwerbbaren Positiven ihrer Kräfte*], *something that is in itself capable of being felt, and, through self – generated representations and through feelings for it awakened by means of these representations, to propose it to the will, as something good or evil, as object of its willing and striving, thus to make it an end.*"

77. *Kritische Briefe* (1793), pp. 414–15. Abicht is vehemently opposed to Kant's distinction between virtue and happiness. He considers the two as naturally connected. Falling back upon God to mediate the two, as Kant does, comes too late to make any difference to the theory (307). Abicht stresses that he is interested in what Kant's calls 'empirical will.' But he then immediately wonders how there could be any other will (64ff.). Assume a metaphysical will, and an insoluble problem of motivation for human action immediately arises (99ff.).

78. See note 68.

79. We shall develop this point in Chapters 3 and 6.

80. *Über Wahrheit und sittliche Vollkommenheit*, Part I, p. 109.

81. *Über Wahrheit und sittliche Vollkommenheit*, pp. 115–18, 124–5.

82. *Hermias, oder Auflösung der die gültige Elementarphilosophie betreffenden Ænesidischen Zweifel* (1794).

83. See note 59.

84. See note 77.

85. Carl Christian Erhard Schmid, *Philosophische Dogmatik, im Grundriß für Vorlesungen* (1796), viii–190, §202. The title on p. 1 reads: "Philosophische Religionslehre."

86. *Grundriß der Moralphilosophie* (Jena: Kröker, 1793) p. 151.

Chapter 3

1. By contrast, I can cite August Gottlob Tittel, whose reaction to Kant in the name of popular philosophy verged on the contemptuous. Tittel suggests to his readers that Kant was pulling their leg. He was offering an example of how sound reason can turn into self-promoting pure reason by dint of obscurity, coined language and ideas, and artificial language. Or perhaps he was being serious. In that case, however, one can understand him only by using his own artificial abstract language and thereby losing track of reality. *Über Herrn Kant's Moralreform* (1786), pp. 3–6. In another short book (a tract more than a book), Tittel accuses Kant of having resuscitated categories that had been originally intended by Aristotle only for classificatory purposes. Kant had warmed them over, so to speak, investing them with an ontological value totally foreign to them. Tittel also defends Locke. *Kantischen Denkformen oder Kategorien* (Frankfurt/Main: Gebhard, 1787).

2. As cited by Lauth (1979), pp. 622, 623.

3. Weishaupt was considered the d'Holbach of Germany.

4. Also spelled as Schulz, Schulze, and Schültz, Schultze. His book, *Erläuterungen über des Herrn Professor Kant Critik der reinen Vernunft* (1784), went through several editions. I shall be citing from that of 1791, which is the most available and just as authoritative as the first. An English translation with informative

introduction and notes, based on the 1791 edition, is available. *Exposition of Kant's* Critique of Pure Reason (1995).

5. Thus Schultz (p. 6). Schultz also says that the book is fated to be, even for the learned public, as if written in hieroglyphs.

6. See note 4.

7. See Morrison's very instructive Introduction to the English translation, pp. xxiiff.

8. There are two chapters in Schultz's book. Each gives a complete account of Kant's Critique – the second, however, in a much briefer and more informal format. This second chapter is where Schultz avoids Kant's technical language.

9. Cf. p. 190. Schultz stresses from the start (pp. 19–20) the presence of intuitively given a priori forms of sensibility, i.e., space and time. Hence, insofar as the mathematical structure of the content of experience is concerned, the possibility of establishing the conformity between any conceptual representations of such forms and the forms themselves can itself be established in principle a priori. The science of mathematics rests on this possibility. But the important issue, for us as well as for Schultz and Kant, is the possibility of establishing that the conformity between any conceptual representations of the dynamic content of experience (i.e., the sequence of sense events) and this content itself is *given* in experience.

10. Cf. pp. 189, 192–3. Also, p. 41: "But now arises the question . . . "

11. Schultz, *Erläuterungen*, pp. 33–9. The schematization of Schultz's deduction is mine.

12. This is the key passage: "Allein, beruht die Einheit der Verknüpfung unserer Vorstellungen auf einem nothwendigen Princip a priori; so muß auch die Verknüpfung unserer mannigfaltigen Vorstellungen selbst auf einem nothwendigen Princip a priori beruhen. Denn, wenn dieses nicht wäre, sondern die Einbildungskraft das Mannigfaltige der Anschauung bloß auf ein Gerathewohl apprehendirte, associirte und reproducirte; so wären diese mannigfaltigen Vorstellungen ohne bestimmten Zusammenhang, bloße regellose Haufen, mithin könnte aus ihrer unbestimmten ganz zufälligen Verknüpfung unmöglich eine nothwendige Einheit a priori werden."

13. The most extensive attempt at this transition was made in his *Metaphysische Anfangsgründe der Naturwissenschaft* of 1786 (*Metaphysical Foundations of Natural Science*). For a brief but very informative account of Kant's struggle for this transition and the critical problem that motivated it, see Förster (1993), especially pp. xxixff.

14. For a brief treatment and a translation of significant texts, see *Between Kant and Hegel*, pp. 36ff., 204ff.

15. I have explored the themes I discuss in this section, but in much broader terms, in the introductory study to *Jacobi*, especially in Section II.

16. *David Hume über den Glauben, oder Idealismus und Realismus. Ein Gespräch* (1787). An English translation with an historical introduction and explanatory notes is in *Jacobi*.

17. *Jacobi*, p. 606, note 13. Jacobi confided these sentiments to Hamann.

18. *Jacobi*, p. 89, note 62.

19. Chapter 1, Section 1.4.

20. This second edition has been the only one easily available to students and commentators and the cause, therefore, of much misunderstanding of Jacobi. The English translation in *Jacobi* clearly indicates the differences between the first and second editions. Jacobi is normally portrayed as an irrationalist. This is at best a one-sided view of him and, at worst, a misinterpretation.

21. That his faith entails knowledge is made quite explicitly by Jacobi later in the dialogue, p. 122.

22. There was some justification, therefore, to the objection raised by the critics that Jacobi had unwarrantedly usurped for religious purposes a purely philosophical strategy of Hume. According to these critics, Hume had made reflective use of the faculty of reason to destroy the illusion that it is possible to demonstrate argumentatively the truth of otherwise spontaneous beliefs. He had never intended to suspend these beliefs but had nonetheless kept reason as the arbiter of truth, even if skeptical doubt was all that reason could ultimately deliver. In this respect Hume belonged, in the opinion of the critics, to the party of the rationalists and was not to be appropriated by a pious enthusiast like Jacobi. Cf. the anonymous reviewer of the dialogue in *ALZ* 2 (1788), no. 92, columns 105–7. Hamann too, though siding with Jacobi and even conspiring with him in the process leading up to the publication of *Letters Concerning Spinoza,* was upset by Jacobi's attempt to construe his appeal to faith as a case of Humean belief. Cf. J. G. Hamann, *Briefwechsel* (1955–79), Letter to Jacobi, 27 April–3 May 1787, vol. 7, p. 167. For another criticism of Jacobi's use of faith in *Letters Concerning Spinoza,* see *ALZ* 1 (1786), columns 292–6.

23. I have already treated this subject in di Giovanni (1997b).

24. See also *David Hume,* pp. 119–20, and the footnote that Jacobi adds to this section in the 1815 edition, *Werke,* II, pp. 215–16. In the 1815 footnote Jacobi claims to have been inspired for his deduction by Spinoza. He then refers, however, to a book on logic by G. E. Schulze (of *Ænesidemus* fame) and to a review of the book in the *Göttingen Erudite Notices,* both of which in fact echo themes from Reid's commonsense philosophy. Cf. G. E. Schulze, *Grundsätze der allgemeinen Logik* (1802), and *Göttingische gelehrte Nachrichten* (1802), especially 1412–13. My paper on Jacobi and Hume (1997b) fails to make sufficient allowance for the influence of Spinoza.

25. "Was heißt: Sich im Denkem orientiren?" AK VIII: 131ff.; cf. 133–4.

26. I have made this point, but in a much narrower context, in di Giovanni (1997b). I closely paraphrase the occasional paragraph in this paper and rely on some of its footnoting.

27. Jacobi cites from a review in *ALZ* 2 (1786), columns 181–3, of Reid's *Essays on the Intellectual Powers of Man.* He turns to the "good David Hume" on pp. 30ff. The reference to Reid is to justify his use of faith.

28. Jacobi indirectly acknowledged his debt to Reid in at least one place, namely, in a passage of the 1784 *Woldemar,* in which he has one of his characters (a Scott named Sydney, who expresses many of the views dear to Jacobi's heart) praise the Scottish philosopher. Part I, p. 80 of the 1796 ed.

(Königsberg: Nicolovius). Cf. *Werke* (1820), vol. 5, p. 71. Jacobi also praises Reid in a letter to Johann Neeb, 18 October 1814, *Friedrich Heinrich Jacobi's auserlesener Briefwechsel* (1825–7), vol. 2, p. 445. For Reid's influence on Jacobi, see Kuehn (1987), pp. 143–9, 158–66, and also Baum (1969), pp. 42–9. In his "Tagebuch der Reise nach dem Reich," Wilhelm von Humboldt reports Jacobi as saying to him in 1788: "There is a big and important difference between perception [*Perception*] and sensation [*Sensation*], between perception [*Wahrnehmung*] of external alterations and the feeling of internal ones – a difference that Kant denies, because, according to him, everything is only a modification of the soul itself, everything is only sensation. We do not perceive, as is usually said, merely the picture of external things [*Dinge*]; we perceive these things themselves (though, to be sure, modified according to the relationship of our position with respect to the thing we perceive and to all other things in the world). This perception occurs, as Reid has said quite correctly, *by a sort of revelation* [English in the original]. Hence we do not demonstrate that there are objects external to us, but believe it. This belief is no acceptance in accordance with probable reasons. It has a greater and more unshakeable certainty than any demonstration could ever afford." W. Humboldt, *Gesammelte Schriften* (1968), vol. 14, p. 58. Cf. p. 61: "We intuit [*schauen . . . an*] the things outside us; these things are actual things, and the certainty intuition affords us we call faith. This certainty is so strong for us, and so necessary, that every other certainty, indeed, even self-consciousness, depends on it. Hence Kant is wrong when he reduces all things to the human being [*den Menschen selbst*], when he explains everything as a modification of the soul and accepts external objects [*Objekte*] in word only while denying their reality [*die Sache selbst*]."

29. Cf. *Essays on the Intellectual Powers of Man*, Essay II, chs. 3 and 4, where Reid argues that 'sensations', understood as mere impressions in the manner of Locke and Hume, are physical events that do not constitute as such consciousness proper, even though God has made them the necessary preconditions of mental life. The latter begins only with perception, and it is clear that "if, therefore, we attend to that act of our mind which we call the perception of an external object of sense, we shall find in it these three things: *First*, Some conception or notion of the object perceived; *Secondly*, A strong and irresistible conviction and belief of its present existence; and *Thirdly*, That this conviction and belief are immediate, and not the effect of reasoning." *Essays on the Intellectual Powers of Man: The Works of Thomas Reid* (1873), vol. 1, p. 258. Cf. also Reid's critique of Hume's theory of ideas in ch. 14.

30. Cf. *David Hume*, pp. 181ff.

31. *Essays on the Intellectual Powers of Man*, Essay IV, Ch. 1. See especially the bottom of the right column on p. 361 and the beginning of the following.

32. *Essays on the Intellectual Powers of Man*; cf. Essay V, ch. 1, pp. 418–19. *David Hume*, p. 182.

33. This is the point in the first edition of *David Hume* that Jacobi later found embarrassing and tried to cover up in the 1815 edition. For the changes later introduced, see the text in *Jacobi*, pp. 298ff.

34. Cf. *Essays on the Intellectual Powers of Man*, Essay VI, ch. 2, pp. 422, 423.

35. The presence and influence of Scottish commonsense philosophy is detailed in Kuehn (1987). See also Kuehn (2001), pp. 130–1. For a German domestic source of common sense, see the Appendix of Kuehn (1987).

36. Though Jacobi left open the possibility of attaining this vision through other, possibly mystical means. Cf. *David Hume*, 186ff.

37. *Versuch einer neuen Theorie des menschlichen Vorstellungsvermögens* (1789).

38. This Preface, under the title "Über das bisherige Schicksal der Kantischen Philosophie" ("Concerning the Fate of Critical Philosophy"), was published in three different venues in the same year, 1789, in *Der Teutsche Merkur* 2 (1789), 3–17, 113–35; as the Preface of *Versuch*, pp. 1–68; and as an independent volume (Jena: Widtemann & Mauke, 1789).

39. The first book, after the Preface, is dedicated to a long defense of the need for a new Theory of Representation. The theory proper begins only with Book II.

40. Pp. 560–79.

41. Cf. Kant's Letter to Sigismund Beck, 20 January 1792, AK XI:315–16.

42. This was a main objection raised by Schulze in *Ænesidemus*, pp. 53–4. See also note 51.

43. I have already presented elements of the following interpretation of Reinhold in di Giovanni (1998).

44. The image that the word evokes in German is that of 'a placing forth'.

45. "Neue Darstellung," *Beyträge*, vol. 1 (1790), p. 265. In *Theorie*, see §VII, p. 200.

46. Hegel borrows this definition of consciousness in his *Phenomenology of Spirit*. *Gesammelte Schriften*, 9:58.25–30.

47. See, for instance, the following proposition, which especially brings out the intentional character of representation: "Representation is possible [. . .] only inasmuch as [. . .] two different 'somewhats' [*zwei verschiedene Etwas*] occur in consciousness united – of which, one belongs to the subject as itself differentiated from what is [thus] united, and the other to the object as [equally] differentiated from it." These primitive distinctions within union are at the basis of further distinctions in representation such as between 'content' and 'form', as Reinhold proceeds to show. *Theorie*, §XVIII, pp. 256ff.

48. Cf. p. 249.

49. Especially pp. 247–52.

50. §VI, p. 199; §VII, p. 201.

51. This is what both Aenesidemus and Maimon denied. G. E. Schulze, *Ænesidemus, oder über die Fundamente der von Herrn Prof. Reinhold in Jena gelieferten Elemetarphilosophie, nebst einer Verteidigung gegen die Anmassungen der Venunftkritik* (1792), pp. 59ff. Solomon Maimon, *Essay Towards a New Logic or Theory of Thought, Together with Letters of Philateles to Aenesidemus* (Berlin: Felisch, 1794), pp. 318–20. English translations of excerpts of both works can be found in *Between Kant and Hegel*. For Fichte's respect for Maimon, see the draft of his letter to Reinhold in Breazeale (1988), p. 389.

52. *Theorie*, §XXXIX, p. 332: "Now, since every consciousness consists in the relating of mere representation to the object and subject, in clear consciousness in general, the object of which is always a representation, this very representation must be represented through another which is different from it

(as the object). In clear consciousness there necessarily occurs, therefore, the representation of representation." An example (my gloss) would be the judgment "A 'rose' is a thing with such and such properties." Only clarity is added to the content of 'rose'.

53. *Theorie*, §XL, p. 333 (Proposition). An example would be (again, my gloss) the claim, *"I say* that 'a rose is a thing with such and such properties.' "

54. *Theorie*, §XLII, p. 340 (Proposition). An example would be "What I say of a 'rose' is what the 'rose' is."

55. It could be argued that here, in principle, is the model of Hegel's analysis of experience in the *Phenomenology of Spirit.*

56. At a later date, when acknowledging some of the weaknesses of his *Theorie*, Reinhold granted that he had failed to draw clear distinctions between form and matter of consciousness and between concept and intuition. As he then clearly recognized, these distinctions must obtain at every level of consciousness, even though at the more reflective levels the matter or content of intuition is itself generated through the spontaneity of the faculty of representation. It is what, at a previous level of representation, was a 'form of receptivity' but, at a more reflective level, is then made the object (i.e., the content) of a representation. With this claim, Reinhold of course relativizes the distinction between form and content. To be sure, he still tries to follow Kant by insisting on a strict distinction between *Anschauung*, or intuition broadly conceived, and *Sinnlichkeit*, i.e., on an ultimate irreducible distinction between 'spontaneity' and 'passivity'. But the question is whether he *can* maintain this distinction once he has granted that neither can form be identified *tout court* with spontaneity nor content with receptivity. Cf. "Erörterungen über den *Versuch einer Theorie des Vostellungsvermögens"* (1790), pp. 389–91, 394–7, 397–8.

57. *Theorie*, §XLVIII, p. 359 (Proposition).

58. *Theorie*, §XVI, pp. 241–42.

59. *Versuch über die Transzendentalphilosophie* (1790), Ch. 2. Also relevant is Maimon's *Essay Towards a New Logic or Theory of Thought* (see note 58). For references, see di Giovanni (1985), pp. 7, 32–6, and notes.

60. *Philosophischer Briefwechsel, nebst einem demselben vorangeschickten Manifest*, in *Streifereien im Gebiete der Philosophie*, 1793, vol. 3.

61. Cf. pp. 247–8; also pp. 252–4.

62. This is what Reinhold does in what appears to be a postscript to Book II of *Theorie*, starting from the bottom of p. 312 and including the theorems XXXIII–XXXVII.

63. Cf. *Theorie*, §XXVII, pp. 294–5; §XXXVIII, pp. 297–8; §XXIX, pp. 300–1.

64. Cf. *Theorie*, §XXII, pp. 276–7.

65. His position on the subject is ultimately inconclusive. In *Theorie*, §XXXVIII, p. 323, he tells us that they differ essentially. But how? If he means (as he seems to be saying on p. 328, see note 67) that representation is *potential* consciousness, then he would be conceding the point that there can indeed be representation without consciousness, and that consciousness is just a more complete form of representation.

66. *Theorie*, §XXXVIII, p. 327.

67. *Theorie*, §XXXVIII, pp. 327–8. Reinhold goes on to say that mere representation is studied in the general theory of representation. When considered in relation to subject and object, it is studied in the theory of cognition.

68. The issue of the continuity, or lack thereof, between the mechanism of nature and the teleology of the human mind was widely discussed before Kant, but especially by H. S. Reimarus (whose relevant works were in Kant's library), mostly with reference to Descartes's alleged automatism of animals. Reimarus repeatedly returned to this issue in *Instinctum Brutorum* (1725), in *Allgemeine Betrachtungen über die Triebe der Thiere* (1762), and in other works in between. On this subject, see Ferrini (2002).

69. Cf. *Theorie*, §XXXVIII, pp. 330–1.

70. Reinhold complained that Kant had failed to define the concept of consciousness adequately, and had restricted 'transcendental unity' to the level of conceptualization alone – as if the I that is the principle of that unity were not present at all level of consciousness, including that of sensation. ("Über das Verhältniß der Theorie des Vorstellungsvermögens zur Kritik der reinen Vernunft," *Beyträge* (1790), vol. I, pp. 305ff.). Such an objection makes sense only on the assumption that the I is a center of real life, a monad in Leibniz's sense. See also *Theorie*, §XLIX, pp. 363–5. Does the *Stoff* of sensibility belong to the natural organism or to representation as such? Apparently to both.

71. See Chapter 2, note 17 and Section 2.2.

72. Although on one occasion Reinhold refers to sense intuition as 'dark' *(dunkel)*, he explicitly and energetically rejects Leibniz's contention that the difference between sensation and concept is one of degree of distinctness of representation. *Theorie*, §XLIII, p. 346; *Theorie*, §XLVII, p. 358.

73. I shall come back to this aspect of Leibniz in the following chapter.

74. In his first eight Kantian Letters, published in *Der Teutsche Merkur*. See Chapter 1, note 29.

Chapter 4

1. *Zum Gebrauch der Vorlesungen in dem Michaelisferien* (Jena: Kröker, 1788).

2. Anonymous; in fact, C. J. Kraus, "Review of Ulrich's *Eleutheriologie,*" (1788). Kraus's main point is that Ulrich fails to bridge the gap between the physical 'can' (however broadly this can is construed to include conceptual activities) and the moral ought. Indeed, he makes things easy for himself by referring the readers for a discussion of the meaning of the absolute ought to his lectures (of which Kraus declares ignorance). AK VIII:454. Kraus also says that Ulrich raises questions that cannot be answered unless one knows not only that freedom is real, but also how it is constituted. AK VIII:459–60. Kant avoids these difficulties by claiming that freedom is real, yet that we are irreducibly ignorant regarding how the physical can and the moral ought are synthesized.

3. *Über die Lehre des Spinoza in Briefen an den Herren Moses Mendelssohn* (1789). Excerpts of the additions are included in *Jacobi*.

4. For the key text, see note 6.

5. Thomas Aquinas, *Summa contra gentiles*, LXXIII.

6. With reference to the *Confessio Philosophi* of 1673 (published posthumously but widely circulated also in his lifetime). *Confessio Philosophi, ein Dialog.* For Steno, see the Introduction, pp. 20–3. A critical text, accompanied by a French translation by Yvon Belaval, is also available (1961). Hunter (2001) also aptly refers to this text of Leibniz, pp. 116–26.

7. "Als ob jemand im Ernst diese Freiheit, sie zu gebrauchen, leugnete! Ich verstehe die Vorstellungen nicht, die sich der Kriticker bildete, als er dies las." *Confessio Philosophi,* p. 175, note 130.

8. Ulrich had already stated his position, in a much more scholastic form in *Institutiones Logicae et Metaphysicae* (1785), in Part II *(Institutiones Metaphysicæ)*, Ch. IV, §§90–109.

9. *Confessio Philosophi,* pp. 129.25–130.2.

10. See note 2.

11. *ALZ* (25 April 1788), no. 100, columns 180–1, AK VIII:457–8.

12. Chapter 1, Section 1.4.

13. I have anticipated the following Schmid–Rheberg–Reinhold debate in di Giovanni (2001b).

14. See note 8.

15. Carl Christian Erhard Schmid, *Versuch einer Moralphilosophie* (1790). There were several later revised editions of this work.

16. Chapter 2, Section 2.4.

17. Cf. §§154, 167–9.

18. Cf. the title of Section I (p. 16) of Ulrich's book. This was the only position assumed at the time to be consistent with the principle of sufficient reason. The principle was universally accepted as synonymous with rationality itself. Cf. Ulrich, *Institutiones,* Part II, §84.

19. We are interested in the following:

    K. L. Reinhold, "Über die Grundwahrheit der Moralität und ihr Verhältniß zur Grundwahrheit der Religion" (1791);

    "Über den bisher verkannte Unterschied zwischen dem uneigennützigen und dem eigennützigen Triebe, und zwischen diesen beyden Trieben und dem Willen" (1790–2b);

    "Erörterung des Begriffes von der Freyheit des Willens" ("Discussion of the Concept of Freedom of Will") (1790–2a).

    Also important is the fourth *Beytrag* in Reinhold's *Beyträge zur Berichtigung bisheriger Mißvertändnisse der Philosophen* (1794b). This contribution is made up of three essays:

    "Über das vollständige Fundament der Moral"; (1794b);
    "Über den Unterschied zwischen dem Wollen und dem Begehren in Rücksicht auf das Sittengesetz: an Herrn Professor Schmid in Jena" (1794c);
    "Über den Zusammenhang zwischen Begehren und Wollen in Rücksicht auf das Sittengesetz" (1794d).

20. Cf. Note 19. The reference here is to the second essay of *Beytrag* IV (Contribution IV).

21. See Note 19, pp. 228–9.

22. Letter VIII (see note 19), pp. 268–9, 276.
23. Letter VIII, p. 264.
24. Letter VIII, pp. 276–7, 290–1.
25. *Versuch einer neuen Theorie des menschlichen Vorstellungsvermögens*, p. 571. Cf. Chapter 3, Section 3.3 and note 40.
26. Letter VIII, pp. 282–4.
27. See, for instance, the attack mounted by Abicht in *Kritische Briefe über die Möglichkeit einer wahren wissenschaftlichen Moral, Theologie, Rechtslehre, empirischen Psychologie und Geschmakslehre, mit prüfender Hinsicht auf die Kantische Begründung dieser Lehre* (1793), Preface, pp. v–xvi.
28. *Die Metaphysik der Sitten*, AK VI: 226.12–16.
29. I have already dealt with this subject in di Giovanni (2001b).
30. For a sketch of Rehberg's place in the Hanoverian school of political thought, see Beiser (1992), pp. 305ff.
31. In 1714, the Hannoverian Electorate had passed over to England by way of the so-called personal union as Georg Ludwig of Hannover became King George I of England. From that time until 1837, when it was annexed by Prussia, Hannover and the surrounding region (*bar* a couple of French occupations) was England's foothold on the Continent.
32. *ALZ* (1788), no. 92, columns 105–7. See *Jacobi*, pp. 90, 362, for more details.
33. August Wilhelm Rehberg, *Cato* (Basel: Thurneysen, 1780), pp. xvi–104; se p. v, where the subject matter is explicitly declared to be "*die Bestimmung des Menschen.*"
34. August Wilhelm Rehberg, *Sämmtliche Schriften*, 4 vols., the third never published (1828, 1829, 1831). "I was one of the first, perhaps even the first, of those who directed to the depths of his [Spinoza's] metaphysical ideas, and the consequentiality of his conclusions, the admiration that has since become a kind of fashion in German philosophy. Not that I, as many a writer following after me, had found Spinoza's doctrine truly satisfactory, or had believed in it" (vol. 1, p. 7). Writing in 1828, Rehberg had, of course, Schelling in mind, or Herder before him, or, in general, the new Romanticism then in vogue.
35. *Sämmtliche Schriften*, vol. 1, pp. 6–7, 9. See also the original text of the essay, August Wilhelm Rehberg, *Abhandlungen über das Wesen und die Einschränkungen der Kräfte* (1779, p. 88). I can briefly summarize Rehberg's essay in this way. Force is equivalent to movement, and its effects to the influence that forces exercise on one another upon coming into collision. But there are conceptual difficulties distinguishing between forces and between their directions. There is no obvious determining ground. It is better, therefore, to consider forces only as objects of representations and to attribute the required distinctions to differences in representations. The same problem emerges, however, with respect to these last. How are we to distinguish between them? It is best to assume, as Leibniz does, that each force is a complete world unto itself, each differing from the rest according to the special degree of clarity with which it reflects what, in fact, every mind reflects in its own way. This assumption presupposes the existence of an infinite mind that perfectly represents what every finite mind also does, but more or less obscurely. But there are

difficulties in maintaining a serious distinction between this infinite mind and the other finite ones. These finite forces ineluctably tend to be absorbed into the one infinite mind as its internal modifications. We thus seem to be faced by an impossible alternative: either no infinite mind or one mind (i.e., to the exclusion of other finite ones). In Spinoza's system (which Rehberg brings into play only at the end), there is a mind that is at once infinite and exclusively one. This is a conceptually attractive position that leads, however, to harmful (i.e., pantheistic) consequences. Hence, we must stay with Leibniz.

It should be noted that Rehberg is very ambiguous, even disingenuous, in stating his conclusion. He turns to Leibniz as if he were the one who found a way of escaping Spinoza's dangerous but otherwise compelling position, ignoring the fact that he had brought Spinoza into the picture in the first place precisely in order to cope with what appeared an impossible conceptual difficulty in Leibniz.

36. *Über das Verhältniß der Metaphysik zur Religion* (1787).

37. For the first time, so far as I know.

38. *ALZ* (6 August 1788), nos. 188a–b, columns 345–52, 353–60. The text was republished by Rehberg in vol. 1 of his *Sämmtliche Schriften*, pp. 62–84. A critical edition can be found in Appendix I of Schultz (1975), pp. 230–56. Christian Gottfried Schütz (an editor of the *ALZ*) sent a copy of the review to Kant before publishing it, to find out "whether you might not like it." Letter of 23 June 1788. AK X:514. We do not have Kant's reply, if there was any

39. Two reviews of Rehberg's book were published in the *ALZ*. The first, (19 June 1788), no. 147, columns 617–21; the second, by Reinhold (26 June 1788), no. 153b, columns 689–96. The first review by Johann Schultz is both unsympathetic and confusing. A footnote to the second says that the author of the book, as well as the readers of the journal, should take it as a sign of the extraordinary attention given to the book that a special issue of the journal was being published in order to make room for a second review of it.

40. "Erläuterungen einiger Schwierigkeiten der natürlichen Theologie" *("Elucidations of Certain Difficulties in Natural Theology")*, *Der Teutsche Merkur* (September, 1788) 215–33; reproduced as "AnhangII" of Schultz (1975), pp. 257–71. The piece was explicitly intended as a reply to Reinhold, and was also so announced in a *Nachricht* (an announcement) published by Rehberg in the *Intelligenzblatt* of the *ALZ* (1788), no. 44, column 384.

41. Reinhold refers to Issues 188a and 188b of the journal, i.e., to Rehberg's review. See note 38. The review, like all reviews at the time, was anonymous, but its authorship was in fact transparent.

42. P. 8. See also *Über das Verhältniß der Metaphysik zur Religion*, p. 109. Rehberg could well think that, on this point, Kant and Spinoza agreed. See, e.g., Kant's statement in the KprV, AK V:94.21–9. Rehberg refers explicitly to this appendix of Book I of the KprV in "Erläuterungen einiger Schwierigkeiten der natürlichen Theologie," p. 665.

43. "The well taken comment has already been made that existence yields absolutely no concept. However, since the particular modes of existence are always appearances, hence contain something subjective in themselves, the

possibility of giving a concept that would indicate the essence of substance falls away," p. 60. Rehberg refers, quite in general, to Kant's *Der einzige mögliche Beweisgrund zu einer Demonstration des Daseins Gottes* (1763). He very likely has AK II:89 in mind.

44. Cf. his review of Kant's KprV, ALZ (1788), no. 188a, column 351 (end): "The principles of morality must be categorical, if there is to be a morality at all . . ."

45. Rehberg does not agree with Kant's way of doing it; this is the point of his criticism, p. 8, footnote.

46. Pp. 132–3. Rehberg does not contrast Kant with Spinoza and Wolff explicitly on this point, but the contrast would follow from Kant's assumption of an autonomous moral principle.

47. See the preceding note.

48. Cf. Rehberg's review of the KprV, *ALZ* (1788), no. 188b, column 357: "It appears indeed, as if by the word *universal* law more is being meant than the action itself to which the law is adapted in each case. But this universality indicates [. . .] only a negative determination . . ."

49. I am basing this interpreting on the fifth section of *Über das Verhältniß der Metaphysik zur Religion*, pp. 108–62.

50. Though 'liberal' in a modern sense of the word, Rehberg was in his own day a typical Tory. He sought rationality first of all in historically well-established situations. The fact that there might be different moral universes bestows authoritative value on the tradition justifying any of them. Rehberg was 'conservative' in the sense that he opposed any social engineering pursued in the name of absolute reason, the kind that was being pursued at the time by the French revolutionaries.

51. On pp. 138–43, Rehberg also attacks moral optimism, or the belief that everything works for the best of all possible worlds on the ground that it blinds us to the uncertainties and the shortcomings that beset any course of action. That kind of optimism fosters intolerance. This is a recurrent theme in Rehberg, but see especially pp. 121–2.

52. Cf. p. 132, note 1. I am expanding on Rehberg's point.

53. See especially pp. 124–31.

54. Review of Kant's KprV, *ALZ* (1788), no. 188b, columns 353–4, 356–7. On this matter, Rehberg had appealed to Kant's own authority. Cf. "Erläuterungen einiger Schwierigkeiten der natürlichen Theologie," p. 221 and footnote (cf. KprV, AK V:102.14–36).

55. *Über das Verhältniß der Metaphysik zur Religion*, pp. 135–8. Also the review of KprV, *ALZ* (1788), no. 188b, column 355.

56. *Über das Verhältniß der Metaphysik zur Religion*, pp. 135–8. Also, the review of KprV, *ALZ* (1788), no. 188b, column 355.

57. Jacobi found Rehberg's historicism just as unacceptable as the rationalism of a Spinoza. In his opinion, it ended up relativizing values. See, on this subject, *Jacobi*, pp. 84–5, note 40.

58. *Über das Verhältniß der Metaphysik zur Religion*, p. 159.

59. This point had been made by Jacobi from the beginning, in the first edition of the *Spinoza-Letters*, p. 59. The argument was presented by Jacobi in an

appendix to one of his letters to Mendelssohn, pp. 56–108. But see also Supplement VII added to the second edition.

60. I have found this same picture of reality, but attributed to Leibniz, in a recent book by an eminent physicist, in an effort to save the appearances of experiences while at the same time bringing quantum mechanics to its logical cosmological conclusions. Barbour (2000).

61. See, for instance, in the second edition, the final pages of Supplement V (357 ff.) and Supplement VI.

62. Mendelssohn was dead by that time.

63. Second edition, p. 365. Re. Fichte, see Chapter 6, Section 6.4 and note 86 and 87.

64. Second edition, p. 366.

65. Second edition, p. 374.

66. Second edition, p. 366.

67. Supplement VI in the second edition.

68. Cf. the first edition, pp. 154–7.

69. In the second edition.

70. How accurate was Jacobi's report of that conversation is, of course, a matter of debate.

Chapter 5

1. For a brief but informative account of this exchange, see Breazeale (1988), pp. 307–12.

2. See the editorial introduction to my translation of the work (Cambridge University Press, 1996).

3. See Kant's account of the genesis of the book in his Letter to Stäudlin, 4 May 1793. AK XI:414–15.

4. Cf. Chapter 4, Section 4.1.

5. Indeed, no less an authority than Daniel Dennett has made a career disputing it.

6. Cf. Kuehn (2001), p. 132.

7. There were, of course, antecedents for it in the nominalistic and voluntaristic tradition both in philosophy and in theology.

8. See Chapter 1, Section 1.4 and note 43.

9. See the texts already cited in Chapter 1, Section 1.4 and note 55. Also, C.pr.V. AK V:99: "If [...] we were capable of another view, namely an intellectual intuition, [...] then we would become aware that this whole chain of appearances, with respect to all that the moral law is concerned with, depends on the spontaneity of the subject as a thing in itself."

10. Poor Casanova was subjected to this psychological torture. He beat the system by escaping from jail. Of course, this line of criticism is in crucial respects unfair to Kant. His theory of moral autonomy was revolutionary and, in the Prussia of Frederick the Great, could have had politically revolutionary consequences as well. It is the theory that in fact animates our modern sense of individualism. At issue here, however, is not Kant's moral inspiration but his critical system. We are saying that this system does not hang together

well, which is exactly what his first critics also contended. One may also have reasons to complain about Kant's moral intuitions, at least as displayed in the casuistry of his *Metaphysics of Morals.*

11. "Only *rationalism* of judgements is suitable to the use of moral concepts, since it draws from sensible nature nothing more than what pure reason can also think for itself, i.e., conformity with law, and transfers into the supersensible nothing but what can, conversely, be really exhibited by actions in the sensible world in accordance with the formal rule of a law in general." AK V:71.

12. Kuehn (2001), p. 318.

13. AK IV:373, note.

14. "The concept of freedom, in so far as its reality is proved by an apodictic law of practical reason, constitutes the *keystone* of the whole structure of a system of pure reason; even of speculative reason." AK V: 3–4. Also, AK V:121; XIX:110 (#6612).

15. The point is made at the very opening, with the claim that "it is impossible to think of anything at all in the world, or indeed even beyond, that could be considered good without limitation except a **good will**" (AK IV:393). The question is what constitutes a good will unconditionally, and this is demonstrated to be 'duty' in a series of three reflections, each constituting one section of the book. The book advances progressively from the standpoint of common rational cognition to that of critique.

16. For Kant's preoccupation with Garve's recent translation of Cicero's ethics, and his possibly taking indirect issue with both Cicero and Garve, see Kuehn (2001), pp. 278ff, p. 485, note 21.

17. For instance, A732/B760: "the mathematical method of definition cannot be imitated in philosophy."

18. AK V:411: "It is clear that all moral concepts have their seat and origin completely a priori in reason."

19. There is an analogy, as we have just indicated, between Kant's method in defining the moral object and the practice of the mathematicians in constructing their objects. A perhaps even more instructive analogy can be drawn, however, between Kant's method and that of the jurists. In their practices, the main concern of the jurists is the authenticity of the law and the consistent application of its norm. The maintenance of 'lawfulness' (law and order) is their overarching interest. This interest, according to Kant, also motivates moral life. The difference, of course, is that for Kant the moral law draws its authority from practical reason itself. Its source is the norm-setting capacity of reason.

20. AK V:46: "The *exposition* of the supreme principle of practical reason is now finished, that is, it has been shown, first, what it contains [. . .], and then what distinguishes it from all other practical principles."

21. AK V:43: "Now, nature in the most general sense is the existence of things under law."

22. See, for instance, the paragraph immediately following V:48, the passage just quoted on p. 47.

23. Cf. Kuehn (2001), pp. 397–8. It is strange that Kuehn finds this doctrine of Kant strange. The doctrine is essential to Kant's idealism.

24. AK IV:421. Cf. AK V:30, §7.
25. The biblical overtones of this position are very clear. In a modern cultural setting, this obligation might just as well be defined as one of having to care for an otherwise fragile nature.
26. "All morality rests on ideas, and its reflection [*Bild*] in the human being is at all times incomplete." AK XIX:108 (#6611)
27. Kuehn (2001), p. 344.
28. He does in *Religion*, AK VI:38.
29. "'Creation' is a concept that does not apply to phenomenal nature, but nature as a noumenon (i.e. such as we have no knowledge of)." AK V:102.
30. *Religion*, AK VI:34–5.
31. "*Mutmasslicher Anfang der Menschengeschlecte*" ("Conjectural Beginning of Human History"), AK VIII:115.
32. Thus Marx, an idealist *malgré soi*, could say that, although reason is itself a product of nature, capitalism became possible as an overriding social force only when natural desires were infinitized by the introduction of the idea of abstract (monetary) value. Kierkegaard, another idealist *malgré soi*, pointed out that it takes the ascetic ideal of the monk for sexuality to become a temptation. Don Giovanni (with his infinite sexual desire) is the heir of the ascetic monk.
33. The most extensive attempt at this transition was performed in his *Metaphysische Anfangsgründe der Naturwissenschaft*, 1786.
34. For a brief but very informative account of Kant's struggle for this transition and the critical problem that motivated it, see Förster (1993), especially pp. xxixff.
35. I.e., "So act that the maxim of your will could always hold at the same time as a principle in a giving of universal law." AK V:30.
36. The two parts of the work were originally published separately in the same year.
37. A posteriori, as Kant famously also says.
38. A priori.
39. It can be argued that in his resolution of the mathematical antinomies Kant has already transgressed his critical brief and has committed himself to a specific metaphysical position. It is one thing to say that our experience of spatial and temporal borders is always ambiguous and reformable. In lived experience, space reaches as far as we can reach and time as far as we have historical or geological memory. It is also one thing to say that the idea of 'world', as the totality of all physical objects, is only an abstract construct that cannot resolve by itself the question of whether the world has or does not have a beginning in space and time, or whether it is or is not made up of ultimately indivisible elements. But it is quite another thing to say that such questions are intrinsically unanswerable. They are indeed unanswerable on Kant's classical assumptions regarding space and time. There is, however, no reason in principle why such concepts as totality, space, and time may not acquire a specific meaning in some theoretical context, such as we do not know yet, that would allow answers to the stated questions for which credible empirical evidence can be adduced.

40. I am, of course, referring to Hegel. Cf. di Giovanni (2003b), p. 375.

41. Ian Hunter quite rightly says the same regarding the political state, according to Kant. The state is at once totally legitimate yet totally illegitimate. Hunter (2001), pp. 375ff.

42. It seems that in the *Critique of Pure Reason*, the postulates are required in order to make the idea of the moral law effective. Cf. A812/B840–A813/B841. In the *Critique of Practical Reason*, the presupposed effectiveness of the law gives credibility instead to the postulates.

43. In one passage of *Religion*, Kant speaks of 'moral happiness', which he contrasts with physical happiness. But this is not a standard usage. By moral happiness, Kant means "the *constancy* of a disposition that always advances in goodness," and from which, therefore, physical happiness should be expected to follow as its due. *Religion*, VI:67.

44. Anonymous, but very likely by W. F. Pistorius, "Review of KprV" (1794); see especially 96–100. Pistorius calls the connection in Kant between moral virtue and natural happiness a "mismatch" *(Mißverhältnis)* that requires God to be held together (99–100). He also points out that by freedom Kant means indeed spontaneity, but a spontaneity of the sort that reason alone supposedly enjoys. Kant is not an indeterminist. Rather, he subscribes to some sort of fatalism of reason. Freedom is understood not in opposition to determinism as such, but to natural determinism, i.e., to external determinism as contrasted to self-willed, self-induced determinism. However, granted this, it follows that, to the extent that man is part of nature, he is in no way free and in no way a subject to whom moral action can be imputed. In Kant we have an individual who actually belongs to two radically different worlds: the intelligible and the sensible. We have in fact two radically different I's: one intelligible and the other sensible. And the great mystery in Kant's philosophy (despite the imagery that Kant uses or the Pauline metaphors of the struggle in man between two principles) is how the two are to be synthesized (101–3). Pistorius makes fun of Kant's distinction between the intelligible and the sensible. He reminds the reader of the story of the farmer who told his bishop, who loved hunting, that it was unseemly for a spiritual ruler to overrun the land of his subjects because of love of sport. And when the bishop replied that he had a temporal side as well as a spiritual one, the farmer went on to inquire where the spiritual side would be when the devil came to take the material one (103–4).

45. See note 44 (re. Pistorius); cf. pp. 104–5. If I understand Rehberg correctly (but I might be interpreting too much), he also makes this point. If the satisfaction of the senses is to be part of happiness, then sensibility too must be part of God's creation, just like freedom. But sensibility is antithetical to freedom. Hence we find ourselves in the impossible situation of having to deny freedom for the sake of obtaining the kind of happiness that moral perfection (predicated on freedom) requires. Anonymous (actually, Rehberg), "Review of the *Critique of Practical Reason*," *ALZ* (1788c); see 356–7, 359.

46. Kuehn (2001), p. 422.

47. This is how wrong the Jena theologians had been in thinking that in Kant they had found a new apologist for their faith.

48. *Anthropologie in pragmatischer Hinsicht* (1798).
49. Kuehn (2001), p. 406.
50. Not, however, according to the order of publication. The feelings associated with the *Critique of Judgement* are treated in the second part, as if bridging the *Critique of Pure Reason* and the *Critique of Practical Reason*.
51. It is "of the utmost necessity to construct a pure moral philosophy which is completely freed from everything which may be only empirical and thus belong to anthropology." AK IV:38852.
52. *Religion*, VI:19ff. I am following Kant's argument as it unfolds. I shall refer specifically only to key texts.
53. My gratitude to Kierkegaard's Climacus, who eloquently gave expression to this state of original sin. Climacus had read his Kant.
54. "Because the law worketh wrath: for where no law is, there is no transgression." St. Paul's Epistle to the Romans, 4.15. "I would not have known sin except through the law." Romans, 7:7. Cf. AK XXVIII:1079.
55. *Religion*, VI:78, note.
56. *Religion*, VI:39: "What the Apostle says might indeed hold true of human beings universally: 'There is no distinction here, they are all under sin – there is none righteous (in the spirit of the law), no, not one'." Romans, 3:9–10.
57. This step is not explicit in VI:61. But see VI:62.
58. This is the subject of Sections IV and V. *Religion*, VI:100ff.
59. This is especially, but not exclusively, the subject of Section VI. *Religion*, VI:109–14.
60. *Religion*, VI:110. Kant does not mention philosophers by title in this context, but they seem to be the only contenders in the field as defined by Kant. Of course, they would have to be critical philosophers.
61. Division II of Book III, *Religion*, VI:124ff.
62. See Kuehn (2001), p. 250, among other places.
63. Cf. Kuehn (2001), pp. 153ff.
64. The last italics are mine.
65. This is the best that I can make out from the account of his daily life.

Chapter 6

1. *ALZ* (March 1794), nos 14, 15, 686–91.
2. AK VI:226.
3. "Einige Bemerkungen über die in der Einleitung zu den metaphysischen Anfangsgründen der Rechtslehre von I. Kant aufgestelleten Begriffe von der Freyheit des Willens" in K. L. Reinhold, *Auswahl vermischter Schriften* (1797); see pp. 383–87. Reinhold's point is that we are not true to the facts of conscience if we do not distinguish (as he implies Kant fails to do) between reason and its use in actual praxis.
4. Ibid. See especially p. 385, where Reinhold speaks of an "elasticity of the I" and of an interplay between the I and a not-I. These are definitely not Kant's terms.

5. One should also include C. B. Bardili, *Ursprung des Begriffes von der Willensfreiheit* (1796). But this article would take us into Reinhold's development past the present controversy.

6. Leonhard Creuzer, *Skeptische Betrachtungen über die Freiheit des Willens, mit Hinsicht auf die neuesten Theorien über dieselbe* (*Skeptical Considerations Regarding Freedom of the Will, in view of the latest theories on the subject*), (Gießen: Heyer, 1793). For a recent study of Creuzer and his historical context, see Tafani (1999).

7. In typical scholastic style, Creuzer divides the concept of freedom into 'metaphysical' and 'moral', and then gives a schema of all positions possible according as the concept is taken in each signification. The schema is organized on the basis of Kant's table of categories. Cf. pp. 30–8. Creuzer's history of the concept follows this schema.

8. E.g., pp. 243ff. For Ulrich and his *Eleutheriologie oder Freyheit und Nothwendigkeit* (1788), see Chapter 4. Section 4.1.

9. I am somewhat editing an otherwise very clumsy construction.

10. Pp. 250–2.

11. *Über die sittliche Güte aus uninteressirtem Wohlwollen* (1792).

12. *Über die sittliche*; cf. pp. 40ff. Gebhard cites Adam Smith as the one who first introduced the system of 'sympathy' to complement the system of otherwise mere 'self-love.' This system of sympathy is a highly honorable one. Gebhard, however, wants to test it against Kant's theory. He grounds it on it. Cf. Introduction, pp. 1–12. The motivation for Gebhard's book was a series of letters published by E. Christian Trapp in the *Braunschweiges Journal* in 1790 and 1791. In these letters, which he entitled "Neue Briefe über die Kantische Philosophie" (1790, 1791), with clear reference to Reinhold's earlier Kantian Letters, Trapp had severely criticized Kant's moral theory. He confessed to being unable to understand Kant. However, to the extent that he could make anything out of his theory, he found it highly unconvincing, hardly a better alternative to traditional eudaimonism. Trapp objected to Kant on many grounds: for his strategy of assuming a law for the sake of then positing a lawgiver (1790, pp. 442–50); for reducing happiness to a mere reward for moral virtue (450–60); for taking the need for either reward or punishment as the basis for our belief in a future life (460–9); and, finally, for thinking that the need for a lawgiver, as required by the law, would constitute a stable foundation for our belief in God (460–9). So far as Trapp was concerned, traditional theory provided a better basis for all the beliefs that Kant was now reintroducing on moral grounds. He found Kant's theory a veritable "garden of errors." These letters were the occasion for Gebhard's book. See the Preface of his book, pp. 5–12.

13. *ALZ* (30 October 1793), no. 303, columns 201–5. GA I.2, 7–14.

14. *ALZ* (31 October 1793), no. 304, columns 209–15. GA I.2, 21–9.

15. This is the chronology of the dispute:

(1) 1793: Creuzer publishes his book with Schmid's introduction to it.

(2) *ALZ* (1793), no. 303: Fichte reviews the book anonymously, accusing Schmid of undermining even the possibility of morality. In the following issue, no. 304, Fichte also reviews Friedrich Heinrich

Gebhard's book. Fichte attacks Gebhard, who had deferred to Schmid for the right answer to the problem of the relation of happiness to morality.

(3) Gebhard is offended by Fichte's tone and publishes an antireview in the *Gothaischen gelehrten Zeitungen* (December 1793). Schmid also publishes a "Declaration" (*Erklärung*) in the *ALZ* (15 February 1794), letting it be known that he was not the author of the review of Gebhard's book (as some might have thought) and also taking the occasion to accuse the reviewer of Creuzer's book of falsifying his own position. By taking issue with the reviews of both Gebhard's and Creuzer's books, Schmid gives implicitly to understand that the author of both was the same.

(4) Fichte replies with a "Counterdeclaration" [*Gegenerklärung über des Hn. Prof. Schmids Erklärung*] in the *ALZ* (26 March 1794), no. 29, declaring his authorship of both reviews. GA I.2, 75–6.

(5) Fichte tries to patch up things with Schmid (cf. Letters to K. A. Böttinger, 2 April 1794; to G. Hufeland, 8 March 1794; to wife, 20 and 26 May 1794). GA III.3, nos. 194, 190, 201, 202.

(6) Schmid points to the dangers of Fichte's idealism, without mentioning him by name, in the Preface to his *Grundriß des Naturrechts* (1795).

(7) Schmid produces the outline of his philosophy: "Bruchstücke aus einer Schrift über die Philosophie und ihrer Principien" (1795a).

(8) Fichte replies with "Vergleichung des vom Hrn Prof. Schmid aufgestellten Systems mit der Wissenschaftslehre" in the same journal (1796b). GA I.3, 235–71. Here's where Fichte proclaims Schmid nonexistent (at the very end). A translation of excerpts can be found in Breazeale (1988), pp. 316ff.

(9) On 23 June 1796: in a notice in the *Reichs-Anzeiger*, Schmid declares that he wants to end his dispute with Fichte and leave the matter up to the judgment of the public.

Others contributed to the debate peripherally. One influential author who summarized the situation and gave perhaps the most sophisticated version of a scholastically reinterpreted Kant was Christian Friedrich Michaelis in his *Über die sittliche Natur und Bestimmung des Menschen. Ein Versuch zur Erläuterung über I. Kant's Kritik der praktischen Vernunft* (1796–7). Michaelis seems to side with Reinhold. Like Reinhold, he reintroduces the traditional cosmology of freedom, but, again like Reinhold, he takes this cosmology to constitute hypotheses rather than knowledge. Moral faith adds no new insight to these hypotheses but a qualitatively new conviction in holding them. See, for instance, vol. 2, pp. 226–7.

16. *ALZ* (1793), columns 204–5. GA I.2, 13:1–14:15. The theory "completely abolishes morality."

17. *ALZ* (1793), column 211. GA I.2, 24:24–9.

18. See note 15, item (8).

19. See note 15, item (8).

20. Reinhold to Erhard, 2 August, 1796. Quoted in Breazeale (1988), p. 355. Kantian philosophy seemed to be undergoing "a hideous change." "More and more [it] seems to be turning into a shameless display of practical egotism."

21. *ALZ* (1793), column 209. GA I.2, 22:3–6.

22. *ALZ* (1793), column 202. GA I.2, 9:1–13.

23. *ALZ* (1793), columns 203–4. GA I.2, 10:30–12:16.

24. *ALZ* (1793), column 203. GA I.2, 10:11–21.

25. Cf. *ALZ* (1793), column 203. GA I.2, 10:4–16. Fichte does offer a quick explanation, however cryptic: "The apparent immediate perception [*Empfindung*] of self-determination is no immediate perception but an undetected consequence of the *non*-perception of the determining force [*Kraft*]." 10:9–10.

26. The first printing omitted the name of the author in the frontispiece (accidentally, as it was claimed). The public took the essay to be Kant's.

27. *ALZ* (1794), nos. 47–9, columns 369–74, 377–83, 385–9. English tr., *Between Kant and Hegel*, pp. 137–57.

28. I have already touched on this issue in di Giovanni (1992), pp. 431–6.

29. Published in Königsberg.

30. Cf. §1, GA I.1, 18.

31. §2, GA I.1, 22–3; §3, GA I.1, 36.

32. §3, GA I.1, 36–7.

33. §3, GA I.1, 37.

34. §4, GA I.1, 41.

35. Cf., for instance, Kant's statements in *Groundwork of the Metaphysics of Morals* (1785), AK IV: 412:27–30: "so ist der Wille nichts anderes als praktische Vernunft" ("and so the will is nothing other than practical reason."). Schelling will claim that it is more accurate to say that practical reason is will. This inversion is significant because it shows how he (and Fichte, whom he was commenting on) thought of reason as a determination of will. Cf. *Allgemeine Übersicht der neuesten philosophischen Literatur* (1797–8), Werke, vol. 4, p. 159 (lines 27–8). In later editions the *Übersicht* was renamed *Abhandlungen zur Erläuterung des Idealismus der Wissenschaftslehre*.

36. §2, GA I.1, 31, 35–6.

37. §2, GA I.1, 33.

38. §3, GA I.1, 38–9.

39. Cf. Fichte's strong statements in *Grundlage der gesamten Wissenschaftslehre* (1794–5), §8, II and III, GA, I.2, 422–5. Also, §4, D, p. 298. However, inasmuch as reflection can also imply an attempt to grasp the mind and its products as if they were mere entities or ready-made facts – a fault to which Fichte, Schelling, and Hegel found Reinhold to be especially prone – the 'standpoint of reflection' often assumes in post-Kantian idealism pejorative connotations.

40. Cf. *Über den Unterschied des Geistes und des Buchstabens in der Philosophie* (Lectures given in the summer semester of 1794), GA II.3, Lecture II, 330:412. Cf. also *Zweite Einleitung in der Wissenschaftslehre* (*Second Introduction to the Wissenschaftslehre*, 1797), GA I.4, 225:10–13. English tr. Breazeale (1994).

41. Klotz's recent monograph (2002) stresses the immanent character of Fichte's idealism with reference to Fichte's unpublished lectures *De nova methodo*.

42. [*Erste*] *Einleitung in der Wissenschaftslehre* (1797), GA I.4, 186–208, §5. English tr. [*First*] *Introduction to the Wissenschaftslehre*, in Breazeale (1994), pp. 7–35.

43. *Second Introduction to the Wissenschaftslehre* (cf. note 40), GA I.2, 219; 217–18 are also relevant. Intellectual intuition cannot be comprehended but must be taken on faith, just as much as sense-intuition.

44. In the following exposition, I shall enter page and line numbers in the text itself.

45. We know that Fichte had been meditating on Reinhold's *Versuch*. See his notes on Reinhold's "Elementarphilosophie," and the comments on this text by its editor, Reinhart Lauth: "Eigne Meditationen über Elementarphilosophie" ("Personal Meditations on the Philosophy of the Elements"), GA II.3, 21–177.

46. Fichte's term is 'subject' as well as *Gemüth*. The latter is normally translated as 'mind'. 'Mental constitution' is also a possible translation.

47. This aspect of desire is made explicit by Fichte in what follows immediately, when he introduces the notion of the pleasant and then of the satisfactory (*Glück*).

48. I am at the end of Section I of §2.

49. It is understood, of course, that the 'form' of representation derives from the faculty itself. It is the active moment of representing.

50. From now on, I am really reconstructing Fichte's otherwise very dense text. Fichte is simply opposing, but at the same time relating, 'impulse' and 'feeling of respect'.

51. "This feeling [of respect] is as it were the point at which the rational and the sensible nature of finite beings flow intimately together." GA I.1 142.23–5.

52. I am interpreting, GA I.1 142:1–19.

53. Fichte says "the law" – but it amounts to the same thing. GA I.1 143:5–13.

54. Cf. GA I.1 143:18ff. The question is whether we should think of respect as being directed in the first place to humanity in general or to oneself. The point, of course, is that, in being directed to oneself, one thereby establishes the universal validity of one's (thereby moral) self.

55. Reinhold had made this distinction the centerpiece of his moral theory. Cf. Chapter 4, Section 4.2 and note 24.

56. GA I.1, 144:10–18.

57. GA I.1, 146:20–40.

58. "We are not the legislators of the human mind but rather its historians – not, of course, journalists but rather writers of pragmatic history." *Über den Begriff der Wissenschaftslehre oder der sogenannten Philosophie* (1794b), §7, GA I.2, 147.

59. See note 45.

60. GA, I,1, 150:22–35.

61. Cf. the concluding pages of §2, GA I.1, 151–3.

62. Cf. the last chapter of the book, where Gebhard criticizes Trapp's objection to Kant. For references, see note 12.

63. "Now Professor Schmid, who is thought to be one of the earliest and most conscientious experts on the Kantian philosophy, removes once and for all any trace of difficulty from this philosophy. He produced the desired eternal peace and engenders the most intimate bond between dogmatic and Critical philosophers. For Professor Schmid, the world is something which is completely finished without any assistance from reason; everything is just as it is. More is thereby conceded to the dogmatist than he ever coveted in his wildest dreams." *Vergleichung,* Breazeale (1988), p. 320. Fichte had already made the point that Hegel was to make again in the Preface to his *Phenomenology* by citing Lessing: "Truth is not a ready-made coin." GW IX.30:28.

64. *Vergleichung,* Breazeale (1988), p. 329.

65. See note 39.

66. Reinhold had found a more lucrative position at Kiel, where he remained until his death in 1823.

67. Fichte himself declared that a better version than any previously published was to be found in his *Grundlage des Naturrechts nach Principien der Wissenschaftslehre* (1796a), GA I..4, 1–165. See Fichte's Letter to Reinhold of 4 July 1797, GA III.3, no. 359, p. 69. Yet another version, arguably even better, was the one that he delivered in a later series of lectures (1796/9) but was never published in his lifetime. It was preserved only in notes. *Wissenschaftslehre nova methodo,* GA III.3, 69, no. 359. English tr., Breazeale (1992).

68. *ALZ,* (1798), no. 5, columns 33–9; no. 6, columns 41–7; no. 7, columns 49–56; no. 8, columns 57–63; no. 9, columns 65–9. The text of the review can also be found appended to Selling (1938).

69. The announcement came in the Preface to *Auswahl vermischter Schriften,* vol. 2 (1797a), pp. x–xi.

70. "If pure science is possible, this is so, indeed *not* THROUGH *critical* philosophy, yet *not* WITHOUT it. Reason must must first learn how to become acquainted with itself, and how to gain insight into itself, in its merely *natural* use . . . before it can think with any *determinateness* of an ARTIFICIAL use." Column 38. Typographical stresses were common at the time but were especially used, and abused, by Reinhold.

71. For the Spinoza–Jacobi pedigree of the notion, see Chapter 3, Section 3.2.2 and note 24.

72. See, for instance, columns 53–8, 60–5.

73. Cf. Fichte to Reinhold, 22 April 1799, Fragment, GA III.3, 330.29–30. Fichte distinguishes between 'real consciousness' and 'speculative thought', or between the standpoint of life and that of philosophy. According to Fichte, the two standpoints have nothing in common. Speculation is only a means of understanding life. The philosopher must therefore cease to philosophize in order to lunge into life (333.2–33). However, this should not mean (as it does for Reinhold) that life is not as it is represented by speculation abstractly. Since ordinary experience of reality is in fact the product of freedom, its day-to-day problems are exactly what speculative reflection diagnoses them to be. Ordinary experience fails to recognize them for what they truly are because it constantly forgets its origin in freedom.

74. [*First*] *Introduction to the Wissenschaftslehre:* "The kind of philosophy one chooses thus depends on the kind of man one is." GA I.4, 434.

75. For sensation (*Empfindung*) as requiring interpretation, cf. *Grundlage*, §10, #20, GA I.2, 437:27–33; §7, C, p. 419.
76. Reinhold to Fichte, 14 February 1797, GA III.3, no. 359.
77. Fichte had signaled this inconsistency to Reinhold in the letter of 14 February 1797.
78. The translation is somewhat free. Reinhold's German is always convoluted.
79. Reinhold will eventually say this explicitly, as we shall see in Chapter 7. Section 7.2.1.
80. The translation is somewhat free.
81. Fichte makes this point quite clearly in the draft of a letter intended for Reinhold. There is a difference between the standpoint of ordinary consciousness, which is also that of science and of traditional metaphysics, and that of the *Wissenschaftslehre* (of 'speculation', as Fichte calls it in this context). The former aims at the actual knowledge of things. This is the standpoint of life, i.e., of those immersed in the actual doing and experiencing of things. It gives rise to the "system of the TOTALITY of OBJECTIVE RATIONAL BEING." The latter, on the contrary, presupposes the freedom of withdrawing oneself from this immersion in immediate experience, i.e., of detaching oneself from it, in order to discover and describe how that experience is possible. It gives rise to the system of the "TOTALITY OF SUBJECTIVE RATIONAL BEING." The two standpoints will never meet except in the mind of a philosopher who assumes the two at once. Nonetheless, neither is possible without the other. And although the standpoint of life might appear as fundamental and independent (this is how Reinhold took it), in fact it entails throughout the kind of freedom (the norm-setting subjectivity, that is) that speculation, for its part, exhibits artificially purely on its own. "LIFE, *understood as active surrender to the mechanism [of nature], is impossible* WITHOUT THAT ACTIVITY AND FREEDOM *(i.e., speculation)* WHICH THUS SURRENDERS ITSELF, *even though not every individual is clearly conscious of it.*" In other words, to be rational means to have set up the subjective norms of meaning that constitute the world within which we are immersed in living experience even before we are reflectively aware of having given rise to that world. See the fragment of Fichte's letter to Reinhold of 22 April 1799, GA III.3, no. 440.
82. This is how Fichte had characterized Reinhold's *Elementarphilosophie* from the beginning. Cf. letter to Reinhold of 28 April 1795, GA II.3, no. 283, Brezeale (1988), p. 389.
83. "Thus, insofar as metaphysics is taken to be a system of real knowledge which is produced merely by thinking, then Kant and I both entirely reject the possibility of metaphysics." Letter to Reinhold of 22 April 1799, GA III.3, no. 440, Breazeale (1988), p. 433.
84. In the early nineteenth century, Schleiermacher's and Fries's forms of neo–Kantianism were really developments of what still was, basically, popular philosophy. The Traugott Krug who took over Kant's chair at Königsberg at his death, and whom Hegel lampooned in one of his earliest essays was himself a self-declared popular philosopher.
85. Letter to Jacobi of 30 August 1795, GA III.3, no. 307, Breazeale (1988), p. 412.

86. P. 351; *Jacobi*, p. 365.
87. GA I.5:48, note.
88. Fichte uses this notion of actuosity throughout his *Second Introduction to the Wissenschaftslehre*. The term '*essentia actuosa*' is in Spinoza. *Ethics*, II, Prop. 3, scholion.
89. Cf. di Giovanni (1994), pp. 88ff., 116.
90. See Chapter 4, Section 4.3.2 and note 47.
91. I am not in any way implying that there was a dialogue between the two men.

Chapter 7

1. *Über die Paradoxien der neuesten Philosophie* (1799b), p. 93.
2. Friedrich Karl Forberg, "Entwickelung des Begriffs der Religion," (1798). As usual, the article was published anonymously. For a quick statement of the situation, see Breazeale (1994), pp. 104–5, note 76. A campaign against Fichte had been waged in the journal *Eudämonia, oder Deutsches Volksglück* since 1796. For this journal, see Beiser (1992), pp. 326–34.
3. The most recent account is found in La Vopa (2001). This study is especially interesting because it portrays Fichte as a rhetorician who was deliberately intent on shaping a new style of philosophical and social discourse. His juridical loss in the atheism case was for him also a rhetorical defeat.
4. Fichte's Letter to Reinhold, 22 April 1799. GA III.3:327.9–26, no. 440.
5. *Sendschreiben an I. C. Lavater und J. G. Fichte über den Glauben an Gott* (1799a), pp. 6–7.
6. Fragments of this section were presented at the 1998 *Reinhold-Tagung* at Bad-Homburgh, and have since appeared in somewhat different form in di Giovanni (2003a).
7. See note 1.
8. See note 5.
9. Jacobi's letter was concluded 21 March; the opening of Reinhold's is dated 27 March. *Jacobi an Fichte* (1799). For the dating, see p. 57.
10. See note 11. Reinhold himself gave to understand in his second writing (pp. 3–4) that he was developing there themes he had already explored in the previous work.
11. See note 12. Reinhold himself gave to understand in his second writing (pp. 3–4) that he was developing there themes he had already explored in the previous work.
12. Reinhold speaks of a "praktisches Selbstdenken in der natürlichen Überzeugung" ("a practical reflective thinking within natural conviction"), pp. 54–55; cf. pp. 48ff., especially p. 52.
13. Cf. pp. 52ff. It is interesting to compare what Reinhold has to say about reflection and abstraction with Jacobi's statements. The two men are saying the same thing, but with different conclusions. See *Jacobi an Fichte*, pp. 19–26.
14. "Freedom's *natural* self-intuition in the consciousness of duty is present in *each* human being. This self-intuition is necessary to the person as person, and to this extent is *mere matter of fact* – a fact that the human being *finds* within himself by himself, without knowing how he got to it" (pp. 70–1).

15. The glosses (*factum, agere*) are mine. See also pp. 54–5: "Philosophical reflective thinking [*'Selbstdenken'*: i.e., literally, 'self-thinking'] is distinguished from this practical reflective thinking [at work] in natural conviction in that, unlike the other, it is in no way presupposed in the field of experience by free actions. It is not necessary to the person as such; it does not in any way belong to the essence of humanity. One can become aware of oneself; one can act freely, perform one's duty, etc., without any philosophizing. And since that [philosophical] reflection cannot, moreover, be compelled through actual perception – on the contrary, it should abstract from it – it must be a free reflective thinking pure and simple." In other words (pp. 56–9), it must be the result of a free resolution to undertake it, an artificial operation (*Kunstoperation*) resulting in a mere artificial product (*Kunstwerk*). See also pp. 70–1: "There is present in every human being, in the consciousness of duty, a natural intuition that freedom has of itself [*Selbstanschauung*]. This self-intuition is necessary to the person as person and is, therefore, mere *factum* [*Tatsache*], such as a human being discovers in himself, without knowing how he got to it. A philosopher's artificial self-intuition of freedom is present only in the philosopher. It is necessary only to philosophy as such. To the human being as human being, this artificial self-intuition is contingent, and is brought about in him only through his voluntary striving for pure knowledge, and through an abstraction which is impossible in natural consciousness. The philosopher knows *how* he got to that self-intuition; it is his own *operation* [*Tathandlung*]." Notice that I translate *Thatsache* with the Latin *factum* because the German word denotes a 'deed' (*That*) considered as 'thing' (*Sache*), and *factum* is the verbal noun of the verb *facere*. I use the Latin *factum* instead of the English 'fact' in order to bring out the original meaning of the latter. *Thathandlung* (an artificial word coined by Fichte) denotes instead a deed precisely as 'action'. In the translation, I have omitted most of Reinhold's excessive, and hence self-defeating, mechanical stresses. Notice also Reinhold's use of the word 'person'.

16. The concept of *Tathandlung* was introduced by Fichte in his review of *Ænesidemus*. GA I.2:46.26.

17. Reinhold is following Fichte, this time his "Zweite Einleitung in die Wissenschaftslehre," the last lines of §1, where Fichte speaks of a *Kunstprodukt*. GA I:4:210.

18. See note 14.

19. See note 14. See also the following texts in *Paradoxien:* "The impossibility to exhaust individuality through the concepts of experience is the true cause of the inadequacy of all merely natural, theoretical conviction – a conviction that, precisely for this reason, is both capable and in need of a progression *in infinitum* through natural explanation" (82). Complete certainty only comes with conscience, when freedom determines the individual for the sake of actions (82–3). "Through absolute self-determination [the philosopher] brings to completion, in an artificial reflective thought, what in natural [determination], through concepts that refer to perception, can never be brought to completion. The philosopher establishes ahead of all possible experience (a priori) the absolute certainty that for actual experience is

contained only in an eternal future (a posteriori)" (84–5). But the philosopher must not forget that his actual conviction does not extend further than his artificial philosophizing (85–6). On pp. 86–7, Reinhold claims that *"individuelle Individualität"* must remain for the philosopher eternally unconceptualizable. The most that the philosopher can do is to deduce the possibility of individuality. This is clearly a reference to Fichte's attempt to deduce the individual in his *Naturrecht.* Cf. Fichte's letter to Jacobi, August 1795: "My *absolute I* is obviously not the *individual.* [. . .] But the *individual must be deduced from the absolute I.* The *Wissenschaftslehre* will proceed to do this in the *Naturrecht* without delay" (GA III.2:391ff.). In fact, in the *Grundlage des Naturrechts* (1796), the presence of the concrete (sensible) individual is still treated as a scandal that can be rationalized only by means of legal relationships and by such pragmatic means as education. See also Fichte's letter to Reinhold, 4 July 1797, where Fichte recommends that Reinhold not invest too much time studying the *Wissenschaftslehre* but instead concentrate instead on the *Naturrecht.* "My Naturrecht is without doubt better" (GA III.3:69).

20. That all thought originates in a certain ethical feeling, a certain inclination, was a position that belonged to Jacobi no less than to Fichte. And that the products of philosophical abstraction should result in works of conceptual art was again a claim to which Jacobi could all too well subscribe, though not exactly in Fichte's spirit. Cf. *Jacobi an Fichte,* pp. 18–23. "Taken *simply* as such, our sciences are games that the human spirit devises to pass the time. In devising these games, *it only organizes its non-knowledge* without coming a single hair's breadth closer to a cognition of *the true*" (p. 24).

21. Reinhold's point is that, though faith is primordial, the speculative standpoint is independent. He develops the point in a long polemic against so-called naturalists and supernaturalists. Cf. pp. 40ff.

22. Appendix 2, entitled "Attempt at a Demonstration That Previous Speculative Philosophy Was Not Speculative Enough." The appendix is in 32 paragraphs (pp. 120–42). See also *Paradoxien,* pp. 50ff.

23. Appendix 2. See also *Paradoxien,* pp. 93–6.

24. But see also pp. 84–7.

25. Letter to Reinhold, 22 April 1799 (GA III.3:327.1–8).

26. See the introductory note to *Send schreiben an I. C. Lavater und J. G. Fichte.* Reinhold writes that one might misunderstand the author of the letter (i.e., himself) as seeking a middle position *("ein Coalition System")* between Jacobi's and Fichte's. But this is not the case. On the contrary, the author recognizes Fichte's standpoint "as the one single standpoint possible on behalf of genuine and thoroughly consequent speculative knowledge, just as he recognizes the opposite standpoint of Jacobi as the original standpoint of conscience's living conviction." The lines cited in the text then follow, pp. 6–7.

27. Pp. 81–2. But see also the introductory pages of the Letter to Fichte, pp. 76–88, the portion penned at Eutin.

28. One passage in which Fichte makes this point most trenchantly is, in my opinion, obscured by the unwarranted emendation of Fichte's original text in the edition of Alexis Philonenko. Breazeale's translation unfortunately follows the editor in this emendation. In the so-called *Zweite Einleitung in die*

Wissenschaftslehre, Fichte says at one point (in Breazeale's translation): "And this freedom, in turn, can be governed by laws or can operate in accordance with rules" (Breazeale, 1994, p. 34). "In accordance to rules" (*"nach Regeln"*) was substituted by Philonenko for Fichte's *"nach Willkühr,"* i.e., "according to free choice" or "arbitrarily," allegedly because it makes more sense in context. The opposite is true. In context, Fichte is saying that the possibility of constraint depends on the spontaneity of thought. The awareness of 'constraint' brings in its train, however, also the awareness of the possibility of contravening the constraint, i.e., of thought exercising its spontaneity arbitrarily, as it indeed happens in 'error'. On Philonenko's emendation, the second part of the sentence is either made redundant (the *'oder'* is treated as inclusive) or taken as playing on the distinction between 'laws' and 'rules'. Any such distinction, though perhaps legitimate in itself, is totally out of context here. Fichte's great insight that is being obscured is that the possibility of error is internal to reason itself, not a circumstance affecting it accidentally.

29. Hence, Fichte's original question, which sets his philosophical reflection in motion: "What is the origin of the system of representations accompanied by a feeling of necessity?" Second Introduction to the Wissenschaftslehre, §2, GA I,4:211.

30. Chapter 7, Section 7.2.1.

31. A prototypical popular philosopher was Christian Garve (1742–98), who was partly responsible for the first review of Kant's *Critique of Pure Reason,* the translator of Adam Ferguson's *Institutes of Moral Philosophy* and of Edmund Burke's *Philosophical Inquiry into the Origin of Our Ideas on the Sublime and the Beautiful,* and the author of such works as *Versuche über verschiedene Gegenstände aus Moral, Literatur und gesellschaftlichen Lebens,* Part I (1792–6). This last work contained essays on such popular subjects as "On Patience," "On Fashion," "On Rochefoucault's Maxim: Bourgeois conceits are occasionally dropped in the army, but never at home," and "On Indecision." Kant's essay "On the Old Saw: That may be right in theory but it won't work in practice" (1793) was written in reply to an objection against his moral theory raised by Garve on pp. 111–16 of this collection of essays in an appended note referring to p. 81. A second volume published in 1796 includes essays on Herodotus, on Shakespeare, on the love for one's fatherland, and on how to think about art.

32. Karl Leonhard Reinhold, *Verhandlungen über die Grundbegriffe und Grundsätze der Moralität,* aus dem Gesichtspunkt des gemeinen und gesunden Verstandes, zum Behuf der Beurtheilung der sittlichen, rechtlichen, politischen und religiösen Angelegenheiten, Vol. 1 (1798b).

33. See, for instance, Reinhold's announcement, "Neue Entdeckung" ("New Discovery"), in *ALZ* (25 September 1788), no. 231a, columns 831–2, in which Reinhold argues that a methodical examination of past history shows that to the question "Does God exist?" humanity has unanimously replied "yes." Reinhold presents this result as a philosophical discovery that should be announced to the public at large just as quickly as any discovery in the physical sciences.

34. He had waged his campaign in innumerable articles and reviews, published anonymously, promoting the secularizing policies of Maria Theresia and Joseph II. These writings have been collected in *Schriften zur Religionkritik und Aufklärung*. See Chapter 2, note 31.

35. Letter to Elise Reimarus, 11 January 1775 [*sic!* It should read], *Friedrich Heinrich Jacobi's Auserlesener Briefwechsel* (1825–7), vol 2, letter 240.

36. *Friedr. Heinr. Jacobi's Briefe an Friedr. Bouterwek aus den Jahren 1800 bis 1819* (1868), letter 11, p. 81.

37. Before being called to the chair of Kantian philosophy just established at the University of Jena, Reinhold had assisted Wieland in the publishing of the *Teutscher Merkur*. He eventually married Wieland's daughter.

38. In a footnote to a softened version of the passage added in the 1816 edition. *Werke* III.

39. In a footnote added in the second edition, he tries to justify his outburst by citing the authority of Ferguson.

40. Mark, 2.23–8.

41. I.e., the special claim to immunity.

42. See Valenza (1994, pp. 51–64) for a very instructive statement on Bardili's position. Bardili conceives thought as a sort of activity of self-reference, not unlike a counting, an *idem per idem*, that slowly absorbs all content of experience, including the subject. This activity proceeds on its own, as if anonymously. For another instructive article on Bardili, see Zahn (1967). As Zahn points out, Reinhold's interpretation of Bardili dispelled the illusion that both Reinhold and Fichte tried at first to promote (perhaps only for strategic reasons) that the difference between the two was minimal.

43. See *Beyträge zur leichtern Übersicht des Zustandes der Philosophie beym Anfange-des 19. Jahrhunderts* (1801b), vol. 1, Contribution VI: "Ideen zu einer Heautogonie oder natürliche Geschichte der reinen Ichheit, genannt reine Vernunft" ("Idea for a Heautogony, or the Natural History of the Pure 'I'-ness, Called Pure Reason"), pp. 134–54. This is a brilliant polemical piece that includes some insightful phenomenological descriptions of how one gets to the standpoint of a Fichte or a Schelling. It is done by relying on one's real individuality while camouflaging this reliance behind the idea of an individuality in general. The whole idealistic standpoint, in other words, is a matter of dissembling – of talking of an individuality in general while in fact meaning one's own concrete self.

44. "Declaration Concerning Fichte's Wissenschaftslehre," Public Declaration No. 6, 7 August 1799, tr. Arnulf Zweig, AK XII:370–1.

Chapter 8

1. *Die Bestimmung des Menschen* (1800), 1956, ed., pp. 83–4. I shall modify the English translation as required and, when there is no risk of confusion, refer to the pagination of the original within the text in parentheses, followed by the pagination of the English translation. The original pagination is indicated in the critical edition, GA I.6.

2. *Bestimmung*, p. 215; English, pp. 98–9.

3. *Bestimmung*, p. 217; English, pp. 99–100.

4. *Bestimmung*, 311–12; English, p. 142.

5. "Glauben und Wissen, oder die Reflexionsphilosophie der Subjectivität, in der Vollständigkeit ihrer Formen, als Kantische, Jacobische, und Fichtesche Philosophie" (1802a), 1–189, p. 173. GW 4, 315–414 (1977, p. 178). We shall cite the original pagination, which is included in both the critical edition and the English translation.

6. *Briefe Von und An Hegel*, ed. J. Hoffmeister (Hamburg: Meiner, 1961), vol. 1, p. 13.

7. An English translation of these early treatises can be found in F. W. J. Schelling, *The Unconditional in Human Knowledge: Four Early Essays (1794–1796)* (1980).

8. But read the editorial notes in the critical edition of the *Bestimmung*. As of 1800, Schelling still seemed to be adopting Fichte's standpoint of practical reason. GA I.6, p. 126, note 27.

9. The same question can be raised with respect to Schleiermacher. He was a disciple of Johann August Eberhard (Kant's strident critic), whom he considered a mentor. See Friedrich Schleiermacher, *On the Highest Good* (1992a), the Postscript by the translator, pp. 105–7.

10. Berlin: Voß 1800. Fichte was acquainted with Spalding's book from his youth. Cf. Fichte, *Appellation an das Publikum* (1799), p. 97: "Might you, honourable Father Spalding, whose *The Vocation of Humankind* cast the first germ of higher speculation in my youthful soul [. . .] – might you be able, and willing, to add your voice in my cause!" (p. 57. GA I.5:447). The "cause" is Fichte's defense against the charge of atheism.

11. It appears, however, that Fichte had forgotten about his early plan when he began to work on the book. See, in this regard, the editors' Preface to the critical edition in GA I.6:147–8 and note 4. The editorial notes in GA are, as usual, detailed and instructive.

12. I am summing up in a few words the whole final part of Book I, 62–70, 30–4.

13. August Ferdinand Bernhardi, in *Berlinisches Archiv der Zeit und ihres Geschmacks*, as cited in GA I.6:162–7, where pp. 205–11 of the original review are reproduced. See p. 165 (second to last line), and the footnotes for similar or opposite views by other reviewers.

14. *Bestimmung*, p. 78; English, p. 37.

15. The whole final section of Book II is relevant, 162–78, 76–82.

16. Cf. *Bestimmung*, pp. 165–6; English, p. 77, where the position of Spinoza is clearly evoked.

17. One wonders how much this work of Fichte is also a biographical account of his spiritual odyssey. According to his own account, Fichte began as a materialist but found through Kant renewed faith in personal freedom. Cf. the fragment of a letter to F. A. Weisshuhn, August–September 1790, GA III:1:167, no. 63; also the draft of a letter to H. N. Achelis, November 1790, GA III:1,193–4, no. 70a. Both texts can be found in English translation. Breazeale (1988), pp. 357–8 and 358–62 (especially pp. 360–1).

18. F. H. Jacobi, *Über die Lehre des Spinoza in Briefen an den Herrn Moses Mendelssohn* (1785), p. 162; *Jacobi*, p. 230. Fichte seems to proceed from dogmatism (necessarily materialist, according to him), to Kant, and then to Jacobi. Hegel follows a similar procession in the final part of Ch. 6 of the *Phenomenology*, where he moves from the materialism of the late Enlightenment (which leads to the spiritualized materialism of the French Revolution), to Kant's moral standpoint, and, finally, to a dialectic of 'conscience' that culminates with Jacobi's position in the *Woldemar*. For the presence of Jacobi in this chapter of Hegel's work, see di Giovanni (1995).

19. Of course, there cannot be certainty without one's being conscious of it. Even the original certainty about the freedom that animates the I must be accompanied by representation from the beginning. This is a point we have seen in Chapter 6, Section 6.2.1. The fact that one has intuition of one's freedom must be, for Fichte, itself an object of faith. Action and representation are inextricably bound together. Fichte, however, assigns to action (to will) genetic priority over representation. Intelligence and intelligibility follow upon the will and are for the sake of willing.

20. Cf.: "My conception and origination of *a purpose* [. . .] is, by its very nature, absolutely free – and producing something out of nothing. With such a conception I must connect my activity if the action is to be regarded as free and as proceeding absolutely from myself alone." *Bestimmung, p.* 186; English, p. 85.

21. *Bestimmung*, p. 215; English, pp. 98–9.

22. According to the editors of the GA, because of what Fichte took to be the universal misunderstanding of his book, Fichte decided not to publish his new "Exposition of the *Wissenschaftslehre*," even though he continued to lecture on his Science in Berlin. GA I.6:181–2.

23. In *Addresses to the German Nation* (*Reden an die deutsche Nation*, lectures at Berlin in 1807), moral education is the central theme.

24. In 1808, Fichte submitted to W. von Humboldt a plan of education reform based on strong authoritarian principles. Schleiermacher presented another, based instead on liberal principles. Humboldt adopted the latter. (Dumont 1994, p. 131). A French translation of the two proposals, and of Humboldt's statement about the organization of higher education, can be found in Ferry, Person, and Renaut (1979).

25. For the following overview, I am relying extensively on the excellent documentation provided by the editors of the critical edition. GA I.6:154ff.

26. Letter to Jean Paul Richter of 13 February 1800, as cited in GA I.6:161.

27. Ibid.

28. Cf. *Über die Lehre des Spinoza*, 212–13.

29. The comment was made by Jean Paul Christian Otto in a letter to Jean Paul Richter of 27 April 1800. *Jean Pauls Briefwechsel mit seinem Freunde Christian Otto* (Berlin, 1829), vol. 3, pp. 270–1, as cited in GA I.6, 156 and note 56. Jens Immanuel Baggesen also thought, at first, that in Fichte's book he had found Jacobi. As he pressed the book to his chest, he felt that he was embracing Jacobi. He, however, changed his mind later. Cf. *Aus Jens Baggesens Briefwechsel mit Karl Leonhard Reinhold und Friedrich Heinrich Jacobi,*

vol. 2 (Leipzig, Brockhaus (1831), Letter to Jacobi of 14 April 1800, no. 71, pp. 286–7.

30. *Aus F. H. Jacobi's Nachlaß*, Letter of 13 February 1800 (cited in Jacobi's letter to Jean Paul Richter, note 26), vol. 1, pp. 234–7.

31. See Chapter 6, Section 6.2.1.

32. One must also keep in mind Fichte's phenomenological dissection of feeling. (Cf. Chapter 6, Section 6.2.2.) As a human phenomenon, feeling is itself normative in structure, for it entails assuming a certain attitude with respect to one's reaction to a given situation. It is for this reason, i.e., because of the inherently reflective (hence normative) nature of feeling, that the philosopher can recognize in it, in some of its forms at least, the experiential counterpart of the self-legislating structure of thought. For some typical texts, see *Grundlage der gesammten Wissenschaftslehre* (1798), p. 301, GA I.2:429; "Zweite Einleitung in die Wissenschaftslehre," *Journal der Philosophies* (1797), GA I.4:219–20; *Das System der Sittenlehre nach den Prucipien der Wissenschaftslehre* (1798), pp. 50ff., 158ff., 220, GA I.5:6off., 120–1, 220.

33. "Was heißt philosophiren? Was war es, und was soll es seyn?" in *Beyträge zur leichtern Übersicht des Zustandes der Philosophie beym Anfang des 19. Jahrhunderts*, pp. 85–7.

34. Cf., for instance, *Bestimmung*, 289ff., 302ff., 332; English, pp. 132ff., 138ff., 152.

35. The anonymous reviewer was Dietrich Tiedemann. *Neue allgemeine deutsche Bibliothek* (1800). Cf. GA I.6:156, 167, 178, and footnotes.

36. *Neue allgemeine deutsche Bibliothek* 60 (1800), 373, 372 ff. GA I.6:167, footnotes 82, 83.

37. *Neue allgemeine deutsche Bibliothek* 60 (1800), 387, 388. GA I.6:174, 178, footnotes 18, 40.

38. *Neue allgemeine deutsche Bibliothek* 60 (1800), 374–9. GA I.6:168–9, footnotes 87–92.

39. The review was anonymous, as was customary, but Fichte took it to be Abicht's. *ALZ* (19 May, 1800), no. 97, columns 774–6. GA I.6:169–70, footnotes 94–9. Abicht was one of those who anonymously accused Fichte's idealism of atheism. Cf. GA I.6:457, footnote 1.

40. For the last point, see *ALZ* (20 May 1800), no. 97, column 779. GA I.6:178 and footnote 39.

41. See Chapter 3, Section 3.4.

42. Fichte thought of Abicht's objections as "nonsense" and pointed out that his denial of the thing in itself was directed at this thing as understood transcendentally by Kant. In any other sense, the denial would have presupposed dogmatism and would have led ineluctably to skepticism. The latter is only the other side of dogmatism. Letter to G. E. A. Mehmel of 22 November 1800. Cf. GA I.6:170 and footnote 99.

43. Schmid's review was published as a chapter of his *Aufsätzen philosophischen und theologischen Inhalts*, vol. 1 (1800), pp. 140–230; p. 225. GA I.6:160, 161 and footnotes 65, 70.

44. *Aufsätzen*, pp. 145, 148. GA 1.6:168 and footnotes 85, 86.

45. Cf. GA I.6:178–9 and footnotes 40, 43–6.

46. *Aufsätzen*, vol. I, pp. 218–19. GA 1.6:178 and footnotes 41, 42. Tiedemann made a similar point. *Neue allgemeine deutsche Bibliothek* 60 (1800), 387. GA I.6:179, footnote 44.

47. *Aufsätzen*, vol. I, pp. 222–4. GA 1.6:180 and footnotes 50, 51.

48. *Clavis Fichteana* (1800). The parody was based on the assumption that by the I Fichte meant the natural individual, and hence that the whole Fichtean system is a form of 'egoism'. Reinhold, who should have known better, writes on the same assumption in his later criticism of Idealism (see note 33). The objection misses the point of Kantian and Fichtean idealism completely. The I is an abstraction. The problem with this kind of idealism (as Jacobi was perceptive enough to notice, even though he fraternized with Richter) is not that there is too much subjectivitys or, for that matter, too much individuality, but that there is not enough of either. In this respect, it was vulnerable to the same criticism that Jacobi had raised against Enlightenment rationalism.

49. *Athenaeum* 3.2 (1800), 283–97. GA 1.6:156, 157 and footnotes 57, 58.

50. GA 1,6:158, footnote 58.

51. GA 1,6:157, footnote 58.

52. GA 1,6:157, footnote 58.

53. *System des transcendentalen Idealismus* (1800), *Sämmtliche Werke* (1858), I.3:633ff.; 1978, ed., pp. 235ff. Also cited in GA 1.6:176, footnote 27. The critical editors suggest that Schelling's apparent change of mind might be due to Hegel's influence.

54. See note 9.

55. See Chapter 2, Section 2.3.

56. "Über die Freiheit," *Friedrich Daniel Ernst Schleiermacher, Jugendschriften 1787– 1796* (1992b); 1984 ed., p. 219. For the dating, see pp. liv–lxii; 1992 ed., p. 3.

57. Cf. Meckenstock (1988), p. 52.

58. "Über die Freiheit," p. 230 (lines 1–6); English, p. 14. The young Schleiermacher might well have put an end to rationalistic theology with his dismantling of Kant's postulates of practical reason, as Meckenstock claims. But he certainly was not thereby breaking loose from the metaphysical tradition of Leibniz and Wolff as embodied in *Popularphilosophie*. Like the popular philosophers, he was simply giving a renewed psychological slant to it. Cf. Meckenstock (1988), p. 154.

59. I am referring to "Über die Freiheit," where the compatibility of a strict system of physical necessity with 'moral accountability' is defended along the lines of Schmid's naturalism rather than of Kant's transcendentalism. Schleiermacher says that accountability must be handled practically rather than theoretically (p. 229; English, pp. 13–14). 'Practically', however, is not being understood here in a Kantian sense, but more in the sense in which a modern compatibilist would use the term (Part II of the Essay, pp. 244ff; English, pp. 29ff.). I am also referring to Schleiermacher's early reflections on Spinoza and Jacobi, *Spinozismus* (1793/4), *Jugendschriften*, 511–97.

60. See note 5. In this essay, Hegel has Fichte's whole philosophical output to date in mind, but he refers most extensively, whether directly or indirectly, to his *Die Bestimmung des Menschen*.

61. Letter to Köppen of 10 August 1802 in Köppen's *Schellings Lehre oder das Ganz der phylosophie des absoluten Nichts*, p. 221. See di Giovanni (1994), *Jacobi*, p. 165.

62. "Glauben und Wissen"; see especially pp. 168–76, (English, pp. 174–80).

63. What Hegel might mean by intellectual intuition at this early stage, or how much the notion is dependent on Schelling's, is an issue open to debate but not one of interest in the present context. In the next few years, the notion faded in Hegel's writings, to be replaced by the dialectical force of the concept.

64. "Glauben und Wissen," pp. 163–4; English, pp. 171–2.

65. "Glauben und Wissen," pp. 181–2; English, pp. 183–4.

66. Cf. "Glauben und Wissen," pp. 153–4, but see also p. 47 (English pp. 164, 85). One might add (though Hegel does not) that in the *Critique of Judgement* another attempt is also made at bridging the distance between freedom and nature at a more immediate level of experience, through 'aesthetic beauty' and the 'feeling of sublimity'.

67. With respect to Kant, Hegel had drawn this distinction explicitly in an essay published in the previous volume of the *Kritisches Journal der Philosophie*. "Verhältniß des Skepticismus zur Philosophie, Darstellung seiner verschiedenen Modificationen, und Vergleichung des neuesten mit dem alten" (1802b); see 69–70. GW 4, 197–238. English tr. in *Between Kant and Hegel*, pp. 311–62.

68. Cf. "Glauben und Wissen," pp. 176–9; English, pp. 180–3.

69. *Differenz des Fichte'sschen und Schelling'sschen Systems der Philosophie*, in Beziehung auf Reinhold's *Beyträge zur leichtern Übersicht des Zustands der Philosophie zu Anfang des neunzehnten Jahrhunderts* (1801); GW, 4, 1–92.

70. I am glossing on Hegel's text. But cf. "Glauben und Wissen," p. 140; pp. 138–42 are also relevant (English, p. 154, pp. 153–6).

71. "Glauben und Wissen," p. 154; English, p. 164. This is really the capping off of an argument that began at p. 143 (English, p. 156).

72. "Glauben und Wissen," p. 157, see also p. 17 and its context (English, p. 167; p. 64).

73. Cf. "Glauben und Wissen," pp. 9–12; English, pp. 59–61.

74. "Glauben und Wissen," p. 173, but see also pp. 171–5; English, p. 178; pp. 177–9.

75. Cf. "Glauben und Wissen," pp. 13–14; English, pp. 61–2.

76. Cf. "Glauben und Wissen," pp. 159–62, 148; English, pp. 168–170; p. 160.

77. "Wie der gemeine Menschenverstand die Philosophie nehme, dargestellt an den Werken des Herrn Krug's" (1802c). Friedrich Köppen, Jacobi's disciple, won a professorship at the very time when Hegel was giving up his ambition for a university career. H. S. Harris, "Glauben und Wissen," English tr., Introduction, p. 29, note 46.

78. "Glauben und Wissen," p. 6; English, p. 57.

79. Hegel's own opinion was that this optimism was an empirical variation on Protestant subjectivism. "This is the basic character of eudaimonism and the Enlightenment. The beautiful subjectivity of Protestantism is transformed into empirical subjectivity; the poetry of Protestant grief that scorns all reconciliation with empirical existence is transformed into the prose of satisfaction with the finite and good conscience about it." *Glauben und Wissen*, p. 12 (English, p. 61).
80. Harris (1972), p. 4.
81. Cf., *Between Kant and Hegel*, p. 267.

Bibliography

For abbreviations used, see the list at the front of the book.

1. Primary Sources

Abel, J. F. (1786) *Einleitung in die Seelenlehre.* Stuttgart: Mezler.

(1787a) *Plan einer systematischen Metaphysik.* Stuttgart: Erhard.

(1787b) *Versuch über die Natur der speculativen Vernunft. Zur Prüfung des Kantischen Systems.* Frankfurt and Leipzig.

Abicht, J. H. (1788) *De philosophæ Kantinanæ habitu ad theologiam. Disseratiatio philosophica pro gradu doctoris.* Erlangen.

(1789) "Über die Freiheit des Willens." *Neues philosophisches Magazin, Erläuterungen und Anwendungen des Kantischen Systems bestimmt,* J. H. Abicht and F. G. Born (eds.). 1 Leipzig: Barth, 64–85.

(1791) *Philosophie der Erkenntnisse.* Beyreuth: Erben.

(1793) *Kritische Briefe über die Möglichkeit einer wahren wissenschaftlichen Moral, Theologie, Rechtslehre, empirischen Psychologie und Geschmakslehre, mit prüfender Hinsicht auf die Kantische Begründung dieser Lehre* (*Critical Letters Concerning the Possibility of a True Moral Theory, Theology, Philosophy of Right, Empirical Psychology and Theory of Taste, with a Scrutiny of the Kantian Grounding of These Doctrines.*) Nürnberg: Felsecker.

(1794) *Hermias, oder Auflösung der die gültige Elementarphilosophie betreffenden Aenesidischen Zweifel* (*Hermias, or Resolution of the Valid Aenesidic Doubts Concerning the Philosophy of the Elements*). Erlangen: Walther.

(1795) *System der Elementarphilosophie oder vollständige Naturlehre der Erkentniss-Gefühl und Willenskraft.* Erlangen: Jakob.

(1800). "Review of Fichte's *Die Bestimmung des Menschen.*" *ALZ* (19 May), no. 97, columns 774–6.

Aquinas, Thomas. (1975) *Summa contra gentiles.* Notre Dame: University Press.

Baggesen, J. (1831) *Aus Jens Baggesen's Briefwechsel mit Karl Leonhard Reinhold und Friedrich Heinrich Jacobi,* K. Baggesen and A. Baggesen (eds.), 2 vols. Leipzig: Brockhaus.

Bardili, C. B. (1796) *Ursprung des Begriffes von der Willensfreiheit* (*The Origin of the Concept of Freedom of the Will*). Stuttgart: Erhard & Löflund.

Bernhardi, A. F. (1800) "Review of Fichte's *Die Bestimmung des Menschen*." *Berlinisches Archiv der Zeit und ihres Geschmacks* (March), 204–11.

Bonnet, C. (1769) *La Palingénésie philosophique, ou Idées sur l'état passé et sur l'état futur des êtres vivants*. Amsterdam: Marc-Michel Rey.

Born, F. G. (1787) "Review of Abel's Works." *Neue Leipziger gelehrte Zeitungen* (15 November).

(1790). "Über den transcendentalen Idealismus." *Neues philosophisches Magazin, Erläuterungen und Anwendungen des Kantischen Systems bestimmt*, J. H. Abicht and F. G. Born (eds.), vol. 1. Leipzig.

Creuzer, L. (1793) *Skeptische Betrachtungen über die Freiheit des Willens, mit Hinsicht auf die neuesten Theorien über dieselbe*. Gießen: Heyer.

Feder, J. G. H. (1787a) "Review of Abel's Works." *Göttingschen Anzeigen von gelehrten Sachen* (17 November).

(1787b) *Über Raum und Causalität: zur Prüfung der Kantischen Philosophie*. Göttingen: Dietrich.

Feder, J. G. H. and Garve, C. (1782) "Review of KrV." *Zugabe zu den Göttingschen Anzeigen von gelehrten Sachen* (19 January), 40–8.

Fichte, J. G. (1793a) "Review of Creuzer." *ALZ* (30 October), no. 303, columns 201–5. GA I.2, 7–14.

(1793b) "Review of Gebhard." *ALZ* (31 October), no. 304, columns 209–15. GA I.2, 21–9.

(1793c) *Versuch einer Critik aller Offenbarung*. Königsberg: Hartung, 1792; 2nd ed. GA I.1, 15–162. *Attempt at a Critique of All Revelation*, G. Green (tr.). Cambridge: Cambridge University Press, 1978.

(1794a) "Review of Aenesidemus." *ALZ* (11–12 February), nos. 47–9, columns 369–74, 377–83, 385–9. GA I.2, 41–67. *Between Kant and Hegel*, pp. 137–57.

(1794b). *Über den Begriff der Wissenschaftslehre oder der sogenannten Philosophie* (*Concerning the Concept of the Doctrine of Science or of the So-Called Philosophy, as Invitations Writing to This Science*). GA I.2, 107–67. *The Science of Knowledge*, p. Heath and J. Lachs (trs.). Cambridge: Cambridge University Press, 1982.

(1794–5). *Grundlage der gesammten Wissenschaftslehre*. GA I.2, 250–451.

(1796a) *Grundlage des Naturrechts nach Principien der Wissenschaftslehre*. GA I.4, 1–165. *Foundations of Natural Right According to Principles of the Wissenschaftslehre*, M. Baur (tr.), F. Neuhouser (ed.). Cambridge: Cambridge University Press, 2000.

(1796b) "Vergleichung des vom Hrn Prof. Schmid aufgestellten Systems mit der Wissenschaftslehre' ("A Comparison between Prof. Schmid's System and the *Wissenschaftslehre*"). *Philosophisches Journal einer Gesellschaft Teutscher Gelehrten* 3.4, 267–320. GA I.3, 235–66.

(1797a) [*Erste*] *Einleitung in der Wissenschaftslehre* ([First] . . . .) GA I, 4, 186–208. *J. G. Fichte, Introduction to the Wissenschaftslehre and Other Writings*, D. Breazeale (tr.). Indianapolis: Hackett, 1994.

(1797b) "Versuch einer neuen Darstellung der Wissenschaftslehre. Attempt at a New Presentation of the *Wissenschaftslehre*." *Journal der Philosophie* 5, 1–49. GA I.4, 183–208. English tr., Breazeale (1994).

(1797c) "Second Introduction to the *Wissenschaftslehre*," *Journal der Philosophie* 5, 319–78, 6 (1798) 1–43. GA I.4, 209–68. English tr. Breazeale (1994).

(1798) *Das System der Sittlichlleit nach den Principien der Wissenschaftslehre* (*System of Ethics According to the Wissenschaftslehre*). Jena and Leipzig: Gabler. GA I.5.

(1799) *Appellation an das Publikum über die durch ein Kurf. Sächs. Confiscationrescript ihm beigemessenen atheistischen Äusserungen.* Jena and Leipzig: Galter. GA I.5, 414–35.

(1800) *Die Bestimmung des Menschen* (*The Vocation of Human Kind*). Berlin: Voß. Frankfurt and Leipzig Voß. GA I.6, 123–309. *The Vocation of Man*, Roderick M. Chisholm (tr. and ed.). New York: Bobbs-Merrill, 1956.

(1807) *Reden an die deutsche Nation.* Hamburg: Meiner, 1955. *Addresses to the German Nation*, R. F. Jones and G. H. Turnball (trs.), G. A. Kelly (ed.). New York: Harper & Row, 1968.

(1962–2005) *Briefwechsel*, R. Lauth and H. Jacob (eds.), GA III.1–5.

(1962–2005) *Eigne Meditationen über Elementarphilosophie.* GA III.3, 21–177.

(1962–2005) *Über den Unterschied des Geistes und des Buchstabens in der Philosophie.* GA II.3, Lecture 2, 330–412.

(1962–2005) *Wissenschaftslehre nova methodo*, GA III.3. Breazeale (1992).

Flatt, J. F. (1789) *Briefe über den moralischen Erkenntnisgrund der Religion überhaupt, und besonders in Beziehung auf die Kantische Philosophie* (*Letters Concerning the Moral Ground of the Knowledge of Religion in General, with Particular Reference to the Kantian Philosophy*). Tübingen: Cotta.

Forberg, F. K. (1798) "Entwickelung des Begriffs der Religion." *Philosophisches Journal einer Gesellschaft Teutscher Gelehrten* 8, 21–46.

Garve, C. (1783) "Review of Kant's KrV." *Allgemeine deutsche Bibliothek*, supplements to vols. 37–52, 838–62. Tr., Sassen (2000).

(1792–6) *Versuche über verschiedene Gegenstände aus Moral, Literatur und gesellschaftlichen Leben* (*Essays Concerning Various Subjects Drawn from Morality, Literature, and Social Life*). 2 vols. Breslau: Korn.

Gebhard, F. H. (1792) *Über die sittliche Güte aus uninteressirtem Wohlwollen.* Gotha: Ettinger.

Goethe, J. W. (1985–) *Dichtung und Wahrheit*, V, *Sämmtliche Werke*, XVI. Munich: Hanser.

Hamann, G. H. (1955–79) *Briefwechsel*, A. Henkel (ed.), 7 vols. Wiesbaden and Frankfurt/Main: Insel Verlag.

Hegel, G. W. F. (1801) *Differenz des Fichte'sschen und Schelling'sschen Systems der Philosophie*, in Beziehung auf Reinhold's *Beyträge zur leichtern Übersicht des Zustands der Philosophie zu Anfang des neunzehnten Jahrhunderts.* Jena: Seider. GW 4, 1–92. *The Difference between Fichte's and Schelling's System of Philosophy*, in connection with Reinhold's *Contributions to a More Convenient Survey of the State of Philosophy at the Beginning of the Nineteenth Century*, H. S. Harris and W. Cerf (trs.). Albany: SUNY Press, 1977.

(1802a) "Glauben und Wissen, oder die Reflexionsphilosophie der Subjectivität, in der Vollständigkeit ihrer Formen, als Kantische, Jacobische, und Fichtesche Philosophie." *Kritisches Journal der Philosophie*, F. W. J. Schelling and

G. W. F. Hegel (eds.), 2.1, 1–189. GA, 4, 315–414. "Faith and Knowledge, or the Reflective Philosophy of Subjectivity in the Complete Range of Its Forms as Kantian, Jacobian, and Fichtean Philosophy," W. Cerf and H. S. Harris (trs.). Albany: SUNY Press, 1977.

(1802b) "Verhältniß des Skepticismus zur Philosophie, Darstellung seiner verschiedenen Modificationen, und Vergleichung des neuesten mit dem alten." *Kritisches Journal der Philosophie* I.2, 1–74. GW 4, 197–238. "On the Relationship of Skepticism to Philosophy, Exposition of Its Different Modifications and Comparison of the Latest Form with the Ancient One," *Between Kant and Hegel*, H. S. Harris (tr.).

(1802c) "Wie der gemeine Menschenverstand die Philosophie nehme, dargestellt an den Werken des Herrn Krug's." *Kritisches Journal der Philosophie* 1, 91–115. GW 4, 174–87. "How the Ordinary Human Understanding Takes Philosophy, as Displayed in the Works of Mr. Krug," H. S. Harris (tr.), *Between Kant and Hegel*, pp. 292–310.

(1807) *Phenomenology of Spirit*. GW IX.

(1961) *Briefe von und an Hegel*, J. Hoffmeister (ed.). Vol. 1. Hamburg: Meiner.

Heydenreich, K. H. *Betrachtungen über die Philosophie der natürlichen Religion* (*Considerations Concerning the Philosophy of Natural Religion*). 2 vols. Leipzig: Weygand.

Humboldt, W. von. (1968) *Gesammelte Schriften*. A. Leitzmann, ed. 17 vols. Berlin: de Gruyter.

Jacobi, F. H. (1782) *Etwas das Leßing gesagt hat. Ein Commentar zu den Reisen der Päpste nebst Betrachtungen von einem Dritten* (*Something That Lessing Said, A Commentary on* The Travels of the Popes, *Together with Observations by a Third Party*). Berlin: George Jacob Decker.

(1785) *Über die Lehre des Spinoza in Briefen an den Herrn Moses Mendelssohn.* (Breslau: Löwe 2nd, much enlarged ed., 1789. *Concerning the Doctrine of Spinoza in Letters to Herr Moses Mendelssohn*, tr. G. di Giovanni, *Jacobi*.

(1787) *David Hume über den Glauben, oder Idealismus und Realismus. Ein Gespräch* (Breslau: Löwe). *David Hume on Faith, or Idealism and Realism, A Dialogue*, G. di Giovanni (tr.), *Jacobi*. Revised 2nd ed., with a Preface to the author's *Collected Works. Friedrich Heinrich Jacobi's Werke*, J. F. Köppen and C. J. F. Roth (eds.), 6 vols. Leipzig: Gerhard Fleischer, 1812–25, Vol. 2, 1815.

(1799) *Jacobi an Fichte*. Hamburg: Perthes. *Jacobi to Fichte*, G. di Giovanni, *Jacobi*.

(1803) Three Letters, see Köppen, *Schellings Lehre oder das Ganze dev Philosophie des absoluted Nichts.*

(1812–25) *Friedrich Heinrich Jacobi's Werke*, J. F. Köppen and C. J. F. Roth (eds.), 6 vols. Leipzig: Gerhard Fleischer. Reprinted Darmstadt: Wissenschaftliche Buchgesellschaft, 1968.

(1825–7) *Friedrich Heinrich Jacobi's auserlesener Briefwechsel*, F. Roth (ed.), 2 vols. Leipzig: Fleischer.

(1868) *Friedr. Heinr. Jacobi's Briefe an Friedr. Bouterwek aus den Jahren 1800 bis 1819*, W. Meyer (ed.), Göttingen: Deuer.

(1869) *Aus F. H. Jacobi's Nachlaß. Ungedruckte Briefe von und an Jacobi und andere. Nebst ungedruckten Gedichten von Goethe und Lenz*, Rudolph Zoeppritz (ed.), 2 vols. Leipzig: Engelmann.

Kant, Immanuel. (1763) *Der einzig mögliche Beweisgrund zu einer Demonstration des Daseins Gottes.* AK II.

(1781) *Kritik der reinen Vernunft* (2nd ed. 1787). AK III, IV. *Critique of Pure Reason,* P. Guyer and A. Wood (trs.). Cambridge: Cambridge University Press, 1998.

(1783) *Prolegomena zu einer jeden künftigen Metaphysik.* AK IV. *Prolegomena to Any Future Metaphysics That Will Be Able to Come Forward as Science,* G. Hatfield (tr.). *Immanuel Kant, Theoretical Philosophy After 1781.* Cambridge: Cambridge University Press, 2002.

(1784) "Idee zu einer allgemeinen Geschichte in weltbürgerlicher Absicht." AK VIII. "Idea for a Universal History from a Cosmopolitan Point of View," L. W. Beck (tr.). Indianapolis: Bobbs-Merrill, 1963.

(1785) *Grundlegung zur Metaphysik der Sitten.* AK IV. *Groundwork of the Metaphysics of Morals,* M. J. Gregor (tr.). *Immanuel Kant, Practical Philosophy.* Cambridge: Cambridge University Press, 1996.

(1786a) *Metaphysische Anfangsgründe der Naturwissenschaft.* AK VIII. *Metaphysical Foundations of Natural Science,* M. Friedman (tr.). *Theoretical Philosophy After 1781.* Cambridge: Cambridge University Press, 2002.

(1786b) "Mutmasslicher Anfang der Menschengeschlechte." AK VIII. "Conjectural Beginning of Human History," E. L. Fackenheim (tr.). *Kant on History.* Indianapolis: Bobbs-Merril, 1963.

(1786c) "Was heißt: Sich im Denken orientiren?" AK VIII. "What Does It Mean to Orient Oneself in Thinking?," A. Wood (tr.). *Immanuel Kant, Religion and Rational Theology.* Cambridge: Cambridge University Press, 1996.

(1788) *Kritik der praktischen Vernunft.* AK V. *The Critique of Practical Reason,* M. J. Gregor (tr.). Cambridge: Cambridge Universtiy Press, 1996.

(1790) *Kritik der Urteilskraft.* AK V. *Critique of the Power of Judgement,* P. Guyer and E. Matthews (trs.). Cambridge: Cambridge University Press, 2000.

(1793a) *Die Religion innerhalb der Grenzen der bloßen Vernunft.* AK VI. *Religion Within the Boundaries of Mere Reason,* G. di Giovanni (tr.). *Immanuel Kant, Religion and Rational Theology.* Cambridge: Cambridge University Press, 1996.

(1793b) "Welches sind die wirklichen Fortschritte, die die Metaphysik seit Leibnitzens und Wolf's Zeiten in Deutchland gemacht hat?" AK XX. "What Real Progress Has Metaphysics Made in Germany Since the Time of Leibniz and Wolff?," H. Allison (tr.). *Immanuel Kant, Theoretical Philosophy After 1781.* Cambridge: Cambridge University Press, 2002.

(1797) *Metaphysik der Sitten.* AK VI. *The Metaphysics of Morals,* M. J. Gregor (tr.). *Immanuel Kant, Practical Philosophy.* Cambridge: Cambridge University Press, 1996.

(1798) *Anthropologie in pragmatischer Hinsicht. Anthropology from a Pragmatic Point of View,* V. L. Dowdell (tr.). London and Amsterdam: Southern Illinois University Press, 1978.

(1999) *Briefwechsel.* AK X–XII. *Correspondence,* A. Zweig (tr.). Cambridge: Cambridge University Press.

Köppen. F. *Schellings Lehre oder das Ganze der Philosophie des absoluten Nichts, Nebst drey Briefen verwandten Inhalts von Friedr. Heinr. Jacobi.* Hamburg: Pethes, 1803.

Kraus, C. J. (1788) "Review of Ulrich's *Eleutheriologie*. *ALZ* (25 April), no. 100, columns 177–84. *Immanuel Kant. Practical Philosophy*, M. J. Gregor (tr.). Cambridge: Cambridge University Press, 1996, pp. 121–31.

Leibniz, G. W. (1673) *Confessio Philosophi, ein Dialog* (*A Philosopher's Profession of Faith, A Dialogue*). (O. Samme, German tr.). Frankfurt/Main: Vittorio Klostermann, 1994. Y. Belaval (French tr.). Paris: Vrin, 1961.

(1949) *New Essays Concerning Human Understanding*, A. G. Langley (tr.). La Salle: Open Court.

Lessing, G. E. (1778) *Nathan der Weise*. S. Prime (ed.). Boston: Heath, 1894.

Maimon, S. (1790) *Versuch über die Transzendentalphilosophie. Essay on Transcendental Philosophy*. Berlin: Voss.

(1793) *Philosophischer Briefwechsel, nebst einem demselben vorangeschickten Manifest. Streifereien im Gebiete der Philosophie. Gesammelte Werke*, V. Verra (ed.). Vol. 3. Hildesheim: Olms, 1970.

(1794) *Versuch einer neuen Logik oder Theorie des Denkens*. Berlin: Felisch. *Essay Towards a New Logic or Theory of Thought, Together with Letters of Philaletes to Ænesidemus*, G. di Giovanni (tr., excerpts). *Between Kant and Hegel*.

Mendelssohn, M. (1785) *Morgenstunden oder Vorlesungen über das Daseyn Gottes. Morning Hours, or Lectures on the Existence of God, Gesammelte Schriften* Jubiläumausgabe, ed. A. Actman. Stuttgart-Bad Cannstatt: Fromann, vol. 3.2, 1974.

(1983) *Jerusalem, or, On Religious Power and Judaism*, A. Arkush (tr.); introduction and commentary by A. Altmann. Hanover: Brandeis University Press.

Michaelis, C. F. (1796–7) *Über die sittliche Natur und Bestimmung des Menschen. Ein Versuch zur Erläuterung über I. Kant's Kritik der praktischen Vernunft* (*Concerning Ethical Nature and the Vocation of Humankind. An Essay in Interpretation of Kant's Critique of Practical Reason*). 2 vols. Leipzig: Beigang.

Pistorius, H. A. (1786) "Review of Johann Schultze's Kant commentary." *Allgemeine deutsche Bibliothek* 66, 92–123. Tr. (excerpts), Sassen (2000).

(1788) "Review of KrV." *Allgemeine deutsche Bibliothek* 81, 343–54.

(1794) "Review of KprV." *Allgemeine deutsche Bibliothek* 117, 78–105.

Rehberg, A. W. (1779) *Abhandlungen über das Wesen und die Einschränkungen der Kräfte* (*Disquisitions Regarding the Essence and the Limitations of Forces*). Leipzig: Weygand.

(1780) *Cato*. Basel: Thurneysen, 1780.

(1787) *Über das Verhältniß der Metaphysik zur Religion*. Berlin: Mylius.

(1788a) "Erläuterungen einiger Schwierigkeiten der natürlichen Theologie." *Der Teutsche Merkur* (September), 215–33.

(1788b) "Nachricht." *ALZ Intelligenzblatt* no. 4, column 384.

(1788c) "Review of KprV. *ALZ* (6 August), nos. 188a–b, columns 345–60.

(1828–31) *Sämmtliche Schriften*. Vols. 1–3. Hannover: Hahn.

Reid, T. (1873) *Essays on the Intellectual Powers of Man: The Works of Thomas Reid*, Sir William Hamilton (ed.). Vol. 1. Edinburgh: MacLachlan & Stewart.

Reimarus, J. A. H. (1762) *Allgemeine Betrachtungen über die Triebe der Thiere*.

(1787) *Über die Gründe der menschlichen Erkenntnis und der natürlichen Religion*. Hamburg: Bohn.

Reinhold, K. L. (1786–7) "Kantian Letters." *Der Teutsche Merkur* 3 (1786), 99–127, 127–41; 1 (1787), 3–39, 117–42; 2 (1787), 167–85; 3 (1787), 67–88, 142–65, 247–78.

(1788a) "Neue Entdeckung." *ALZ* (25 September), no. 231a, columns 831–2.

(1788b) "Review of Rehberg's *Über das Verhältniß der Metaphysik zur Religion.*" *ALZ* (26 June), no. 153b, columns 689–96.

(1789) *Versuch einer neuen Theorie des menschlichen Vorstellungsvermögens* (*Essay of a New Theory of the Human Faculty of Representation*). Prague and Jena: Widtemann & Mauke.

(1790a) "Erörterungen über den *Versuch einer Theorie des Vostellungsvermögens.*" *Beyträge zur Berichtigung bisheriger Mißverständnisse der Philosophen.* 2 vols. Jena: Mauke. Vol. 1, 373–404.

(1790b) "Neue Darstellung der Hauptmomente der Elementarphilosophie." *Beyträge zur Berichtigung bisheriger Mißverständnisse der Philosophen.* 2 vols. Jena: Mauke. Vol. 1, 165–254.

(1790c) "Über das Verhältniß der Theorie des Vorstellungsvermögens zur Kritik der reinen Vernunft." *Beyträge zur Berichtigung bisheriger Mißverständnisse der Philosophen.* 2 vols. Jena: Mauke. Vol. 2, pp. 255–338.

(1790–2a) "Erörterung des Begriffes von der Freyheit des Willens." "Discussion of the Concept of Freedom of Will." *Briefe über die Kantische Philosophie.* 2 vols. Leipzig: Göschen. Vol. 2, Letter 7, 220–61.

(1790–2b) "Über den bisher verkannte Unterschied zwischen dem uneigennützigen und dem eigennützigen Triebe, und zwischen diesen beyden Trieben und dem Willen" ("On the Hitherto Misunderstood Distinction Between Disinterested and Interested Drive, and Between These Two and the Will"). *Briefe über die Kantische Philosophie,* 2 vols. Leipzig: Göschen. Vol. II, Letter VII, 220–61.

(1791a) *Über das Fundament des philosophischen Wissens. Concerning the Foundation of Philosophical Knowledge.* Jena: Mauke. Tr. of excerpt, *Between Kant and Hegel.*

(1791b) "Über die Grundwahrheit der Moralität und ihr Verhältniß zur Grundwahrheit der Religion." ("On the Fundamental Truths of Morality and Their Relation to the Fundamental Truths of Religion"). *Der neue Teutsche Merkur* (March), 225–80.

(1794a) "Review of Kant's *Religion.*" *ALZ* (March), nos. 14, 15, columns 686–91.

(1794b) "Über das vollständige Fundament der Moral." ("Regarding the Complete Foundation of Morality"). *Beyträge zur Berichtigung bisheriger Mißverständnisse der Philosophen. Contributions to the Corection of Philosophers' Misunderstandings to Date.* 2 vols. Jena: Mauke. Vol. 2, 207–29.

(1794c) "Über den Unterschied zwischen dem Wollen und dem Begehren in Rücksicht auf das Sittengesetz: an Herrn Professor Schmid in Jena" ("Regarding the Distinction Between Willing and Desire with Reference to the Moral Law: Addressed to the Herr Professor Schmid in Jena"). *Beyträge zur Berichtigung bisheriger Mißverständnisse der Philosophen.* 2 vols. Jena: Mauke. Vol. 2, 230–64.

(1794d) "Über den Zusammenhang zwischen Begehren und Wollen in Rücksicht auf das Sittengesetz" ("Regarding the Connection Between Desire and Willing with Reference to the Moral Law"). *Beyträge zur Berichtigung bisheriger Mißverständnisse der Philosophen.* 2 vols. Jena: Mauke. Vol. 2, 265–94.

(1797a) "Einige Bemerkungen über die in der Einleitung zu den metaphysischen Anfangsgründen der Rechtslehre von I. Kant aufgestellten Begriffe von der Freyheit des Willens" ("Some Comments Regarding the Concept of the Freedom of the Will Advanced in Kant's Introduction to the Metaphysical Principles of the Doctrine of Right"). *Auswahl vermischter Schriften.* 2 vols. Jena: Mauke. Vol. 2, 364–400.

(1797b) Preface to J. G. Fichte, *Auswahl vermischter Schriften*, vol. 2. Jena: Mauke, pp. x–xi.

(1798a) "Omnibus Review of Fichte's Works to Date." *ALZ* (4–8 January), nos. 5–9, columns 33–69.

(1798b) *Verhandlungen über die Grundbegriffe und Grundsätze der Moralität (Negotiations Concerning the Fundamental Concepts and Principles of Morality).* Vol. 1. Lübeck and Leipzig: Friedrich Bohm.

(1799a) *Sendschreiben an I. C. Lavater und J. G. Fichte über den Glauben an Gott.* Hamburg: Friedrich Perthes.

(1799b) *Über die Paradoxien der neuesten Philosophie (Regarding the Paradoxes of the Latest Philosophy).* Hamburg: Friedrich Perthes.

(1801a) "Ideen zu einer Heautogonie oder natürliche Geschichte der reinen Ichheit, genannt reine Vernunft." *Beyträge zur leichtern Übersicht des Zustandes der Philosophie beym Anfange des 19. Jahrhunderts.* Vol. 1. Hamburg: Perthes. *Beytrag 4*, 134–54.

(1801b) "Was heißt philosophiren? Was war es, und was soll es seyn?" *Beyträge zur leichtern Übersicht des Zustandes der Philosophie beym Anfange des 19. Jahrhunderts (Contributions to a Simplified Overview of the Situation of Philosophy at the Beginning of the 19th Century).* Vol. 1. Hamburg: Perthes.

(1977) *Schriften zur Religionkritik und Aufklärung, 1782–1784*, Z. Batscha (ed.). Bremen and Wolfenbüttel: Jacobi.

Richter, J-P. (1800) *Clavis Fichteana seu leibgeriana. Jean Paul, Werke.* Vol. 3. Munich: Hanser, 1965–7.

(1829–33) *Jean Pauls Briefwechsel mit seinem Freunde Christian Otto.* Berlin: Reimer.

Schelling, F. W. J. (1797–8) *Allgemeine Übersicht der neuesten philosophischen Literatur.* Later retitled *Übersicht*, was renamed *Abhandlungen zur Erläuterung des Idealismus der Wissenschaftslehre. Sämmtliche Werke.* Vol. 4. Stuttgart and Augsburg: Cotta, 1858.

(1800) *System des transcendentalen Idealismus, Sämmtliche Werke.* Vol. 3. Stuttgart and Augsburg: Cotta, 1858. *System of Transcendental Idealism*, P. Heath (tr.), M. Vater (ed.). Charlotteville: University of Virginia Press, 1978.

(1980) *The Unconditional in Human Knowledge: Four Early Essays (1794–1796)*, F. Marti (tr.). Lewisburg: Buchnell, 1980.

Schleiermacher, F. (1793–4) *Spinozismus. Friedrich Daniel Ernst Schleiermacher, Jugendschriften 1787–1796*, G. Meckenstock (ed.). Berlin and New York: Walter de Gruyter, 1984.

(1800) "Review of Fichte's *Bestimmung des Menschen*." *Athaeneum*, 3.2, 283–97.

(1992a) *On the Highest Good*, H. V. Froese (tr. and ed.). Lewiston, Queenston, and Lampeter: Edwin Mellen.

(1992b) "Über die Freiheit." *Friedrich Daniel Ernst Schleiermacher, Jugendschriften 1787–1796*, G. Meckenstock (ed.). Berlin and New York: Walter de Gruyter, 1984. English tr. *On Freedom*, A. L. Blackwell (tr.). Lewiston, Queeston, and Lampeter: Edwin Mellen, 1992.

Schmid, C. C. E. (1788) *Wörterbuch zum leichtern Gebrauch der Kantischen Schriften. Lexicon for an Easier Use of Kantian Writings*. Jena: Kröker.

(1790) *Versuch einer Moralphilosophie. An Essay in Moral Philosophy*. Jena: Kröker.

(1793) *Grundriß der Moralphilosophie*. Jena: Kröker.

(1795a) "Bruchstücke aus einer Schrift über die Philosophie und ihrer Principien" ("Fragments of a Script Concerning Philosophy and Its Principles"). *Philosophisches Journal einer Gesellschaft Teutscher Gelehrten* 3, 95–132.

(1795b) *Grundriß des Naturrechts*. Jena and Leipzig: Gabler.

(1796) *Philosophische Dogmatik, im Grundriß für Vorlesungen*. Jena and Leipzig: Gabler.

(1800) *Aufsätzen Philosophischen und Theologischen Inhalts*, 2 vols. Jena: Kröker.

Schultz, J. (1784) *Erläuterungen über des Herrn Professor Kant Critik der reinen Vernunft*. Königsberg: Hartnung; 2nd ed., 1791. *Exposition of Kant's Critique of Pure Reason*, J. Morrison (tr. and ed.). Ottawa: University of Ottawa Press, 1995.

(1788) Review of Rehberg's *Über das Verhältniß der Metaphysik und der Religion*. *ALZ* (19 June), no. 147, columns 617–21.

Schulze, G. E. (1792) *Ænesidemus, oder über die Fundamente der von Herrn Prof. Reinhold in Jena gelieferten Elemetarphilosophie, nebst einer Verteidigung gegen die Anmassungen der Venunftkritik (Ænesidemus, or, Concerning the Foundations of the Philosophy of the Elements Issued by Prof. Reinhold in Jena, Together with a Defence of Skepticism Against the Pretensions of the Critique of Reason)*. Tr. (excerpts), *Between Kant and Hegel*.

(1801) *Kritik der theoretischen Philosophie*. 2 vols. Hamburg: Bohn.

(1802a) *Grundsätze der allgemeinen Logik*. Helmstädt: Fleckeisen.

(1802b) Review of G. E. Schulze's *Grundsätze der allgemeinen Logik*. *Gottingische gelehrte Nachrichten*, 111, 1409–21.

(1803) "Aphorismen über das Absolute, als das alleinige Prinzip der wahren Philosophie, über die einzige mögliche Art es zu erkennen, wie auch über das Verhältniß aller Dinge in der Welt zu demselben." *Neues Museum der Philosophie und Litteratur*, F. Bouterwek (ed.). Vol. 1, 110–48. Reproduced in Jaeschke (1993a).

(1805) "Die Hauptmomente der skeptischen Denkart über die menschliche Erkenntniss." *Neues Museum der Philosophie und Litteratur*, F. Bouterwek (ed.). Vol. 3, 2–57. Reproduced in Jaeschke (1993a).

Selle, C. G. (1788) *Grundsätze der reinen Philosophie*. Berlin: Himburgh.

Spalding, J. J. (1774) *Die Bestimmung des Menschen*. Leipzig: Erben und Reich.

Spinoza, B. de. (1677) *Ethica ordine geometrica demonstrata. Opera omnia priora et posthuma*. Vol. 2. Amsterdam.

Tiedemann, D. (1800) Review of Fichte's *Die Bestimmung des Menschen. Neue allgemeine deutsche Bibliothek* 60, 369–89.

Tittel, G. A. (1786) *Über Herrn Kant's Moralreform*. Frankfurt and Leipzig: Pfhäler.

(1787) *Kantischen Denkformen oder Kategorien*. Frankfurt/Main: Gebhard.

Trapp, C. H. E. (1790, 1791) "Neue Briefe über die Kantische Philosophie" ("New Letters Concerning the Kantian Philosophy"). *Braunschweiges Journal* 2 (1790), 442–78; 2 (1791), 199–218.

Ulrich, J. A. H. (1785) *Institutiones Logicae et Metaphysicae*. Jena: Kröker.

   (1788) *Eleutheriologie oder über Freiheit und Nothwendigkeit*. Jena: Kröker.

Weishaupt, A. (1787) *Über Materialismus und Idealismus*. Nürnberg: Grattenhau.

   (1788a) *Über die Gründe und Gewisheit* [*sic*] *der Menschlichen Erkenntnis. Zur Prüfung der Kantishen Kritik* (*Concerning the Grounds and the Certainty of Human Cognition. Towards a Reconsideration of the Kantian Critique*). Nürnberg: Grattenhau.

   (1788b) *Zum Gebrauch der Vorlesungen in den Michaelisferien*. Jena: Kröker.

   (1793–7) *Über Wahrheit und sittliche Vollkommenheit. Concerning Truth and Ethical Perfection*. 3 vols. Regensburg: Montag & Weiß.

2. Secondary Sources

Albrecht, M. (1989) "Thomasius – kein Eklektiker?" *Christian Thomasius 1655– 1728. Interpretationen zu Werk und Wirkung*, W. Schneiders (ed.). Hamburg: Meiner.

Allison, H. E. (1973) *The Kant–Eberhard Controversy*. Baltimore and London: Johns Hopkins University Press.

   (1983) *Kant's Transcendental Idealism*. New Haven and London: Yale University Press.

Ameriks, K. (2000) *Kant and the Fate of Autonomy*. Cambridge: Cambridge University Press.

Barbour, J. (2000) *The End of Time: The Next Revolution in Physics*. Oxford: Oxford University Press.

Beiser, F. C. (1992) *Enlightenment, Revolution, and Romanticism: The Genesis of Modern German Political Thought 1790–1800*. Cambridge, MA, and London: Harvard University Press.

Baum, G. (1969) *Vernunft und Erkenntnis: Die Philosophie F. H. Jacobis*. Bonn: Bouvier.

Borowski, L. E. (1804) *Darstellung des Lebens und Charakters Immanuel Kant's*. Königsberg. Deutsche Bibliothek.

Breazeale, D., ed., tr. (1988) *Fichte. Early Philosophical Writings*. Ithaca: Cornell University Press.

   ed., tr. (1992) *Fichte: Foundations of Transcendental Philosophy*. Ithaca: Cornell University Press.

   ed., tr. (1994) *J. G. Fichte. Introductions to the Wissenschaftslehre and Other Writings*. Indianapolis and Cambridge: Hackett.

di Giovanni, G. (1985) "The Facts of Consciousness." *Between Kant and Hegel*, pp. 2–50.

   (1992) "The First Twenty Years of Critique: The Spinoza Connection." *The Cambridge Companion to Kant*, P. Guyer (ed.). Cambridge: Cambridge University Press, pp. 417–48.

   (1994) *The Unfinished Philosophy of Friedrich Heinrich Jacobi. Jacobi*, pp. 1–167.

(1995) "Hegel, Jacobi, and Crypto-Catholicism, or, Hegel in Dialogue with the Enlightenment." *Hegel on the Modern World,* A. Collins (ed.). Albany: SUNY, pp. 53–72.

(1996) *Religion within the Boundaries of Mere Reason,* tr. G. di Giovanni in *Immanuel Kant, Religion and Natural Theology,* ed. and tr. G. di Giovanni and A. Wood. New York: Cambridge University Press.

(1997a) "... *Wie aus der Pistole*...: Fries and Hegel on Faith and Knowledge." *Hegel and the Tradition: Essays in Honour of H. S. Harris.* Toronto: University of Toronto Press, pp. 212–41.

(1997b) "Hume, Jacobi, and Common Sense: An Episode in the Reception of Hume in Germany at the Time of Kant." *Kant-Studien* 88 (1997): 44–58.

(1998) "The Jacobi–Reinhold Dialogue and Analytical Philosophy." *Fichte-Studien,* 14: 63–86.

(2001a) "Jacobi," sub voce: http://plato.stanford.edu/contents.html

(2001b) "Rehberg, Reinhold und C. C. E. Schmid über Kant und moralische Freiheit." *Vernunftkritik und Aufklärung: Studien zur Philosophie Kants und seines Jahrhunderts,* M. Oberhausen (ed.). Stuttgart-Bad Canstatt: Fromann-Holzboog, 2001, pp. 93–113.

(2003a) "1799: The Year of Reinhold's Conversion to Jacobi," *Die Philosophie Karl Leonhard Reinholds,* M. Bondeli and W. Schrader (eds.). *Fichte-Studien, Supplementa.* Amsterdam and New York: Rodopi, pp. 259–82.

(2003b) "Faith without Religion, and Religion without Faith: Kant and Hegel on Religion." *Journal of the History of Philosophy* 41.3 (2003): 365–83.

di Giovanni, G. and Harris, H. S., trs., eds (1985; new ed., 2000) *Between Kant and Hegel: Texts in the Development of Post-Kantian Idealism.* Indianapolis and Cambridge: Hackett.

Dumont, L. (1994) *German Ideology: From France to Germany and Back.* Chicago: Chicago University Press.

Ferrini, C. (2002) "Kant, H. S. Reimarus, e il problema degli *Algoa Zoa.*" *Studi Kantiani,* Vol. 15. Rome and Pisa: Istituti editoriali e poligrafici internazionali.

Ferry, L., Person, J. P., and Renaut, A., eds. (1979) *Philosophies de l'Université: L'idéalisme allemande et la question de l'Université.* Paris: Gallimard.

Förster, E. (1993) "Introduction." *Immanuel Kant. Opus postumum,* E. Förster and M. Rosen (trs.). New York: Cambridge University Press.

Fuchs, G. W. (1994) *Karl Leonhard Reinhold – Illuminat und Philosoph.* Bern: Peter-Lang.

Goethe, J. W. von. *Dichtung und Wahrheit,* V. *Sämmtliche Werke,* Münchener Ausgabe. Vol. 16. München: Heinser, 1985–.

Harris, H. S. (1972) *Hegel's Development: Toward the Sunlight, 1770–1801.* Oxford: Clarendon Press.

(1977) "Introduction." *G. W. F. Hegel, Faith and Knowledge.* Albany: SUNY Press.

(1965) "Leutwein über Hegel. Ein Dokument zu Hegels Biographie." *Hegel-Studien* 3 (1965), 39–77.

Hinske, N. (1994) "Moses Mendelssohn und die Kreise seiner Wirksamkeit." *Wolfenbütteler Studien Band 19.* Tübingen: Max Niemayer.

(1995a). "Die Kritik der reinen Vernunft und der Freiraum des Glaubens. Zur Kantinterpretation des Jenaer Frühkantianismus." *Jenaer philosophische Vorträge und Studien,* W. Hogrebe (ed.). Erlangen and Jena: Palm & Enke.

(1995b) "Ausblick: Der Jenaer Frühkantianismus als Forschungsausgabe." *Der Aufbruch in den Kantianismus. Der Frühkantianismus an der Universität Jena von 1785–1800 und seine Vorgeschichte,* N. Hinske, E. Lange, and H. Schröpfer (eds.). Stuttgart-Bad Canstatt: Fromann, pp. 231–43.

Humboldt, W. (1916) *Wilhelm von Humboldt Tagebücher, 1788–1798,* A. Leitzman (ed.), in *Gesammelte Schriften,* vol. 16. Berlin: Behr.

Hunter, I. (2001) *Rival Enlightenments. Civil and Metaphysical Philosophy in Early Modern Germany.* Cambridge: Cambridge University Press.

Jaeshke, W., ed. (1993a) *Der Streit um die Gestalt einer Ersten Philosophie (1799–1807), Quellenband.* Hamburg: Meiner.

ed. (1993b) *Der Streit um die Gestalt einer Ersten Philosophie (1799–1807).* Hamburg: Meiner.

Klotz, C. (2002) *Selbstbewußtsein und praktische Identität.* Frankfurt/Main: Vittorio Klostermann.

Korsgaard, C. M. (1996) *Creating the Kingdom of Ends.* New York: Cambridge University Press.

Kuehn, M. (1987) *Scottish Common Sense in Germany, 1768–1800: A Contribution to the History of Critical Philosophy.* Kingston and Montréal: McGill-Queens University Press.

(2001) *Kant: A Biography.* New York: Cambridge University Press.

La Vopa, A. J. (2001) *Fichte: The Self and the Calling of Philosophy, 1762–1799.* Cambridge: Cambridge University Press.

Lauth, R. (1979) "Nouvelles recherches sur Reinhold et l'Aufklärung." *Archives de philosophie,* 42: 593–629.

Le Forestier, R. (1914) *Les Illuminés de Bavière et la Franc-Maçonnerie allemande,* Paris.

Mahfouz, N. (1992) *Sugar Street.* New York: Random House.

Meckenstock, G. (1988) *Deterministische Ethik und kritische Theologie: Die Auseinandersetzung des frühen Schleiermachers mit Kant und Spinoza 1789–1794.* Berlin and New York: Walter de Gruyter.

Meist, K. R. (1993) "'Sich vollbringende Skeptizismus': G. E. Schulzes Replik auf Hegel und Schelling." In Jaeschke (1993b), pp. 192–230.

Negri, A. (1962) *Alle origini del formalismo giuriolico: studio sul problema della forma in Kant e nei giuristi kantiani tra il 1787 e il 1802.* Padova: CEDAM.

Nietzsche, F. (1922) *Gesammelte Werke, Erster Band, Jugendschriften 1858–1868.* München: Musarium Verlag.

Nuzzo, A. (1994a) "Metamorphosen der Freiheit in der Jenenser Kant-Rezeption (1785–1794)." *Evolution des Geistes: Jena um 1800,* F. Strack (ed.). Stuttgart: Klett-Cotta.

(1994b) "Transformations of Freedom in the Jena Kant Reception (1785–1794)," A. Bunch (tr.). *The Owl of Minerva,* 32 (2001), 135–67.

Pozzo, R. (1989) *Hegel: "Introductio in philosophiam." Dagli studi giovanili alla prima logica (1782–1801).* Firenze: La nuova Italia.

Sassen, B., ed., tr. (2000) *Kant's Early Critics: The Empiricist Critique of the Theoretical Philosophy*. Cambridge: Cambridge University Press.

Schultz, E. G. (1975) *Rehbergs Opposition gegen Kants Ethik*. Köln and Wien: Böhlau.

Selling, M. (1938) *Karl Leonhard Reinholds Elementarphilosophie in ihrem philosophis- chegeschichtlichen Zusammenhang*. Lund: Ohlsson.

Strawson, P. F. (1966) *The Bounds of Sense*. London: Methuen.

Stroud, B. (2003) "The Dissatisfactions of Metaphysics." Paper read at McGill University, Montréal.

Tafani, D. (1999) *Christoph Andreas Leonhard Creuzer. La discussione della dottrina morale di Kant alla fine del settecento*. Genova: Erga.

Valenza, P. (1994) *Reinhold e Hegel. Ragione storica e inizio assoluto della filosofia*. Padova: CEDAM.

Van Dülmen, R. (1975) *Der Geheimbund der Illuminaten, Darstellung, Analyse, Doku- mentation*. Stuttgart-Bad Cannstatt: Fromann.

Zahn, M. (1967) "Fichte, Schelling et Hegel en face du 'Realisme Logique' de Christoph Gottfried Bardili." *Archives de philosophie*, 30 (1967), 61–88, 199– 230.

Index

Abel, J.F., 311–12
Abicht, J.H., 55–8, 66, 77, 83, 119, 206
  and Locke, 59
  and Reinhold, 313
  and Schmid, 58
  and Weishaupt, 58–9
  critique of Fichte, 289, 343
  critique of Kant, 55, 60, 314
  Hermias, 60
  reform of Kant, 59–60
abstraction
  and Fichte, 287
  and Jacobi, 138, 146
  and Reinhold, 248, 258, 287
action
  and Fichte, 241
  and Hegel, 294
  and Jacobi, 13
  and Kant, 164
  and Rehberg, 131–2
actual, the
  and Kant, 19
actuality
  and possibility, 18–21, 85, 141
Aenesidemus, *see* Schulze, G.E.
affection (*Empfindung*)
  and Fichte, 215–17, 219
afterlife
  and Kant, 9
  and Spalding, 9

agency
  and Jacobi, 14–15
  and Kant 14–15
  and Reinhold, 256
Allgemeine deutsche Bibliothek, 37
Allgemeine Literatur-Zeitung, 37, 108,
  117, 125, 126, 127, 207, 225, 289,
  331
Allison, H.E., ix–x
Ameriks, K., ix, 306
Analogies of Experience, 72–3, 74,
  174
anthropology, 65
Antinomy of Pure Reason,
  153–5
appearance(s), 4
  and Kant, 19, 177–8
apperception, 57
  synthesis of, 71
  unity of, 71, 227
apprehension
  synthesis of, 71
Aquinas, Thomas, 6
  Summa Theologiae, 6
arbitrary choice (*Willkühr*)
  and Fichte, 209, 221
  and Kant, 189, 191–2, 193,
  259
  and Reinhold, 124
  and *Wille*, 205

atheism
  and Fichte, 10, 25, 242
  and Kant, 25
  and Reinhold, 256–7, 258, 262
  and Spinozism, 11
atheism dispute (*Atheismusstreit*), 242,
    244
  and Jacobi, 242–3, 244
  and Reinhold, 242, 243–4
Athenaeum, 291
Aufklärung (*see* Enlightenment)
  and Kant, xii
  religion of the, 193
authority, religious
  and Kant, 201
autonomy
  and Kant, 164

Baggesen, J.I., 342
Bardili, C.B., 265, 269, 330, 340
Beck, S., 75, 269
belief
  and faith, 79
  and Kant, 183
  ecclesiastical, 200–1
Berlin Academy, 125
Berliner, the, 77
Berlinische Monatsschrift, 37, 152
Bonnet, C., 46
Born, F.G., 60, 312
Breazeale, D., 338

categorical imperative, 168–9, 172,
    213
categories
  and 'I think', 75
  and Jacobi, 82
  and Kant, 18
  and things, 172
  and Weishaupt, 53
  application of, 74, 173, 174
  of the understanding, 69–70, 72–4
causa sui, 22, 184
causality, 121
  and Kant, 20, 22, 154, 156–7, 159,
    176, 178–9
  and Reinhold, 209

  and Spinoza, 142
  category of, 72
Christianity
  and Kant, 186
  and popular philosophy, 38
church
  and Kant, 200, 201, 202
Church Universal, 200
Cicero, 326
cognition
  and faith, 78
  and Reinhold, 95–6
'common sense', 41, 96
  and Hegel, 296
  and Jacobi, 87, 89–90
  and Kant, 48
  and Mendelssohn, 48, 87, 89, 91
  and philosophy, 41
  and popular philosophy, 48
  and Reid, 89
  and Reinhold, 89, 235
'common sense' philosophy, 77
  and popular philosophy, 9, 47–8
community
  and Fichte, 239
compatibilism, 157
  and Kant, 159
concept(s), 71
  and classical metaphysics, 36
  and Kant, 36
  and Reinhold, 100
  and sensations, 36, 68
  and Weishaupt, 45
  speculative, 247, 249
conscience
  and Reinhold, 253–4
consciousness
  and Reinhold, 93, 101–2
  'clear' and 'distinct', 95
corpus mysticum, 19
creation
  and Leibniz, 109–10
Creuzer, L., 205–6, 207
  and Schmid, 207
'critical ignorance', 121
Critique of Reason, 301
  destabilizing effects of, 10

novelty of, 34
problems with, 161–2, 325
response to, 5, 29, 32
Crusius, C.A., 40, 42, 43, 304

Dennett, D., 325
Descartes, R., 22, 43, 45, 50, 97, 320
and Fichte, 276–7, 278, 279
desire
and Fichte, 215, 216–17, 218, 219, 221, 274
determinism
and Creuzer, 206
and Schleiermacher, 292
and Ulrich, 112–13, 114, 142–3
Dilthey, W., 292
dogmatism, 227
and Fichte, 224–5
doubt, 276, 277
and Reinhold, 253
duty
and Kant, 164, 165
and religion, 201–2
sui generis, 199

Eberhard, J.A., 41, 49, 292, 341
eclecticism
and popular philosophy, 41, 42, 43–4
and system, 43
education
and popular philosophy, 299
and Reinhold, 300
elementary philosophy
and Abicht, 55–6
and Reinhold, 56
empiricism, 41 (*see also* Purism, Kantian)
and judgment, 69
and popular philosophy, 9
British, 262
classical, 74, 80
Locke's, 45, 50, 52, 53–4, 59
Enlightenment, the, 37, 65, 66, 276, 279, 292, 296, 297
and Fichte, 7, 215

and Hegel, xi
and Kant, 4–5
and popular philosophy, 37
view of humans, 2
ens perfectissimum, 109, 110
ens realissimum, 109, 110
entia rationis (*see* noumena)
eudaimonism, 7, 131, 292
and Fichte, 217
and Gebhard, 207
and Kant, 330
Kant's critique of, 3
evil
and Kant, 129, 187–91, 192–4, 198
propensity to, 189, 190, 191
evil genius, 276–7, 278, 279
existentialism, 7
experience, 80
aesthetic, 171
and Fichte, 222–3, 334, 335
and Jacobi, 82, 86–7, 238
and Kant, 68, 69–75, 155
and Leibniz, 32
and Reinhold, 96–7, 246, 286
and Schmid, 71
extension
and Spinoza, 143–4

fact of consciousness, 91, 92, 233, 235, 296
and Fichte, 218–19
and Gebhard, 224
and Reinhold, 246–7, 261
fact of reason, 167
and freedom, 167
faith
and Abicht, 289
and Enlightenment, 26, 297, 298
and Fichte, 233, 236, 238, 250, 251, 280, 287–8
and Hegel, 294
and Jacobi, 13, 78, 149, 237–8, 250, 251
and Kant, 10, 26–7, 36–7
and knowledge, 25–6
and Lessing, 26
and reason, 34–5

faith (*cont.*)
 and Reinhold, 248, 250, 251–2,
  253–4, 257
 in Kant's system, 30
 seeking understanding (*fides qaerens
  intellectum*), 33–5, 36
fall, the, 192
fatalism
 and Ulrich, 114
 and Weishaupt, 53–4, 105, 114, 275
 empirical, 206–7
 intelligible, 245
Feder, J.G.H., 41, 49, 308, 312
feeling(s)
 and Abicht, 56–7, 58–9, 60
 and Enlightenment, 55
 and Fichte, 219–20, 221, 230, 343
 and interest of reason, 76
 and Jacobi, 338
 and Kant, 55
 and moral conduct, 169–70
 and Weishaupt, 59
Fichte, J.G., 1, 58, 66, 76, 84, 118, 126,
  133, 140, 150, 162, 205, 271
 and Jacobi, 215, 237–9, 257, 280–1
 and Kant, 28, 30–1, 213–14, 215,
  222, 226, 229–31, 233, 236, 277,
  285, 289–90
 and Rehberg, 240–1
 as Jacobin, 240
 Critique of All Revelation, 209,
  210–12, 215, 230, 240, 241, 298
 critique of Creuzer, 208–9, 223–4
 critique of Gebhard, 208, 223, 224
 critique of Kant, 209, 221, 278
 critique of Reinhold, 209, 221,
  223–4
 defense of Kant and Reinhold, 208
 dispute with Schmid, 207–8, 223,
  224–5, 233, 330–1
 System of Ethics, 239
 The Vocation of Humankind, 1, 7, 30,
  272–83, 285, 288, 293
 Wissenschaftslehre, 205, 210, 215,
  225, 226, 231, 232, 233, 234, 235,
  236, 237, 238, 245, 253, 258, 263,
  267, 270, 280

Flatt, J.F., 26, 49
 *Letters Concerning the Moral Ground of
  Knowledge of Religion*, 49
Forberg, F.K., 242
formalism
 and Fichte, 297, 298
 and Kant, 53, 55, 84, 171–6, 297
Free Masonry, 37, 44
 and Reinhold, 263, 265
freedom, 16, 108
 and Creuzer, 330
 and Fichte, 208, 212–15, 216, 218,
  221, 251, 274, 281–2, 284
 and God's omnipotence, 109–12
 and Jacobi, 12, 105, 142–3, 144–5,
  148–9
 and Kant, 6, 14, 29, 30, 117, 118,
  154, 155, 158, 179, 180, 184, 194,
  195, 198, 203, 304, 328
 and Leibniz, 110, 111
 and medieval theology, 111
 and Rehberg, 132, 328
 and Reinhold, 106, 122, 123, 124,
  141, 246, 247, 248, 249–50,
  255–6
 and Spinoza, 141–2
 and Ulrich, 112, 113–14, 141, 142
 and Weishaupt, 105
 comparative, 121, 130
French Revolution, 125, 240, 263,
  264
Fries, Jakob Friedrich, 1, 78, 269
 as popular philosopher, 335

Garve, C.J., 49, 308, 326, 339
Gebhard, F.H., 207, 330
 and Fichte, 331
 and Kant, 207
God, 80, 108–10
 and Fichte, 210–11, 251, 259, 277,
  288
 and freedom, 2–3
 and Herder, 239
 and Jacobi, 15, 25, 148, 239, 251,
  268
 and Kant, xi, 181–2, 183, 187, 195,
  196, 197, 199, 203, 240

and moral law, 211–12
and Reinhold, 252, 254, 256, 286
and Schmid, 61
and Spalding, 8
and Spinoza, 85, 138, 139–40
belief in, 251
in medieval theology, 111
proofs of existence, 85–6, 302
Goethe, J.W., 3, 11, 12, 128, 185, 272
and Jacobi, 13, 23, 150, 303
Prometheus, 2, 3, 11, 24, 27
good, the
and Spalding, 8
Kant and the highest, 182, 183, 292
perfect, 135
good principle, 198
goodness
human, 188
guilt, 275

Hammann, G.H., 240
and Jacobi, 316
Hannover school, 125
happiness
and Abicht, 60
and Enlightenment, 297
and Fichte, 217, 224, 251, 298
and Hegel, 297
and Jacobi, 251
and Kant, 3–4, 135, 182, 183–4,
314, 328
and Rehberg, 328
and Reinhold, 251
and Spalding, 8
and Ulrich, 114
and virtue, 182, 183
and Weishaupt, 46, 59, 313
Hegel, G.W.F., 76, 237, 262, 271,
328
and Fichte, 221, 272, 342
and Jacobi, 293
and Krug, 306
and Reinhold, 259, 261, 296, 318
and Schelling, 311, 344
and Schulze, 311
as social educator, 300
critique of Fichte, 293–5, 296–8

critique of Jacobi, 298
critique of Kant, 294–5, 296–7
critique of popular philosophy, 37
Faith and Knowledge, 293
Logic, x
Phenomenology of Spirit, x, 311, 318,
342
Heine, H., xii
hen kai pan, 13
Herder, J.G., 108, 140, 149
heteronomy, 180
Heydenreich, K.H., 304
history
and Fichte, 65
and Hegel, 65
and Kant, 6, 22, 27, 214
and Mendelssohn, 13
and philosophy, 65
and Reinhold, 65
and system, 6
Holbach, P.H. d', 46
Holy Will, 180, 182, 187, 284
homo noumenon
and *homo phaenomenon*, 5, 64,
179–80, 283, 284
human nature
and Kant, 186, 190–1
humanism, 1–3, 12
and Fichte, 220, 292
and Jacobi, 11–12
and Kant, 3–5, 10, 12
and Spalding, 106
humanity well pleasing to God, 196,
197
Humboldt, W. von, 317, 342
Hume, David, 71, 80, 81, 84, 88–9
and Jacobi, 79–81, 82–3, 84
critique of Locke and Leibniz, 40
Hunter, Ian, xii, 304

'I', the
and Abicht, 289
and Fichte, 281, 344
and Schmid, 121
'I think', 71, 72, 73, 75–6, 166, 171,
174
and Fichte, 229, 277–8

idealism, 288
  and Fichte, 223, 224–5, 264, 285
  and Hegel, 295, 296
  and Kant, 175, 176
  and Reinhold, 237, 244, 269
  and Schmid, 290
  and Schulze, 311
  critical, x
  fundamental thesis of, 35
  post-Kantian, x
  Romantic, 272
  transcendental, 52, 82
Identity Philosophy, 300
ignorance
  critical, 18
Illuminati, 38, 44, 66, 226, 263
  and Reinhold, 263–4
  and Weishaupt, 263
imaginary constructs, 64
imagination, 70
impulse (*Trieb*)
  and Fichte, 216, 219
  and reason, 217
incentive (*Triebfeder*), 169–70
individual, the, 2–3
  and Enlightenment, 283
  and Fichte, 275–6, 278, 284–5
  and Jacobi, 12–15, 239, 245, 246,
    267–8
  and Kant, 5, 16, 27, 73, 160, 162,
    174–5, 192, 194–5, 198, 202, 278,
    283, 328
  and Mendelssohn, 13
  and popular philosophers, 73, 283,
    299
  and Reinhold, 337–8
  and Schmid, 53–4
  and system, 6
  and Weishaupt, 53–4
  concrete, 65, 66, 72
  dual nature of, 5
individuality
  of things, 45–6
infinite and finite
  and Reinhold, 255, 256
intellect
  and medieval theology, 34

interest
  and Kant, 169–70
intuition
  faculty of, 177
  sensible, ix
intuition, intellectual
  and Fichte, 213
  and Hegel, 345
  and Kant, 22–3, 36, 213
irrationality
  and Jacobi, 79, 105, 316
  and Kant, 26, 30, 204
  of human situation, 194

Jacobi, F.H., xi, 10–12, 27, 54, 58, 77,
    92, 105, 116, 118, 125, 126, 204,
    278, 292, 299
  and Hume, 316
  and Kant, 265, 270
  and Kant reception, 11
  and Leibniz, 90, 105, 144
  and Spinoza, 84, 105, 137–8,
    139–42, 143–7, 239
  common ground with Kant, 14–15,
    85–6
  critique of Enlightenment, 11–12,
    14
  critique of Fichte, 25, 28, 265–8,
    285–6
  critique of Herder, 143, 150
  critique of Kant, 14, 15, 17, 18, 25,
    77, 82–3, 84, 86–7, 91, 243, 267,
    299
  critique of popular philosophers,
    37, 38
  critique of Rehberg, 136, 324
  *David Hume on Faith or Idealism and
    Realism, a Dialogue*, 77–91, 93, 95,
    97, 105, 125, 137, 144, 147, 150,
    151, 238, 239, 244, 268
  his project, 29
  religious concerns, 24–5
Jena theologians, 25, 156, 313
  and Kant, 27, 270, 328
Jesuits, 37
Jesus, 201
Judaism, 201

judgment
  and experience, 68, 69–70, 73
  and Kant, 166
  of experience, 82
jurists
  and Kant, xii, 306, 326

Kant, I. (*see also* Critique of Reason)
  and critical ignorance, 25, 176
  and dogmatists, 173–4
  and Locke, 62
  and 'transcendental story', ix–x, xi,
    29, 30, 194–5
  as empiricist, 74
  as metaphysical thinker, x, xi, 20–1,
    133, 134, 160
  as phenomenologist, 75
  *Anthropology from a Pragmatic Point of
    View*, 186
  critique of Fichte, 269–70
  critique of his moral vision, 164, 171
  Critique of Judgment, 295, 329, 345
  Critique of Practical Reason, 23, 126,
    127, 137, 154, 164, 165–6, 169,
    182, 185, 328, 329
  Critique of Pure Reason, 1, 2, 4, 6, 12,
    16, 29, 67, 70, 73, 76, 77, 86, 118,
    134, 153, 166, 173, 182, 328, 329,
    339
  critique of Reinhold, 124, 205
  *Groundwork for the Metaphysics of
    Morals*, 164
  his Copernican revolution, 28
  his *Übergang*, 173
  immodesty, 35, 185
  Metaphysics of Morals, 173, 205, 326
  modesty, 20, 153, 176, 304
  originality, 158, 163
  practical postulates, 191–2
  Prolegomena to Any Future Metaphysics,
    67
  psychological model, 64
  psychologizing of, 50
  reception of, x, 14
  *Religion within the Boundaries of Mere
    Reason*, 152–3, 193, 195, 198, 201,
    202, 203, 328

vision of the universe, 283–4
"What Does It Mean to Orient
    Oneself in Thinking?", 87
Kierkegaard, S., 327, 329
Kingdom of Ends, 168, 180
Kingdom of God
  and Kant, 196, 200
knowledge
  and Fichte, 213, 273, 282
  and Jacobi, 79
  and Kant, 17, 20–1, 35–6, 226,
    277
  and Leibniz, 47
  and Locke, 47
  and Reinhold, 227–8
  and Weishaupt, 46
  of transcendant objects, 76
  representational theory of, 35
Köppen, F., 345
Kraus, C.J., 108
  critique of Ulrich, 117–18, 320
Kritisches Journal der Philosophie, 299,
    345
Krug, W.T., 37, 262, 298
  as popular philosopher, 335
Kuehn, M., xi, 307, 326

La Vopa, A.J., 336
language
  Fichte on religious, 285
  Kant on moral, 21
Lavater, J.K., 79, 245, 251, 252–3, 257,
    286
Law, the
  and Fichte, 208, 210, 213
  and inclinations, 170
  and Jacobi, 267
  and Kant, 3–4, 129–30, 133, 165,
    167, 173, 174, 197
  and Rehberg, 130–1
  and Schmid, 119–20
  idea of, 118
Leibniz, G.W., 50, 84, 87, 95, 98, 103,
    108, 117, 139, 262
  ideal of universal harmony, 60
  Monadology, 104
  Theodicy, 141

Lessing, G.E., 11, 13, 27, 54, 85, 105, 107, 140, 149, 242, 243, 256
life
  and Fichte, 223
Locke, J., 16, 41, 45, 50, 71, 97, 98, 102
  and popular philosophy, 39, 47, 50
  Essay on Human Understanding, 47
logic
  formal, 27
  transcendental, 17, 40
  Transcendental, 62, 64, 65, 73, 261
Luther, M., 259

Maimon, S.
  critique of Kant, 98
  critique of Reinhold, 98–9, 318
Marx, K., 327
materialism, 46
mathematics, 98
  and Kant, 165–6
maxim, 168, 169, 188
meaning
  and Fichte, 290
  and Kant, 20
mechanism
  and Jacobi, 142, 145
Meckenstock, G., 344
Meiners, C., 41
Mendelssohn, M., 10, 85, 86, 106, 143, 243, 281
  and German philosophy, 43
  and Jacobi, 11, 14, 77, 78, 87, 137, 140, 141
  and Kant, 12, 27, 302, 303, 304
metaphysics
  and Fichte, 260–1
  and Kant, 32–3, 64, 158, 178, 184–5, 195
  and Rehberg, 125, 128–9
  dissatisfaction of, x
  dogmatic, 32
  rationalistic, 34
  scholastic, 84, 90, 140
method
  transcendental, 59
  phenomenological, 83
Michaelis, C.F., 331

mind
  and Abicht, 60
  and Fichte, 222
  and Leibniz, 61, 63–5, 97
  and Locke, 62
  and Schmid, 51, 61, 64
  and Weishaupt, 64
morality
  and Fichte, 282
  and Gebhard, 207
  and Kant, 30, 129–30, 157, 160, 162–71
  and principle of non-contradiction, 131
  and Reinhold, 122–4
  and Schmid, 119–22
moral life, 60
  and Abicht, 57–8
  and Hegel, 293–5
  and Kant, 23–4, 283–4
  and Reinhold, 246
Moses, 201
mystery
  holy, 203–4
myth
  and Fichte, 260
  and human nature, 34

naturalism
  and Fichte, 262
  and Kant, 262
  and popular philosophers, 262
  and Schmid, 120–2
  ethical, 14–15
nature
  and Fichte, 228, 229–30, 259, 273–5, 282, 290, 299
  and Hegel, 261, 262, 293–4, 295
  and idealism, 35, 175
  and Kant, 3, 18, 23, 168–9, 173, 175, 299
  and moral law, 3, 164, 168, 170, 171
  and popular philosophers, 2
  and Reinhold, 256, 261, 296
  ethical state of, 198–9
  juridical state of, 198

necessity
and Ulrich, 112–13
Neue allgemeine deutsche Bibliothek, 288
Nietzsche, Friedrich, 301
nominalism
and Kant, 306
normativity
and Fichte, 259, 287
and Reinhold, 286–7
noumena (*see also* world), 4–5, 33, 63, 64
and phenomena, 74

object
and Hume, 296
and Kant, 17, 18–19, 35, 177, 178
and Kantian Purism, 50, 51
and Locke, 296
and Weishaupt, 53
of experience in general, 69–70
obligation
and Ulrich, 113–14
optimism
and Rehberg, 324
order
Spalding and universal, 8–9
other, the
and Fichte, 220, 231
and Jacobi, 268
Otto, J.P.C., 342
'ought', the
and Kant, 157

pantheism
and Herder, 239
and Schleiermacher, 292
People of God
and Kant, 199, 200, 201, 202
phenomena (*see also* noumena)
and Kant, 74
phenomenology
of the genesis of experience, 94
of the genesis of the self, 76
of the mind, 59
Philonenko, Alexis, 338
philosophy
and Jacobi, 13, 147, 149, 244, 265

and Fichte, 236, 238, 258–9, 334, 335
and Reinhold, 227, 228, 235, 247, 249–50, 254–7, 258, 286
practical, 257
Pietism
and Kant, 30
Pistorius, W. F., 49, 328
Platonism, 185
Plattner, E., 41, 102, 309
pleasure
and Fichte, 217
Pope, A., 185
popular philosophy, xi, 28, 59, 77, 78, 107, 262
and critics, 37–8
and Fichte, 222–3, 236
and Hegel, 262, 296
and Jacobi, 29, 244, 268
and Kant, 48, 50, 62–3, 64
and Leibniz, 39, 47, 52
and Reinhold, 29, 38–41, 42–4, 47, 102, 225, 244, 262, 269, 286
its mistake, 222
nature of, 38
origins of, 41
tension in, 2–3
possibility
and Kant, 18–19, 21
in moral context, 19–20
poststructuralists, 7
predispositions
and Kant, 188–9
principium compositionis
and *principium generationis*, 85
principle
of contradiction, 39, 43
of morality, 166–7
of sufficient reason, 114, 118, 124–5, 137, 206, 208
psychology
and Abicht, 55
and Fichte, 222
and Kant, 169
and popular philosophy, 62, 63
Purism, Kantian, 64, 72
and Empiricism, 50–2

rationalism, 41, 45, 74
rationality
  and Fichte, 220
realism, 86, 175, 277
  and Kant, 176
reality
  and Kant, 6, 20
  and Reinhold, 255
reason
  and Fichte, 211, 220–1, 223, 236,
    239, 259, 260, 268, 291
  and Jacobi, 15, 27, 88–9, 146–7,
    243, 268
  and Kant, 4, 15, 17, 33, 34–5, 116,
    165–6, 170–1, 172, 204, 226–7,
    236
  and Rehberg, 126–7
  and Reinhold, 27, 122, 123, 127,
    233–5, 236, 247, 254–5, 264, 300
  and Schelling, 331–2
  and Schmid, 51
  and Spalding, 30
  artificial use of, 227, 228, 231–2,
    233–5, 247, 250, 255
  natural use of, 227, 255
recognition, 70, 71
reductionism
  and Kant, 159–60
reflection, philosophical
  and Fichte, 250, 266–7
  and Jacobi, 336
  and Reinhold, 247, 248–50, 251–3,
    254, 255–6, 257, 260–2, 337
Rehberg, W.R., 156, 158, 290
  and Herder, 322
  and Jacobi, 151
  and Leibniz, 126, 322–3
  and Reinhold, 126–7, 323
  and Schelling, 322
  and Spinoza, 127–9, 140, 323
  Cato, 125
  *Concerning the Relation of Metaphysics
    to Religion*, 126
  conservative tendencies, 324
  critique of, 136
Reid, T., 84, 144
  and Jacobi, 88–9, 316–17

Reimarus, J.A.H., 41, 312, 320
Reinhold, K.L., xi, 77, 132, 221
  and Bardili, 340
  and Fichte, 102, 215, 218–19, 222,
    225–6, 228, 234–5, 247, 253, 257,
    258, 261, 262, 286–7
  and Jacobi, 245, 246, 252, 256, 257,
    264–5
  and Kant, 4, 12–13, 14, 42, 50, 193,
    205, 206, 226–7, 229, 262
  and Leibniz, 101
  and Michaelis, 331
  and Schmid, 122, 127, 135–6, 143
  and Weishaupt, 66
  as mediator, 28, 106, 243–4, 257
  as quietist, 264
  as realist, 296
  *Concerning the Paradoxes of the Most
    Recent Philosophy*, 244, 245, 250,
    251, 253, 256, 258, 261, 262
  Contributions, 122
  critique of, 91–2, 93
  critique of Fichte, 233–4, 249, 286,
    287–8
  critique of Jacobi, 247–8
  critique of Kant, 43, 91, 95, 227, 320
  critique of Weishaupt, 263, 308
  *Essay of a New Theory of the Human
    Faculty of Representation*, 91, 92, 94,
    96, 97, 98, 99, 103, 107
  his project, 29
  Kantian Letters, 122, 123, 127, 143
  *Letter to I.C. Lavater and J.G. Fichte
    Regarding Faith in God*, 245, 257
  *Negotiations Regarding the
    Fundamental Concepts and First
    Principles of Morality*, 263, 264
  *The Foundation of Philosophical
    Knowledge*, 47
Reinhold–Schmid controversy
  and Fichte, 152
religion, 6
  and Enlightenment, 16
  and Fichte, 210, 211, 241
  and Jacobi, 16
  and Kant, xi, 16, 187, 200, 201, 211,
    240

and philosophy, 252
and Rehberg, 129, 136, 240–1
and Reinhold, 16, 25
and Schmid, 62
and Spalding, 7
in Kant's system, 7
repentance
and Fichte, 275
representation(s), 39, 68
and feeling, 56–7
and Fichte, 215–16, 221, 281
and Jacobi, 80–1, 83
and Kant, 36
and Locke, 39–40, 94
and Mendelssohn, 94
and popular philosophy, 41
and Reinhold, 42, 56, 91–3, 94–5,
99–102, 320
form and material of, 100–1
innate, 39
reflective, 73
unity of, 72
reproduction
synthesis of, 70
respect
Fichte and feeling of, 219, 220–1
responsibility
and Fichte, 217
and Kant, 157, 163, 164
revelation
and Fichte, 210, 211, 212, 213
Richter, J-P., 285
and Fichte, 291
Rousseau, J-J., 157

salto mortale, 13, 14, 149, 303
satisfaction (*Glück*)
and Fichte, 217
Schelling, F.W.J., 150, 237, 269, 272,
291, 300
and Fichte, 341
critique of Fichte, 292
Schlegel, A.W., 291
Schleiermacher, F., 78, 269, 310, 341,
342
as popular philosopher, 335
critique of Fichte, 291–2

Schmid, C.C.E., 25, 52, 55, 66, 83,
123, 130, 132, 141, 206, 208, 292
and Kant, 205
critique of Fichte, 289–90
Philosophische Dogmatik, 61
scholasticism, 45, 64, 163
Schultz, J., 29, 74, 75, 76, 84, 91, 174
and the self, 73
*Elucidations of Professor Kant's Critique
of Pure Reason*, 67–8
review of *Critique of Pure Reason*,
68–72
Schulze, G.E./Aenesidemus, 210
Aenesidemus, 49
and Abicht, 59
critique of Kant, 49, 56, 103
critique of Reinhold, 103, 318
Schütz, C.G., 323
Schwärmerei, 78, 79, 128, 135, 136
science
and Jacobi, 103
and Kant, 161–2
and Reinhold, 42, 245–6
and Schmid, 61
and Weishaupt, 46
Scriptures, 191
'self', the, 80–1
and Fichte, 221, 229, 230–1, 232–3
self-determination
and Fichte, 218
Selle, C.G., 41, 312
sensation(s), 70, 102–3
and concepts, 68, 96
and Kant, 62, 102–3, 233
and Locke, 87
and Maimon, 97–8
and Reid, 88, 104, 317
and Weishaupt, 104
sense(s), 91
and experience, 84
and feelings, 76
and Kant, 62, 75
impressions, 39
sensibility
and Fichte, 216, 220
and Kant, 169, 172
and Schmid, 50, 51

Shaftesbury, Lord, 43
sin, 109
  and Fichte, 259–60
  and Hegel, 260
  and Kant, 193, 195, 197, 259
  and Leibniz, 110–11
skepticism, 35, 41, 227
  and Hume, 40, 41, 45, 48, 87, 88,
    103, 105
  and Jacobi, 80
  and Kant, 176
  and Maimon, 98, 103
  and Rehberg, 136, 151
  and Weishaupt, 46
skeptics, the, 52
Smith, A., 330
solipsism, 53, 58
'Son of God'
  and Kant, 196, 197, 198
soul
  and Abicht, 56
  and Weishaupt, 45, 46
space
  and Kant, 154–5, 177, 327
  and Spinoza, 138, 139
Spalding, J.J., 1, 7–10, 27, 33, 125, 158,
    275, 276, 277, 299
  and Fichte, 30–1, 272, 273
  and Kant, 9–10, 30
speculation (*see* reflection,
  philosophical)
Spinoza, B. de., 10, 22, 54, 90, 108,
    115, 116, 131, 266, 278,
    292
  and Fichte, 267
  and Kant, 21–2, 31, 129
Spinoza dispute, 11–14, 106, 242–3
  and Descartes, 143–4, 145
  and Jacobi, 10–12, 13–14, 87
  and Kant, 12, 27, 243
  and Leibniz, 140–1, 143–4
Spinozism, 10
  and Herder, 150
  and Lessing, 11
  and Rehberg, 125, 126
Starck, J.A., 37, 38

state
  Kant on juridico-civil, 199, 200
Steno, Bishop Nicholaus, 117
  critique of Leibniz, 112
Strawson, P.F., ix, x
Stroud, B., x
subject, 53
  and Hume, 296
  and Kant, 4, 50, 52, 175, 179–81
  and Locke, 296
  and popular philosophy, 50
  and Weishaupt, 52
  concrete, 63
  logical, 65, 66
  of experience, 71
'subjective interest of reason', 76
subjectivism
  and Jacobi, 78
  and Kant, 52
  and Schmid, 52
subjectivity
  and Fichte, 277–8, 287
  and Jacobi, 80
substance, 128, 129, 138, 266
sympathy (*Wohlwollen*), 207
system
  and Kant, 9–10, 18, 19
  and popular philosophy, 42, 43
  and Reinhold, 42
  and Spalding, 7

Tathandlung, 210, 222, 228, 229, 231,
    235, 296
  and 'I think', 228
  and Reinhold, 247, 250, 261
  as a myth, 236
Tatsache, 210, 222, 296
  and Abicht, 55, 56
  and Reinhold, 247
teleology
  of nature, 21–2, 295
Teutscher Merkur, 122, 126, 132, 340
theology
  and Fichte, 210
  and metaphysics, 33, 34
  and Schleiermacher, 344

thing-in-itself, ix, x, 4, 134
  and appearance, 70, 176
  and Fichte, 223, 231, 236, 288
  and Jacobi, 16, 18
  and Kant, 16–18, 19, 20, 75, 160,
    176, 230, 231, 283–4
  and morality, 159
  and popular philosophy, 49
  and Reinhold, 93–4, 97, 99–100
  and Schmid, 52
  and Schulze, 16
  and substance, 129
  as meaningless, 74
things
  and Fichte, 282
Thomasius, C., 42, 304
thought
  and Fichte, 259
Tiedeman D., 41, 343
Tittel, G.A., 314
time
  and Kant, 115, 154–5, 177, 327
transcendance
  and Fichte, 214
transcendental deduction, 73, 74, 75,
    95, 134
  Schultz's presentation of, 70–2
Trapp, E.C., 330
truth
  and idealism, 35
  and Reinhold, 43, 94

Ulrich, J.A.H., 49, 108, 112–18, 120,
    123, 124, 130, 156, 157, 161, 206,
    292, 310
  and Kant, 114–15, 310
  and Leibniz, 114
  critique of Kant, 114, 115–16
  *Eleutheriology, or Of Human Freedom
    and Necessity*, 108, 122
  misunderstanding of Kant, 116, 193
unconditional, the
  and Jacobi, 147–8

understanding, 71, 75, 78
  and Schmid, 51

vocation, human
  and Weishaupt, 104
volition (*Wollen*)
  and Fichte, 215, 216, 218, 221, 222,
    224
Voltaire, F-M. A. de, 207, 297

Weishaupt, A., 44–7, 66, 83, 104, 139,
    226, 228, 264, 283, 292
  and Fichte, 273
  and Leibniz, 47, 104–5
  and Locke, 47
  and Schmid, 58–9
  as popular philosopher, 44
  Concerning Materialism and Idealism,
    44
  critique of Kant, 52–3, 54
Wieland, C.M., 340
will (*see also* Holy Will)
  and Abicht, 57, 60
  and Fichte, 209, 211, 274
  and Kant, 164, 169–70
  and moral law, 211–13
  and Reinhold, 123–4, 127
  and Schelling, 332
  and Schmid, 290
wisdom
  and Kant, 24
Wolff, C., 42, 43, 102, 262
world(s)
  and self, 72
  and Weishaupt, 45–6
  Jacobi and external, 81–2, 83
  Kant and intelligible, 21, 22
  noumenal and phenomenal,
    134–5
  possible, 44
  two worlds view, 5, 6

Young Hegelians, 212